# Barrios Norteños

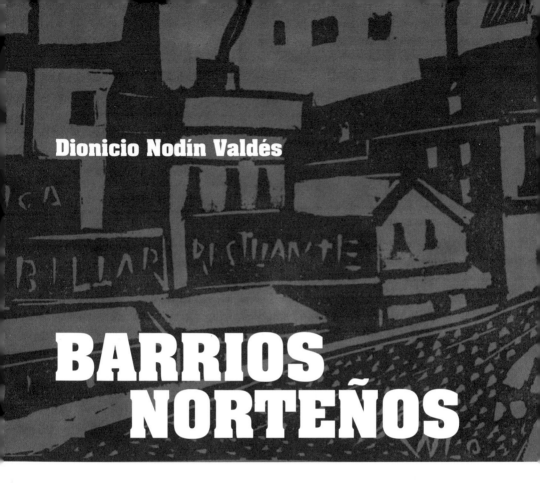

Dionicio Nodín Valdés

# BARRIOS NORTEÑOS

St. Paul and Midwestern
Mexican Communities
in the Twentieth Century

University of Texas Press

AUSTIN

Publication of this book was made possible in part
by support from the Pachita Tennant Pike Fund for
Latin American Studies.

First edition, 2000

⊗ The paper used in this book meets the minimum
requirements of ANSI/NISO Z39.48-1992 (R1997)
(Permanence of Paper).

Valdés, Dennis Nodín.
    Barrios norteños : St. Paul and midwestern Mexican
communities in the twentieth century / Dionicio Nodín
Valdés. — 1st ed.
        p.      cm.
    Includes bibliographical references (p.      ) and
index.
    ISBN 0-292-78743-X (cloth : alk. paper). —
ISBN 0-292-78744-8 (pbk. : alk. paper)
    1. Mexican Americans—Minnesota—Saint Paul—
History—20th century.    2. Mexican Americans—
Minnesota—Saint Paul—Social conditions—20th
century.    3. Saint Paul (Minn.)—Social conditions—
20th century.    4. Hispanic American neighborhoods—
Middle West Case studies.    I. Title.
F614.S4V35    2000
977.6'5810046872073—dc21                          99-36269

# Contents

# Acknowledgments

I wish to thank friends, colleagues, and students who have long reminded me of the compelling need to write an urban history of midwestern Mexicans. The vast scale of such a project, combined with the practical and theoretical utility of a specific focus convinced me to offer a local history, in which St. Paul's West Side, the oldest and largest barrio in Minnesota, provides a window to Mexican communities in the region. In particular I acknowledge the efforts of the members of the Twin Cities–based Teatro Latino de Minnesota and the Teatro del Pueblo, whose sustained efforts have helped to maintain and enrich cultural presence and historical awareness. In response to a request by the latter group to discuss the history of the St. Paul barrio as an introduction to performances of their inaugural production, I had an opportunity to examine materials I had been gathering over the years and to enter local archives once again. The public lectures that resulted provided me the incentive to commit myself to this work.

I am also grateful to Mario Compean, Joe González, Guillermo Rojas, and Jaime Duarte for sharing thoughts and access to items from their own private collections. Thanks to Diana Huizar Rivera and her students Hugo Piña and Nathan García for creating the maps in this book. I also thank Sr. Francisco Reyes and Sr. Secundino Reyes for allowing me to use the cover photo. I appreciate the valuable criticism and suggestions of friends and colleagues who read drafts of this work: Guadalupe Luna, Lars Olsson, Peter Rachleff, and students in my Chicano history seminar, Laura Espondaburu, Cindy Navarro, Arcela Nuñez, Anne Martínez, Alda Saute, May Fu, and Karin Jacobson. The staff of the University of Texas Press again have been most helpful. I also thank Patrick Anzelc, of the archives of the Archdiocese of St. Paul and Minneapolis, and staff members of the Minnesota Legislative Reference Library, the Immigration History Research Center, and the Minnesota Historical Society for their assistance.

Finally, I am grateful for the efforts of individuals responsible for a project sponsored by the Minnesota Historical Society a generation ago on the Mexican community in St. Paul. The reports, oral interviews, and manuscript collections they gathered allowed access to *colonia* residents, many no longer alive, who discussed their experiences and offered their visions of the world. This book is a personal contribution to an ongoing dialogue initiated by the students of La Raza Student Cultural Center at the University of Minnesota, *Contando Nuestras Historias,* as a collective story of our history in the Midwest and its local, regional, national, and international contexts. It is the first history of midwestern Mexican communities to cover the entire twentieth century, but it will not be the last.

# Barrios Norteños

# Introduction

This is a history of Chicanos and their spaces in the urban Midwest during the twentieth century, with a specific focus on the West Side of St. Paul, "called 'San Pablo' by the Mexicans," as one English-speaking investigator observed in 1927.[1] It stems in part from my earlier investigation of the history of farmworkers in the Great Lakes region. My original intent in *Al Norte* was to examine the experiences of people who came north from Mexico, Texas, and elsewhere to the fields of the Midwest, their working lives in agricultural settings, and their settlement into the cities and towns of the region. Those plans were unduly ambitious, and I was forced to concentrate on their experiences as agricultural workers. This book starts where the former ended, with the farmworkers who left the fields and the labor camps to settle in nearby cities and towns. It also examines the lives of individuals and families from Mexico and Texas who came directly to midwestern urban settings to work and live. Like my earlier book, this work is written from the bottom up, but it focuses more directly on issues of ethnicity, race, and nationality, simultaneously examining how those forces intertwined with gender and class. I focus on St. Paul primarily for strategic reasons, including accessibility to local materials. It permits me to relate a history emanating from a medium-sized urban community while addressing specific and more general aspects of Mexican life in midwestern communities framed simultaneously in local, regional, national, and international contexts.

The story of midwestern barrios reveals again that the distinction made by academics, politicians, and popular writers between rural and urban settings, and between agricultural and city life, commonly has been blurred for Mexicans since the first farmworkers came north in the early years of the century. Most of the early settlers in St. Paul originally were agricultural workers who did not cut their ties with the fields immediately. For many years they often worked and lived in rural settings when employment was available and then returned to their urban homes after the harvest ended. The experience of sharing urban and rural residences took place in many parts of the Midwest, the Great Plains, the Southwest,

California, and elsewhere. Over the years workers gradually severed their ties with agriculture, and their working and living experiences became increasingly diverse. In the cities, adults could find a wider variety of employment opportunities and more stable lives, children could attend school, and together they could create a more varied social and cultural life. Unlike in rural settings, in cities the physical presence and memories of each generation of new arrivals were added cumulatively to those of its predecessors. Furthermore, the urban Mexicano population became progressively more diverse, while in midwestern agriculture the earlier farmworkers were continually being replaced, and they left few physical traces of their presence.

In the large cities, where no single industry dominated employment, agricultural and nonagricultural workers were attracted to a range of jobs in industries and services, while others were self-employed or unemployed, reflecting a much greater range of working experiences than Mexicans in the midwestern fields. While the process of class and social formation was more varied and complex than in agriculture, Mexicans in the Midwest remained overwhelmingly a working people. Although they widened their social and cultural relations in the cities, they did not attain material equality with the majority population, even after many generations.

Mexicans in St. Paul and other urban barrios were more visible than rural farmworkers and attracted greater attention from governmental authorities, institutions, and other urban residents. They retained links with their past, but their experiences at work, at home, in school, and in social and cultural activities became increasingly diverse. This social history focuses on how they created ethnic spaces and how their lives and their communities changed during the course of the twentieth century.

The *colonia* in St. Paul has been the heart of the Mexican community of the Twin Cities, Minnesota, and the Upper Midwest since the early twentieth century, when large-scale Mexicano migration to the region began. Although the first settlement was confined to a small neighborhood on the Lower West Side, the Mexican population expanded and the community spread out geographically. Elsewhere in the Midwest, small numbers of Mexicans moved into urban neighborhoods, industrial suburbs, and scattered small-town and rural settings. In many places, including Minnesota, Mexican farmworkers often were present for several generations without becoming permanent residents.

In this book I interpret the history of Mexicans in midwestern communities in particular, and the twentieth-century urban history of Chicanos in general. The published historical literature includes only a handful of detailed works on urban communities. It does not address whether the urban experience of Mexicans in Los Angeles, El Paso, and San Antonio, the settings most often studied, were typical; nor does it seek to establish systemic links among different communities. Academic literature on the urban Midwest is scattered and with few exceptions does not venture beyond the early years of the Great Depression. To date, not a single Chicano urban history has examined the entire twentieth century, a perspective making it possible to compare different approaches to chronology and assess change over time. Many authors have criticized linear approaches to history as being Eurocentric and male dominated, yet they commonly fail to offer alternative frameworks while making generalizations based on restricted chronologies.[2] I am concerned about relationships among linear, sometimes referred to as "traditional" techniques (yet not all lines are straight); emphases on continuity, or a view that history does not change; as well as discontinuous and cyclical approaches.

Chapter 1 examines inequality, a constant feature of Chicano history and Chicano studies social science literature, and particularly its applicability to settings outside the Southwest. Chapters 2 and 3 deal with the first cycle of twentieth-century midwestern Chicano history, specifically the formation of Mexican communities between the early 1900s and the Great Depression. In Chapter 4 I examine the second cycle, encompassing World War II and its aftermath, when midwestern Mexicans established a firm foothold in the industrial working class. Chapter 5 focuses on the Chicano Movement and struggles in communities and academic institutions that broke out erratically in time and space in Minnesota and elsewhere in the Midwest during the 1960s and 1970s. The final chapter deals with the third cycle of twentieth-century midwestern Chicano history, the final decades of the century, characterized by industrial restructuring and unprecedented migration and population growth.

During the twentieth century, popular and academic observers have been unable to agree on whether to identify Mexicans as an ethnic group, a culture, a nation, a race, or a class. Some have even suggested psychic and cultural identity crises resulting from the physical proximity of the Mexican population in the Southwest to the political border immediately to the south, a topic that would seem scarcely applicable to the more than two million Mexicans residing in the Midwest. My own concerns about the historical construction of identities are informed by Eric Hobsbawm, who suggests that "the unity of classes and nations is defined by what they have in common as against other groups, and not by their internal homogeneity," as such constructions are relational.[3]

The variety and frequent changes in terms of identity stem from the U.S. conquest of Mexico in the War of 1846–1848, the imperfect incorporation of Mexicans into the body politic, their uneven and limited assimilation into the national cultural matrix, and the continued material inequality which informed relations between Mexicans and dominant European Americans. When European immigrant groups entered the country, they were also subjected to competing identifiers, many disparaging. Their acceptance by the dominant population was uneven.[4] Eventually Europeans were universally treated as White, whereas the place of Mexicans has not yet been resolved a century and a half after conquest. Mexicans and other groups involuntarily incorporated into the United States struggled to claim an identity for themselves while new terms were continuously imposed from above. As a consequence, they have experienced ambiguity, confusion, and ambivalence over how to identify themselves.

From the mid nineteenth century on, non-Mexicans created many terms to identify the conquered population and later arrivals from Mexico, including *Spaniards, Hispanos, Indians, Mexicans, peons, greasers,* and the self-identities of *Mexicana* and *Mexicano.* Around the time of World War I, in Minnesota and elsewhere in the country, European American agents of assimilation inconsistently applied the term *Mexican American,* which bore little immediate relationship to the increasingly important border between the United States and Mexico. Rather, Americanizers were applying the term to Mexicans as they were to Irish, Germans, Swedes, and other European ethnic groups. Yet it did not stick well in the Midwest, as many outside observers confirmed, even in the 1960s and 1970s. Historian Julie Leininger reported during her research in South Bend, Indiana, that the identifier *Mexican American* "is not heard in the barrio as often as some other terms." In the Midwest, Mexicans responded to the term inconsistently, with acquiescence or challenge, often an indication of differential assimilation or internal class and cultural differences.[5]

Perhaps the most concerted and forceful challenge to impositions of identity in the twentieth century was posed by youthful Mexicans coming of age in the 1960s, who reintroduced the term *Chicano* as a self-identifier, aware of its political, ideological, and cultural implications. They argued that to accept imposed identities, including that of Mexican American, represented a blind acceptance of a narrow U.S. "American"—more appropriately European American—way of life. Such an imposition neither understood nor respected the distinctiveness of Mexican culture on either side of the political border and allowed dominant society to create confusion and maintain control while destroying a culture. Chicanas and Chicanos believed that such an imposition was another feature of dominant ideological weaponry intent on keeping them subordinated.

Although many people considered the term *Chicano* new, it had a long history in the United States. In the early years of the twentieth century, working-class immigrants entering the country had used it to identify themselves in relationship to people who were not Mexicans. In 1927, Gilberto Hernández recalled that in Arizona, "we were picking cotton when I had a serious difficulty with an American who was the manager and he wished to cheat me on the weight . . . We had an exchange of words and we even called each other names. Then all the *Chicanada* [translated in the text as "Mexicans"] came to my help and we came mighty near lynching him."[6]

The effort by youth in the Chicano Movement to claim their own identities was only partially successful. European Americans quickly rejected the term which was not their own, while many older Mexicans who recalled its class-based context continued to view it pejoratively. Meanwhile, fearing its connotations, dominant interests in government and business soon tried to popularize other terms, particularly Hispanic. They were joined by academics who quickly imposed the term Hispanic backward in time in reference to Mexicans in the seventeenth, eighteenth, and nineteenth centuries, when the elite in Mexican society more commonly identified themselves as "Español" or "Español Mexicano." Thus the scholars added confusion to the contemporary debate on identity among people of Mexican birth and descent in the United States.

In this book, I will use *Mexican, Mexicana,* and *Mexicano* to identify people of Mexican birth and descent, the most popular self-identifiers in the Midwest throughout the twentieth century. In keeping with usage popularized in the region, I will apply the labels *Latina* and *Latino* when referring to people of various Latin American backgrounds collectively.[7] I will employ the terms *Chicana* and *Chicano* specifically to the generation of Mexicans who came of age during the Chicano Movement and to the academic literature that accompanied it, to which this story belongs.

# 1 Mexican Inequality and the Midwest

I seek to accomplish two major objectives in this book. The first is to reconstruct the twentieth-century history of midwestern Mexican urban communities, with a particular focus on St. Paul, Minnesota. The second is to discuss group inequality, a central theme in Chicano studies social science literature. It is paradoxical that attention to the topic has attracted less interest in recent years, a time of rapidly increasing material levels of inequality, both between Mexican and European American populations in the United States, and among Mexicans. That reason alone justifies its centrality.

My research has been guided by two related questions, namely, what has been the place of Mexicans in the twentieth-century urban Midwest, and how has it been portrayed and understood by Mexicans and non-Mexicans? In addressing these issues, I examine interactions among race, class, gender, physical spaces, and the ethnic organizations and other cultural activities in which midwestern Mexicanos participated.[1] Theoretical discussions of inequality in the social sciences too often have been posited and debated as a series of discrete and timeless models, often in isolation from each other rather than in the historical contexts in which they took place. In this chapter, I will first examine how those discussions were applied to Mexicans in the United States and how they unfolded during the twentieth century. I will then turn to the geographic setting of the Midwest and its relationship to the Southwest-based framework for most theoretical Chicano social science literature. In subsequent chapters, I examine in greater detail the interaction and applicability of theory with the experiences of midwestern Mexicans and the communities they created.

## Modeling Chicano Inequality

Popular and academic interest about group adjustment and inequality in the United States had a long history before the first major cycle of Mexican immigration to the Midwest. The two most popular interpretive tendencies at the turn of the twentieth century were assimilationist and deficiency theories, generally representing liberal and conservative viewpoints, respectively, in their day. Assimilationist ideas, including the melting pot notions articulated by J. Hector St. John de Crèvecoeur in the late eighteenth century, dominated popular ideas regarding immigrant adjustment from the early years of the republic, when it was assumed that Europeans could be made into good citizens of the United States.[2] Although not all Europeans were treated equally, they were generally considered malleable enough to be assimilated and soon accepted into the dominant culture. People of non-European origins—Africans, Native Americans, and later Asians—were considered less adaptable or capable of assimilation, and they and their descendants did not enjoy equal protection of the laws.

European American attitudes and policies toward Mexicans were ambivalent from the earliest systematic contacts in the nineteenth century. The Treaty of Guadalupe Hidalgo of 1848, which established the legal framework under which Mexicans were to be incorporated following the U.S. conquest, contained explicitly assimilationist assumptions. Its Article VIII declared that all Mexicans who remained in the territories acquired by the United States automatically had achieved legal equality: "without having declared their intention to retain the character of Mexicans, shall be considered to have elected to become citizens of the United States." Many invading European American soldiers shared assimilationist expectations. Colonel George Archibald McCall, who participated in the conquest of New Mexico, wrote that although technical and mechanical accomplishments of New Mexicans were "primitive," it was not because of "deficiency of aptness and manual skill or dexterity, as to the want of proper instruction and better models. . . . Gradual improvement in this branch may therefore be looked for, if their natural indolence can be overcome or their love of gain be stimulated through the influence of our own enterprising countrymen."[3]

Yet many European Americans strongly disagreed with McCall and expressed the belief that the conquered Mexicans were incapable of assimilation and did not deserve to participate in the dominant political culture of the nation. Some argued that the United States was "fundamentally Anglo-Saxon in its institutions, its culture, its modes of thought, and the temper of its people" and that African slaves, American Indians, Asians, and Mexicans posed a threat. They justified the inequality of people who had been conquered, subjugated, and/or enslaved on the grounds of biological or mental characteristics or deficient cultures. Frank Edwards, a member of the Missouri Volunteers who also participated in the conquest of New Mexico, characterized the Mexican men he encountered in Santa Fe as "the meanest, most contemptible set of swarthy thieves and liars to be found anywhere. The rich ones will cheat and swindle; and the poor sneakingly pilfer anything."[4] Afterward, purveyors of dominant popular thought continued to regard assimilation as a necessary step toward overcoming inequality, and they remained ambivalent regarding possibilities for Mexicans.

Some European American observers resolved their ambivalence by seeking to establish internal racial differences, by accepting those people they considered assimilable as White, or "Spaniards," while rejecting the remainder on the basis of ostensibly Indian traits. In 1901, A. H. Naftzger, president and general manager of the Southern California Fruit Exchange, asserted that "Mexicans don't want to work at all, and they will not work so long as there is a little of anything in the house to eat, or their stomachs are full." He added that "the Mexican is chronically indolent and indifferent," while "the Spaniard is a somewhat different type." Naftzger had incorporated what Carey McWilliams later characterized as the "Spanish fantasy heritage," which romanticized the "Spanish" past and presence in the Southwest. The separation of Mexicans into different racial categories did more than resolve individual identity crises. It permitted a basis for policy makers to establish racial standing according to the law and thus influenced Mexicans' possibilities for retaining land, achieving legal rights equal to those of the dominant population, remaining segregated or becoming integrated residentially, obtaining schooling, and other matters. Mexicans represented as Indians, regardless of their own personal identities, were more likely to be deprived of rights accruing to European Americans. Later variants of the "Spanish" terminology, including *Hispano, Spanish-American,* and *Hispanic,* indicate continuity despite changing constructions of identity, as well as the ongoing tension between indigenous and European among Mexicans dating from the European conquest of the Americas.[5]

In the late nineteenth century, dominant thought and policy generally accepted the notion that European immigrants were capable of assimilation. Immigrants from Sweden, a group closely identified with Minnesota and several parts of the Midwest, represent an important case. While many Swedish immigrants were able immediately to invest in property and businesses, a larger number entered the country with few resources, often first residing in humble urban quarters. Employers seeking unskilled and skilled workers generally welcomed Swedes, who were accepted by earlier European immigrants and their descendants as White. Swedes quickly entered the building trades and were readily admitted into labor unions in Chicago, Minneapolis, St. Paul, Omaha, and other cities in the region. Many experienced rapid upward mobility, encountering little systematic resistance in purchasing homes in the cities or farmsteads in the countryside. As historian Ulf Beijbom concluded, for Swedes coming to the United States, "the transition was very easy."[6]

While dominant culture in the late nineteenth century welcomed Europeans unevenly, it applied deficiency theories more consistently to non-Europeans. Chinese immigrants, concentrated mostly in California, attracted attention far beyond their numbers. Academics and purveyors of popular ideas applied a range of biological and cultural arguments to support a political movement aimed at restricting immigration from China. Their efforts were highlighted by the 1882 Chinese Exclusion Act, which curtailed the immigration of Chinese workers—but not merchants or students—to the United States. In California and nearby states, laws and ordinances subjected Chinese immigrants and their descendants to other forms of institutionalized discrimination involving work, residence, land ownership, marriage, and other matters that European immigrants did not encounter.[7]

Supporters of deficiency theories who led campaigns to restrict foreign immigration found it more difficult to curtail Southern and Eastern Europeans, who formed a majority of immigration to the United States at its peak in the 1890s and first two decades of the twentieth century. Dominant popular and academic thought was inconsistent about race, although it distinguished a hierarchy among Europeans. It tended to place Nordic and Germanic races on top, followed by Mediterranean and Slavic races, with non-European races consistently below them. Restrictionists claimed that the unlimited entry of Eastern and Southern Europeans threatened to dilute the purity of the Aryan race, which, they felt, had made the nation's greatness possible. They buttressed their arguments with the increasingly widespread notion that the nation's vast frontier was finally closing, an idea popularized in the writings of University of Wisconsin historian Frederick Jackson Turner. Political and economic forces in the world economy furthered their ends, as industrialization and rising living standards in European nations narrowed the income gap with the United States and reduced its attractiveness to Europeans. Restrictionists gained further support as a result of rising xenophobia that accompanied World War I, which enabled them to convince Congress to pass legislation in 1917, 1921, and 1924 to severely reduce immigration from Southern and

Eastern Europe. Their success in restricting immigration was due not entirely to their own efforts but also to pressures operating simultaneously in many parts of the world.[8]

In debates over European immigration, restrictionists failed to convince Congress of threats posed by immigration from countries of the Western Hemisphere. Dominant attitudes about deficiencies of Mexicans generally ran deeper than those toward Southern and Eastern Europeans, but the scale of migration from Mexico was not considered significant enough to merit concerted congressional action. As immigration from across the Southern border of the United States accelerated and showed increasing signs of permanence in the 1920s, restrictionist-minded politicians, policy makers, and academics directed intensified attention toward Mexico.

Liberal and conservative opinions were not entirely antagonistic, and they did not divide neatly over restriction of immigration from Mexico. Both accepted the thesis that the nation's frontier was closed and that its natural resources were limited. They also agreed that Mexicans were not equal to the majority population in levels of material culture, education, or the contributions that Mexico had made to the world. Labor leaders, like Edgar Walls of the American Federation of Labor, argued: "I have nothing against the Mexican. I do not say he is inferior, but he is dissimilar. He is unassimilable, and would bring another race problem . . . into this country." More sympathetic to Mexican immigration, U.S. Representative C. B. Hudspeth, a rancher from West Texas, asserted that many Mexicans came to the United States because they sought democracy and a better life, and that they made good citizens. But in response to a hostile question, if he thought "Mexicans as good as whites," he responded in anger: "You know I don't believe that, so why ask me the question? No Texan has ever said that."[9] He clearly understood that identity as a Texan was reserved only for White people and could not be attained by place of residence, birth, or citizenship alone.

Many European Americans were more explicit in articulating a racial basis for Mexican deficiency, including leading academics in eastern and midwestern universities. In 1927 a dozen professors from Princeton and Harvard, as well as University of Michigan president C. C. Little and University of Wisconsin professors Edward A. Ross, William H. Kiekhofer, J. E. Irelin, John R. Commons, and Henry R. Trumbower, submitted a statement to Congress. They favored a quota from all countries of North and South America "from which we have substantial immigration and in which the population is not predominantly of the white race . . . for a reasonable degree of homogeneity . . . (so) civilization can have its best development." The statement referred to Mexico, the only country from which a substantial migration to the United States was taking place. Harvard-educated Lothrop Stoddard, writing that same year, was more explicit: "the Mexican peon is about the most 'alien,' unassimilable creature that could be imagined. His temperament and outlook on life are absolutely opposed to those of the typical American. Low in intelligence and almost devoid of individual initiative, the Mexican Indian is likely splendid potential revolutionary material, because he is a born communist." He concluded that "what is thus true of European immigrants, most of whom belong to some branch of the white racial group, most emphatically does not apply to non-White immigrants, like the Chinese, Japanese, or Mexicans; neither does it apply to the large negro element which has been a tragic anomaly from our earliest times. Here, ethnic differences are so great that 'assimilation' in the racial sense is impossible." In a similar vein, Professor Roy Garis of Vanderbilt University argued that "we did not restrict immigration from Europe in order to let in people who have proved even more alien and even less easily assimilated than European immigration: people whose threat to the American standard of living, and to the future organization of American civic life, is as great as anything we had from Europe." Elsewhere Garis wrote of Mexicans: "their minds run to nothing higher than the animal functions—eat, sleep, and sexual debauchery. In every huddle of Mexican shacks one meets the same idleness, hordes of hungry dogs and filthy children with faces plastered with flies, disease, lice, human filth, stench, promiscuous fornication, bastardy, lounging, apathetic peons and lazy squaws, beans and dried chili, liquor, general squalor and envy and hatred of the Gringo." While restrictionists failed to obtain the legislation they desired, tightened administrative procedures by immigration officials and the onset of the Great Depression in 1929 combined to reverse the direction of migration for several years, as hundreds of thousands of people of Mexican birth and their children left the United States.[10]

Although supporters of deficiency theories temporarily won the battle over immigration from Mexico, their ideas faced increasingly vigorous attack from mainstream political and academic circles. During the Great Depression, the difficulties faced by middle-class institutions and millions of European American individuals offered powerful evidence that the environment and even luck, rather than inborn weaknesses or character flaws, might account for failure. The cause of deficiency theories was further upset by the compelling political need to challenge premises of extremist biological deficiency theories like Fascism and Nazism during World War II. After the War, arguments based on biological deficiency largely went into abeyance in academia, and conservative explanations focused more on cultural and psychological factors. In later years some academics attempted to resurrect biological and genetic theories, but they faced strong opposition.[11]

Liberal academics and politicians tended to accept the notion that Mexicans could be assimilated, emphasizing environmental factors as accounting for inequality. Deriving their arguments from those applied earlier to European immigrants, they suggested that Mexicanos came from a poorer and more backward land, but that individuals could adjust if they adopted a strategy of seeking acceptance and imitating the U.S. American way of life and its culture. In order to hasten the process, they encouraged Mexicans to participate in Americanization educational programs to help mold them into good citizens, again following the experience of European immigrants. Liberal assumptions that Mexicans and others considered recent arrivals can eventually achieve equality once they assimilate became a dominant trend in academic and popular thought in the middle decades of the twentieth century.

A variant of assimilation theory, cultural pluralism, merits specific attention because of its widespread influence. Educator Horace Kallen, a student of John Dewey, adopted cultural pluralism as a challenge to deficiency theories in the early twentieth century. Adherents of cultural pluralism suggest that assimilation is not a simple process that can be measured by a single indicator, like attitudes or language use. They also suggest that as immigrants and their children assimilate, they can retain a degree of cultural, linguistic, and religious autonomy. A well-known version of cultural pluralism, formulated by sociologist Milton Gordon in the 1960s, insisted on the need to examine several matrices simultaneously, including language, attitudes, the political behavior of immigrants and their descendants, and the role of the dominant European American population, particularly its attitudes (prejudice) and behavior (discrimination). Gordon explicitly stated that African Americans, Native Americans, Mexican Americans, and Puerto Ricans, who were incorporated by force and conquest, experienced outcomes distinct from those of Europeans. Because assimilation was much more than an act of human will, he suggested, a cultural pluralist model could not be applied equally to European immigrant and formerly conquered and/or enslaved non-European-descent populations.[12]

While Gordon acknowledged that cultural pluralism might not be universally applicable, academics influenced by the new social movements involving Blacks, Chicanos, and Native Americans in the 1960s and 1970s took the argument farther. They criticized cultural pluralism as a variant of assimilationist thought with many of the same critical flaws, starting with conditions of incorporation. While Europeans entered the United States voluntarily, Blacks, Chicanos, and Native Americans were enslaved and/or conquered. These critics also challenged the assumption that assimilation is linear and inevitable. Another significant flaw they found in assimilationist and cultural pluralist analyses was a tendency to confuse individuals with groups as units of analysis.[13] A final criticism was that both theories avoid economic and other material indicators and the interrelated equation of adjustment or adaptation with equality. In short, the critics asserted that cultural pluralism and other assimilationist theories are not capable of dealing systematically with inequality among the formerly conquered and/or enslaved non-European-descent peoples.

Chicano studies social science literature, when it first appeared in the late 1960s and 1970s, accepted many premises of critics of assimilationist and cultural pluralist thought. Simultaneously, it sought to examine in tandem several factors, particularly race, class, gender, and the historical concentration of Chicanos in the Southwest. Interest in race and its leading representative model, internal colonialism, had roots at least from W. E. B. DuBois in the early twentieth century. A more immediate inspiration came from writers influenced by anticolonial and national liberation struggles in Asia, Africa, and Latin America, including Frantz Fanon, Albert Memmi, and Che Guevara. The Cuban Revolution of 1959, because of its proximity and immediacy, touched a particularly responsive chord in the Chicano Movement and other antihegemonic struggles in the United States in the 1960s.[14] The anticolonial movements helped legitimize the histories of non-European peoples, their demands for entry into academia as students and scholars, and academic programs focusing on Chicano, Afro-American, American Indian, and non-European American studies, which had been largely neglected in mainstream academia. Similar to the shifts of the 1930s and 1940s, the appearance of Chicano studies literature reframed political and academic debates about Mexican inequality in the United States.

Internal colonial models posit a direct link between the conquest and subjugation of the Third World and the unequal relations between the descendants of Europeans and Third World peoples in the United States. The models suggest that conquest and involuntary incorporation enabled the conquerors to distinguish themselves from and subordinate the conquered, including those in the United States, whom they identified as non-White races. Discriminatory legal codes, popular representations, and the imposition of a foreign language and culture helped confine the latter to a limited and inferior range of employment options and to distinct "internal colonies," particularly ghettoes for African Americans, reservations for Indians, and barrios and *colonias* for Chicanos and Puerto Ricans.[15]

Class-based studies also influenced early Chicano writings, although works by Mexicans and other Latino Marxists were already appearing in the early twentieth century. In 1929, Communist Party authors León Slavin Ruiz and Alberto Moreau argued that U.S. imperialism, as it gained political and economic sway in Latin America, was also responsible for migration within and from those countries. Capitalists sought not only raw materials and markets but also cheap labor for their fields and factories in Latin America and the United States. The authors suggested that while imperialism had made Mexicanos and Puertorriqueños part of an international working class, White racism of employers and workers in the United States further subordinated them while it hindered efforts at labor unity. By the 1930s, Mexican and other Latino activists were engaged simultaneously in writing about and organizing Mexican workers, often outside the established labor movement.[16] These early authors typically were organizers and activists, and their writings did not display the weaknesses which haunted many later Marxists, who were often isolated in academia or who reverted to a simplistic economic determinism that failed to address race and other complex societal interactions.

A more immediate influence on early Chicano studies scholarship was socialist Carey McWilliams, a journalist, activist, and author of books including *North from Mexico,* considered by many the original Chicano history text. He argued that the class-based exploitation of Mexicans in the Southwest was distinctive because of its pattern of racial discrimination rooted in the U.S. invasion and conquest of Mexico. The victors and their heirs subordinated Mexicans politically and economically by using race and racism as tools· of control. McWilliams's influence was evident in much early Chicano social science and historical literature, which included the works of Rodolfo Acuña, who stressed the importance of racism in the colonization and subordination of Mexicans in the nineteenth century and of class oppression in the twentieth, and of Mario Barrera, who stressed the interaction of race and class in maintaining inequality in the Southwest.[17]

Early writings in the field were not very interested in gender until Chicana scholars, dissatisfied with both Chicano studies and Women's studies literature, posited the need for a theoretical matrix simultaneously examining inequality at the intersection of race, class, and gender as interactive rather than distinct factors. Their focus on the relationship between production and reproduction, from daily to intergenerational activities, and their interest in families and communities, also bridged the gap between the individual-based assimilationist analysis and the abstract national and international levels stressed in race- and class-based theories.[18]

## Mexicans and Midwestern Geography

Theoretical literature in Chicana and Chicano studies is still largely confined by Southwest-based geographic perspectives, although more than two million people of Mexican birth and descent reside elsewhere in the United States, with a continuous history in the Midwest since the early twentieth century. Leading theoretical and interpretive social science literature continues to stress the critical role of the geographic concentration of Mexicans along the United States–Mexican border, formerly Mexican territory, as influencing the distinctive conditions that Chicanos encounter. By focusing on the Midwest, located far from the border and lacking an established Mexican presence prior to the U.S. conquest, I question the role of that distinctive geography in accounting for inequality. The geographic focus of this book consists of the ethnic spaces created by Mexicans in the urban Midwest, whose appearance and evolution during the course of the twentieth century heretofore have not been examined systematically.

The most popular current geographic perspectives in the literature, focusing on the "Homeland" and "Greater Mexico," suffer from important shortcomings. The former, refined by geographer Richard Nostrand, suggests a dichotomy between the "Hispano Homeland," a region where Mexicans resided at the time of the U.S. conquest, and more recently established settlements beyond. Nostrand distinguishes the "Hispano Homeland" by its long settlement by Spanish-speaking peoples, its dense population, and its cultural concentrations. He suggests that beyond the "Homeland" a shorter history and less dense population concentrations resulted in a weaker culture. A variant of the "Homeland" thesis, proposed by historian Sara Deutsch, offers a cultural twist to World-Systems schema, whose "regional community" distinguishes a Hispanic "core" in northern New Mexico (within Nostrand's Hispano Homeland), a "semi-periphery" in Southern Colorado, and a "periphery" in northern Colorado and neighboring areas. Deutsch suggests that the three zones are distinguished by history of settlement, population, and cultural density, and that semi-periphery and periphery are incomplete and partial versions of the core. The model would consider the Midwest an external area because of its extremely limited links with the "core" in New Mexico, or a "periphery" because of its links with a Texas core. While a "Homelands" geographical model has the virtue of explaining regional variations in Chicano experiences, it fails to recognize the vital role of Mexico, which influenced not only the Hispanic "core," but also the "periphery" and "semiperiphery" in distinct ways. By the late twentieth century, Mexican population density, Spanish language use, and cultural symbols have become much greater in many midwestern locations than in many parts of the "core"—possibilities not considered in the "Homeland" models.[19]

A "Greater Mexico" model, as adopted recently by many scholars in Chicana and Chicano studies, is based on a larger geographic unit, presumably the Mexican nation of the 1820s. An improvement on the "Hispano Homeland," it also offers the potential virtue of transcending the distinct historical subfields addressed in Chicano history, including Mexico, the United States, the West, and the Spanish borderlands, in the tradition of Herbert Eugene Bolton.[20] It compensates for a critical flaw in the "Homeland" thesis by placing Mexico at center stage. Yet it also suffers from a hazy geography and fails theoretically to address regions like the Midwest, which were not included in the political boundaries of early-Republican Mexico. Like deficiency and assimilationist models, its leading proponents adhere to modernization theory, which assumes that Mexico and Mexicans are backward and inferior to the United States and its citizens and that modernization is linear, positive, inevitable, and essentially immune to the actions of common people.

The Midwest, external to extant Hispano Homeland and Greater Mexico models, offers an important theoretical challenge to the Southwest-based geographic premises of Chicano social science theory. Many observers have argued that while Mexicans might be a race and class apart in the Southwest, because of distinct historical, demographic, political, and social factors, Mexicans in the Midwest can be best understood in the context of European-based models of assimilation. First, because large-scale Mexican settlement in the region was subsequent to that of Europeans, Mexicans might be more accurately portrayed as the last of the immigrants. Second, Mexicans who came to the Midwest in the early twentieth century did not share the collective memory of conquest, land loss, or the mechanisms of subordination imposed on Mexicans in the

Southwest, suggesting that perspectives based on colonialism are less applicable. As Carey McWilliams wrote, "in Chicago and Detroit, Mexicans are merely another immigrant group; in the Southwest they are an indigenous people." Third, midwestern Mexican employment patterns differed from those in the Southwest; as Gilbert Cárdenas has suggested, "the predominant industrial and other manufacturing related employment and the urban settlement of Mexican immigrants to the Midwest more closely parallel the European immigrant pattern than the earlier patterns of [Mexican] immigration to the Southwest."[21] Fourth, Mexicans entered a region characterized by a much greater degree of ethnic diversity among European Americans than in the Southwest, blurring potential Anglo unity. Furthermore, the much larger and more visible African American population made African Americans, rather than Mexicans, the most numerous racial "other" with which the dominant White population contrasted itself. Finally, Mexican population densities in the Midwest historically have been lower than in the Southwest, creating a less visible population, not as subject to recriminations, while permitting conditions conducive to assimilation.

A number of observers have interpreted the history of Mexicans in the Midwest within the context of European-based assimilationist models, as distinct from the southwestern models. Historian Susan Diebold asserted that "Mexicans were merely the most recent of the many immigrant groups to settle on 'the flats,'" of St. Paul's West Side. Diebold added that "Minnesota has gained a reputation . . . for offering a good quality of life to those who live here and a high level of services to assist those who wish to settle." In 1950 John McCulley wrote in the *Reporter* that a "great peninsula" of Mexican immigration was pushing northward from Texas and the Southwest, adding that "on the peninsula's northern fringes, the migrants are being absorbed, but at its base they are still holding on to their language, culture and mores." In 1966, José Hernández Alvarez concluded that the midwestern environment resulted in "a unique phenomenon within the Mexican population of the United States," whose residents, unlike those of the Southwest, "developed in an environment similar to that of the large majority of [European] immigrants in the United States." Some Mexican settlers shared those opinions, including Sra. María Bósquez, who immigrated from Jalisco to Minnesota in 1928 when she was twenty-two years old. She claimed that "the state of Minnesota is one of the states that helps 'La Raza' the most. . . . I have seen it on television and in the paper." Unfortunately, she based her belief in Minnesota exceptionalism on dominant popular media and acknowledged, "I have not lived in any other state" of the United States, for when she crossed the border she went directly to the Twin Cities to join her family.[22]

Portrayals of Mexicans in the Midwest as the last of the immigrants, with accompanying assimilationist premises, date from the early years of large-scale settlement. In the late 1920s, Paul Taylor suggested that Mexicans in the urban Midwest "have come into contact more fully and more sharply than in rural areas with a mental and material culture different from their own, and in it they are remaining less a class and race apart." In 1957 reporter Harvey S. Ford of the *Toledo Blade* wrote that Mexicans were "the most recent addition to the many nationality groups" in the region. Thirteen years later Father Michael Bradley of St. Paul suggested that "the Spanish-speaking settlers in this area at the present are in a position similar to that of the European peoples of some years ago." In 1981, Mexicans in the Stockyards district of Chicago were described as "the newest 'Back of the Yards' emigrant group."[23] If midwestern Mexicans had successfully assimilated in the 1920s, why were they still perceived as the last of the immigrants in the same neighborhoods three generations later?

Assimilationist notions and implicit modernization theory also pervade studies on gender and families in the Midwest. Sociologist Norman Goldner suggests that Mexicanas in the Twin Cities were hindered by "the traditional Spanish patriarchal family system" yet claims that the hierarchical, male-dominated family structure brought from Mexico and Texas quickly began to "break down when their migrancy began, and, later, in the city," allowing them to assimilate. The degree to which male domination differed in Anglo families has not yet been systematically addressed.[24]

Several authors challenge interpretations that midwestern Mexicans migrated in the tradition of Europeans and sought to emulate them. Francisco Arturo Rosales writes that although Mexicans in Chicago represented "one more in a long line of immigrant groups who fulfilled the labor needs of the huge industrial city," they "were seeking neither refuge nor the start to a new life. They came to earn money and wanted to return home. Many did, but even those who remained harbored a dream of someday going back, an attitude which promoted immigrant cohesion based on identification with Mexican nationalism." Similarly, anthropologists Barbara June Macklin and Alvina Teniente de Costilla suggest that in the case of Toledo, Ohio, Mexicans, the decision to "settle out," or establish permanent residence locally, commonly was not based on a desire to improve their lives and assimilate but rather was "completely situational."[25]

Studies emphasizing the primacy of race and ethnicity, including internal colonialism, have had less influence on studies of Mexicans in the Midwest. Concurring with Paul Taylor's earlier observations, sociologist Norman Humphrey in the 1940s argued that in the northern United States, race prejudice against Mexicans was not as developed as that against Blacks in the South or Mexicans in the Southwest. He suggested that "germinal elements for a Mexican caste are present" but less systematic due to "simply the small size of the Mexican group, which prevents the Mexicans from being defined by the dominant American group as threatening its economic position." Mario Barrera asserted that during the mass migration to the Southwest during the period 1900–1930, "Mexican immigrants were fit into the existing colonial structure," but he does not mention whether similar conditions applied to Mexicans in the Midwest. In his study of Chicago during the 1920s, Mark Reisler more explicitly argued that racism was the most important determinant of inequality, adding that "to the Mexican, the United States was not the promised land. He stayed only because work was available. . . . Only his effort to preserve his native identity and his hope of returning to the homeland alleviated the despair of the culture of poverty." In the 1980s historian Edward Escobar, in his work on Northwest Indiana, suggested that selected features of an internal colonial model do apply: particularly occupational stratification, employers' use of Mexicans as a "reserve labor force," and the targeting of them as "shock absorbers" in times of economic dislocation.[26]

Midwestern studies have placed a greater emphasis on class as critical to Mexican inequality than have southwestern ones, and have delineated other important differences between the two regions. First, the experience of conquest and systematic subordination in the Southwest was not replicated in the Midwest. Second, the sharpest race-based historical division in the region has been between Black and White, rather than Mexican and Anglo. Third, because of the smaller and more scattered Mexican population, there were fewer opportunities for a tradition of mutual and systematic hostility based on racial features or competing identities to develop. Fourth, Mexican migration to the region remained overwhelmingly a function of employer demands for unskilled labor. As Norman Humphrey observed, even people who had skills and professions in Mexico "tended to become common laborers" in the North, "as a consequence of the specialized character of American production." Meanwhile, a landowning class did not appear, and there were few opportunities for the appearance of a midwestern middle class or petite bourgeoisie. George Edson, a U.S. Department of Labor investigator who conducted a very detailed survey of Mexican communities in the region in 1926 and 1927, noted that their residents included "practically no men of capital. A very limited number have been men of means or position." More recently, Juan García and Angel Cal similarly concluded that in the Midwest "Mexicans from the middle class quickly learned that their education and background were of little value in helping them achieve a higher standard of living, improved employment opportunities, or respect from members of the host society."[27] Thus even after nearly a century of continuous presence, midwestern Mexican communities tend to be much less diverse than in the Southwest, with workers concentrated at the lower occupational levels.

Approaches based on World-Systems analysis, including the present study, offer opportunities to include a distinct midwestern geography in Chicana and Chicano studies literature. Formally articulated in the 1970s from a Marxist framework, it has since been adopted and modified by scholars of various political persuasions. Many of its central features, including the intersection of racism and class in an international setting, were applied to Mexican workers in writings by León Slavin Ruiz and Alberto Moreau in the 1920s, but largely neglected for more than a generation afterward. As articulated by Immanuel Wallerstein, it suggests that a world economy appeared during the "long" sixteenth century as part of the process of capital accumulation, and it has been constantly expanding, intensifying, and changing. The modern world system is based on unequal relationships between the imperialist, or "core" countries, and their colonies and former colonies of the "periphery" in the political, economic, and cultural arenas. Furthermore, capitalists' efforts to control the forces and relations of production, circulation, and reproduction systematically subordinate workers. But the system simultaneously establishes conditions that permit resistance and challenges to inequality.

As applied to the United States and Mexico, the nineteenth-century invasion and conquest permitted the former to forcibly acquire land and other means of production, to subordinate Mexico politically, economically, and culturally, and to incorporate a reserve labor army. Capitalists from the United States intensified economic, political, and cultural penetration of Mexico while they set in motion a system of exploitation and circulation of Mexican workers between the two countries. In times of need the labor force in Mexico could be readily tapped, while in times of excess it could be released. An exploitative relationship between the two countries was replicated in popular culture, as notions of White superiority and racist attitudes rooted in conquest facilitated European American acquisition of land and control of Mexican workers. But it contradictorily created conditions permitting Mexican workers to develop oppositional political and cultural forums for their own liberation. While some critical observers suggest that global models can obscure local variation and distinctiveness, the present examination of midwestern Mexican communities and the barrio on the West Side of St. Paul offers an opportunity to examine links involving global, regional, local, and microlevel geography.[28]

# 2 Reckoning with Winter

Industrial expansion in the late nineteenth and early twentieth centuries unleashed a phenomenal rate of urbanization in the heartland of the United States, led by Chicago, Detroit, Milwaukee, and two pairs of urban twins, the Kansas Cities of Kansas and Missouri, and Minneapolis and St. Paul. Immigrants from Europe filled the needs of the handful of major industries that dominated the region, namely railroads, steel, automobiles, and food processing. The railroads required thousands of workers to operate the trains and maintain cars, tracks, and railroad beds that linked the cities and their products to each other, to their agricultural hinterlands, and to the rest of the country. The more recently established steel and automobile plants that transformed the region and the world required even more workers. By the 1920s, the industrial belt extending along the South Shore of Lake Michigan was the largest steel-producing center in the nation, and Michigan produced "more autos than the rest of the world combined."[1] Workers in the cities also represented a major market for a rapidly expanding food production and processing industry that established a meat-based diet, making the United States the envy of much of the world. The meat processing industry in the industrial heartland employed thousands of additional workers.

Capitalists adopted production strategies oriented toward the burgeoning domestic market by concentrating plants and workers in large factories and specific urban districts. In those plants they developed a drive system to push workers harder. They also established a highly regimented job hierarchy, hired workers from many countries, and used reserve labor pools to discipline and divide workers and hinder industrial unionism. In the mid nineteenth century their largest labor pools came from Germany and Ireland, but these soon were outnumbered by arrivals from Scandinavia and southern and eastern Europe. As immigration accelerated, dominant groups in the United States increasingly expressed disenchantment with changes they attributed to the new arrivals, while politicians in Europe expressed concern over the fate of their compatriots, which resulted in more exclusionary immigration policies between the two continents. By the time of World War I, capitalists had turned to more readily accessible labor sources from the southern United States and along the United States–Mexican border, inducing the first major wave of labor migration from Mexico to the Midwest. In cities throughout the region, Mexican workers formed *colonias,* as they identified the neighborhoods where they took up residence.[2]

As Mexicans replaced European workers, their actual place in midwestern society and their relations with their predecessors became the subject of some dispute among popular observers and academics. One view is that Mexicans were the "last of the immigrants" who migrated north to improve their lives, and in general they could expect to achieve a degree of upward mobility. A second view holds that their choices were much more constrained and that because of widespread discrimination, "employment was available in only the least desirable jobs." Furthermore, "except for a fortunate few, . . . migration imposed broad social leveling," segmenting Mexicans into to the bottom levels of the working class, whereas Europeans had a much greater range of employment opportunities. A third opinion, articulated by George Edson, offered a still bleaker assessment. He suggested that Mexicans were "brought in as supernumerary laborers," and even among those who remained, "the duration of a Mexican on a job was relatively short," because they were confined to the function of an unstable labor reserve.[3]

These differences in interpretation reflect both different expectations of observers and local variations, for Mexican experiences in the communities they formed were not uniform. In some cities Mexicans had several employment options, while in others they worked overwhelmingly for one employer or a single industry. In some cities they formed a number of barrios, while in others they were confined to a single neighborhood as a company town, or an "urban village." Some enjoyed a varied social and cultural life, while others' experiences outside of work were much bleaker. In some settings their work and cultural lives were separated geographically, as in Minnesota, where most were recruited to the sugar beet fields in the southern and northwestern sections of the state, but they established only one important barrio, the Lower West Side of St. Paul. In this chapter I will discuss the formation of Mexican *colonias* and how patterns of work, family, social, and cultural life unfolded in the early-twentieth-century urban Midwest.

## Last of the Immigrants

Industrial capitalism, which stimulated migration from many countries to the United States, also encouraged hundreds of thousands of workers to

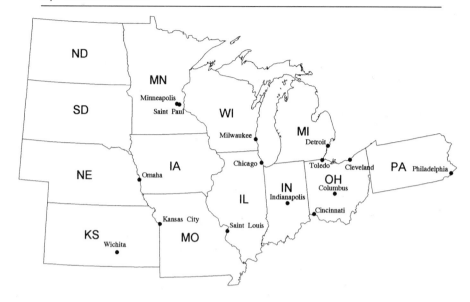

MAP I. MAJOR CITIES OF THE
MIDWEST AND PENNSYLVANIA.

cross national borders within Europe in search of employment in industrial cities and agriculture. An early stage of this process in both Europe
and North America was the construction of a railroad system, which
reached its peak in Mexico during the age of dictator Porfirio Díaz, the
*Porfiriato* (1876–1910). Workers left rural settings and smaller towns to
build a railroad network from the United States to the larger cities, including Guadalajara, Mexico City, and Monterrey, offering easy access to the
border and beyond.[4]

Mexican railroads stimulated international investment and commerce
while making possible a rapid increase in labor migration between Mexico
and the United States. The largest numbers passed through El Paso beginning in the 1880s, followed by Laredo, Eagle Pass, and other Texas
border towns shortly afterward. Prior to World War I, a majority of migration to the United States was destined for Texas, which became the
gateway for Mexican migration to other parts of the country. The location
of railroads also influenced the regional origins of Mexican immigration
to the United States. The largest concentration of people who settled in
Texas came from northeastern Mexico, while those heading to California
originated largely in western and west-central Mexico and passed mostly
through El Paso. Individuals who headed for the Midwest mostly came

from central Mexico and were more likely to pass through Laredo. They worked their way north and east from Texas gradually and had reached the cotton-growing sections of Oklahoma in the first years of the century.[5]

Midwestern Mexican *colonias* appeared in three distinct phases in the early twentieth century. The first, between 1906 and 1910, was associated with recruitment by railroad companies already employing Mexicans in the Southwest. Employers transported workers to settings on the Great Plains for seasonal track maintenance and repair work and permitted them to spend winters in bunkhouses or boxcars usually located on adjacent company-owned properties. A second phase, from 1916 to 1919, was linked to railroad and industrial employer demands during the wartime economic boom and labor shortages that resulted from restricted immigration from Europe. In 1916 several railroad companies brought hundreds of Mexicans to the Near West Side of Chicago. In 1918 the Ford Motor Company in Detroit hired a large contingent of Mexican student apprentices, who were soon joined by a greater number of unskilled countrymen. In 1919 the steel mills of South Chicago, the Indiana Harbor section of East Chicago, and Gary, Indiana, recruited unsuspecting Mexicans to break the nationwide steel strike that year. A third phase of *colonia* formation took place after the postwar industrial depression of 1920–1921. The *colonia* in the Stockyards district of Chicago appeared when employers seeking to break the packinghouse workers' strike in 1921–1922 hired a contingent of Mexicans. Steel mill companies also lured Mexicans to work in some of their foundries farther east, including those in Lorain, Ohio; Homestead and Bethlehem, Pennsylvania; and Buffalo, New York. In St. Paul, a few Mexican workers had settled in the railroad yards of the Lower West Side prior to the war. The *colonia* took on a visible form when the American Beet Sugar Company (later American Crystal) directed families there in the fall of 1923, after harvest ended.[6]

Early midwestern *colonias* shared several features in common. First, they appeared in direct response to employer efforts to attract "labor to build and maintain the basic industries of the United States." Their size and location was largely determined by available work. In numerical terms, the largest nonagricultural employers were steel mills and the closely related automobile industry, where most Mexicans worked in foundries. Next in importance were railroads, building and highway construction, and packinghouses. Smaller but still significant urban employers included cement and brick plants, tanneries, and restaurants.[7]

Second, residents of midwestern barrios came primarily from the Mesa Central, especially Michoacán, Jalisco, Guanajuato, and Mexico City, with a second important clustering from the north-central states of Zacatecas, Chihuahua, Coahuila, and Nuevo León. The Mesa Central, with its very high population density, offered limited opportunities for small or aspiring landowners, according to Father James Ward, a longtime priest of the Mexican parish in St. Paul. He noted that on large holdings workers received little more than lodging and food for wages, while owners of small ranchos had difficulty sustaining their families without outside employment. Demographic and political tensions, culminating in *La Cristiada* (the Cristero Rebellion) in the late 1920s, a conservative Catholic uprising, encouraged additional departures. Railroad recruiters and employment agents took advantage of the presence of several railroads that traversed the zone to lure workers north in the early years of the century, and the movement soon developed a momentum of its own.[8]

A third distinguishing feature of midwestern *colonias* was their greater homogeneity than that found in barrios of the Southwest. In the early years they were composed overwhelmingly of young adult Mexican-born males. At first the men clustered in company housing or family-run boarding houses (*casas de asistencia*), which became "an institution, a center for recreation and social life," sometimes providing food or making arrangements with local Mexican restaurants. Yet many young men quickly developed their own culinary skills. One Gary man stated, "I did not know how to cook when I came here, but I have learned so that now I can cook better than a woman." The northern barrios exhibited less occupational diversity than those in the Southwest, where greater opportunities existed for Mexican businesses and professionals because of longer-established communities, larger populations, and sharper segregation. In midwestern cities, Mexicans commonly purchased goods and services from establishments owned by Europeans and European Americans or Spanish-speaking entrepreneurs from Spain, Puerto Rico, the Philippines, and Cuba. When employers sought out Spanish-speaking office workers, Chicago social worker Agnes Fenton observed, "usually an industry prefers a Cuban, a Porto Rican [*sic*], or a native Spaniard for their work, as they are better educated and more accustomed to business methods."[9]

Fourth, despite popular impressions that the Mexican Midwest, in contrast to the Southwest, was urban, Paul Taylor recognized in the late 1920s that in the Midwest "most of the Mexicans came originally from agriculture." Prior to the 1950s, the cotton industry hired more Mexicans than did any other employer in the zone running from Arkansas and Texas to California, while the sugar beet industry played a similar role on the northern Great Plains and the Midwest. Mexican agricultural workers commonly spent the period between spring and fall preparing fields, weeding, tending plants, and harvesting cotton or sugar beets. While some wintered in rural *colonias,* others moved to large cities, including Los Angeles, El Paso, San Antonio, Denver, Kansas City, St. Paul, Chicago, and Detroit, or they returned to Mexico. The sharp distinction between city and countryside, well articulated in the popular cultures of both Mexico and the United States, did not apply to hundreds of thousands of Mexicans who moved frequently among large and medium-sized cities, small towns, and rural locations in search of employment and more stable lives.[10]

Within midwestern states the rate of urban and rural settlement varied widely. According to the 1930 census, the resident Mexican population of Indiana was 96.4 percent urban, while that of Missouri was 88.7 percent; Illinois, 87.3 percent; Wisconsin, 86.9 percent; Michigan, 86.8 percent; Iowa, 72.9 percent; Kansas, 56.8 percent; Nebraska, 41.6 percent; and Minnesota, 36.2 percent. Censuses underestimated the impact of agriculture, particularly because counts took place in early April, preceding the annual migration of sugar beet workers from Texas, Mexico, and midwestern cities. Many who were counted as city dwellers spent much of the year and gained almost all their income from work in the fields. Census takers also undercounted unmarried Mexican males, who were usually away during the day when canvassers arrived. As an astute observer noted, landladies "very frequently deny any knowledge of the nationality of their roomers when they are Mexicans."[11]

The location, size, and characteristics of specific midwestern *colonias* resulted from interaction among workers and employers, local social and economic conditions, and the attitudes and behavior of non-Mexican populations. Much initial large-scale migration was linked to earlier U.S. entrepreneurial investment in Mexican railroads, mines, agriculture, and other industrial activities. Several large employers in the United States had earlier experiences with workers in Mexico, including one of the first manufacturing concerns to hire Mexicans in the region, based in the North Side of Chicago. Mexicans already formed an international working class, suggesting serious flaws in dominant economic models and political rhetoric of the twentieth century that separate capital flows from the migration of workers.[12]

Railroads were the first major employer in the Midwest to take advantage of international networks, often sending labor agents into the Mexican interior to attract workers. By 1910, Mexican immigrants already dominated track labor in the Southwest and had begun to move northward. Kansas City, Dodge City, Topeka, and Omaha became funnels through which a much greater wave of migration passed when demands for labor intensified in the Great Lakes states during and after World War I. Mexican railroad *colonias* soon appeared farther north and east, including Council Bluffs, Des Moines, East Des Moines, Fort Madison, Davenport, and Bettendorf, Iowa; and Moline, East Moline, Silvis, Rock Island, Aurora, and Joliet, Illinois. By 1928, Mexicans represented 43 percent of track and maintenance workers on sixteen major railroads in the Chicago and northwestern Indiana region and were working on the railroads in the string of cities from Toledo to Saginaw, with smaller numbers farther east. A detailed survey of early 1927 calculated that about eight thousand Mexicans worked on railroads in the zone from Ohio to Minnesota and Iowa, with an additional ten thousand in Nebraska, South Dakota, Montana, Wyoming, Colorado, and Kansas. They formed a labor reserve for higher-paying work in other industries. Santa Fe Railroad Chief Engineer R. A. Rutledge asserted that "the Mexicans cannot be driven like the Negro, but anyone who knows how to manage the Mexicans can get more out of them than any other class."[13]

Several steel companies "discovered" Mexican workers during World War I and tried to use them to break the nationwide steel strike of 1919, which had the overwhelming support of workers in fifty-five cities in ten states, despite its mixed success. A steel industry labor recruiter born in Chihuahua who had come to Illinois in 1917 via California and Colorado reported that he was working as a translator and that "the workers at the mills had been ready to go on strike but waited only for the end of the war. Soon after the armistice they struck. The Mexicans went out too. The mills were deserted. The companies sent me to get our Mexicans to work for them. I got some at Chicago, others at Omaha, Kansas City, a few at St. Louis. I even went down to El Paso and some cities in Texas. ... Mexicans as a rule are not strike breakers." After the postwar recession, the industry intensified its recruitment efforts, in part because of the reduction of the working day to eight hours in 1923. By 1927 more than seventeen thousand Mexicans worked in steel mills and foundries in the Great Plains and Great Lakes region, almost half the total number of Mexicans employed outside agriculture.[14] The steel and automobile industries that hired Mexicans primarily as foundry workers were responsible for the appearance of many barrios, particularly in the industrial belts extending from South Chicago to Gary; from Toledo through Detroit to Saginaw; and in a few cities farther east. Mexicans were much more selectively employed in the mills and foundries than on the railroads.

A smaller number of Mexicanos were attracted to packinghouses, especially during World War I and again in 1921–1922, when they were recruited by several companies to break an industry-wide strike. Labor demands in meatpacking were not as great as in steel, and employment in the industry declined by more than 25 percent during the 1920s; yet by late 1927, more than one thousand Mexicans worked in the region's packing-houses. The largest single concentration appeared in the Back of the Yards district in Chicago, where, as Rick Halpern observed, in comparison with African Americans, Mexicans faced greater discrimination and "had far fewer opportunities to advance up the job ladder." Confined to the worst jobs in hide cellars, freezers, glue houses, and fertilizer departments, Mexicans were, according to Halpern, "the most exploited segment of the packinghouse workers." Smaller numbers of Mexicans also found work in the packing plants of Omaha, Kansas City, and Sioux City, Iowa.[15] During the 1920s, packinghouses in South St. Paul offered the most important urban employment available to Mexicans in the Twin Cities.

The sugar beet industry, which had been luring Mexicans to the region since World War I, also influenced the process of community formation. Although work in the beets was more seasonal than in factories and rail-roads, Methodist minister Robert McLean observed that "every city located in or near a beet area can be counted upon to develop a Mexican colony." In the fall, employers directed *betabeleros* (beet workers) to find winter refuge in rural *colonias* and nearby cities including Saginaw, Detroit, Toledo, Chicago's Hull House district, Milwaukee, Des Moines, Kansas City, and St. Paul.[16]

By the late 1920s, there were several clusters of urban settlements in the Midwest, each with distinct characteristics. The oldest was in Kansas, with the largest concentrations in the metropolitan Kansas City area, spreading to Nebraska, particularly Omaha, and several medium-sized Iowa cities. A second cluster, the most important in the region, centered in Chicago and took in the extensive steel mill district in northeastern Illinois and northwestern Indiana, including several *colonias* associated with railroads and other industries. A third cluster of settlements centered on Detroit, extending from Toledo in the south to Saginaw in the north, representing the automobile and its affiliated industries. Farther to the east, a smaller number of Mexican *colonias* appeared in response to railroad or foundry work.

Large-scale Mexican migration to Kansas began around 1903 when the Santa Fe Railroad brought in track workers from its southwestern lines as an experiment. During the economic boom in 1907, its recruitment increased, and other companies soon followed suit. Visible *colonias* appeared

MAP 2. SELECT CITIES OF THE
MIDWEST —WESTERN SECTION.

in and near railroad yards in smaller communities, including Lyons, Ot-
tawa, Emporia, Newton, Wellington, and Horton. In Dodge City, a *colonia* formed on Santa Fe Railroad property, consisting of small shacks on
its two principal streets, and workers paid 50 cents per month for rent. In
Garden City, Mexicans were clustered in a section south of the railroad
tracks referred to as "Little Mexico," consisting of two distinct barrios
popularly called *La Nalga,* on the west side of Main Street, and *La Garra*
on the east. *Colonias* also appeared in and around larger cities, including
the south side of Wichita, and Topeka, where by 1910 Santa Fe railroad
workers had begun to construct a "Little Mexico" in the southeast corner
of the railroad yards. The *colonia,* which survived until 1939 when it was
finally torn down, consisted of shacks, barns, sheds, and garages, and
dwellings had spaces for gardens and animals. Additional Kansas *colonias*
appeared in response to employment in salt mining in Hutchinson, Lyons, Little River, and Kanopolis, where White and Mexican miners lived

MAP 3. SELECT CITIES OF THE MIDWEST AND
PENNSYLVANIA — EASTERN SECTION.

in segregated neighborhoods. Mexicans also lived near the meatpacking plants where they worked in Kansas City, Topeka, and Wichita.[17]

In metropolitan Kansas City, six Mexican neighborhoods had appeared by the 1920s, each originally formed as a railroad camp. On the Kansas side of the Missouri River, Mexicans formed a boxcar camp in the northeast section of Argentine, a company town of the Santa Fe railroad and site of railroad car repair shops and administrative offices. They had begun to settle around 1905, and the barrio reached seven hundred residents by 1907, though its population fluctuated afterward. Argentine Mexicans concentrated on both sides of the railroad yards primarily between 24th and 27th streets, while smaller groups also resided in the yards, and along 39th and 40th streets. Home to a large contingent of former residents of

Tangancicuaro, Michoacán, Argentine was the largest barrio in the metropolitan area until the 1920s. In subsequent decades until the 1951 flood, its residents became "more separated from the rest of the community and more concentrated in the barrio." The nearby barrio in Rosedale began as a camp of the Frisco (St. Louis and San Francisco) Railroad. The barrio in the bottoms along Turkey Creek began as a camp of the Katy (Kansas and Texas) Railroad and soon extended into Armourdale, home of meatpacking workers employed in the four huge plants located there in the 1920s.[18]

Three barrios on the Missouri side of the river included a small railroad workers' camp of the Chicago, Burlington and Quincy Railroad in North Kansas City; another along the Blue River in the Sheffield area; and the Westside Bluffs. The Westide barrio was the largest, extending from the Missouri River eastward to Summit, concentrated between 20th and 25th streets. As German, Irish, and Swedish predecessors departed, Mexicans moved in, and by the 1920s the Westside surpassed Argentine in population and became the principal Mexican commercial and cultural district in the Kansas City area. A temporary chapel offering Mexican masses was set up in 1914 and became permanent in 1919 when the Swedish Lutheran church moved out. In 1926 the Guadalupe Center was established to offer recreation, crafts, and classes in the community. The Mexican population in the Kansas City area reached its peak around 1920 at about ten thousand but had declined to between six and seven thousand by the end of the decade. Throughout the 1920s and the early 1930s, historian Judith Fincher Laird concludes, "segregation was the rule, whether in residential, educational, religious, recreational or social circles" for Mexicans in the several urban *colonias* of the Kansas City area. Because of its early formation, its location at the intersection of several railroads, and the instability of railroad employment, Kansas City became an important recruitment center for Mexican workers headed to fields and factories farther north and east.[19]

In 1925, 95 percent of Mexicans in Kansas were classified as laborers, and in 1930, almost 75 percent of employed Mexican and Mexican American males in the state still worked for railroads. Typically employment was seasonal, between May and October, mostly on section gangs in maintenance and repair of rails and railroad beds. Mexicans in many midwestern cities found similar "shovel work" in gangs working construction and maintenance of roads and street railways. As one observer noted, "railroads were the lowest-paying of the major industrial employers," and work on section gangs was the least stable. Mexican railroad workers also experienced the greatest degree of segregation from their European and European American counterparts, both on work gangs and in railroad camps.[20]

In Nebraska, sugar beet and railroad workers clustered in a number of cities and towns, including Lincoln, where in the mid 1920s about fifteen Mexican families formed a *colonia* near Salt Creek, around 1st and I streets. The largest settlement was in Omaha, where railroad workers arrived in 1908 and 1909 from Kansas City. Omaha railroad workers clustered in several districts—near the Burlington Station around Sixth Street; in Carville, just north of Gibson on the banks of the Missouri, where most lived in railroad car bodies on Burlington property; along Spring Street; and in adjoining Council Bluffs, Iowa, near the Union Pacific Shops. By 1925 the Mexican population of the city exceeded fifteen hundred, with the largest concentration in the packinghouse district of South Omaha, near the eastern edge of the city. Mexicans lived among Hungarian, Bohemian, Italian, Greek, and African American families in one of the most stable *colonias* in the region, employed mostly at the Swift, Armour, and Cudahy plants. A 1926 survey found that Mexicans in those plants had been employed for an average of seven years and that 85 to 90 percent lived in separate households, although most were young and unmarried. The South Omaha *colonia* had a grocery store, two pool halls, and a barbershop and was a center of recruitment for sugar beet workers in the Great Plains and industries in the Chicago area. Because no Mexican church had been established in Omaha at the time, Mexicanos rarely attended services.[21]

In a 1924 study, geographer T. Earl Sullenger asserted that Mexicans in Omaha "lack confidence in the American, as they think that the average American thinks of them only as inferiors." Their thoughts were widely confirmed by many observers, including Edson, who reported that police in Omaha "used to arrest Mexicans they found in restaurants, dance halls, theaters or street corners [without cause]. Mexicans were frequently railroaded by judges, insulted by neighbors and cheated by lawyers," while youth attending school "were spat upon and called 'greasers' by other children," an epithet popular throughout the region. Sullenger attributed the inequality of Omaha's Mexicanos to cultural deficiencies, claiming that "they seem to accept their lot as ordinary laborers in good faith. Their ambitions are not high." Suspicion and mistrust were widespread among European Americans, including Thomas Diouhy, a grocery store owner in Carville who catered to the Mexican trade: "I don't trust them. They're not to be blamed; they're to be pitied. They're just children and don't know any better." Yet Carville resident María Hernández, who had recently dropped out of school and still lived with her parents, understood inequality differently. She asserted, "I'd give anything to get out of here and live uptown, like in one of those houses I saw up there when I was going to school (in Omaha). The younger folks, they know better and want to get out, to be free. They know we're not free, not when we have to live this way."[22]

Mexicans first came to neighboring Iowa in small numbers to work on the railroads around 1910, and by the winter of 1926–1927 about eleven hundred were reported in the vicinity of Sioux City, Mason City, Fort Madison, Des Moines, and Valley Junction. Most worked on the railroads, with smaller numbers in cement and meatpacking plants, in addition to the sugar beet fields in northern sections of the state. In the Quad Cities area, they clustered in Davenport, West Davenport, Bettendorf, Moline, East Moline, Rock Island, and Silvis. Most local Mexicanos were employed by the Rock Island and other railroads except those in Bettendorf, who worked at the automobile plants of the Bettendorf Company, which had a close and paternalistic relationship with its workers. Silvis, with almost four hundred Mexican residents, had the largest *colonia* in the Quad Cities area, "a veritable Mexican town of its own." They resided in modest cottages rented from the Rock Island Railroad, or in boxcars and coach bodies they fixed up with materials mostly salvaged from old railroad cars. Typical of smaller urban *colonias* in the region, those of the Quad Cities and elsewhere in Iowa were "detached settlements," often exhibiting many characteristics of company towns, including close supervision by employers. They were often too small to sustain Mexican businesses or professionals and had few sharply marked internal divisions. Exhibiting comparatively fragile social and political life and tight employer control, according to Edson, "the field for a political agitator or a patriotic journalist would be thin."[23]

A massive wave of immigration during and immediately after World War I permitted Chicago, already the second most populous city in the nation, to gain distinction for the largest concentration of Mexicans beyond the border states. Informed estimates ranged from 15,000 to 20,000 by the late 1920s, the fourth largest urban concentration of Mexicans in the United States, following Los Angeles, San Antonio, and El Paso. In 1926, about three years before its pre-Depression population peak, Mexican officials reported that more than 45,000 Mexicans resided in the zone extending from the northern and western industrial suburbs of Chicago into northwestern Indiana. An additional 25,000 were reported in Lower Michigan and Ohio; 3,000 in Upper Michigan, Wisconsin, and Minnesota, and about 12,000 in Missouri, Iowa, and Western Illinois. At least 25,000 more Mexicans resided in Kansas and Nebraska at the time, for a total of about 110,000 in the Great Plains and Great Lakes region. These estimates excluded thousands of workers employed in the sugar beet fields and other scattered locations, increasing the population an estimated 50 percent. There were perhaps 10,000 additional Mexicans then residing in Pennsylvania, West Virginia, New York, Connecticut, and New Jersey.[24]

In the 1920s there were several concentrations of Mexicans in Chicago, of which three stood out, all south of the Loop—the Near West Side (Hull House), the Stockyards district (Back of the Yards), and South Chicago. The largest was on the Near West Side, extending from Halsted to Blue Island between Harrison and 15th Street. It centered around Hull House, the settlement house founded by Jane Addams. The oldest Mexican neighborhood in Chicago, it appeared around 1916 when several railroad lines brought in maintenance-of-way workers, and by 1919 more than one thousand had been imported to the area from Mexico, most under special exemption of the 1917 Immigration Act. In addition to local railroads, many men found employment locally in meatpacking plants, beading factories, miscellaneous metal and small packing plants, and hotels on the Loop. Women commonly worked at Cracker Jack and other candy factories and as machine operators in several bedding and rug factories. The Near West Side was the poorest Mexican neighborhood in Chicago, and most residents there had unstable and irregular employment. It was also the major residence in the Chicago area for families of sugar beet workers from Michigan, Wisconsin, Minnesota, and neighboring states after the harvest ended, who "seldom have enough for a period of idleness." Yet as social worker Anita Jones observed, despite their own meager resources, Mexicanos more established in the colony "lend a neighborly hand and do all they can to alleviate the suffering" of unemployed beet workers. Mexicans were not the majority in this very diverse ethnic neighborhood, also home to large numbers of Bohemians, Italians, Poles, and other southern and eastern Europeans, who were already beginning to move westward toward the suburbs.[25]

Hull House had more in common with the *colonia* that formed on St. Paul's Lower West Side than other Chicago-area Mexican neighborhoods, as both were important ports of entry for newly arrived immigrants, centers of Mexican social and cultural activities, and winter homes for *betabeleros*. Their residents lived in "crowded and unsanitary buildings." One observer noted that "Mexicans live in the poorest houses in the neighborhood," in rear houses, basements, and other undesirable sections of apartment buildings, and "some families have been known to sleep with guns under the bed to shoot rats in the night."[26]

The Near West Side was the region's Mexican business, literary, and cultural capital, and despite the poverty it was described as "one of the gayest and most colorful of Chicago's foreign colonies." It had more than twenty-five active Mexican clubs and societies in the mid 1930s, despite the devastation of the Great Depression. Many groups met in the formerly Italian St. Francis of Assisi Church, which was assigned its first Spanish-speaking priest and became a Mexican church in 1928, while others met at Hull House, where it was reported, "we never had better mannered guests." A market on the plaza next to Hull House was described as "very similar to a Mexican market," where vendors spoke Spanish, sold Mexican fruits, vegetables, and groceries including items like chiles, *cajeta* (candy made from goat milk), *pan dulce* (sweet bread), and Mexican chocolate. The immediate neighborhood had several Mexican restaurants, El Arte Mexicano music store, and a music school operated by Professor Francisco Calderón. Even Mexicans of the middle class and entrepreneurial groups exhibited a strong urge not to assimilate; as Edson observed, "they do not care to learn our language or our manners or our attitude toward wealth, all of which they consider barbarous."[27]

A second major Mexican neighborhood, the Back of the Yards district, associated with the Stockyards since the 1860s, was the site of Upton Sinclair's 1906 muckraking exposé, *The Jungle*. It had three distinct Mexican neighborhoods, the largest centering around 46th and Ashland, also referred to as the University of Chicago Settlement Colony. Mexicans appeared almost suddenly when a number of meatpacking companies, including Armour, Swift, and Wilson, began recruiting them to break the packinghouse strike of 1921–1922. They also worked for the Crane Brothers Manufacturing Company, the American Can Company, and a number of railroads. Offering greater opportunities for regular employment, it was more stable than Hull House, but its longer-established European and European American residents, often homeowners with a greater vested interest in the neighborhood, were more reluctant to accept Mexicans as neighbors. As one observer noted in the 1930s, "a great deal of neighborhood hostility was felt toward this Mexican migration into the community, and older nationalities made every effort to keep the Mexicans away from the area."[28] As in many sites of ethnic confrontation, local opposition alone did not determine the neighborhoods Mexicans would occupy, for with the tacit support of employers and social workers at the University of Chicago Settlement House, the *colonia* survived.

The third major Mexican district was in South Chicago, where Mexicans were concentrated in two neighborhoods. In Millgate, located to the east of the Illinois Steel mill (a U.S. Steel subsidiary, later USX South Works), and extending to Commerce, Mexicans resided between 83rd and 93rd streets, particularly between 89th and 92nd. A second South Chicago district was the Irondale neighborhood, across from the Wisconsin Steel mill (owned by International Harvester), where Mexicans concentrated along Torrance Avenue between 106th and 109th streets. The South Chicago settlement was more recent than the other major Chicago barrios, first appearing when employers brought in several hundred Mexicans from Kansas City and the Southwest during the 1919 steel strike, and growing much more rapidly in 1922 and 1923. The steel companies made paternalistic gestures to maintain control over workers and prevent unionization, including cheap meals in company cafeterias, selling coal at below-market prices, and supporting mutual aid societies and other recreational activities, including baseball and football teams. Illinois Steel also supported efforts to establish Our Lady of Guadalupe Church, which was formed in 1924 at 89th and Mackinaw Streets and supplanted by a larger church in 1928 at 91st and Brandon, to help maintain worker loyalty.[29]

During the 1920s the South Chicago *colonia* was comprised overwhelmingly of males residing in boarding houses, who, like residents of comparable neighborhoods, were constantly exposed to prostitution, bootlegging, police harassment, and discrimination in churches, housing, and rent. Local settlement house activities were associated principally with the Congregational Church's Bird Memorial Center, which offered Mexicans space for clubs and recreational activities. The district had a number of small Mexican businesses, often started by families who ensured their own sustenance by working in the steel mills. They included *casas de asistencia*, a common starting place for Mexican business activities, as well as pool halls, restaurants, and barbershops. There was a drug store on South Buffalo owned by Sr. Galindo, originally from Jalisco. He reported that his Mexican customers came from as far as Joliet to "buy more herbs than medicines," indicating that they had not assimilated the ideology of modernism in the form of industrial-scientific remedies commodified by the dominant medical community.[30]

Several smaller concentrations of Mexicanos appeared elsewhere in Chicago, typically located close to places of employment. They included the Pilsen district on the near South Side above 22nd Street, which continued to be inhabited largely by Bohemians until after World War II. There was little indication that later massive immigration from Mexico would make it the largest midwestern barrio in the late twentieth century. Mexicans also concentrated in many locations less visible to outsiders, including at least seven railroad camps within city limits, fifteen more immediately to the west, and several more to the east. The camps of the Santa Fe; the Chicago, Milwaukee and St. Paul; and the Rock Island in Blue Island were the most important. They confirmed the observations of sociologist Ruth Camblon, in 1928, that Mexicans headed *al norte* principally because of capitalists' desire for cheap labor, but neither employer nor worker expected permanent Mexican settlement, and "he seldom becomes a definite part of the community life because of his short period of residence."[31]

Mexicans in the Chicago area commonly encountered resistance to settlement from their European and European American neighbors. In addition to less physical encounters like refusal to rent and verbal threats, they experienced physical assaults, smashed windows, attacks on property, and fires started by rags saturated with oil thrown into dwellings, often with the tacit and sometimes overt support of local police. In 1929 the Chicago Chamber of Commerce discussed steps to establish formal segregation of Mexicans but decided against it, according to one account, for two reasons: "[f]irst, the legal case for such separation is not so clear as for separation of the Negroes. We understand that the Mexicans are legally classed as white. Second, the Mexicans do not present a general problem throughout the entire Chicago community as the Negroes." Similarly, a banker from Indiana Harbor asserted, "[w]e have been trying to make restrictions here to separate the Mexicans by themselves, but have not got very far with it yet." Consequently, despite verbal hostility, physical violence, and unwritten codes, systematic opposition by Whites to restrict places of Mexican residence in Chicago and neighboring cities was less formal than that against African Americans.[32]

Mexican settlements also appeared in several industrial suburbs of Chicago; the most important, as Juan García has perceptively observed, were the "satellite centers" that developed along the major rail transportation routes leading to and from the city, notably Waukegan, Elgin, Aurora, Joliet, and Chicago Heights. The *colonia* in the northern suburb of Waukegan reached about 500 people by 1926, concentrated in a swampy district between Lake Michigan and the Chicago & Northwestern railway tracks, where it was reported: "in this neighborhood, smoke-begrimed and uncharming, dwell Mexicans, negroes and the ragged edge of humanity." About 250 Mexicans worked in a local tanning plant where they washed fresh hides in a chemical bath that reportedly caused serious kidney injury.

Others were employed in an asbestos plant manufacturing shingles, where "the air is filled with dust" that filled workers' lungs, although the link between asbestos and deadly respiratory illnesses was not yet widely understood. About 80 percent of Waukegan Mexicans were single men who lived in boarding houses. One dwelling was described as "a mixture of smoke, steam, Hungarian tobacco smoke and foreign languages [that] might make some people think these places weren't like home, but they never had to go through a melting pot."[33]

In the southwestern industrial suburb of Joliet, railroad workers employed on the Santa Fe, Rock Island, Chicago & Alton, C. M. & G., and Joliet and Eastern lines formed a *colonia* along the Santa Fe tracks. The largest local employer was Illinois Steel, and a *colonia* appeared near the mill on Collins Street, while other workers scattered in railroad camps closer to work. The Mexican population rose from a handful in 1921 to more than two thousand by 1924, declined over the next two years, but in later years increased again as farmworkers from Will County settled out.[34]

Farther northwest in Aurora, most Mexicans were attracted by the Burlington Railroad to work as track laborers, in shops, roundhouses, and storehouses, or in the railroad foundry. More than one thousand Mexicanos resided in Aurora by the late 1920s, with the largest concentration north and east of the Burlington shops on low ground near the Fox River, in the midst of railroad tracks and lumber yards. A boxcar *colonia* also formed in Eola, just north of Aurora, where residents were employed by a metal-scrap works that served the Burlington and Quincy lines. Aurora lacked Mexican businesses at the time, and a contemporary observer noted that Mexicans "are looked at with askance and are discriminated against somewhat" in barbershops and theaters.[35]

The *colonias* in Elgin to the northwest of the city and Chicago Heights to the South, initially associated with railroad workers, were substantially smaller. In Chicago Heights, an Inland Steel plant constructed in 1893 employed a diverse group of European immigrants, later hiring Black and Mexican workers who were confined to the East Side, a largely immigrant district and the poorest part of town.[36]

Immediately across the state line in Indiana, larger barrios appeared in East Chicago and Gary. The Indiana Harbor section of East Chicago was a classic company town dominated by Inland Steel, which first brought in large numbers of Mexican workers during the 1919 steel strike. Heavy recruitment in 1923 and 1924 made it the largest single employer of Mexicans in the United States, a distinction for which it vied with the Ford Motor Company later in the decade. Other major local employers included

Youngstown Sheet & Tube Company and the Universal Portland Cement Company.[37]

The heart of the barrio was in the oldest part of town, just outside the factory gates, with its heaviest concentration on Block, Pennsylvania, and Grant avenues, whose intersection with Michigan Avenue was popularly referred to as the "bucket of blood," due to its reputation for violent fights and shootings. It had an overwhelmingly young male adult population crowded in bunkhouses, rooming houses, and small dingy dwellings, and "some compared the facilities to a prison." Historian Francisco Arturo Rosales observed that in Indiana Harbor "life for the Mexican workers was grim from the outset." In addition to unfamiliar work routines that "imposed a rigid structure to which they had never been exposed," the Indiana Harbor barrio, with its highly unbalanced sex ratios, prostitution, gambling, speakeasies, police brutality and discrimination, "took on the atmosphere of a frontier town." Benjamín Figueroa, a factory worker who tried to establish himself as a publisher after working all day in the factory, asserted that for all the wealth Mexican workers produce, "they get little more than a miserable existence, snubbed by their neighbors, abused by the authorities and exploited by everybody. With all the asperities that we suffer here we realize that the United States is a great country, and we cannot hate it. It is winning our affection and alluring our children." [38]

In late 1920s, the Indiana Harbor barrio became the first major urban neighborhood in the Great Lakes region with a Mexican majority and "one of the most dense concentrations of Mexicans in the United States." It was home to about five thousand Mexicanos in an area of less than one square mile, while an equal number lived elsewhere in the city. They controlled Park Avenue so completely that "the rest of the city is willing to concede it to them." Despite the bleak physical conditions, Indiana Harbor offered a rich social and cultural life. The parish of Our Lady of Guadalupe, formally established in 1927, had been preceded by Spanish-language masses in a local storefront. Although there were few Mexican professionals, Indiana Harbor had about forty restaurants, six poolrooms, six barbershops, and five groceries that catered to Mexicans. Several Mexican shops produced tailored clothing, chocolate, *pan dulce, chorizo,* and corn tortillas for local consumption.[39]

Only eight miles to the east stood Gary, whose Mexican *colonia* had grown to about twenty-five hundred by the late 1920s. It was founded as a company town around 1906, when the Gary Land Company, a subsidiary of U.S. Steel, built "a sprawling slum of shacks, barrack-like boarding houses, and cheap frame houses" for workers. Indiana Steel, American

Sheet & Tinplate Company, and Gary Tube, also subsidiaries of U.S. Steel, were the major employers, while lesser numbers of Mexicans worked on railroads and in smaller factories and shops. The *colonia* was concentrated between 10th and 20th avenues along Washington, Adams, Jefferson, and Madison streets, where housing was considered "indescribably wretched." A Mexican parish was established in 1924, in part because of hostility in established churches from European parishioners and local priests. As in most other large communities, a number of Protestant groups conducted missionary efforts, while the local International Institute, the Neighborhood House, and the Gary-Alerding settlement house also sought to attract Mexicans. The primary lure of Gary in the 1920s, as historians Neil Betten and Raymond Mohl observed, was that Mexicanos could find "fairly steady employment" in the mills.[40]

In part because of its population and comparative diversity of employment, the Chicago area had the largest Mexican business and professional class in the region. Each barrio typically had several Mexican-owned restaurants, pool halls, grocery stores, bakeries, and other shops, most of which catered to local clientele. Yet a contemporary noted that even in Chicago, "the businesses in which Mexicans are engaged are rudimentary," and few in proportion to the population they served.[41]

In Milwaukee, which boasted the largest concentration of Mexicanos in Wisconsin, workers were lured to Inland Steel and Illinois Steel plants during World War I, while in 1920 the largest employer of the pre-Depression era, the Pfister and Vogel tannery, initially imported a contingent of about one hundred Mexicans as strikebreakers. Others worked for local railroads, construction companies, and packing plants. By the end of the 1920s they approached four thousand residents, clustered in five neighborhoods bordering the Milwaukee or Menominee Rivers. The largest was in the factory district on the near South Side, with a second important *colonia* near the tannery on the North Side. As in many other northern cities, Milwaukee also was an important winter residence for sugar beet workers. Yet Milwaukee's Mexican population was reportedly "not well organized socially or politically" in comparison with many midwestern cities, despite its Sociedad Hispano-Azteca and the Guadalupe mission on Grove Street.[42]

Farther to the east, Detroit, the nation's fourth largest city at the time, had the second largest regional concentration of Mexicanos. Railroads and sugar beet companies first lured workers to the area, but more permanent urban *colonias* appeared in direct response to the automobile industry and its affiliated factories and foundries. During World War I, seeking to extend his automobile empire around the world, Henry Ford recruited several hundred young Mexican men of middle-class background as students in the Ford School of Technology to learn the particulars of automobile production and repair. School director E. M. Hutchins gave the impression that Ford himself considered it an "effort to help the little brown brother." The men were trained to learn Ford operations so they could operate agencies and garages in Mexico and the Ford assembly plant in Balbuena, outside Mexico City. These students were soon joined by thousands of men who came from nearby beet fields, other midwestern cities, and directly from Texas and Mexico, attracted by Ford's legendary high wages. By the late 1920s, an estimated fifteen thousand Mexicans resided in Detroit.[43]

In the early 1920s, most Detroit Mexicanos lived near downtown, one group residing east of Woodward Avenue for a mile along Congress and nearby streets. A greater number resided on the near Southwest Side, clustering in Corktown, formerly inhabited by Irish immigrants. A contemporary described it as "an area of deterioration" characterized by "high mobility, poor housing and transiency." The barrio moved southwest over time, largely in response to the expansion of the Central Business District and its accompanying warehouse zone. This ethnically diverse neighborhood was bounded on the south by the Detroit River, on the north by Grand River Avenue, on the east by Sixth Street, and on the west by a line formed by Clark Park and Junction Avenue. Mexicans also clustered near the Ford plants located downriver, in Highland Park and in Dearborn.[44]

Scattered sites of employment and the highly selective hiring practices of midwestern industry were evident in Detroit. More than two thousand Mexicans worked at Ford, distributed among the Fordson plant in River Rouge, the assembly plant in Highland Park, and the tractor plant in Dearborn. At their peak in the 1920s they represented slightly more than 2 percent of Ford employees in the area. Other major automobile manufacturers, all of whom also employed thousands of workers, hired substantially fewer Mexicans. In 1926 the second largest employer was Briggs Manufacturing on Mack Avenue (later Chrysler), which made automobile parts, with about four hundred Mexican workers, who stayed on the job an average of less than six months. The next important employer, Dodge Brothers, on Joseph Campau in Hamtramck, had about three hundred Mexicans on the payroll. By contrast, there were only about two dozen Mexicans each at Cadillac and Continental Motors, and fewer still at Hudson, the Motor Products Company, Fisher Body, and Chrysler. Small numbers of Mexicans also found employment with private construction projects, the Detroit Department of Public Works, and the Michigan Central Railway, further discouraging highly concentrated settlement patterns. Many Mexicano employees of Michigan Central resided in a boxcar *colonia* at Michigan Avenue and 20th Street. The *colonia* was surrounded by meatpacking plants belonging to Hygrade Products, Sullivan Packing, Hammond-Standish, and Gunsburg, none of which reported Mexican workers.[45]

The combined impact of employment and residential patterns, poor public transportation, and low car prices quickly made Detroit Mexicans dependent on automobiles. For recreation, they liked to "play pool, ride in automobiles, attend the motion pictures and go visiting," the last activity considered "a great thing in a Mexican's life and compensates him for the hours of toil in the dreary foundry." According to Mexican consul Joaquín Terrazas, "the automobile exerts such a strong influence that many Mexicans have acquired cars, and generally when they return to Mexico they drive down, preferring it to the train." Young men often pooled resources to make purchases, yet one observer astutely noted that "the machines most of them own wouldn't hold together any farther than Ypsilanti," thirty miles to the west.[46] The automobile industry of Detroit, which afforded Mexicans a greater degree of physical mobility than their compatriots enjoyed elsewhere, was already beginning to dig a grave for the city, as became abundantly clear in subsequent generations.

The large contingent of middle-class Ford students enhanced the rapid development of Mexican social and cultural organizations and small businesses, particularly pool halls, barbershops, and restaurants that catered to the young and largely unmarried male population. As in many midwestern cities, other Spanish-speaking immigrants, particularly Spaniards, toward whom Mexicans had "much more friendly feelings than toward other European nationalities," were more influential than immigrants from other countries in the economic, political, and cultural life of Mexican communities. The first priest in the Detroit *colonia*, the Rev. Juan Pablo Alanís Gómez of Nuevo León, Mexico, helped establish a Mexican chapel in 1920. A Mexican church was established in 1923, located at Kirby and Roosevelt, away from the major concentrations of Mexicanos in the city.[47]

One could expect that the Mexican automobile workers of Detroit would be the first group to integrate into the industrial proletariat. According to some observers, they represented the aristocracy of the Mexican working class in the United States in the 1920s. Detroit was the heart of "Fordism," foreshadowing post–World War II patterns of monopoly capital. Ford experimented by offering high pay and creating a stable workforce in an effort to eliminate worker unrest and strengthen company control, a strategy that included recruiting a diverse workforce to discourage worker unity. The fame of high wages spread so rapidly that men crossing the Mexican border often expressed a desire to head directly to Detroit and work for Ford. In 1927 George Edson acknowledged that the *colonia* was "assuming almost a permanent form" in comparison with other Mexican communities in the region and that there were "quite a number of Mexicans possessing some education, ability and ambition," which resulted in, "a noticeably high civic standard." [48]

Yet high wages, comparative job stability at Ford, and the middle-class students who worked there suggest a largely illusory exceptionalism among Mexicans in Detroit. High wages offset the taxing demands of heavy physical labor, "drudgery and industrial hazard," made more unpleasant by the repetitive drive system, speed-ups, close control, and discipline by supervisors. Mexican workers were commonly cheated "what was due them," particularly in cases of accident compensation. They faced prejudice and discrimination and were "known among the Detroit workmen as 'spicks.'" They also encountered denigrating representations from agents of the state, including Miss Tillet of the Detroit Public Welfare Bureau, who claimed that they had "very low morals," while Police Inspector Raymond claimed that "much petty thievery is attributed to them." As in other midwestern settings, Mexicans were denied access to most city neighborhoods, although those able to pass as "Spaniards" had a somewhat wider range of options. Consequently, they occupied the worst housing the city offered, and one observer asserted that "in Detroit the Negroes are preferred to the Mexicans as neighbors." Mr. Fitzgerald of the St. Vincent de Paul Society reported that "they live in quarters even the negroes would not live in." [49]

Mexican men and women in Detroit were selectively prohibited from entering public places that welcomed working-class Europeans. Young men who were unable to pass as Spaniards were barred from dance halls, including the Graystone Ballroom on Woodward Avenue. Those who gained entry had problems because White girls refused to dance with them, according to Miss Hutzel of the Detroit Police Department. To compensate, enterprising operators set up dance halls where young Mexican men paid European-born "nickel-snappers" for each dance, though the "girls" were considered "quite inferior to the Mexican boys." Even Father Castillo reported "a good deal of race prejudice against the Mexicans," recalling a case in which he raised money to send a young Mexicana to an Episcopal camp for poor youth, "but they didn't accept her because they didn't want anything to do with any Mexican."[50]

Like other midwestern Mexican industrial workers, those of Detroit were an unstable population, and in the late 1920s about 80 percent were men between the ages of 18 and 36, of whom about 75 percent were unmarried. Following the boom period of 1923–1926, it became more difficult to find work, and most Mexicans were unemployed for between three and five months each year. Furthermore, Detroit was badly devastated during the Great Depression, possibly more than any other large city in the industrial Midwest. Most Mexicans employed by Ford and other urban industries quickly lost their jobs, and repatriation siphoned off many of the civic leaders of the 1920s. The lack of long-term upward mobility was confirmed by sociologist Norman Humphrey, who observed in the early 1940s that "Mexicans in Detroit have remained on the lowest rung of the industrial ladder."[51]

Mexican *colonias* associated with automobiles and their foundries appeared in several other eastern Michigan cities and extended into northwestern Ohio. By 1926 the *colonia* in Pontiac had about five hundred residents, concentrated on the South Side, with a single Mexican restaurant on Wilson Avenue. It was near the Wilson Foundry, which was considered "friendly to Mexicans," and as T. A. Meehan of its Employment Department wrote, their turnover "is not as great as Americans." Several hundred Mexicans in Pontiac also found work on construction projects for roads and buildings.[52]

In nearby Flint, then a clean and rapidly growing city dependent on Buick and Chevrolet, Mexican railroad and sugar beet workers started settling during the war and were first hired systematically by Buick in 1922. Most resided initially in company bunkhouses but soon moved into private housing behind the plant in the northeastern part of town, along Stewart Avenue, Michigan Avenue, and St. John Street, amidst African Americans, Hungarians, Romanians, and other immigrant groups. Leither Street was the center of Mexican business, with several restaurants, barbershops, and a pool hall. By 1926 the *colonia* reached about one thousand, about half of whom worked at Buick, while Chevrolet, across town, had only about seventy-five Mexican workers.[53]

Saginaw, immediately to the north, was in the heart of Michigan's sugar beet country, and Mexicans moved constantly between the fields and the city. In October 1926, its Mexican population was estimated at 1,000, excluding hundreds of workers soon due to arrive after beet topping ended. About 550 were employed by the Gray Iron foundry, a division of General

Motors, while another large group worked on the Pere Marquette and Michigan Central railroads. Smaller numbers worked for road construction contractors, the streetcar line, and a handful of small factories. More than in other settlements in the state, Mexicans in Saginaw were segregated residentially because of discriminatory landlord practices. They clustered in the First Ward east of Washington Avenue near the Pere Marquette railroad and the Gray Iron foundry. The Sociedad Mutualista Mexicana appeared in the mid 1920s, but many workers did not join because the foundry paid for basic health needs and death benefits. The Potter Street business district was described as "essentially Mexican," with two restaurants, a tailor shop, and a pool hall, as well as other enterprises that catered mostly to Mexicans. Earlier in the decade there had been an even larger Mexican colony in South Saginaw, near the Saginaw Malleable Iron Foundry, also part of General Motors, but it soon stopped hiring Mexicans, and by 1927 only a few continued to live in the vicinity. E. G. Rust wrote, "I have been informed by the foundry people that they are better laborers than either the negroes or the whites, because they can stand the heat better." Additional reasons for their employment, particularly in older mills like Gray Iron, were the unsafe working conditions and longer working days. The day shift lasted from 7 A.M. until 10 P.M., and the evening shift from 5 P.M. until 5 A.M., with wages of 45 cents per hour and no extra pay for overtime. In addition to long hours, low wages, and physically exhausting work, Edson reported, conditions were particularly trying on hot summer days, when "the Mexican boys frequently faint at their task. The Italian foremen 'give them hell.' . . . Tuberculosis results from inhaling the gas and from going out from the hot room into the cold air, sometimes with their clothes wet with sweat." He concluded that "young men go to work for the Gray Iron Foundry in the full bloom of health, and within a year or two they fade and die." The health risks in the foundry convinced many Mexicanos to return each spring to the sugar beet fields with their own attendant hazards and lower pay.[54]

Mexicans were also attracted to the southern end of this industrial belt in Toledo during World War I, when sugar beet and railroad companies began recruitment. By the mid 1920s, about four hundred resided in the city, even more on its outskirts, employed mostly by railroad companies whose lines traversed the city. The largest Mexican camps belonged to the Toledo Terminal Railroad on the Old Middle Grounds, site of Union Station; and the New York Central at Walbridge. They also resided in scattered "dumps" on the urban fringe consisting of shacks and railroad cars. Toledo's largest employer, the Willys-Overland automobile plant (later Jeep), with a payroll of more than sixteen thousand in 1926, had hired a large contingent of Mexican workers during the labor shortage in 1923. According to Willys official C. S. Dence, the company stopping hiring in part due to opposition from other employees representing the forty-five European nationalities employed by the company, who didn't like to work with Mexicans. He also reported difficulties stemming from a War Registry questionnaire the company distributed in connection with the "Americanization enthusiasm." In response to a question whether they would fight for the United States or their own country in the event of war, he asserted, "all the Mexicans stated that they would fight for their own country," and most were soon fired or quit.[55]

Only a few clusters of Mexican settlement appeared elsewhere in Ohio, the largest at Lorain, which emerged in 1923 as a result of recruitment by the National Tube Company, a subsidiary of U.S. Steel. More than 90 percent of Mexican workers in the city were employed by National Tube in 1925, residing primarily in two sections of South Lorain near the company plant. One was an ethnically diverse neighborhood of European immigrants, the other a shabbier district dominated by African Americans. Local elementary school principal C. F. Creamer claimed that Mexican students were "the poorest we have," rarely going beyond sixth grade. He attributed their low achievement to the inborn deficiency of being "a backward, indolent race." Yet during a celebration of the Diez y Seis de Septiembre of 1926, Edson reported: "to one looking in it would have the appearance of a Sunday school program and the audience that of the average and better citizenry." A handful of Mexican businesses appeared in South Lorain, including two restaurants, two tailor shops, a barbershop, and a bakery that catered mostly to their countrymen. A contemporary report observed that Spaniards "get the bulk of the business." Edson also estimated three hundred Mexicans residing in Cleveland and several hundred in Youngstown, most employed in steel mills.[56]

Farther to the east, Mexicans were fewer and more scattered. Most were initially recruited and transported directly from the Texas cities of San Antonio, Fort Worth, Dallas, or El Paso by the Pennsylvania Railroad or various steel companies. The railroad workers typically resided in small camps along the tracks or in railroad yards. In Pennsylvania, the steel industry, longer established than that of the Chicago-Calumet area, hired much smaller numbers of Mexicanos than its counterparts on the south shore of Lake Michigan. Only a few visible *colonias* appeared, the largest at Homestead and Bethlehem, the latter a result of recruitment by Bethlehem Steel in 1923 through an arrangement with the Mexican consul in

San Antonio. Single workers initially resided in company bunkhouses, where they also could purchase meals prepared by Mexican cooks, while some families moved into company-owned cottages at the coke plant; but the majority soon dispersed into town. By 1924 the Bethlehem *colonia* population exceeded one thousand, but it had already fallen to fewer than four hundred by the end of the decade. In the late 1920s the Bethlehem *colonia* had a Mexican grocery store, pool hall, restaurant, and newspaper stand. In late 1926 in other major Eastern urban centers, only about two hundred Mexicans resided in Philadelphia, the third largest city in the country; while in New York City there were perhaps twenty-five hundred Mexicans, widely scattered and largely indistinguishable among the ethnically diverse working population of the nation's largest city. While several Eastern employers had engaged in labor recruitment during the war and the early 1920s, by the middle of the decade the number of Mexicans was already declining, in contrast to settings to the west.[57]

Employer decisions to hire Mexicans largely explain the scattered and infrequent appearance of *colonias* in the northern states in the early twentieth century. Even in large factories and foundries that hired them in large numbers, Mexicans typically were only a small portion of the workforce. As C. M. Brading of Wisconsin Steel in Chicago, which had 660 Mexicans in a workforce of 3,049, stated, "when I hire Mexicans at the gate, I pick out the lightest among them. No, it isn't that the lighter colored ones are better workers, but the darker ones are like the niggers." Other companies had "policies opposed to hiring Mexicans," and emphatically refused to employ them, even for unskilled work. A staff member of the Free Employment Bureau of Illinois informed anthropologist Robert Redfield that "none of the employers he had anything to do with would hire a Mexican and he no longer tried to place one. Many employers, when they called him up to apply for a gang of men prefaced further remarks by saying, '[b]ut don't send us Mexicans.'" Mr. Mitchell, of the State Employment Bureau in Pittsburgh, concurred: "we have few if any calls for Mexicans, and none apply to us. They are generally regarded as undesirable." In sum, employer attitudes, often overtly racist, generally determined whether and how many Mexicans were employed in different settings and profoundly influenced the size and location of Mexican communities throughout the northern United States.[58]

## Urban Farmworkers

A study by the International Institute of St. Paul concluded that "the sugar beet industry, with its demand for cheap labor, is responsible for the presence of Mexicans in Minnesota in large numbers." Located more than two hundred miles from the center of sugar beet production in the Red River Valley, the emergence of the barrio on St. Paul's Lower West Side appears at first glance to have been an anomaly. Mary Bishop of the Guild of Catholic Women explained the discrepancy, noting that most *colonia* residents "have been lured there from Mexico or Texas by the promise of work in the sugar beet fields, during the summer. The winter was not often reckoned with until it came."[59]

Between World War I and the Great Depression, the American Beet Sugar Company adopted three successive strategies in dealing with Mexican workers after harvest ended. During the first stage, under special exemptions of the 1917 Immigration Act, employers were permitted to hire Mexicans temporarily, on condition that they guarantee workers' return at the end of the contract period. Company recruiters contracted Mexicans in Texas for fields around Albert Lea, Chaska, and Savage in the Minnesota River Valley. The exemption ended in 1920 with the onset of the postwar industrial depression and the return of unemployed Europeans to the beet fields. Thousands of Mexican industrial and agricultural workers had drifted into cities, and social service agencies and employers in many communities devised plans to repatriate Mexicans, while others departed on their own accord. In the Chicago area, Mexican employment reportedly declined by two thirds in 1920 and 1921, accompanied by a sharp depopulation. In the Kansas City area, at least four thousand Mexicans departed in the spring of 1921 alone, returning to the border by special trains at public expense. In Detroit, in March 1921, the number of Mexicans employed was only 44 percent that of twelve months earlier. The St. Vincent de Paul Society, the Detroit Board of Commerce, and several companies contributed funds to permit the return of thousands of unemployed men and their families to Mexico.[60] At the time, the Mexican population of St. Paul was too small to attract much attention from authorities.

When the economy recovered, American Beet Sugar initiated a second stage in its dealings with Mexican workers, which involved encouraging settlement. It coincided with the onset of large-scale sugar beet production in the Red River Valley of Minnesota and North Dakota. Using agents in San Antonio, Houston, Dallas, and Fort Worth, the company offered field workers a set rate of $18 per acre, which held fairly constant through the 1920s. Wages included costs for transportation to the fields by train, housing, and the use of a garden plot for the workers. The company also guaranteed credit at nearby stores and settled disputes "between the farmer and the Mexican," according to a 1936 International Institute study, suggesting that European Americans in Minnesota considered the term "Mexican" practically interchangeable with "beet field worker." As an earlier report acknowledged, "the Mexican in beet work has become a recognized institution in this part of the country," a social construction that remained deeply embedded in local dominant popular thought for many decades.[61]

Seeking a resident agricultural proletariat, American Beet Sugar experimented "with a plan of keeping many of their Mexican beet workers in the territory the year round," a strategy the Great Western Sugar Company had successfully adopted in Colorado. It provided company housing, consisting of apartment buildings or small houses, in Chaska, Albert Lea, East Grand Forks, and elsewhere and encouraged farmers to permit workers to remain during the winter in the ramshackle dwellings that already housed them in the summer. During this second stage, workers also drifted into nearby cities, including St. Paul, Des Moines, Mason City, Kansas City, Milwaukee, Chicago, and Detroit. Yet as late as 1928, American Beet Sugar Labor Superintendant E. F. Heckman asserted, "we do not recommend Minneapolis and St. Paul as winter work is scarce there." The seasonal cycle began again the following spring, when company agents went to the urban *colonias* to recruit workers, sign contracts, and arrange for transportation to the farms. To encourage them to remain during the winter, the company paid an extra five dollars per acre, or $23 for those hired locally, and an additional dollar per acre if they could arrange their own transportation to the fields. Employers calculated that the higher wages offset the "expense and trouble of recruiting a new supply in the Southwest every spring." In the winter of 1926–1927, Edson calculated that only 35 percent of the *betabeleros* who came to the Great Lakes and Plains states in the spring returned to Texas or Mexico at the end of the season. Fifteen percent remained in the beet country, while 50 percent went to nearby cities, and half of them remained the entire winter. In large part because American Beet Sugar encouraged workers from the Minnesota and Red River Valleys to settle locally and discouraged them from heading to the Twin Cities, the ratio of beet workers residing in rural sections of Minnesota in the late 1920s was substantially higher than elsewhere in the region.[62]

Mexicans who came to Minnesota at the time seldom had to contend with authorities concerned about their mode of entry into the United States. Guadalupe Cruz, born in Jalisco in 1894, took a train to El Paso in 1915 and later recalled that "then there were no documents needed. All you had to do was put a nickel in the box and that was it." She moved first to California, where she remained six years, and then to Arizona, and later to Brush, Colorado, working in the sugar beets. In 1929 she signed a contract to work in Chaska and moved to St. Paul at the end of the season. Even after the Immigration Act of 1924 established the Border Patrol, documented entry was not a pressing concern. As Marcelino Rivera, born in Mexico City in 1906, recalls, on crossing the border in 1927, there was no need for passports. In Texas he picked cotton and cleared tree stumps from fields and then found railroad work in Louisiana. There he signed a contract in 1931 to work the beet fields near Lafayette, Minnesota, and in the winter he moved to St. Paul.[63] Through the late 1920s, employer demands took precedence over politicians' concerns about verification of legal status, and neither worker nor employer was penalized for failure to comply with entry requirements. Although the notion of an international border gained political, economic, and social importance in the early twentieth century, popular interest in the legal status of Mexicanos in the United States developed more slowly and erratically. In a contradictory fashion, intensified international economic relations and greater demand for Mexican workers accompanied more stringent regulations for individual Mexicans crossing the political border, one legal barrier to civic assimilation in the United States.

By the end of the 1920s, the sugar beet industry initiated a third strategy for wintering Mexicans by encouraging them to settle in St. Paul rather than in rural sections of the state. American Beet Sugar was responding to pressure from European and European American residents of rural communities whose fear of permanent Mexican neighbors encouraged them to send local police and sheriffs to dwellings where Mexican workers stayed to ensure they vacated after the harvest ended. Such unwillingness to accept Mexican neighbors suggests a failure of attitudinal and behavioral assimilation by the dominant population. As acreage increased, American Beet Sugar realized that its plan to create a resident rural Mexican workforce was costly and entailed too much organized opposition. Sr. Jesús Méndez, son of a carpenter and born in Zamora, Michoacán, in 1910, crossed the border with his parents at Laredo in 1927. The family was recruited almost immediately to work in the beet fields around East Grand Forks. They spent their first winter in company housing but one year later were offered housing in St. Paul and a promise of work in the fields the following spring. Sr. Méndez stated that "if you stayed, you would get a better price the next year." Furthermore, he acknowledged, Mexicans had difficulty finding jobs elsewhere, suggesting that many workers remained in Minnesota more out of resignation than a sense of opportunity.[64]

Manuel Contreras Prieto, born on a rancho in Durango in 1904, crossed the border at Piedras Negras during the Mexican Revolution and worked for several years in Texas, shearing sheep, picking cotton, and clearing land. In 1924 an acquaintance in Cisco, Texas, experienced in Minnesota sugar beets, showed Contreras Prieto a paper permitting him to return on "any train he wanted" and encouraging him "to bring people from Mexico." He and his sister Abelina, who were willing to go "wherever we could find work," agreed to join him in the beet fields. He recalled that the decision to return to Texas or stay in Minnesota at the end of the season often depended on family resources: "some cannot afford it, so they stay." He noted that "people came from all over to work the beets," including his eventual wife, who had come from Chicago. He remained in sugar beet territory between Lake Lillian and Chaska, where his wife died, until 1933, when he moved to St. Paul. In his and many other cases it was not necessarily the most successful, but often the most desperate who remained in the Midwest, and they were encouraged by their corporate employers.[65]

Alfonso de León, born in 1902 in the rancho of Antila de Nogales, Catorce de Real, San Luis Potosí, Mexico, worked in local silver mines for three years before he migrated to Texas at age sixteen. He worked wherever he could find employment, including the coal mines around Bridgeport from 1920 to 1922, until "the union was broken up." In 1923 he began a pattern, which lasted six years, of wintering in Texas and then migrating north to the beet fields of Minnesota, Wyoming, Colorado, and Iowa in the spring. He recalled that in 1929 he decided to remain in Minnesota permanently because his son broke his leg and was hospitalized and because "they asked us to stay, because it cost so much to go back and forth." They spent their first winter on the West Side of St. Paul renting a house on State Street, in the heart of the rapidly growing *colonia*, where they remained.[66]

The gender and household composition of different midwestern Mexican communities varied according to local hiring patterns. Most urban industries recruited only young adult males, while agriculture consciously attracted families as a unit. In states where agricultural employment predominated, particularly Minnesota, sex ratios were more balanced and there were higher proportions of children. A detailed report on Mexicans in the region between Ohio and Kansas conducted in the fall and winter of 1926–1927 calculated that the population was 59 percent adult males, while among adults the sex ratio was 83 men to 17 women. In Minnesota, the resident Mexican population in the sugar beet territories, centering on

East Grand Forks and Albert Lea, was only 27 percent adult males, while the adult sex ratio was 52 men to 48 women. For St. Paul and Minneapolis combined, the Mexican population was 38 percent adult men, with an adult sex ratio of 65 men to 35 women. These figures contrasted sharply with most midwestern industrial barrios, where 80 percent or more of the total population typically were adult men. Minnesota's Mexican population rose rapidly in the late 1920s in response to an increase in sugar beet acreage, which doubled in the spring of 1927 alone, when another factory was completed in East Grand Forks. That year the resident Mexican population of the state was estimated at five thousand Mexicanos, which increased to seven thousand the following year, a majority residing in rural locations.[67]

Unlike other midwestern industries, where they were a small portion of the total labor force, one report noted, "Mexicans constitute the bulk of the sugar beet workers" throughout the region. In the Twin Cities, Mexicans also worked in smaller numbers on railroads, particularly the Burlington, Rock Island, and Milwaukee, and in the Cudahy, Swift, and Armour meatpacking houses located in the Stockyards district of South St. Paul, adjacent to the Lower West Side. In the early winter of 1927, a survey of Mexican packinghouse workers in St. Paul reported that although they had resided in the United States for an average of 8.2 years, their employment in those plants averaged only 143 days. Yet Mexicans in urban settings considered packinghouses as "among the steadiest" sources of employment and often preferred them to higher-paying but less stable jobs like steel mills, tanneries, and cement and brick plants.[68]

Mexican women commonly came to the Midwest because of family decisions, not individual preferences. As one Chicago Mexicana stated, "I did not want to come to the United States at all. My two oldest sons came first and stayed about two years; one of my nephews came about the same time. At the end of two years my sons came back to Mexico to bring me and the rest of the family to the United States, but I could not bear to leave my tierra." Like their male counterparts women usually migrated to the Midwest to work, the majority in family units recruited by the beet companies. Sra. Felicitas Herrera, born in 1909 in Pátzcuaro, Michoacán, recalls that as a little girl she used to go to the market to sell tortillas her mother made at home. She accompanied her family to the United States following the international influenza pandemic of 1918–1919, which had a deadly influence on her country, still beset by the effects of revolution and widespread hunger. In 1920 they crossed the border at Laredo and began working in the cotton fields of Texas, which provided the major source of family income until 1926. The following year they contracted in Fort Worth to work in the sugar beet fields in Round Lake, near Worthington, and for the next six years they worked in the beet fields of Minnesota and Michigan, spending several winters in Chicago. In 1933 they moved to St. Paul and decided to stay permanently, while continuing to work in the beet fields each season until 1940.[69]

Outside of agriculture, women's employment for wages in Minnesota was relatively restricted, with the important exception of domestic labor. Sebastián Jara, born in Monterrey, Nuevo León, in 1906, entered Texas as an infant and worked on a ranch with his family until he was eighteen, then contracted for the Minnesota beet fields. In 1927 the family settled in St. Paul. When he and other male relatives could not find work, his mother secured employment as a housekeeper for a Jewish fruit vendor in the neighborhood, which enabled her to support the family.[70]

Hiring practices in the United States, particularly in the sugar beet industry, contradicted contemporary domestic ideals in popular bourgeois ideology and culture of both Mexico and the United States that limited women to the domestic sphere. Many midwestern scholars emphasized that patriarchy was much more entrenched in Mexico, but did not agree on the impact of the United States. Agnes Fenton saw little change, claiming that in contrast to the European American, the Mexican wife in Milwaukee "is wholly under the control of her husband. She is for his pleasure in the first place, she has children just as fast as she can, she almost never goes out at night without her husband or son. She never goes to a function without him." Sociologist Norman Goldner claimed positive changes in Minnesota, suggesting that the traditional "patriarchal and authoritarian" Mexican family changed because of the experience of shared labor in the beet fields, which served a function of "leveling and democratizing of the family." Paul Taylor, by contrast, emphasized disruption. He suggested that Mexicans came to the region "with a conception of family relations which is distinctly patriarchal, and buttressed in part by religious sanctions." The experience of migration, laws and customs, employment patterns, and regular attendance of children in schools gave midwestern Mexicanas greater independence than their counterparts in Mexico or the Southwest. As a result, he noted, "the family unit is subject to more disintegrating influences" in the Midwest.[71]

In midwestern settings, Mexican women played a greater direct role in deciding family matters, including working outside the home and choosing mates. A Chicago Mexicana from Jalisco found employment cleaning casings in a Wilson meatpacking plant because her husband, who was experienced in the leather and harness business, had lost his job. He lamented, "My wife resolved to go to work even though in Mexico she had never, never worked. I felt at first very much ashamed of myself because I was not able to support her. I often wonder what my father would say if he knew she was working? I would never have approved of it but what can you do? Economic circumstances in this country are different from Mexico." Most observers considered higher rates of divorce disruptive, and some, like Chicago social worker Anita Jones, claimed that it was largely the result of frivolous decisions by individuals unaccustomed to freedom: "the scarcity of women in the community leads to many temptations for the young girls of the families." Jones added that "divorce, almost unknown in Mexico, seems to be like a new toy to both men and women here." Other observers were aware of systematic preferences and consistent patterns of behavior within the range of options and agreed that midwestern Mexicanas "never stayed single very long except by choice." Furthermore, as a Bethlehem, Pennsylvania, account confirmed, Mexicanas were clear regarding their preferences. In that city, where Mexican men greatly outnumbered Mexican women, and where association between the former and "women of other nationalities was comparatively frequent," not a single Mexicana had intermarried. The unbalanced sex ratios had permitted Mexicanas greater freedom to make and break relations with partners, but regardless of prior experiences they preferred Mexican men or none at all.[72]

The marriage patterns of early-twentieth-century midwestern Mexican men and women suggest instructive comparisons with those of Mexicans during the first generation of contact between Anglos and Mexicans in California, Texas, and New Mexico in the early and mid nineteenth century. Perhaps reflecting sharp gender imbalances within their own group, Mexican men of the early twentieth century Midwest, like Anglo men of the early nineteenth century, were more likely to mingle with women from the numerically dominant population. Yet Anglo men of the earlier period sought out wealthy Mexican women, who afforded them social influence and land, while later midwestern Mexican men tended to mingle with the poorest European immigrant women, presumably for love. Among Mexican women of the early and mid nineteenth century, propertied fathers frequently arranged for their daughters' marriages with early Anglo immigrants. By contrast, Mexican daughters from families with little or no land found spouses overwhelmingly among Mexicans and sometimes Indian men in the nineteenth century, a pattern more consistent with the behavior of their working-class midwestern Mexicana counterparts in the early twentieth century. In both cases, such intermingling slowed quickly, in the earlier instance following conquest, in the latter with the Great Depression and attendant repatriation. In both settings Mexican and Anglo societies became more evenly balanced in gender but increasingly separated from each other.[73]

In the Twin Cities of the early twentieth century, Mexicans resided in several locations but were heavily concentrated on the West Side of St. Paul. The barrio, located on the west bank of the Mississippi River, across the Robert Street Bridge from downtown, was variously referred to as the Flats, the Lower Westside, Riverview, or the West Side, of which it was part, and its business district was on Fairfield Avenue and State Street. Mexicans also resided downriver in the Burlington railroad yards at Dayton's Bluff, near the Fish Hatchery; in South St. Paul, site of several packing plants; and at Inver Grove Heights, where the Rock Island had a terminal. In Minneapolis, Mexicans clustered in two locations. The first was the Milwaukee Railroad yards at 22nd Avenue South in the Seward neighborhood. The second was located north of the Chicago, St. Paul, Minneapolis, and Omaha railroad tracks, centering around 6th Avenue North and 5th Street, where several families of railroad and sugar beet workers resided. Edson reported that "nobody wants these beet workers to come to Minneapolis to spend the winter but they come anyway."[74]

The Lower West Side, like many barrios, had mixed industrial, commercial, institutional, and residential land use patterns. It had served as a port of entry for European immigrants to St. Paul for several generations after the forcible removal of Lakota from the area and the 1851 Treaty of Traverse de Sioux. It was a predominantly working-class neighborhood from the time the first White people settled. Between the 1850s and the 1880s, French, German, and Irish immigrants moved into the area, followed by a cycle between the 1880s and World War I when arrivals originated mostly from Eastern Europe, including Jewish immigrants from Russia. Mexican railroad workers had begun trickling into the area shortly before World War I, but railroad employment alone was not sufficient to create a visible and distinct Mexican presence. The 1920 census listed only 237 Mexican-born residents in Minnesota, of whom 70 resided in St. Paul, most on the Lower West Side. With the economic upturn following the depression of 1920 and 1921 and the expansion of sugar beet acreage in the Red River Valley, the *colonia* started to take visible form.[75]

Observers consistently agreed that Mexicans had the worst housing of any ethnic group in the region, and St. Paul was no exception. Conditions in the railroad *colonias* and the "boxcar camps" were particularly notorious.

Located in railroad yards or along sidings, housing included dismounted or abandoned boxcars, sometimes equipped with a stove or supplied with steps to permit easier entry. For protection from the cold, occupants banked cars with dirt, filled cracks with newspaper, and covered them with tar paper. Railroad yard dwellings also included "uncomfortable shacks made from scrap pieces and cheap, second-hand materials including old ties, rails, and sheet metal," or railroad section houses. Housing in the Burlington Yards camp in Dayton's Bluff in St. Paul included boxcars divided into two apartments of three rooms each and a number of makeshift shacks. At the Rock Island terminal in Inver Grove Heights, an informed observer commented, "in giving a blue ribbon to the worst company-furnished house in the country, a judge should not overlook" a shanty occupied by two men working for the railroad and their families, totaling sixteen people. Because railroad camps like Carville, near Omaha, lacked indoor plumbing, like many Mexican barrios of the 1920s, water from hydrants was "carried to the far ends of the streets by the women." Similar camps were often located within the corporate limits of even the largest cities. In Detroit, in 1920 more than five hundred Mexicans lived in a camp in the Detroit River Yards of the Grand Truck Railroad. A nearby camp in the Michigan Central Yards at Michigan Avenue and 20th Street was located in a packinghouse district, where the odor was described as "frightfully offensive," and "refuse and filth were scattered along the track." The boxcar dwellings, located near "filthy chicken cars," were within six feet of the railroad tracks and lacked sewerage and sanitary facilities. Crude shacks served as outhouses: "when filled they are picked up and moved another few feet, where another hole is dug in the ground and the former location filled up with dirt, but no lime or other disinfectant used."[76]

When they moved into residential neighborhoods, Mexicans were confined to the worst sections, often residing in basements, back rooms, attics, shacks along alleys, and second- and third-story rooms above stores and businesses. Because of poverty and overcharging by landlords, a family often crowded into units with only one or two rooms or shacks without basements, while frequently several families piled into a single-family house. In the Twin Cities it was reported that few homes were wired for electricity and most had outdoor privies, usually obtaining water from nearby city water hydrants. Conditions were particularly difficult during cold weather, and as a West Side resident recalled, one winter "the floors froze and it was miserable," and "many people were sickly, especially the children," who suffered from pneumonia, tuberculosis, and rickets.[77]

Discrimination contributed to poor housing, for Mexicans could rarely enter new neighborhoods without encountering resistance from local residents, landlords, and real estate agents. In Milwaukee they faced frequent harassment from gangs of Eastern European immigrants on the South Side, while police often of the same nationality typically sided with the attackers. Turf wars were not uncommon, and as one observer noted, "landlords in certain neighborhoods refuse to rent to Mexicans." When allowed admission, Mexicans were confined to the worst units and paid "outrageous rents," which contributed to further overcrowding.[78]

When housing standards existed, exceptions excluded most dwellings with Mexican occupancy. The 1902 Chicago housing code for tenements was not retroactive, and an estimated 80 percent of Mexicans lived in the city's older dwellings not covered by the law. In a Chicago study, housing expert Homer Hoyt established a "ranking of races and nationalities with respect to their beneficial effect on land values," based on popular local attitudes, and placed Mexicans at the bottom of all ethnic and racial groups examined. He found that popular opinion conformed to a "last of the immigrants" model in which new immigrants, as their social standing improved, could expect to achieve upward mobility in housing, with two exceptions. He observed that "except in the case of negroes and Mexicans, racial and national barriers disappear when the individuals in the foreign nationality groups rise in the economic scale or conform to the American standard of living."[79]

Attitudes and behavior of the dominant population isolated Mexicans, even in public and private agencies charged with care for the poor. Charity and welfare organizations consistently tried to evade caring for Mexicanos, who consequently did not generally seek assistance. Furthermore, the same agencies commended Mexicans for caring for their own: "very few Mexicans ask for help, as they help one another. Social workers have observed that the Mexicans have a willingness to share their means with any of their unfortunate countrymen and a marked reluctance to ask for public assistance." In a study of attitudes and opinions in Flint, Michigan, sociologist William Albig interviewed Mexicans' European immigrant neighbors. A twenty-year-old Hungarian woman who had recently moved from Detroit stated, "I keep away from the whole district now as much as possible. I don't like it, and I wish we'd move. I dislike the Mexicans very much." A male twenty-year-old Serb student asserted that "the neighbors don't like them as they say the Mexicans and Negroes depreciate the value of property. The Mexicans are favored in the giving out of jobs." A nineteen-year-old male student who lived next door to a house occupied by Mexicans claimed that "the women are pretty dumb, they never do learn to talk." A seventeen-year-old student stated, "I'm glad we're going to move . . . I'm not comfortable any more. They're all terribly dirty and crowded." An older Hungarian, Mr. J., who worked at Chevrolet, claimed that "a couple of them are pretty good fellows, though I'm scared of the rest." Albig found that "young adults were, in general, much more critical of divergent customs than were the elders," suggesting that Americanization made the children of European immigrants more intolerant of Mexicans than their parents. In a similar vein, a Chicago settlement house worker challenged discriminatory actions by an Italian woman who was trying to keep Mexicans out of the neighborhood: "in Italy you would not be prejudiced against the Mexicans because of their color." The latter responded, "no, but we are becoming Americanized."[80]

Another pervasive opinion about Mexicans was related to crime; as Edson commented, "the only way of lot of people know there are any Mexicans in the United States is when they hear of one murdering another." L. H. Burnett, a Pittsburgh executive at Carnegie Steel, stated, "Mexicans are unjustly the victims of the impression given by popular stories typifying the Mexican as a deep-dyed villain." Portrayals of Mexican criminals were particularly widespread in law enforcement agencies. Chicago social worker Agnes Fenton claimed that "a Mexican is law-abiding as long as he knows he is being watched." A Chicago police sergeant claimed, "every one of these Mexicans carries a knife. Why, they can throw a knife fifty feet, and they'll cut you every time. You know, Indian and Mexican blood does not mix very well. That is the trouble with the Mexican; he has too much Negro blood." In Chicago Mexican arrest and conviction rates far surpassed those for Whites, while in Omaha it was reported that crime among Mexicans "ranks higher than that of any other immigrant class born in the city."[81]

Several factors account for such statistics, including poverty, as a 1931 study of Mexican prisoners in Illinois found that 78 percent lacked money to hire a lawyer. Another was language, as in Omaha a 1927 report indicated that a high proportion of arrests were dismissed on the grounds that the Mexicanos did not understand English and therefore could not follow the orders of police. Still another factor was police politics, particularly the lack of Mexican law enforcement officers. Hiring police in large cities was a critical facet of urban ethnic politics, as police tended to share opinions with and favor their own ethnic groups. Lacking representation left Mexicans particularly vulnerable to brutal police tactics. Anthropologist Robert Redfield, reporting on a raid at a Mexican dance at Brighton Park in Chicago, observed that the raid was conducted with "such needless and indiscriminate vigor that the neighbors' feelings were outraged by the brutality of the police." Criminologist Paul Warnshius reported that in Illinois police were systematically biased against Mexicans and that it was standard practice in many precincts to prohibit those who were detained from contacting friends or lawyers, in violation of their constitutional rights. Warnshius also discovered a "favorite plan," in which a group of police would visit pool rooms frequented by Mexicans, "line every one up against the wall, and search them. When asked if they had warrants, the answer is that it was not necessary, since it was a public place." Similar cases of arrest without cause took place in restaurants and on the streets. In one instance a Mexican carrying a jackknife was arrested on the grounds that it was a concealed weapon, but in court the judge threw the case out. Police then altered the charge to disorderly conduct, and he was fined $31.50. Mexican prisoners in Illinois testified that they were subjected to torture and beatings in jail and deprived of food for several days in order to extract "confessions." One man testified that after they arrested him, detectives punched him in the chest, stomach, and face on several occasions, but before they took him to court the police made him wash the blood off his face so the judge would not see it. Another Mexicano reported that police punched him in the face about a hundred times, pushing a revolver in his mouth and threatening to blow his head off, but he confessed nothing because he was innocent.[82]

The courts posed additional problems for Mexicans because of interpreters, attorneys, and judges. Mexicans went to court with few interpreters, and those who appeared were commonly unqualified or biased to the point of consciously distorting testimony in translation. Given the difficulty of finding lawyers, they occasionally called on the Mexican consulate to investigate abuses, but with questionable value. In one case when Mexican employees of the Michigan Central Railway were attacked and beaten by White employees of the company, the consul informed investigators that police actions were within the law, although "on this occasion justice was not done since even the complainants were not called for their testimony." Mexicans regularly experienced unequal application of the law in the legal system. In the case of a flare-up of interethnic tensions in South Chicago, one informed European American observed that "the Mexicans get little protection in the courts. The Mexicans are now learning that you must buy justice. The police searched the Mexican houses without warrants and let the crowd hit their Mexican prisoners while they were in custody. The Mexican is in the same position as the Negro in the South.

He is always wrong unless there is a white man to speak for him." Furthermore, Taylor calculated, in Chicago the probability of conviction of Mexicans for misdemeanors in 1927 and 1928 was 65 percent greater than average.[83]

A final factor in understanding criminality included the selective nature of general statistics. In Chicago most arrests involved disorderly conduct charges rather than more serious offenses. As Paul Warnshius noted, disorderly conduct "provides the police with what appears to be a convenient, colorless charge to which they can have recourse when the original accusation can not be proved." A 1925 study in Chicago found that of more than five thousand cases of juvenile delinquency, only four involved Mexican youth. In several midwestern cities, Mexicans were not considered particularly prone to crime. Detroit Mexicans were reportedly "a small factor" in criminal activity, and even Inspector Knauth of the Detroit Police Department acknowledged, "Mexicans do not give us much trouble." Similarly, European Americans in St. Paul, including the police, frequently expressed surprise at the low crime statistics among Mexicans, which conflicted with the stereotypes they had learned. Overall, Edson concluded, Mexicans "are not regarded as particularly vicious," as most of their offenses were misdemeanors involving misconduct.[84]

St. Paul police acknowledged that the barrio had the lowest crime levels in the city, and one report asserted that among local Mexicans, the "crime record is exceptionally good." The statistics were noteworthy because the Lower West Side was one of the "bad delinquency areas and the worst housing of the city." In several years not a single Mexican juvenile under age eighteen was placed on probation, and there were few arrests even for minor infractions like drunkenness, petty larceny, and disorderly conduct. As Sr. Ramedo Saucedo, born in St. Paul in 1930, recalled,

> no one that we knew locked their doors. We knew where everyone lived. We knew our neighbors by name, first name. We knew how many members of the family there were. We knew what each family owned. We knew if someone was riding a bike, we knew who it belonged to right away. . . . We didn't envy, because no one had any more than we did. No one had any less than we did. . . . We just didn't think there was such a thing as stealing. . . . This was pounded into our heads when we were small.

Sr. Manuel Contreras recalled somewhat nostalgically that "the people were more united and they cooperated with each other. . . . Some of the people have changed just because they have a little more than someone else. How foolish that can be. . . . Now each person stays in their own little cubby hole."[85] The social organization of the barrio involved internal mechanisms of control that permitted a greater degree of security than elsewhere in the city and prevented youth, though mostly born and reared in Minnesota, from assimilating competitive, materialistic, and individualistic values conducive to crime.

Police attitudes and actions further inhibited opportunities for assimilation. In Gary in 1924 there was "an avowed effort on the part of the police department to run the Mexicans out of the city." It involved "wholesale arrests of Mexicans without cause," which led to the formation of the Sociedad Mutualista Feminina to challenge police actions. Tension with law enforcement officials was heightened by different cultural patterns, according to one observer, for "Mexicans resent the rudeness of policemen," which was contrary to their own upbringing and experience. As Ruth Camblon observed in Chicago, "it is as natural for the Mexican to be polite as it is for him to eat." Luis García, originally a shoemaker from Michoacán who arrived in Chicago via the sugar beet industry of Minnesota and the South Shore Railroad of River Rouge, Michigan, recalled, "My friends made me drunk with moonshine; when I saw the police coming I threw the empty bottle on the floor. The policeman hit me on the head with his gun. I didn't say nothing to him; I didn't fight. I didn't say nothing in court; they didn't ask me anything," although he was fined $14. In Mexico, he observed, "the police wouldn't do that. They would just take a drunk man by the arm, take him to jail, and let him out the next day."[86]

Imbued with negative stereotypes and the arm of the police, custodians of public spaces denied Mexicans access inconsistently. Historian Robert Oppenheimer noted that until the 1950s, "in virtually every Kansas town and city, Mexicans and Mexican-Americans remained segregated" residentially and had restricted access to barbershops, hotels, swimming pools, churches, theaters, railroad cars, sections of city parks, and other public facilities. The University of Kansas Hospital in Lawrence and the Bell Memorial Hospital in Kansas City segregated darker Mexicans with Blacks and lighter ones with Whites, for whom care was superior. Many restaurants refused to serve Mexicans or permitted them to eat only in the kitchen. Even in death, Mexicans were often segregated in municipal cemeteries. In many cities Mexicans were denied entrance to Catholic churches, forced to sit in pews in the back, or permitted space only in the basement to hold services. While allowed unrestricted access to the shabbiest theaters, they were more commonly denied entry to those in more affluent neighborhoods, indicating that racism against Mexicans was at least as entrenched as and functioned more effectively among the rich than among working-class European Americans and European immigrants.[87]

Segregation of Mexican children in the public schools, practiced inconsistently, took on a variety of forms across the region. In Kansas City, Kansas, the school system "established rigidly segregated educational facilities for them." In other districts, including St. Paul, Mexicans often were segregated into special classrooms, justified on the grounds that they were migrant sugar beet workers whose seasonal attendance interfered with the normal functioning of the classroom and that their mingling placed them and other children at a disadvantage. The St. Paul strategy acknowledged an unwillingness to enforce compulsory school attendance laws, and as Taylor noted, "wherever Mexican laborers have colonized in the United States, their children are under pressure of one kind or another to terminate their education early." While nonattendance was the rule in rural locations, it was not uncommon in cities and occurred with the full knowledge of school authorities. A Chicago social worker reported that "in the railroad camps the children don't go to school regularly. Truant officers say there are so many of them they can't enforce the law." Children from a boxcar *colonia* in Detroit did not attend school, and a truant officer visited the father of one family to discuss their absence, but "when told that he didn't have the money to send them to school the truant officer departed and nothing further had been done."[88]

Negative portrayals of Mexicans by Europeans and European Americans included epithets like "dirty Mexican," applied throughout the region, "more or less irrespective of physical cleanliness to despised persons or nationalities." Children were more affected than parents because of more frequent contacts with assimilated individuals. Such cruel language and treatment were not applied equally across nationalities, as a social worker from the University of Chicago Settlement House observed, for Mexican boys were "constantly insulted. I cannot help but feel that handling them separately pleases them better because of the harshness they receive at times from other boys." Another social worker reported that "they play ball in tiny places on the street because they are not allowed the usual places by other boys." An Omaha study observed that at "social gatherings of the schools and churches Mexican children were spat upon and called 'greasers' by other children." In Milwaukee a contemporary report asserted that more Mexican children were coming from Texas who "are darker skinned, more Indian and of a lower type of intelligence," a stereotype that affected the expectations of schoolteachers.[89]

An accommodationist strategy frequently employed by Mexicans was to identify as Spaniards and pass as Whites individually in order to obtain jobs, rent dwellings, and enter public places that excluded Mexicans. A Chicago man acknowledged, "I am ashamed to say that in order to get work which wasn't on a railroad, I used to say that I was Spanish. . . . While I was there they fired four Mexicans as soon as the foreman found out they were Mexicans." Another individual similarly asserted, "I was ashamed to tell the employment man that I was Mexican, I was afraid." A man experienced as a machinist in Mexico who was one of the few who obtained the same work in Chicago claimed that "sometimes even now when people see that I am a machinist, they say to me, 'you are not a Mexican.'" Sr. Carlos Pérez López of Chicago, president of the Mutualista Fraternal Mexicana, stated, "The humble Mexicans never deny their nationality. Those who have had better opportunities and on account of their appearance can pass as Spaniards and call themselves Spanish."[90] While identifying as Mexican often limited individual opportunities, many were unwilling to deny their national origins and asserted their Mexican identity collectively.

## Organizing and the Community

Mexican participation in political, social, and cultural organizations in the Midwest has been explained by various motivations, according to academics and dominant popular thought. Some observers considered it an escape from oppressive conditions and discrimination, often articulated as an exaggerated love for Mexico. Others have viewed such participation as celebration of culture for its own sake. Another view suggests that Mexican organizations were tools of others, including the Mexican government, the Catholic Church, employers, or agencies and institutions involved in Americanization, each of which sought its own ends. A final interpretation is that it represented political, social, or cultural resistance by Mexicans.

While individual motivations varied, it is clear that Mexican involvement in midwestern organizational life was highly selective, particularly in non-ethnic-specific organizations and activities. In the important case of organized labor, the American Federation of Labor (AFL) had been encouraged by the U.S. government to address Mexican workers as an instrument of foreign policy. Yet Mexicano participation in the labor movement in the Midwest prior to the Great Depression was quite limited. Lack of involvement has been attributed variously to the lack of skilled Mexicans in the workforce, prejudices and discrimination by European and European American workers, and successful efforts by employers to pit workers against each other, particularly by hiring Mexicans as strikebreakers. The AFL catered principally to skilled workers, and Mexicans in the Midwest were recruited overwhelming as unskilled labor. Yet organized labor was not particularly receptive to those who were skilled; as one Mexicano in Waukegan complained, "there are Mexicans here who have trades, such as painters and carpenters, but they are barred from the unions because they are not citizens." A junior executive from a Chicago plant claimed that prejudice and discrimination by European workers kept Mexicans in subordinate roles, and "a lot of these ignorant Germans called the Mexicans 'niggers.'" Another Chicago manager asserted that "we haven't any Mexicans; our workmen are practically all Swedes and object to the Mexicans." While many midwestern central labor bodies had no Mexican members, some were more accepting, such as the cigar makers' union, which included twenty-five Chicago Mexicans, residing mostly in the Stockyards district.[91]

Employers frequently hired Mexicans as part of a divide-and-rule strategy. President Charles Schwab of Bethlehem Steel acknowledged the utility of hiring a diverse workforce because "they fight each other, not us." A Chicago employment manager agreed that "it isn't good to have all of one nationality; they will gang up on you, even the Scotch. We have Negroes and Mexicans in a sort of competition with each other. It is a dirty trick," he acknowledged. W. H. Baird, superintendent of a Mason City sugar beet factory predicted: "I look for the development of separate cultures. It will stimulate the whites to greater effort to maintain their domination and will provide healthy competition for us."[92]

Many observers, including sociologist Edward Bauer, observed that because Mexicans often were originally recruited as strikebreakers, "they were the object of bitter antagonisms by the other workers." Employers' hiring of Mexicans in the 1922 strike of railway shopmen in the Newton and Wellington, Kansas, shops of the Santa Fe railroad "caused deep rooted hostility, which lasted for many years against Mexican residents in these cities, often resulting in much discrimination." Yet claims of Mexican strikebreaking were highly exaggerated. Even though they were not admitted into the skilled workers' unions, many Mexicans supported the railroad strikers in 1922 and in other cases. An earlier instance of employer recruitment of Mexican scabs in Chicago involved the Illinois Malleable Iron Company, which hired a large contingent through an El Paso agent in April 1916, four days before a strike began. Given assurances that there was no strike, when other workers walked out, "they all quit work" immediately and remained out for its two weeks' duration, despite pressure and coercion by employers. Even though some were skilled workers and had union cards, "Americans would have nothing to do with them and also refused to take them into the union."[93]

During the nationwide 1919 steel strike, although employers imported them as strikebreakers, one executive recalled, "the Mexicans mostly followed the lead of the Spanish, and there were a good many radicals among the Spanish," and most supported the strike. Similarly, during the 1921–1922 stockyards strike, many Mexicans hired as scabs were sympathetic to the strikers' cause. Challenging the reputation of midwestern Mexicans as strikebreakers, many contemporary observers had precisely the opposite opinion. One priest claimed, "there are 560 organized communists in Gary and they consist almost wholly of Mexicans and Russians." Other informed observers agreed that assessments of Mexicans as strikebreakers were inaccurate, as confirmed by their widespread participation in union organizing drives during the 1930s.[94]

Mexicans in the Midwest participated even less in electoral politics than in labor organizations. Because most were very poor, engaged in unstable work, and had low rates of citizenship, they rarely attracted the attention of politicians seeking votes. During the 1920s they were more likely to be drawn into politics involving Mexico, particularly the struggle between the federal government and the Catholic Church, centered in Jalisco, Michoacán, and neighboring states, the major source of immigration to the Midwest. They were encouraged to forgo supporting the rebellion by the Mexican government, which had established sixty offices throughout the United States by the end of the 1920s, including the midwestern cities of Milwaukee, Chicago, Detroit, St. Louis, and Kansas City, in addition to honorary or part-time consular representatives in many smaller cities. Despite their avowed concern of promoting loyalty and defending the interests of Mexicans in the United States, midwestern consular officials exerted greater energies in promoting business contacts between the two countries than in assisting working-class Mexicans. Yet several did provide information about employment and supported some worker actions, including boycotts against businesses that discriminated against Mexicans.

Countering the pressures on Mexican immigrants to maintain loyalty toward their native land, social workers, educators, church officials, and employers engaged in programs aimed at Americanization. While motives often varied, they shared in common a desire to socialize and control

Mexican labor. As Servando I. Esquivel of the Y.M.C.A. observed, the thrust of its Americanization efforts were aimed at enhancing better understanding, "to increase the economic efficiency of the workman," and "to avoid economic disturbances." Methodist Reverend Vernon McCombs, superintendent of the Latino-American Missions in Southern California, asserted that Mexicans "hold fine possibilities of citizenship." He added, however, that lacking formal schooling, they are "grossly misinformed about the United States," and "I.W.W. agitators find it comparatively easy to play upon their ignorance and to convince them the United States is a tyrannical country." He considered that the primary goal of church efforts was "to combat this sinister propaganda, but the Government should recognize the necessity for such efforts [at Americanization] and tackle the problem on a big scale," for "the economic future of the entire Southwest depends more and more upon the Mexicans." As historian Zaragoza Vargas observed, a central goal of Americanization programs was "to make immigrants equate factory discipline with good citizenship." [95]

Aimed initially at European immigrants, the Americanization movement quickly spread to Mexicans in cities and towns throughout the Southwest and Midwest. Employers and public school officials held special classes for children and adults, churches hired social workers, and settlement houses established programs to Americanize Mexicans. In East Chicago the public schools held evening classes attended by immigrants from several countries, including Mexico. Omaha schools offered special classes for Mexican women in the afternoon and Mexican men at night, but it was reported that progress at Americanization was "slow." Many large employers also adopted Americanization campaigns replete with English language and citizenship classes aimed at "wooing workers away from ethnicity" while gaining greater employee loyalty. [96]

The Americanization movement became much more defensive and rigid as the United States entered World War I. It reflected increasing fear within dominant popular culture and political leadership about foreign subversion and the "vast unassimilated mass of alien population whose national affiliations were uncertain, whose political ideals were unformed, [and] whose social and economic life was unrelated to American standards and American needs." Its leadership of Anglo-conformist "100 per cent Americans" claimed the need to demand immediate assimilation, eliminate all distinctive features of foreign cultures, and enforce an unquestioning allegiance toward the United States of America. Anglo-conformists considered Mexicans as a particularly acute "Americanization problem." Allied with Prohibitionists who were energized by the enactment of the

Eighteenth Amendment in 1918, they also sought to control morality, viewing the consumption of alcoholic beverages as distinctly foreign, although most informed observers agreed that Mexicans were not particularly heavy drinkers. A contemporary critic suggested that from the perspective of immigrants, "the spectacle of the rabid and ignorant Americanizing efforts was disheartening," for it did not respect languages or cultures, it lacked spontaneity, and it made no "recognition of national rights of the home county." Some industrial capitalists, including the U.S. Steel Corporation, believed that the "moral and political danger" Mexicans posed could be overcome by Americanization. Employers continued to hope that such programs would increase worker efficiency and eliminate absenteeism. As one observer noted, "in these prohibition days a man is wasting good time when he stays up after 10 o'clock."[97]

The drive to Americanize Mexicans in Minnesota in the 1920s involved a number of institutions, including the Neighborhood House, the public school system, and the International Institute. While they agreed on the general goals of converting Mexicans into loyal U.S. citizens and good workers, their methods and understanding of meanings of Americanization differed. The Neighborhood House, a settlement house with branches in many cities, was modeled after Jane Addams's Hull House in Chicago. In St. Paul it appeared on the Lower West Side in 1897, created by Mount Zion Temple on behalf of Jewish immigrants. The St. Paul Neighborhood House reorganized in 1903 as an agency of the Community Chest, a private social service funding agency, and adopted a nonsectarian emphasis, catering to all immigrant groups in the neighborhood and promoting assimilation.[98]

In 1923 the Neighborhood House in St. Paul first turned its attention to "the Mexican problem and the probability of even more of them coming to the city next fall." Already thirty-eight Mexicans were attending its night school classes, while an additional ninety-four went to evening sessions at the nearby Lafayette Grade School. In addition to offering instruction on the principles of the U.S. government and the American way of life, its classes, movies, and other activities aimed at enhancing immigrants' integration and productivity. Its staff taught language, citizenship, sewing, cooking, health education, music, and arts and crafts and offered athletics and social clubs for boys, girls, and young adults, a Mexican Doll Club for girls, as well as a camp, festivals, and other unorganized activities. Settlement house philosophy allowed a degree of group autonomy, permitting local residents to use facilities for their own events and clubs. As early as 1924 Sr. Zamora and other elders initiated Mexican activities, including performances of the *Pastorelas,* also known as *Los Pastores* (The Shepherd's Play) during the Christmas season.[99] The St. Paul Neighborhood House's view of Americanization was not as narrow as that promoted by the wartime Anglo-conformists.

Americanization programs in the Midwest had mixed results among Mexicans, and local leadership and staff sometimes sought to exclude them systematically. In Detroit, the Neighborhood House had made little contact with Mexicans until the late 1930s, when Reverend López initiated an effort to enlighten local staff. But its Protestant board, in harmony with the staff of the maternal health clinic located in the same building, successfully thwarted the Reverend's efforts, as they were not interested in encouraging Mexicans to become their kind of Americans.[100]

Although non-Mexican observers consistently noted that Minnesota Mexicans assimilated more slowly than any European immigrant group, from the earliest years there were clear signs of U.S. influence in the northernmost urban *colonia* in the United States. During the Mexican Fiesta de Navidad (Christmas party) held at the Neighborhood House in 1926, a *St. Paul Pioneer Press* reporter took careful note of attire. Elderly women maintained dress and hair styles common in Mexico, while young children, whose parents made most of their clothes, also conformed with Mexican fashion. "But the girls and youths and also the older men, are noticeably Americanized. Girls bobbed and with dresses of style, young 'sheiks' with glossy, well-sleeked, black hair, gay neckties and well pressed suits, indicate that Americanization is an engrossing ambition in the Mexican colony." Many young men who donned the 'sheik' style also wore *patillas,* short pointed side-whiskers, in emulation of movie star Rudolph Valentino. The Hollywood actor, as one observer noted, "was a great hero to the Mexicans, the psychological explanation being that he popularized the Latin type . . . which redounds to the self-satisfaction of the Mexican, who has always feared that the fair Saxon looked with disdain upon dark skinned people." Young Mexican sheiks also appeared in Omaha, Chicago, and other midwestern cities, while in smaller communities, like Mason City, "the sale of good clothes is limited, and the sheik class is very small." The Mexican sheiks of the 1920s—older brothers, uncles, and fathers of the youth of the late 1930s and 1940s who donned "zoot suits"—adopted a commercial fashion popular in its day. Yet their choice of apparel suggests a selective response to forces of assimilation, indicating that commercial culture could provide a niche that distinguished Mexican from Anglo ideals of the American Dream.[101]

Another major institution, the Catholic Church, had long utilized ethnicity as a means of organizing, fund-raising, and expansion, and its nationality-based parishes attracted European immigrant populations. Yet as Chicago Archbishop John Cardinal Cody observed, in contrast with Mexicans, "the Europeans brought their priests and sisters with them." Historian Mark Reisler has suggested that "the Roman Catholic Church played a much less significant role in the life of the Chicago Mexican community than it did for most ethnic groups." Furthermore, Juan García argued, its Americanization programs were halfhearted, instituted to counter charges that the church was a papist tool controlled by foreign interests. He added that "the Americanization crusade was the chosen instrument of their defensive and self-legitimating strategy" to justify that it was a "genuinely American church."[102]

While Mexican parishes were established in many midwestern Mexican cities, their appearance and survival was contingent on several factors. The first and most important was economic, for parishioners were expected to sustain their churches financially, and midwestern Mexicans included few people of means and fewer priests. In Lorain, Ohio, the Cleveland Diocese regarded the formation of a special parish as a means of organizing the Spanish-speaking community and encouraged parishioners to contribute five dollars each to initiate the effort, plus a dollar per month to support it. In Gary, the U.S. Steel Corporation, in collaboration with the Catholic Church, donated funds to help establish a Mexican parish in their efforts "to create the institutions of social control." A second factor was fear within the Catholic hierarchy of "losing" Mexicans to more vigorous Protestants, who established dozens of Mexican missions and churches throughout the region. There were also six Spiritist centers in Chicago alone in the late 1920s catering to Mexicans. Support for Mexican parishes was part of an "important Catholic counter-offensive" against Protestants, and because of frequent hostility from established Catholic priests and parishioners, it often sustained separate spaces for Mexicans. A third factor was the attitude of local bishops and archbishops, who ruled supreme in deciding to permit or prohibit separate nationality parishes.[103]

Catholic Church hierarchy based decisions about whether to support separate parishes in part on whether they thought it would enhance Mexican assimilation. In Chicago in the late 1920s, the Templo de Guadalupe, formerly St. Judas Tadeus, claimed more than eight thousand Mexican members, offering masses and a range of social and educational activities, including language classes in both English and Spanish. According to its priest, Padre Catalina, it promoted assimilation and loyalty, not only toward U.S. ideals but also toward employers. He asserted, "I can say that we benefit the City of Chicago by educating the people and making them good citizens; socially as well as morally, to be good workers and faithful to their jobs." In Detroit, by contrast, in 1938 Archbishop Edward Moody prohibited the establishment of a Mexican parish in the community (the old one had gone into abeyance because of its inconvenient location) on similar grounds. He argued that if Mexicans had their own parish and other nationality-based organizations within the church, they would not mingle with other groups, which would delay their assimilation.[104]

In St. Paul the archdiocese was alerted to the rapidly growing Mexican *colonia* in the late 1920s. Until that time, Mexican families who attended mass chose St. Michael's, St. Matthews, or the St. Paul Cathedral, which were within reasonable walking distance in good weather, "but in winter very few people attended. Most of them did not have warm clothing for the long walk." Church hierarchy determined that in St. Paul, as in other Mexican communities lacking their own church, attendance was low regardless of weather, and in 1931 it permitted the establishment of a Mexican mission, the prelude to a Mexican parish. In comparison with other local institutions, the Catholic Church was a late entry into the St. Paul barrio.[105]

Another agent of Americanization, the International Institute of Minnesota, appeared in St. Paul in 1919, through the efforts of European American women members of the local board of the YWCA. It offered social services, including English language and citizenship classes, casework, and social activities for foreign-born women. The International Institute identified itself as nonpolitical, interfaith, and interracial in orientation and retained its close ties to the YWCA until 1938, when it became independent and shifted its focus more to casework and folk arts. Under director Alice Sickels, it conducted important studies of Twin Cities Mexicans in the 1930s and 1940s, working closely with Neighborhood House staff. In many midwestern cities the International Institute attracted Mexicans to its classes, and they were reported as good students. Yet they often dropped out suddenly; as one observer noted, "the reason was that some hundred-percent American would make an eloquent speech before the foreigners' class and tell them how overjoyed he was to find them making such wonderful progress and that they would soon be ready for American citizenship. He might as well have injected pellagra fungus into the Mexicans, for he made them very sick. They quit attending class. They did not wish to be made into American citizens, and if learning the English language meant becoming naturalized they would let the English language alone."[106]

Institutional efforts to Americanize Mexicans were problematic, according to Edson, because of their anti-authoritarian and anarchist tendencies and an inherent belief that "all laws are bad laws." Like many contemporaries, Edson did not consider the melting pot imagery applicable. He asserted that "it was apparent to some employment men that the Mexicans did not want anybody trying to make them happy and they looked with a foxy eye on anyone who might have an idea he was going to put them in a pot, melt them up with a little applesauce and mold them into Americans." Expressing a less charitable assessment, an Austrian-born priest, John deVille, who organized the Catholic Instructional League as part of Americanization efforts in Gary, complained in 1927 that "we have shut out European immigrants and have accepted the uncivilized Mexican in his place. . . . You can Americanize the man from southeastern and southern Europe, but [you] can't Americanize a Mexican." The priest faced a direct challenge from Gary resident José Gallardo, who asserted: "we do not have to become American citizens because we are Americans bone and flesh." Gallardo's internationalist perspective embracing an understanding of America as applicable to two continents, widespread among Mexicans, considered the logic of the agents of Americanization as narrowly nationalist, crude, and uninformed.[107]

Dominant political and popular culture hindered assimilation by its own attitudes and by discriminatory behavior, as evident in patterns of Mexican work and housing. Midwestern Mexicanos almost invariably worked separately from other groups in the sugar beet fields and commonly were isolated on the railroads, while they intermingled more often with European immigrants and African Americans, but not European Americans, in urban factories and residential neighborhoods. They were generally restricted in housing options. Paul Taylor noted that "in practically every major colony of Mexicans in the region, there were or had been efforts by landlords, real estate men, and residents of other nationalities, to drive out the Mexicans or to isolate them by restricting the boundaries of their residence," with some success. Mexicans typically were isolated in railroad *colonias*, company towns, and small cities where employers controlled housing. In larger cities, they tended to cluster in poorer neighborhoods on the same streets in houses and apartments with European immigrants and often with Blacks. Mexican separation from African Americans varied in specific settings. In Detroit, it was reported, "they mix very little with negroes" socially or residentially, while in Waukegan they resided among both Europeans and African Americans. In Lorain, Mexicans resided in both European and African American neighborhoods. In the cafeteria at National Tube, Lorain's largest employer, African Americans were required to eat on one side of the dining room apart from Whites, while Mexicans could eat where they desired, and about a third of them "voluntarily took seats at the table with the negroes." In Bethlehem, Mexicans identified themselves as distinct from European immigrants and European Americans, both of whom they identified as White, and from African Americans. In Chicago it was reported that "Slovaks and others regard the Mexicans as colored men." A Chicago school principal stated that "the Negroes resist segregation, and when the Mexicans came they asked us if the Mexicans were white. We told them that they were." A Mexican in Chicago stated, "it is true that the Mexicans feel alone in the United States, and about the only people who talk to them are the Negroes, who speak to them smilingly."[108]

The Mexican consulate challenged the Americanization effort by participating in the establishment of Mexican social, cultural, and self-help organizations, including the Comité Patriótico Mexicano and the Cruz Azul, an organization composed chiefly of women and aimed at providing charity for the sick and needy. Consular representatives sometimes assisted in the formation of theater groups, including the Artistas Unidos Mexicanos de Chicago and the Cuadro Dramatico in Indiana Harbor. In St. Paul, which did not have a full-time consular office, a volunteer was appointed to represent the Mexican government and promote social, cultural, and educational activities and to provide a link between *colonia* residents and public and private agencies.[109]

As honorary chair of the local Comisión Honorífico or Comité Patriótico, the consul promoted *mexicanidad,* an awareness and pride in being Mexican, by sponsoring Mexican organizations, social and cultural activities, and the celebration of Mexican national holidays, with an ultimate goal of encouraging immigrants' return to Mexico. The explicit Mexican cultural nationalism promoted by the consulate, heightened by the pervasive influence of the Mexican Revolution, sought to counter Americanization campaigns and the cultural influence of the United States. Even ardent cultural nationalists in the United States like Lorain, Ohio, resident Gustavo del Río expressed concern that people in the northern *colonias* were losing their identity and urged, "*hay que Mexicanizar a esos mismos Mexicanos*" (it is necessary to Mexicanize these very Mexicanos). Benjamín Figueroa, publisher of *El amigo del hogar* in East Chicago, feared that "children are being educated in the schools and taught to be Americans. They will never return to Mexico now." Mexican cultural organizations, furthermore, were often poorly developed, particularly in settings where consular officials were not active. In Milwaukee, George Edson reported that "the chief reason for the lack of organization is the lack of time available to the consul in Milwaukee to foster the spirit."[110] Such grim assessments of Mexicans' capacity to sustain a distinct culture in the United States would have surprised most social workers, Catholic priests, and other agents of Americanization, who considered the Mexican culture as a greater obstacle to their own efforts than any European cultures they encountered.

Mexicans' reluctance to heed the agents of Americanization also reflected their perceptions of European Americans' sense of superiority and individual experiences. They encountered condescending attitudes even from individuals who considered themselves sympathetic, like geographer T. Earl Sullenger, who asserted that "as human beings these Mexicans are sociable, friendly, approachable, grateful, charitable, and simple-minded." Many individuals had bitter memories, including Sr. Sebastián Jara, who recalled that his mother "never gave me the opportunity to learn English because she had sworn, that during her lifetime, she would never change her feelings about white people. She didn't like them at all. My mother was a Tarascan Indian." After his family moved from the beet fields to St. Paul, he became involved in the YMCA English language programs, but he recalled, "I didn't like it at the Y too much, because there was a lot of discrimination. This I have never liked, because I feel we are all equal and that we are all sons of God or sons of the Devil." Yet resistance to Americanization was a doubled-edged sword, according to Edson, who asserted that "the fact that he [the Mexican] resists attempts to Americanize him is very pleasing to capitalists, for it will be a happy day when they find a class of laboring men with intelligence enough to do their work well but without sense enough to rise out of their primitive condition."[111]

Midwestern Mexicanos formed dozens of nationality-based organizations. At the end of the 1920s one observer counted twenty-three Mexican societies in Chicago, eight in Indiana Harbor, four in Gary, fourteen in Detroit, and several elsewhere. While some were creations of the Mexican government, the Catholic Church, local agencies, settlement houses, and employers, Paul Taylor observed that most "were of entirely independent origin and affiliation."[112]

The most popular were *mutualistas,* patterned after similar organizations in Mexico and Europe whose major functions were to provide charitable aid while promoting social, cultural, and recreational activities. Their role and importance, nonetheless, has been subject to debate. In the 1940s Frank Paz offered a critical assessment based on his Chicago experiences, asserting that "in reality they all have been only social clubs, with dances as their principal activities." More recently, historian Juan García offered a more positive assessment, emphasizing that they provided support systems otherwise lacking "that they could turn to in time of need." The charity function was particularly important because the federal government did not accept responsibility for public welfare until the enactment of New Deal legislation in the 1930s. Private and public local agencies that provided social welfare rarely accepted responsibility for indigent Mexicans. The public welfare section in South Chicago acknowledged in reference to Mexican cases that the "number appears unreasonably small." Welfare providers simply assumed that Mexicans would care for their own, as Detroit Assistant Director of Immigration Isador Weishaar observed: "wherever there is a group of Mexicans in this country they rarely permit one of their number to become a public charge." Paul Taylor concluded that "Mexicans are not regarded as a serious charity problem."[113]

In St. Paul the Sociedad Mutua Benefica Recreativa Anahuac formed in 1922, with eligibility open to Spanish speakers who supported the goals of the organization and paid an initiation fee of three dollars, plus dues of ten cents per month. In return, members with temporary illnesses or injuries received fifty cents per day for a maximum of fifteen days, contingent on prior notification of committee members, plus five dollars for medicine. Dues commonly were inadequate for individual emergencies, and organizations typically foundered during hard times. In such cases, St. Paul Sociedad Anahuac member Sra. Crescencia Rangel recalled, "they would take up collections to help each other among the same members of the society. When anyone needed help, such as food or clothing, the members of the Women's Auxiliary would get together and take the needy families food, clothing and money." Local Mexican societies, composed of workers holding unstable jobs, were partially able to offset the failure of local welfare providers to handle workers in distress, while outside observers concurred that conditions among Mexicans during the winter in large cities like Chicago were "distressing."[114]

*Mutualistas* also offered spaces of refuge, Juan García contends: "more important than the financial aid was the social and psychological support" they provided by sponsoring dances, holiday celebrations, parades, funerals, weddings, and baptisms. They were particularly critical in the earliest years, as Sra. Rangel recalled, because "none of us could speak English to defend ourselves." *Mutualistas* also offered friendship, according to Sr. Sebastián Jara. On arriving in St. Paul in 1927, he "decided to see what the Anahuac Society did. . . . Being a member of this society, I was able to meet people of La Raza." Through its close-knit organization and maintenance of a Mexican nationalist ideology, García suggests, Mexicans could "stave off" assimilation. He noted that "even the names of the organizations were designed so as to foster pride in the mestizo-Indian heritage of Mexico," as in the case of Anahuac, the Aztec name for ancient Mexico.[115]

Members voluntarily sustained social and cultural activities in their communities. *Anahuac* members Sr. Luis Garzón and Sra. Crescencia Rangel directed choruses of Mexican men and children. Sr. Garzón, himself an accomplished professional musician, also formed and directed the Sociedad Anahuac's *orquesta,* which performed at social events, holiday celebrations, and benefit dances to raise money for people in need and to purchase Christmas toys for Mexican children. The children's choir performance in Spanish impressed the *St. Paul Pioneer Press,* which reported that "sub-zero temperatures, scant coal bins, food costs, are forgotten in the culmination of the festival, reviving the communal spirit that is so inherent in tropical lands." The talented children convinced the newspaper that Mexicans had inherently exceptional musical abilities, an idea that contrasted with current cultural deficiency theories.[116]

The Sociedad Anahuac also sponsored social and cultural events aimed at preserving and enhancing Mexican identity and culture, and the women's auxiliary, whose members held equal voting power with men, played a crucial role in organizing events and cooking and selling food. Both Sra. Crescencia Rangel and Sr. Francisco Rangel taught youth the mechanics of planning, staging, and performing plays and consciously worked to attract entire families. Despite its cultural nationalist sympathies, the Sociedad Anahuac was not isolationist, nor did it encourage members to repatriate to Mexico, and its leaders frequently challenged exploitation and mistreatment of their compatriots in the United States. Unlike *mutualistas* in many larger cities, where competition and division accompanied the proliferation of organizations, the Sociedad Anahuac, through its social and cultural functions, helped create an "urban village" in which few Mexican residents of St. Paul and Minneapolis failed to participate.[117]

The Sociedad Anahuac took on roles not typical of *mutualistas,* for its president was also ex-oficio representative of the Mexican consul in Minnesota, a part-time voluntary position. Not distracted by concerns over Mexican foreign policy or foreign investment, the representative instead focused on promoting local cultural events and defense of *colonia* interests. Members of Anahuac's Women's Auxiliary performed functions that La Cruz Azul Mexicana was resonsible for in larger cities. The organization also adopted the role of the Comité Patriótico Mexicano, organizing Cinco de Mayo and Diez y Seis de Septiembre celebrations. Sra. Juanita Rangel de Morán, the daughter of former Sociedad Anahuac president Sr. Francisco Rangel, recalled: "my father would say that he did this so that people would remember the customs followed in Mexico and also so that the young people could learn and preserve important aspects of our Mexican culture."[118]

Sociedad Anahuac members also accepted the consular responsibility of defending the interests and rights of Mexicans against discriminatory abuses and practices. Sra. Crescencia Rangel recalled an incident in which her husband presented documentation that countered school officials' assertions that Mexicans were only worthy of work in the beet fields, including those of teachers who berated students with negative comments like: "What do you know? You are like the animals that work the soil. What civilization do you have? What business do you have in school?" Anahuac members also took up cases of worker rights by meeting officials to discuss and publicize abuses. They also wrote editorials challenging a hostile press in order to educate an uninformed public and shed popular misconceptions about Mexico and its people.[119]

While Sociedad Anahuac represented a fairly homogeneous group of workers, midwestern *mutualistas* also reflected diverse class and political interests. Los Obreros Católicos San José of East Chicago, composed of conservative Catholic exiles, shared both elitist leadership and goals. Similarly, the earliest *mutualista* in Kansas City, the Unión Mexicana Benito Juárez, had relatively affluent professional leaders. In Detroit, the elitist Círculo Mutualista Mexicana sponsored activities like the Debutantes Ball, but it competed with the more progressive, working-class membership of Obreros Libres.[120]

Musical groups, particularly Mexican brass bands, were also common in midwestern communities in the 1920s. While some professional musicians organized and led these musical groups, they were composed overwhelmingly of workers and youth. There were four brass bands in the Chicago-Calumet area. In the Hull House district, Francisco Calderón headed the local Mexican band for several years. The South Chicago Mexican Band, directed by Professor Gumaro Ortiz, was supported financially by Illinois Steel, which gave members preference in employment while enhancing its own influence. The Indiana Harbor band was organized by Cirilio Rodríguez, formerly a flautist in the Mexican National Army Band, while Gary had its own Banda Anahuac. In Kansas City, the Guadalupe Center on the West Side had its own parish band, while in

Silvis, Illinois, the Rock Island Railroad helped employees form a community band, purchase instruments, and clean up land for a park to hold performances and other gatherings. Other bands and *orquestas* appeared, particularly in the larger cities. By the early 1930s, Chicago was home to the Chapultepec Jazz band, "composed wholly of Mexicans," and *orquestas* sponsored by the Latin American Cultural Club and the Aztec Club. *Orquestas* appeared even in small communities like Dodge City, Kansas, while an informed observer claimed that Detroit had thirty orchestras of its own in 1926, most supported by *mutualistas* or employers. The Mexican orchestra and choir in St. Paul, directed by Sr. Luis Garzón, appeared without the support of a Mexican consul or company paternalism. Its volunteer members provided friends, neighbors, and relatives another respite from the commercial culture that pervaded their communities.[121]

Leadership played an important role in the maintenance of *bandas, orquestas,* and other organizations in the early midwestern *colonias.* Many leaders could be considered "organic intellectuals" and often were referred to as the community's informal "Mexican Mayor." The leadership reflected diverse class backgrounds and included storekeepers, local ministers, professionals, and skilled or common laborers. The earliest leader of the West Side *colonia* in St. Paul, Sr. Luis Garzón, according to popular lore was the first Mexicano to settle in Minnesota. A professional oboist in the Mexican National Police Band, he came to Minneapolis to play in the city's Industrial Exposition in 1884, decided to stay after becoming ill on tour, and soon gained employment with the Minneapolis Symphony Orchestra. In the early 1920s, as the barrio formed on the Lower West Side, he opened a Mexican grocery store on Fairfield Street, which became a local institution for many years and was reported to be the "intellectual center" of the community. In Detroit, Sr. José Alfaro, who arrived in 1923, spent his entire adult life as an auto worker and devoted more than sixty years as a volunteer in community activities, teaching dance, music, and art. In Indiana Harbor, self-styled leaders included the brothers Benjamín and F. J. Figueroa, and J. Jesús Cortez, who formed a *mutualista,* Los Obreros Católicos San José, and spent countless volunteer hours publishing a newspaper, *El Amigo del Hogar,* in the late 1920s. Although they clearly expressed an elitist and paternalistic vision, these Indiana Harbor leaders worked as proletarians in East Chicago in a local cement plant and tube mill. In the small railroad *colonia* of Carville just north of Gibson, near Omaha, Sr. J. B. Hernández, whose family was identified as "the aristocrats of Carville," was a railroad worker like his neighbors and was acknowledged as their leader. The leadership of this generation did not expect remuneration for teaching classes, publishing newspapers, directing choirs and bands, organizing social and cultural events, or helping neighbors in need after a hard day at work.[122]

In St. Paul, another long-active *colonia* leader, Sr. Francisco Rangel, for many years secretary of the Sociedad Anahuac, was born in Jalisco and orphaned as a child. Sent with his brother to live with a priest, he learned to read and write before being adopted by a family. His skills enabled him to become secretary of an independent railway workers union that eventually affiliated with the Confederación Regional Obrero Mexicano (CROM) in Aguascalientes, Mexico, after the Mexican Revolution. In 1926 he entered the United States, and after a brief residence in Kansas, he moved to St. Paul in 1927, where he soon found employment with the Cudahy Packing Company and joined the Sociedad Anahuac. Like many other Mexicanos, he was laid off during the Great Depression and for several years was forced to engage in the annual trek between St. Paul and the beet fields until recalled by Cudahy. Despite his writing skills and organizational experience, Rangel remained a packinghouse laborer for more than twenty-five years in addition to many more years as a beet worker. As his daughter observed of Mexicanos in St. Paul, "none of us had any wealth. All of us worked."[123]

Sr. Rangel, although never identifying with the middle class, was named the first St. Paul voluntary consular representative, in which capacity he volunteered time to political, social, and cultural events while assisting individuals in need. He helped recent arrivals settle, assisted individuals in acquiring residency papers, and submitted formal complaints in cases of discrimination and police brutality. His daughter also noted "that when anyone in the community had any problems, such as lack of food or their husband had been deported, they would come to my father so he could arrange something. My father was very good at putting thoughts together and then writing them down, so he would help everyone in need."[124]

Local leaders in midwestern Mexican communities were particularly important in smaller cities lacking consular offices, where they often functioned in its stead without pay or other material rewards. Most sustained themselves by employment in working-class jobs, despite talents that included writing and speaking skills and a willingness to take responsibility for needs they perceived in their community. Had they been Europeans, or reared in a later generation, they would likely have acquired more formal schooling and been professionals or "academic" intellectuals. Systematic discrimination against midwestern Mexicanos stymied whatever middle-class aspirations they might have entertained. After completing a working day in shops and factories, they devoted their energies to the needs of their friends and neighbors. As a result of New Deal reforms, demands for the services they offered diminished, and many of their organizations disappeared. Later, the War on Poverty and the struggles of the Chicano Movement, combined with the appearance of a professional class of Latinos and Hispanics in nonprofit and government agencies, institutionalized additional social services and reduced the need for such organizations.

Despite the efforts of their members, Mexican organizations in the Midwest, including *mutualistas,* typically had short lives, and according to one study, more than 80 percent collapsed within a year of formation. Observers and participants have variously attributed their lack of continuity to internal factionalism caused by individuals willing to participate only as leaders; business competition in which leaders became involved only "to aid one's business"; conflicts between the Mexican government and the Catholic Church; and poverty and unstable employment among members. Many *mutualistas* collapsed because of workers' shifting employment or the drain on funds resulting from members' illness. Class conflict also presented a problem, as one Chicago mechanic asserted, for "the lower classes don't want to join with the middle and upper classes." Paul Taylor observed that the frequent collapse of individual organizations did not end community activities, and "new societies arose, however, from the ashes of the old."[125]

While individual motivations varied, Mexicans entered the northern United States in the early twentieth century en masse as a reserve labor army to perform unstable, unpleasant, and seasonal work in the sugar beet fields, on the railroads, and in factories. Prior negative social constructions of Mexicans by the dominant political and social culture were reinforced in the Midwest, limiting life chances at work and in other settings. Their stay on any single job generally was short, and to survive they typically were compelled to shift from one place of residence to another. Apart from agriculture, the Mexican urban Midwest was largely a man's world in its earliest years. Highly unbalanced sex ratios further suggest that Mexicanos in the 1910s and 1920s were not following the path of earlier Europeans nor being recruited to become part of stable communities. The largest single contingent, sugar beet workers, unlike thousands of their European predecessors, had no opportunities to climb the mythical "agricultural ladder" and become farmers. As Edson observed of Mexicans in the region, rural or urban, "not one in a hundred owns his own home." [126] Only a miniscule portion of midwestern Mexicanos found a stable place in the industrial proletariat in the early twentieth century.

As railroad track workers, Mexicans averaged about seven months' employment per year, despite substantial individual variation. In Omaha, in 1928 ten railroad companies employed between 800 and 1000 Mexican workers in the summer, but only 250 in the winter. Factory employment was slightly less erratic, and automobile plants in Detroit offered an average of between five and eight months' of work during the year, with the exception of Ford, which presaged a more stable future relationship with employees. Most Mexican auto and steel workers were unemployed during the winter, but even in summer, many worked only three or four days per week. A 1925 study estimated that more than 30 percent of Mexicans in Chicago were also without work during the summer. Obtaining employment in the winter was particularly difficult for Mexicans because of its often political context. As Mrs. Kembell of the United Charities in Chicago observed, the city would not even employ Mexicans to shovel snow, for "labor men say, 'they demoralize a crew.'" [127]

Employers benefited from hiring Mexicans as a reserve labor army. In the steel foundries, Mexicans were assigned the most dangerous jobs and suffered high mortality rates resulting from the emission of gases and fumes in metal casting. Even when workers were injured or died, employers usually avoided paying compensation, with the help of nativist legislation in several states that exempted them from paying claims to dependents residing in foreign countries. Another notable feature was the rarity of upward mobility among unskilled Mexican workers and employers' refusal to recognize skills they had already acquired. Mexicans complained widely about unfair hiring and promotional practices in the factories and railroads. Railroad workers hired in the early twentieth century often remained section or extra gang laborers after thirty or forty years, as employers refused to promote them to positions as foremen and assistant foremen. Even skilled and middle-class Mexican workers were "obliged to enter the ranks of common labor" without opportunities for upward mobility after many years' employment, in contrast with European immigrants. One Bethlehem Steel executive observed, "If it were not for the color of their skins I don't see why some Mexicans couldn't rise to positions of responsibility." [128]

A 1927 survey of eighty-six major employers reported that midwestern Mexican workers averaged $2.80 per day, with substantial variations. Workers understood a hierarchy in Mexican employment options, mitigated by several factors. The sugar beet industry stood at the bottom, with wages averaging $23 per acre plus lodging for individuals able to provide their own transportation. An average adult male tended about ten acres per season, adult females about three-fourths of an adult male, and children lesser amounts depending on age. Sugar beets offered advantages of readily available employment and opportunities to offset low wages by the labor of women and especially children, who were not bound by legal restrictions current in factories. A level higher, work on railroad gangs (principally performing track maintenance), tended to average between 35 and 40 cents per hour, or between $2.50 and $3.20 per day. Despite the low pay, workers like Luis García preferred it to the Wisconsin Steel plant in South Chicago: "I want track work, but not where I have to be boarded. I want to board myself. I want tortillas and frijoles and chili. I don't like white beans, and biscuits not done enough; they make me sick. I don't like roast beef."[129]

The next higher-paying major category of employment included urban packinghouses. In Omaha, wages in 1924 averaged 42 cents per hour, or $3.36 for a standard eight-hour day, while in Chicago they ranged from 42.5 to 47 cents per hour. It was more stable than on the railroads, but with fewer available jobs. At the top of the scale, the steel mills and foundries commonly paid between 45 cents and 50 cents per hour. On the negative side, it was notoriously unstable employment, as one steel mill worker in Chicago complained: "we live here like birds of the air. As long as there is work in the steel mills, we stay; when work closes down, we are away to any place we can hear of steady work." Most Mexicans employed by automobile companies worked in foundries. Ford in Detroit offered the highest reported pay, at 75 cents per hour, or six dollars for an eight-hour day, and employment sometimes lasted twelve months per year, with standard eight-hour shifts and five days' work each week. The Ford reputation lured thousands of workers, so the company did not have to recruit, and obtaining employment was difficult. Neighboring auto plants typically paid four or five dollars per day, with ten- or twelve-hour work days, and only five to eight months' employment per year. Yet the large factories were not always the most attractive, as Sr. Roberto Cortina recalled of his father's experience at Briggs in Detroit: "He saw so many people get cut up, get their arms cut up, their fingers cut up. That's why he gave up on that kind of work." Most workers, nonetheless, were influenced by the possibility of stability, which made Ford attractive, as Javier Tovar observed, because "Mexicans like steady work when they can get it."[130]

While Mexican men generally earned lower wages than European immigrants by virtue of exclusion from more skilled and higher-paying categories of employment, an explicit dual wage policy for comparable work commonly was applied to women. In a typical Chicago confectionary, men started at 45 cents per hour, women at between 30 and 35 cents. Furthermore, Mexicanas were excluded from many occupations where their male counterparts found work, particularly in heavy industry and on the railroads. Women's work as domestics paid an average of seven or eight dollars per week plus room and board, but in the Midwest there were "very few" Mexicanas in that category in comparison with the Southwest. Much larger numbers worked in *casas de asistencia* with their families, as cooks where young Mexican male employees resided, and particularly as part-time or temporary workers. Formal contract provisions also hid the presence of much greater numbers of Mexicanas in the sugar beet fields. When the sugar beet industry is included, it is evident that most Mexican girls and women in the early-twentieth-century Midwest worked for wages for many years.[131]

Mexicans were much less likely to establish businesses than European immigrants, even in the largest cities, where opportunities were greatest, and the number of Mexican professionals was infinitesimal. In Chicago, Paul Taylor found that 33 percent of Mexican establishments were pool halls, 23 percent restaurants, 12 percent barbershops, and 9 percent groceries. Even in Chicago it was reported that "no Mexican appears to be making a very large income," and "business mortality was high." The number of Mexican businesses was further masked by Spanish and Latin American businessmen who set up shops and establishments like Indiana Harbor's Botica Mexicana (Mexican drugstore), "a camouflage title under which the International Drug company at the corner of Washington and Pennsylvania Avenue masks its non-Mexican ownership." As in the Southwest, an observer noted, "opportunities for Mexicans to become clerks depended on the patronage of Mexicans," yet even then there were relatively few Mexican clerks.[132]

For entrepreneurial-minded individuals, there were often greater opportunities in the informal economy. In Detroit a woman named Trini, of "humble social background" but great intelligence, had "one of the most important bootlegging centers" in the city operating out of her house and several men, "American and others," under her orders. In Etna, Pennsylvania, a group of Mexicans in a *casa de asistencia* reportedly had a lively trade in home brew. During these years of prohibition, Mexicans also gained inroads into the distribution of marijuana, referred to in English as "Mary Juana," "Mexican weed" or "Indian hemp." Negative popular representations of Mexicans in the trade were widespread, and a St. Paul observer claimed, "just as the Chinese carry the opium habit wherever they migrate, Mexicans carry marijuana," which another described as "a kind of dope which many of the West Side Mexicans were using." While it was reportedly available in most midwestern neighborhoods, including every drugstore of Indiana Harbor, its importance was the subject of debate. Some observers claimed that its popularity was due to the influence of Mexican railroad and beet workers, as it "spread in a wild state in Kansas, Nebraska and other midwestern states. Some tough Mexicans make a business of peddling it." In Kansas, "a patch of it was found thriving within the walls of the state penitentiary." Inspector Knauth of the Detroit Narcotics Squad asserted that "quite a little is grown down south and they bring it up," and in addition, "Mexicans who work in the beet fields raise it on the side. I have heard that one of them made as much as $3800 in a season." In some locations it was reported that European American men went to Mexican pool halls in search of the weed, while at Homestead, Pennsylvania, where cigarettes sold for 25 cents, the Police Court reported that "some of them smoke hemp and get wild." Yet even in Homestead it was not a Mexican monopoly, as men of several nationalities engaged in its growing and distribution. While it offered opportunities for entrepreneurs lacking access to more established networks, most often it had not even reached the underground economy. A Chicago report suggested that "the source of supply is often somebody's garden or window-box," while at Indiana Harbor, "one old lady had it growing in her yard and the police destroyed it." [133]

Patterns of Mexican *colonia* formation in the early-twentieth-century Midwest stand between the Southwest, where *colonias* were much more widespread, and the East, where they were rare and highly unstable. Large-scale industry in the Midwest was youthful in comparison with that of the eastern United States, and Mexicans were attracted to the region's most vibrant industries, particularly sugar beets, steel, and automobiles. The larger unskilled European immigrant population in the East may account for the low numbers of Mexicans there, even on the railroads, in contrast with the Southwest, where they dominated. As in the Southwest, *colonias* often appeared in the Midwest near railroads, which were the first to hire Mexicans.

Dominant popular thought influenced the way Mexicans were received, and in the early-twentieth-century Midwest attitudinal extremes ranged from comparatively sympathetic social workers to openly hostile eugenecists. As Agnes Fenton observed in Milwaukee in 1930, "while the social workers are afraid that the peons will not mix with our native populations, the eugenists [*sic*] are afraid that they will." Opposition by European immigrant workers does not adequately explain the failure of Mexicans to enter specific occupations or establish *colonias* in many midwestern locations, for such hostility was not absent in any specific part of the nation. While the relatively smaller numbers of European immigrants in Southwestern cities may have permitted Mexicans access to a greater range of occupations, resistance was much more effectively organized by skilled workers, who often prevented skilled Mexicans from being hired in jobs for which they were qualified. Still more successful were employers, who may have been reluctant to hire Mexicans but were more concerned about running profitable operations. They were most able to limit occupational choices of Mexican workers while delimiting the neighborhoods in which they resided by rent gouging, in alliances with bankers and realtors. Taunting, violence, and threats by working-class immigrants to keep Mexicans out of their neighborhoods were much less successful. Although segregation in the Midwest was less systematic than in the Southwest, prejudice and discrimination in the more ethnically diverse Midwest, Taylor noted, contributed to a "strong emotional resistance" to naturalization. As in the Southwest, midwestern Mexicans had the lowest naturalization rates among all foreign-born groups.[134]

Mexicanos assimilated selectively, and midwestern observers consistently reported that they were much slower to adopt dominant patterns of behavior than any European immigrant group, a view consistent with their place in the expanding world economy. Working seasonally in the beet fields as families, or as single men on railroads and in factories, they found their assimilation also delayed by the small numbers of children among them who were likely to bring the English language and other midwestern habits as they returned home from school and other settings. Men commonly lived in isolated single rooms, company barracks, railroad *colonias,* boarding houses, or *casas de asistencia,* separated from their families in Texas and Mexico, where the lower cost of reproduction and opportunities to sustain themselves outside of the market nexus ultimately kept costs down for midwestern employers. They were not recruited to the Midwest to assimilate into the nation's urban proletariat, and the messages of their employers, agents of assimilation, and European Americans further isolated them from dominant culture while it simultaneously lured them into the expanding world economy.

Mexicans' limited opportunities in employment, plus the generally hostile treatment by agents of Americanization and assimilated European neighbors, were not positive inducements for proclamations of loyalty to the United States. Nevertheless, their communities continued to expand and stabilize in the 1920s. The long periods of unemployment and frustrated opportunities for upward mobility encouraged them to develop a vibrant and self-sustaining social and cultural life and to establish roots in communities throughout the region. As Robert McLean suggested, "it is probable . . . that the northern Mexican can be considered a permanent increment to the population in the community where he lives."[135] The trend toward stability was greatly enhanced by the increasing presence of women and children but was severely tested by the Great Depression.

# 3 Memory of Hunger

Midwestern Mexicans had established only a tenuous presence in the region following World War I and were particularly vulnerable to the ravages of the Great Depression. As part of President Herbert Hoover's national campaign to "Hire American," Mexicans quickly were "eked out by white labor" with the assistance of nativist politicians and the dominant media. Unable to continue providing for the needs of their unemployed compatriots, Mexicans drew attention for draining private and public welfare resources throughout the nation.[1] To deal with the perceived problem, the U.S. Department of Labor's Bureau of Immigration contrived a campaign of terror and intimidation to deport Mexicans who entered the country without proper documentation, while seeking to convince permanent residents and even U.S. citizens of Mexican descent to depart voluntarily. Simultaneously, welfare officials and social workers concerned about reducing the costs of charity, public schooling, and other services devised numerous community-based repatriation schemes. Some employers, nonetheless, were reluctant to discharge workers who had demonstrated competence and loyalty, and a few political organizations and settlement house workers defended their right to remain. As individuals and as families, Mexicans faced contradictory pressures due to the hard times.

## The Drive to Repatriate

The Midwest played a critical role in the intensifying political debate over Mexican immigration which culminated in the repatriation movement, for it broadened the controversy from a regional southwestern setting to the national arena. As Paul Taylor observed in 1931, there existed "a feeling in the Southwest that were it not for transportation of Mexicans to the beet fields, scattering them over the North, the rest of the country would raise little outcry against Mexican immigrants." Anti-Mexican sentiment in the Midwest intensified sharply in the late 1920s, and northern politicians, policy makers, and academics were among the leaders in national discussions over the restriction of Mexican immigration. Chicago Mu-

MEXICANS IN THE MIDWEST, 1930

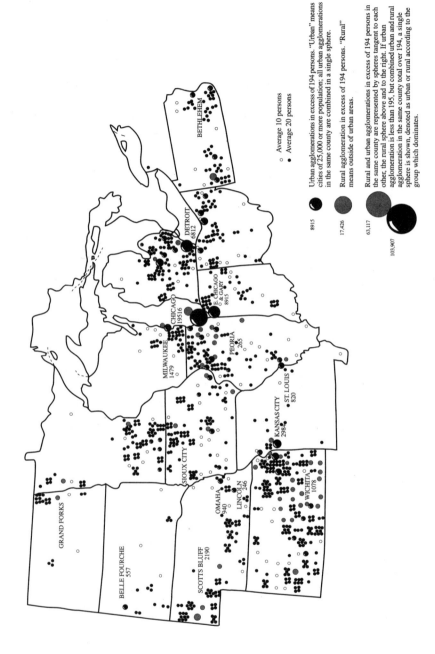

- ○ Average 10 persons
- ● Average 20 persons

Urban agglomerations in excess of 194 persons. "Urban" means cities of 25,000 or more population; all urban agglomerations in the same county are combined in a single sphere.

Rural agglomeration in excess of 194 persons. "Rural" means outside of urban areas.

Rural and urban agglomerations in excess of 194 persons in the same county are represented by spheres tangent to each other, the rural sphere above and to the right. If urban agglomeration is less than 195, but combined urban and rural agglomeration in the same county total over 194, a single sphere is shown, denoted as urban or rural according to the group which dominates.

8915

17,426

63,117

103,907

MAP 4. MEXICANS IN THE MIDWEST, 1930 (FROM PAUL SCHUSTER TAYLOR,
*MEXICAN LABOR IN THE UNITED STATES: MIGRATION STATISTICS, IV*).

nicipal Judge Thomas Green asserted in 1931, "we have a great deal of trouble with vagrant Mexicans, who require watching. They come here to take work away from the Americans and later become vagrants and create a problem." The best-known congressional proposal aimed at restriction, popularly associated with John Box of Texas, was cosponsored by Thomas Jenkins of Ohio. Many midwestern public figures articulated similar sentiments, including Indiana lawyer, orator, and educator Oswald Ryan. In 1927 he asserted, "the rapidly swelling stream of unassimilable mass immigration now soaring into this country from Mexico and lands to the south, unless stopped, will create a political and social problem of utmost gravity to our country in the near future."[2]

Their opinions were shared by influential captains of midwestern industry, including R. E. Wood of Chicago, president of Sears Roebuck, who complained in 1929 that "the Mexican immigration has been steadily increasing. The presence of this cheap, ignorant labor, which cuts under our standards of living and forms an unassimilated mass, is dangerous to our institutions." The underlying fear was that Mexicans were heading north and staying, as Charles Thomson wrote: "European immigration has been restricted, but the cheap labor vacuum that is thus created is quickly sucking the Mexicans out of the Southwest and into the North and East. Soon the man from next door may actually live next door to many of us."[3]

Although politicians and their allies failed to pass legislation restricting Mexican immigration, they found other means to achieve their ends. In 1929 Congress redefined conditions of entry into the United States, prior to which an individual who entered without the "customary bow to the immigration officials was not even guilty of a misdemeanor." The new law considered undocumented entry a misdemeanor and increased the cost of obtaining citizenship by 300 percent. More important were administrative decisions on both the state and national levels. In 1930, for example, the governor of Kansas wrote to the six largest railroad companies requesting that they "dismiss Mexican aliens" in favor of European Americans. On the federal level, in 1929 the State Department made a determination to tighten up the ease of obtaining visas, sharply reducing the entry of Mexicans. The Department of Labor also issued an administrative decision requiring Border Patrol agents to more strictly enforce existing statutes that prohibited entry of individuals liable to become a public charge. The decision affected a young mother born in San Pedro Caro, Michoacán, who initially entered the United States in 1909 as an infant with her recently widowed father and moved with him to Topeka, where he found railroad employment. They moved in 1918 to St. Paul, where he found work on the Burlington Railroad, and she briefly returned to Mexico and rejoined him in Minnesota in 1924. In 1928 she secured employment at the Cudahy packing plant and, though not married, soon gave birth to a daughter. She took another trip to Michoacán in 1929 and left her daughter with her father. On attempting to cross the border at Laredo the following year to rejoin her father and daughter in St. Paul, the Border Patrol refused her entry. The father appealed to the American Consular Service, claiming he could support her, as he had worked continuously for the Burlington for more than ten years, and that she was needed to help him care for her St. Paul–born daughter. The service "found her inadmissible to the United States," on the grounds that she was liable to become a public charge.[4]

Another Labor Department directive authorized immigration officials to use their discretionary powers to conduct a deportation campaign aimed at removing undocumented entrants from the country. Major media outlets throughout the nation, including the *Chicago Herald-Examiner* and the *Detroit News,* supported the drive with exaggerated reports on the numbers of Mexicans who had not established legal residence. According to the 1924 Immigration Act, people who had entered the country prior to July 1, 1924, unless they committed criminal offenses, regardless of their mode of entry or declaration of intent to become citizens, were not subject to deportation. Upon demonstration of five years' continuous residence they were eligible for naturalization. This meant that the overwhelming majority of Mexicans in the Midwest and other parts of the United States were legal residents of the country. Yet they formed the majority of Mexicans who were the focus of the deportation campaign, which began in Texas in late 1928 and soon extended to the Midwest and other parts of the country.[5]

The repatriation campaign was also directed at aliens liable to become public charges, whose numbers increased as the Great Depression deepened, for "most Mexicans were discharged" from jobs in automobile plants, foundries, packinghouses, railroads, and other urban enterprises where they had often been employed for several years. In Rockdale, Illinois, a group of workers in a brick factory complained of being laid off "for the simple fact of being Mexican to give work to North Americans and Europeans." In the Stockyards district of Chicago, a local report observed that "unemployment among the Mexicans, as expected, is more felt than in any other group in the neighborhood." In Port Huron, Michigan, an estimated six to seven hundred Mexicans were employed in 1928, primarily in foundries, but only one hundred remained at the end of 1932, of whom only eighteen were still working an average of ten to fifteen hours per week at 30 cents per hour. In Detroit, by 1932, only 15 percent of Mexican adults were employed. As the economic crisis continued, even the largest employers in the region, including Indiana Steel in East Chicago, U.S. Steel in Gary, and Ford in Detroit, decided to require permanent residency, and later U.S. citizenship, as a prerequisite for employment. City and state governments also enacted ordinances requiring citizenship to continue working and discharged almost all their Mexican employees from jobs primarily in "shovel labor" and track maintenance.[6]

As unemployment soared, the "altruistic spirit" increased in Mexican communities, particularly on behalf of the unemployed and the ill. In Chicago, the Cruz Azul Mexicana sought volunteer doctors and nurses to attend to the sick, while the Sociedad Feminil Mexicana held voluntary collections. Women from the Josefa Ortiz de Domínguez society held dances and other functions, donating proceeds to help the sick in hospitals and others in need, while social and cultural events became fund-raisers, like the 1930 Cinco de Mayo celebration at Eagle Hall. Local newspapers joined the effort, and in December 1930 *El Nacional* of Chicago reported that there were many "children who suffer from lack of food and clothing. It is our duty to assist any family which finds itself in such straitened circumstances. We must contribute liberally to aid at least one poor Mexican family," and if not money, "let us get clothes from our friends." Meanwhile, Narciso González of Chicago's *México* cajoled readers, "let us not forget; all the Mexicans who today enjoy a partial security, that perhaps tomorrow or a day after they may be in their ranks."[7]

Such efforts were inadequate, and destitute Mexicans increasingly requested assistance from local governments, employers, and the Mexican consulate for food and clothing. In St. Paul, hungry families on relief borrowed food and coal from neighbors, although "they had to return the borrowed amount" when they received their monthly allotments from the Transient Bureau. In many cities they formed groups like the Confederación Pro-repatriación in Kansas City, seeking assistance for a return to the homeland. A group from Chicago wrote to President Pascual Ortiz Rubio: "These unhappy, ragged, dirty, suffering people, half dead from hunger and humiliated . . . have been scourged by bad luck and now are barely surviving in the most profound misery, despised by the people of the United States and their authorities." Mexican consular officials, through the Secretaría de Relaciones Exteriores (Foreign Relations Secretariat), agreed to assist in the repatriation of those who wanted to return, on condition that they had a means of support in Mexico. Consular authorities arranged with U.S. Customs to permit repatriates to take personal items across the border without paying duties, including automobiles and musical instruments, radios, pianos, phonographs, and other personal belongings. They also negotiated special discount fares with railroad lines for the trip to the border at Laredo, typically for $15 from midwestern cities, and with the Mexican National Railroad to the Mexican interior for a fare of one cent per mile. While some individuals were eager to return once the Cristero Rebellion subsided in 1929, consular officials were motivated primarily by responsibility to protect their compatriots from further mistreatment by local, state, and federal officials in the United States. As historian Moisés González Navarro observed, "the peak of the repatriation movement in 1931 coincided with an intense nationalist campaign in favor of *la raza,* our economy and our culture."[8]

Several northern employers, religious figures, social workers, and political groups were not swayed by arguments that Mexicans should return. Henry Ford used the seniority system to avoid firing healthy Mexican workers, and instead laid them off with the proviso to rehire them when economic conditions improved. Santa Fe railroad officials "helped shelter local Mexican enclaves" by claiming that they were U.S citizens from New Mexico. Robert McLean, superintendent of Mexican work for the Presbyterian Church, and active in northern *colonias,* was an outspoken critic of repatriation. He denounced Border Patrol officials for hypocritically allowing Mexicans to enter when employers claimed shortages of labor that "no white man will do." Later, during hard times, they beefed up their staff and ousted people who had contributed so much to the nation's wealth and included children who had never seen Mexico. Considering the state of the world economy, he asked rhetorically: "is anyone so simple as to believe in this period of world depression that Mexico is able to absorb an army of new laborers every month?" Among the political groups that spoke forcefully in opposition, the Communist Party was particularly vigorous, arguing that repatriation represented U.S. imperialist exploitation of Mexico's resources, economy, and people, justified on racist grounds that Mexicans were inferior.[9] The repatriation campaigns further confirmed that Mexicans were considered merely a reserve labor army and a colonized labor force that could be removed to their homelands when no longer needed by capitalists.

Formal repatriation campaigns in the Midwest took place in 1931 and 1932, after thousands of individuals had already departed, sometimes voluntarily and with the assistance of the Mexican government, or as a result of the federal immigration deportation campaign. Local circumstances occasionally shielded communities, including the barrio in Argentine, Kansas, according to Judith Fincher Laird, because of support from the Santa Fe Railroad and the Methodist Mexican Mission.[10] Furthermore, local conditions influenced repatriation campaigns in midwestern cities conducted by federal, state, and local officials, often operating in tandem, as evident in Gary, East Chicago, Detroit, Chicago, and St. Paul.

In Gary and East Chicago, located in Lake County, local officials dissatisfied with the earlier U.S. Department of Labor campaign "to deport all aliens who were subject to deportation," initiated local drives. Conditions were particularly difficult in Lake County, where a federal investigation found that relief funds were depleted because of "the straight-out theft of hundreds of thousands of dollars of county funds by corrupt officials and the failures of a number of public depositories" where the money had been stored. In Gary, industrialists including the presidents of U.S. Steel, Bethlehem Steel, the Gary Commercial Club, and the Gary Chamber of Commerce led the drive, with support from several private and public agencies. While publicized as an effort to induce Mexicans to depart voluntarily, it involved widespread coercion and actions of questionable legality, "to the disgust of the International Institute," which turned its earlier support into opposition. By the end of 1932, when the operation terminated, more than fifteen hundred Mexicans had been repatriated, excluding those forced to leave earlier.[11]

The local repatriation drive in East Chicago was the most thorough in the region and encountered the least overt opposition. Members of American Legion Post #266 initiated the effort in response to a recommendation from national headquarters urging local posts to plan an offensive and "proceed to the attack" on problems of unemployment and relief in their communities. East Chicago legionnaires served in prominent public and private positions of power, including the North Township Trustee and the Emergency Relief Association of the Community Chest, which were responsible for local relief. They also belonged to the East Chicago Chamber of Commerce and the East Chicago Manufacturers Association, which included major employers like Indiana Steel, the largest Mexican employer in the region during most of the 1920s. Members of Post #266 determined that the most effective way to meet the directive of the national office "would be a removal of the nationalists, especially the Mexicans . . . with a view of repatriating as many of them as possible."[12]

They justified their actions on the grounds that Mexicans were unassimilable, took jobs away from U.S. citizens, and drained relief and social services, thus denying work and assistance to more deserving people. They also portrayed Mexicans as lazy idlers. Russell F. Robinson, former commander of Post #266, chair of the Emergency Relief Administration, and local director of the repatriation effort, asserted that "these Mexican people will be content to sit idly by and let us feed and maintain them." Members of the East Chicago Chamber of Commerce expressed concern about a growing "housing problem" in the city, claiming that the recent influx of Mexicans and African Americans was "debasing property values." Yet they failed to secure funds from federal officials more concerned about further straining international relations.

Consequently they devised a plan to offer scrip to local capitalists to loan them money for the drive. The scrip could be used to pay for future taxes, meaning that the drive was funded by local rather than federal taxes. The East Chicago repatriation drive in the summer and fall of 1932 resulted in the departure of 505 men, 155 women, as well as 372 children under eighteen years, sent to the Mexican border on trains. Arturo Rosales and Daniel Simon noted that repatriates generally were the least rooted and mostly from the old core of the barrio, the "traditional first area of residence for new arrivals." Although the drive was publicized as repatriation, Indiana Harbor resident Sr. Vernon Fernández recalled, "we weren't asked voluntarily if we wanted to go," for when people lost their jobs and were taken off welfare, they were given a choice: "starve or go back to Mexico." Legionnaires proudly claimed to have met the mandate of the national office by reducing unemployment and lowering welfare and educational costs for the township and city, resulting from the departure of about 3,000 people from Indiana Harbor, half the *colonia* population at its peak in the late 1920s.[13]

In Michigan, many individuals departed voluntarily until 1931, when a Comité Pro-repatriación formed whose members requested assistance from the Mexican consulate. But federal immigration authorities were not satisfied, and after an investigation, with the assistance of welfare officials and police in several cities, they sought to uncover and "drive" out Mexicans "who entered the country illegally." Immigration authorities, with the support of local police, even intimidated individuals who had established legal residence and did not wish to leave. They deported only a small number formally, but the campaign had a positive effect, in the opinion of Detroit Immigration Director John L. Zubrick. He asserted that a tour of the barrio in Saginaw's First Ward "showed scores of empty houses that previously had been occupied before the investigation started." He added that "in reducing the city's population by this method, a real service is being extended to the people of the city, for all of these people have little to contribute to a community and frequently take much from it." Such an attitude showed little regard for the contributions in labor, purchases of goods, rent, and other services made by local Mexicanos over the years.[14]

Local repatriation efforts in Michigan began in October 1931, when representatives of the Detroit Department of Public Welfare contacted the Mexican consulate to encourage Mexicans arriving after 1923 and unable to support themselves to depart, assuming they had secure places in Mexico. In early 1932 Michigan Governor Wilbur M. Brucker and the state's welfare department took control, supported by several local government agencies. Michigan authorities offered to pay for train fares to the border for destitute individuals, while the Mexican government agreed to cover costs from the border to repatriates' homes in the Mexican interior. Unlike those in charge of the campaigns in northwest Indiana, Michigan industrial leaders maintained a low profile. The drive gained greater attention in 1932 when Mexican artist Diego Rivera arrived under contract to paint a mural at the Detroit Institute of Arts. He helped establish La Liga de Obreros y Campesinos, aimed at protecting the interests of local Mexicans and assisting those willing to return by establishing repatriate *colonias* in Mexico. Nevertheless, coercion intensified, and in August 1932, Detroit welfare officials set up tent cities, "to house evicted welfare families." The first tent colony in the city was not coincidental, located in Clark Park in the heart of the Mexican district. The Michigan National Guard provided tents, while the mayor's unemployment committee supplied cots and blankets, and as local resident Sra. Carmen Cortina recalled, "it was a sad sight to see." Opposition to repatriation in Detroit was more organized than in northwest Indiana, and the International Labor Defense of the Communist Party played a prominent role, condemning the actions as "gigantic wholesale illegal kidnappings." The Mexican consulate estimated that about four thousand Mexicans were repatriated from the state under formal auspices in 1932, by which time Detroit's Mexican population had declined to about three thousand, only a fifth of its size five years earlier.[15]

Chicago differed from East Chicago, Gary, and Detroit, as Louise Año Nuevo Kerr observes, because Mexicans "were not singled out for arbitrary repatriation" by local or state authorities. The lack of organized pressure did not reflect greater even-handedness than in the Southwest or a more diverse midwestern urban population, as demonstrated by the drives in neighboring Indiana and Michigan, which were also home to people from "every other kind of nationality." It is also questionable whether

Chicago's more diverse economy "helped offset organized repatriation pressures," and welfare officials encouraged Mexicans individually to depart and, as in neighboring locations, funded trips for many indigent people to the border. As elsewhere, Chicago-born Frank X. Paz observed that repatriation was "forced upon the Chicago Mexican through false promises by the local Mexican Consular offices, coercion on the part of relief authorities, and by industries where Mexicans had been employed in large numbers." In Chicago a Comité Organizador de Repatriación formed in 1931 to obtain assistance from the Mexican government, including special fares and certification that repatriates would not be abandoned at the end of the train ride from the Dearborn Street Station to the border at Laredo.[16]

As in many locations, Chicago Mexicans experienced a campaign of harassment by federal immigration officials in 1931 and 1932, often in contravention of the laws the officials were supposed to enforce. In the Stockyards district, immigration agents entered poolrooms and other places where Mexicans congregated in search of individuals without proper documentation, not infrequently forcing their way into private residences. In a celebrated case in August 1932, two immigration agents raided the "luxurious North Side apartment" of Sr. Ignacio Romero and his family without a warrant and "without determining whether or not Mr. Romero was legally in the country." After "upsetting the whole house," agents took him to immigration offices and questioned him for another thirty minutes until they were convinced of his claims that he was a naturalized citizen. Individuals with fewer resources and weaker legal standing than Sr. Romero could expect much greater abuse.[17]

In Chicago, more than in other midwestern cities, organized opposition to abusive agency efforts to remove Mexicans developed. An active Spanish-language press, Mexican organizations, the Immigrants Protective League (IPL), political groups including the Communist Party, and local settlement houses, many of which had Mexican officers and employees, led the way. IPL secretary Sra. H. Sahagún de la Mora asserted that many Mexicans did consider repatriation "to end the cruel stay" in the United States. Sra. Sahagún also warned them against making a hasty decision simply because they might "see in a return to the homeland a panacea for their ills and needs," suggesting instead that they determine "whether such a means of livelihood really does exist" in Mexico. Meanwhile, settlement house staff pointed to the raids as another reason why Mexicans should take out citizenship papers to protect themselves. Chicago's Mexican population fell from an estimated 20,000 in 1930 to 12,500 in 1934, a much lower proportionate decline than in Detroit and northwest Indiana. As in other midwestern locations, it recovered partially later in the decade, yet by 1940 there were about 25 percent fewer Mexicans in Chicago than in the late 1920s. While the activities to protect Mexicans against arbitrary deportations in Chicago did not prevent suffering and abuse, those efforts, rather than ethnic diversity, even-handed agencies, or impersonal economic forces, prevented an organized local campaign in 1932 and reduced the scale of repatriation from Chicago in comparison to that from neighboring cities.[18]

In St. Paul, the small *colonia* of the late 1920s and early 1930s did not attract as much attention as those in larger cities, and the volunteer Mexican consul lacked resources to offer assistance in repatriation. Nevertheless, a modest local drive took place in late 1932, when the Ramsey County Board of Public Welfare, which was concerned about rising costs, worked with federal authorities and the staff of the Neighborhood House to establish an office in search of indigent families who might be induced to depart. On November 10, 1932, they boarded eighty-six people from sixteen families on a train to the Mexican border. Although the drive was much smaller than in Gary, East Chicago, or Detroit, it nevertheless removed approximately 15 percent of the total Mexican population residing in the city. In the case of St. Paul, most individuals that welfare officials claimed had been "returned" to Mexico were children born in the United States who had never seen the country where their parents were born. While Neighborhood House staff permitted the Board of Public Welfare to establish a branch office in its building, like the staff of the International Institute in Gary, they soon lamented the decision. Neighborhood House Director Constance Currie regretted that "the ultimate effect" of permitting relief officers to operate was to disrupt its activities and relations with local residents. When it became obvious that coercion was involved, it withdrew its support.[19]

Throughout the Midwest, efforts by federal immigration agents and local officials to remove Mexicans were much more widespread than the written record indicates. Many local roundups did not receive attention, including one involving Sr. Francisco Guzmán. Born in Guanajuato, Sr. Guzmán and his young bride, Sra. Dolores Guzmán, who grew up in Ojinaga, crossed the border at Presidio, Texas, in 1922. They worked at different jobs in the state, especially the cotton fields, until 1929, when they signed a contract in Fort Worth for the sugar beet fields around Chaska, where they remained for several years. Around 1932, Sra. Guzmán recalled, "after we finished our work, the farmer that we worked for told us that they were rounding up all the Mexicans in Chaska to take them back to Mexico. He took us to Chaska to see if they would take us back." To ensure worker departures, the company would not hand over paychecks until they boarded the trucks that were to take them away. Sr. Guzmán instead went to the company offices to demand his pay, and to his surprise he received his check. As Sra. Guzmán observed, "we did not know why they gave it [the paycheck] to him and not the others. We did not know what was going on," but as a result the Guzmáns did not board the trucks that took the others to Mexico. They were not personally opposed to repatriation, Sr. Guzmán recalls: "we did not mind going back to Mexico, because that was our country," but they preferred to stay in Minnesota. After receiving their pay, the family traveled to St. Paul, where they settled permanently.[20]

More flexible local repatriation strategies would have enticed many more families to depart, including that of Juan Diego Rosario. Arriving in Detroit in 1927, he had worked earlier in the cotton fields of Texas, the railroads of the prairie states, the slaughterhouses of Kansas City, and the sugar beets of the Saginaw Valley. Rosario also worked in track labor for the Michigan Central Railroad and street paving for the Detroit Department of Public Works before finding employment in Ford's River Rouge foundry. After he lost his job and his infant child died, he "would gladly have returned to Mexico in 1933 if the Welfare Department had supplied him with gas for the truck." Instead he remained, struggling through the Great Depression in Michigan.[21] Poorly coordinated and often arbitrary agency actions had a disrupting and contradictory effect on repatriation, forcing many to leave against their will, often unaware of their rights, or allowing others to remain who wished to depart.

The highly publicized local repatriation drives in the Midwest ceased after the Democratic election victory in November 1932, because the Roosevelt administration did not scapegoat Mexicans systematically as had its predecessor. Discussions about repatriation continued sporadically on the local level, where social workers and charities devised schemes to pressure individuals and families to leave, despite an official policy of recommending repatriation only for specific individual cases when initiated by Mexican clients. In 1933 the Bureau of Immigration asked the national board of the International Institute to gather information on the results of repatriation, which social workers in cities including Gary considered justification for their efforts to continue pressuring Mexicans to leave by refusing relief. In St. Paul, social workers continued to discuss how to remove Mexicans, and a drive was reported in 1934. Again in 1937, governor Elmer Benson announced a plan to deport fifteen hundred Mexicans from Minnesota, but state officials quickly aborted the project. Local relief workers often took matters into their own hands, including one Miss Jones of St. Paul, who pressured many people to leave because, as a social worker claimed, she "dislikes or doesn't understand Mexicans." Their persistence was evident in a 1933 case of a United Charities relief worker who claimed she was not forcing Mexicans to leave; "she was just making arrangements for repatriation as they themselves had requested it. She had to pin them down on a date because Mexicans are very changeable. It was arranged that they be ready today but not that they were compelled to go." The case involved a man who was working part-time at Swift and stated emphatically that he did not want to depart. Although eligible for relief, a social worker reported, "he hesitates asking for it because he will be urged to return to Mexico or groceries [will be] denied." In a 1939 case, a St. Paul resident complained to the Ramsey County Welfare Board that he had been trying to take out citizenship papers since 1934. He would have succeeded, he continued, "but every time you have stopped me by telling me to take my family to Mexico . . . because I have ten children born here and because there is no work and we are on relief. . . . Do you think it is best for me to take them to Mexico, where they have no one waiting for them or to stay here and become a citizen?"[22]

Throughout the Great Depression, Mexican consular officials were sympathetic to repatriation. In 1929, President-Elect Pascual Ortiz Rubio visited Chicago, where a speech at the Hotel Blackstone "drew enthusiastic applause" for his statement that one object of his government "would be to help establish conditions in Mexico that emigrants might return to their country without economic sacrifice." During the presidency of Lázaro Cárdenas (1934–1940), the Mexican government was even more eager to encourage its citizens to return and sent agents to recruit individuals for proposed new colonization schemes, but it attracted few Mexicans from the Midwest. The last large-scale exodus of Mexicans from the region took place during the fall and winter of 1932–1933, and relatively few left afterward due to "less confidence in finding a good adjustment in Mexico and to fewer ties with the home country." Furthermore, under Franklin D. Roosevelt the Democratic administration altered policies of its Republican predecessors. It sought to improve the public image of the United States in Latin America, particularly though the Good Neighbor Policy. As historian Daniel T. Simon noted, Democratic leaders were "concerned with the diplomatic repercussions that might follow government financing of repatriation." Despite the continued local climate of fear and uncertainty, midwestern Mexicans were more entrenched and determined to resist pressures to repatriate after 1932.[23]

Paul Taylor observed that Mexicans in the Midwest repatriated at rates far above those of the Southwest. Mexicans in Michigan, Illinois, and Indiana comprised only 3.6 percent of the total Mexican-born population of the United States, but 10.5 percent of repatriates. The higher rates can be attributed to several factors, including greater competition with non-Mexicans for higher-paying industrial jobs, greater unemployment, the instability of northern Mexican communities, a weaker communal "safety net," and more determined pressures by local and state authorities to reduce higher welfare costs. In the first half of 1931, monthly per capita welfare was calculated at $6.59 for Detroit; $3.40 for Los Angeles; $2.41 for Chicago; $1.69 for Minneapolis, but only $.15 for San Antonio. The insistent efforts of local repatriation activities in the Midwest suggest both an economic incentive and a greater fear of Mexicans within dominant local culture than in the Southwest.[24]

As in other parts of the country, the impact of repatriation in the Midwest was not even, nor was it uniformly devastating. Between the onset of the Great Depression and 1934, Chicago's Mexican population fell by an estimated 40 percent, with attendant declines in East Chicago of 50 percent, Gary of 60 percent, and Detroit of at least 70 percent. By contrast, the St. Paul *colonia* grew continuously, even in 1932, as families of *betabeleros* were leaving rural residences in the Minnesota and Red River Valleys to settle on the Lower West Side. As one report provided, Mexicans were not welcomed, but there was no way to prevent them from coming to St. Paul, for "they are not deportable, repatriation has been tried and is rarely successful."[25] Furthermore, the economic downturn severely reduced their employment options and they became even more dependent on agriculture or non-wage labor for sustenance.

### The Internal *Colonia*

By the end of the 1930s Mexicans were the largest group on St. Paul's Lower West Side, which had changed markedly from the previous decade. Because there was less demand for their labor, observers acknowledged that in St. Paul as elsewhere, Mexicans faced systematic "discriminations in employment." As they lost jobs on the railroads, in packing plants, and at factories, they traveled to Chicago and other cities as well as to the Minnesota beet fields. Finding work was particularly difficult, and employers increasingly posted signs reading, "only white labor employed."

The sugar beet industry did not indulge in such exclusion because Mexicans would accept what others would not; as a St. Paul report on Mexicanos concluded, "theirs is a seasonal occupation in which there are many abuses, especially in the hire system, and life is extremely hard." [26]

Working conditions in the fields deteriorated sharply as the beet industry fell into turmoil, despite reduced labor costs and temporarily not having to recruit from Texas and other distant locations. On the verge of dissolution in 1932, the American Beet Sugar Company reorganized as American Crystal and instituted new relations with workers. It no longer guaranteed wages for specific tasks, nor provided transportation or guaranteed credit. It eliminated its agents and no longer sold winter staples to workers at wholesale. Corporation strategy aimed at making it appear that farmers were henceforth responsible for hiring and employment decisions while allowing it to evade employer responsibility. Rather than hire workers directly through its own agents, the company hired a labor contractor who arranged with owners of local businesses to recruit workers from the Lower West Side. Recruiters came to the barrio each spring, contacted workers, and if necessary arranged for transportation to the fields. Once workers reached their destination, the recruiters presented company-written contracts signed by workers and farmers. The corporation also removed itself as arbiter in disputes between farmers and workers, permitting more abuses in housing arrangements, working conditions, wages, and field measurements. As one report concluded, the company was ultimately able to reduce wages and avoid earlier responsibilities because, in comparison with the 1920s, "labor is plentiful." [27]

In the early 1930s, prior to the federal relief programs of the Roosevelt administration, many Europeans and European Americans displaced Mexicans from the fields. New Deal welfare and work relief programs offered modest but stable incomes and greater annual earnings than the sugar beet fields. Local administrators commonly denied relief to Mexicans except in emergency and temporary situations, or with the stipulation that they return to the fields in the spring. Additional federal laws enhancing workers' rights in urban industries explicitly excluded agricultural workers from the right to organize for collective bargaining, social security and unemployment compensation, and minimum wages. The major relief program, the Works Progress Administration (WPA), increasingly took over relief responsibilities, beginning in 1935, from local relief agencies. As amended by the Relief Appropriation Act of 1937, the WPA excluded aliens who had not taken out citizenship papers, and its administrators dismissed thousands of Mexicans. Restrictions against Mexicans increasingly appeared in public projects, including those of the Civilian Conservation Corps (CCC), even for individuals with long-standing residence. State and local laws made it increasingly difficult for Mexicans to establish residency required for welfare. In Illinois, until 1932, any person with a year's residency in the state was eligible for local relief, but by 1939 the state denied relief to any person who had not resided in the same location for three consecutive years. The legislation and policies excluding Mexicans from public welfare and work programs and pushing them into the beet fields increased disparities and sharpened race and class distinctions between Mexicans and European Americans.[28]

Mexican children were increasingly pressured to seek work so their families could survive. Frank Rodríguez, born when his family was employed in the Wyoming sugar beet fields in 1920, moved to St. Paul with his parents as a child and spent several additional years in the fields of Minnesota. Unlike his father, who was a Mexican citizen, he was able to secure employment in 1936 with the CCC in Ely, Minnesota, asserting that he was sixteen, the minimum age for acceptance, although he was only fifteen. He sent his parents twenty-five dollars of his thirty-dollar monthly paycheck, using the rest for personal needs and periodic family visits.[29]

Lacking alternatives, Mexicanos were increasingly compelled to return to the fields. Sra. Juanita Morán, born in Aguascalientes in 1921, entered Texas with her family when she was five years old and moved to Kansas the following year. Her uncle had already found employment at the Cudahy packinghouse and convinced her parents to come to Minnesota in 1928. Her father quickly found employment at Cudahy, working continuously until early 1931, when he was laid off. To survive they became beet workers, departing for the fields around Bird Island in the spring before the school term ended, returning late in the autumn. Because she missed so much school, Sra. Morán recalled, "I had to repeat the same grade."[30]

Finding winter work was rare, as Father James Ward of Our Lady of Guadalupe parish explained, and "there was much misery, much want and much poverty." Manuel Contreras, who moved to St. Paul in 1933 after several years in the sugar beet area around Chaska, was similarly impressed by the poverty of *colonia* residents: "There was much misery among them. . . .[w]hen we came to St. Paul, we rented some old homes without windows for $5 a month." He recalled that "nobody had any money only the rich," adding, "I came to look for work. There was no work, but people came in the hopes of finding work." A 1936 Neighborhood House report concluded that "the Mexican situation is a serious problem."[31]

Wage data confirm the importance of the sugar beet industry among Mexican families in St. Paul. With an average of 5.62 members in 1936, families earned $315.68 for a season in the fields, and $48.41 in additional winter employment. Most men, women, and children above age eight worked in the beet fields for about half of the year but could find little gainful employment during the time they resided in the city.[32]

To survive, many people turned to the informal economy. Sr. Marcelino Rivera moved from Mexico City to Texas in 1927, where he grubbed roots from trees or worked in the cotton fields. Later he worked in Louisiana and Michigan before coming to the beet fields around Lafayette, Minnesota, in 1931. When the family moved to St. Paul that winter, he could not find a job, according to his wife, Sra. Irene Rivera, "so he would cut trees and sell wood" to heat houses. A number of people picked up "gleanings from [the] junk yard," where they also found wood or coal for heating and other scraps. One man told his welfare worker that "he thought he could pick up enough coal in the railroad yards" to heat the family dwelling. A welfare report noted that a man who worked with his family in the fields in the summer "goes to the dumps daily . . . sorts out the different metals and sells them." He earned about 15 cents per day, and "if he finds food there he washes it and brings it home and eats it." The case worker wrote, "we expect they are just one of these families that come in and out of the city each year as their work is completed in the beet fields."[33]

Mexicanos also relied increasingly on domestic production for their own sustenance, Sra. Esiquia Monita recalled. When her family returned to St. Paul from the beet fields, "we barely had enough to buy a sack of flour, beans, and lard, and all of those things of the winter time." Like other families engaged in beet work, they were allotted garden plots to engage in home-based production of vegetables, which they ate fresh on the farm, or canned on return to St. Paul. One season she and her husband together canned two hundred fifty quarts of tomatoes and four bushels of green peppers and garlic, "and none of it ever went bad." Sra. Monita directed the family-based division of labor: "I would toast the peppers, then we would peel them. My husband was good at peeling the peppers, and I would boil them. Then I would have the jars ready for canning. . . . I liked the green peppers because they were really hot." To make salsa, she ground the peppers with a *molcajete* (grinder) and then added tomatoes and garlic. Their labor thus provided a major portion of subsistence throughout the winter. The case further suggests that tasks performed by women and men were not always clearly separated, nor did they conform to middle-class ideal types in which women worked inside the home and men worked outside, particularly during the hard times of the Great Depression.[34]

During the Great Depression, the incipient Mexican middle class in the Midwest was badly weakened. In Chicago, small proprietors were compelled to seek wage employment to sustain themselves and their businesses. Eduardo Hidalgo, owner of El Esfuerzo Mexicano grocery store on Burley Avenue had to work at Illinois Steel because the business alone could not sustain the family. Theodoro Lomelí and Pedro Gutiérrez, who operated a billiard room and adjoining restaurant on Buffalo Avenue, also worked at the steel mill, while Mauro Esquivel, who owned El Rancho Grande restaurant nearby, had to work while his wife attended to most of the details of the business. Sr. Equihua, who started publishing the newspaper *La Lucha* in 1934 in South Chicago, could only produce two editions per month because he had to work at another job to cover his expenditures for the paper. Even in St. Paul, where the rapidly growing barrio offered potential new opportunities for businesses and professionals to serve its needs, a 1936 survey of the Lower West Side reported that it did not have a single establishment owned or operated by Mexicans. The handful of enterprises formed in the 1920s had disappeared, indicating that the Mexican ascent into the middle class had been reversed.[35]

As conditions deteriorated and as dominant sentiments against Mexican residence in rural communities intensified, more Mexicans opted for the city. Sra. Guadalupe Cruz, who first came to Minnesota to work in the beet fields around Chaska in 1929, explained that at the onset of the Great Depression, "we could have gone back to Mexico, but if we stayed they offered to help us. They would give us a home to live in and we got a raise of five dollars per family member. We lived in Chaska for three years." She recalled that "there were some people that did not have anything to eat." Meanwhile, "our *compadres* were already here and kept telling us to move to St. Paul because the schools were much closer here. In Chaska we lived in the company hotel and the children had to walk into town to go to school in the cold and snow. We came to St. Paul and we never went back."[36]

In the fall, workers returned to the Lower West Side, as Alice Sickels of the International Institute observed in 1934: "truckloads of Mexican people, just off the beet fields, most of them children, are piling into the old houses" that otherwise would have remained vacant. They "rapidly filled all that were left of the worst houses in the city, for no one else would take Mexicans." Yet even in the worst neighborhood in the Twin Cities,

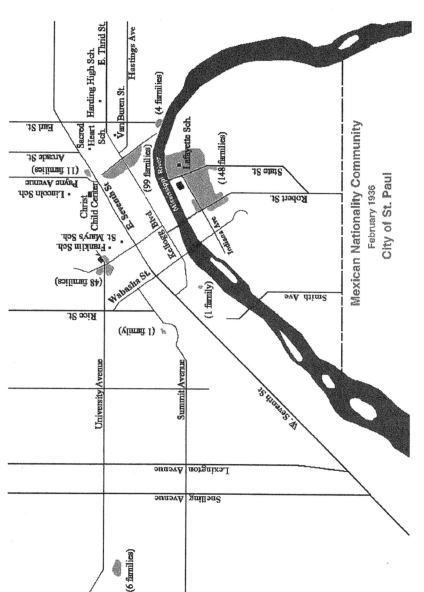

MAP 5. MEXICAN FAMILIES IN ST. PAUL, 1936 (ADAPTED FROM INTERNATIONAL INSTITUTE, "THE MEXICAN NATIONALITY COMMUNITY IN ST. PAUL").

*St. Paul Pioneer Press* reporter Eugene Cook observed, Mexican renters were forced to accept discriminatory clauses, including a requirement that "landlords take rent in advance for the winter." Discrimination resulted in rural depopulation and concentration of the Minnesota Mexican population into the St. Paul barrio. This informal apartheid peaked in the 1930s as Minnesota Mexicans became a seasonal urban population, according to one member of the Comité de Reconstrucción, for "most of us are not here in the summer."[37]

Claims that Mexicans moved to St. Paul because they sought relief were inaccurate, an International Institute report noted. Rather, rural welfare authorities and law enforcement officials "refuse to let them remain for the winter," through force and threats of deportation to ensure their departure. It added that "Mexicans have come in increasing numbers because living costs are lower in the cities than in rural communities, because there are better schools and health services." Meanwhile, welfare in St. Paul commonly was granted as emergency, transient, or work relief, as in 1932 when a group of Mexican men was employed for three weeks by city welfare officials to construct a playground, in exchange for payment in meat and groceries. Welfare officials systematically cut Mexicans off in the spring when sugar beet company recruiters came to the barrio. A contemporary account observed, "the relief agencies have carefully scrutinized the residence of every St. Paul Mexican family who is on relief. Every person was sent away for whom legal residence could be found in any place willing to accept them except for a few families who for special reasons . . . were allowed to remain until the spring work opened [and] have been warned by the relief agencies not to return."[38]

Welfare for people of all backgrounds, including Mexicans, rose sharply from the previous decade. Between 1927 and 1930, only thirty-five Mexican families in St. Paul had applied for relief, but with the outbreak of the Great Depression, when Mexican labor "was early displaced by white labor," demands for assistance increased, including transient relief, county relief, W.P.A. employment, and basic health services. In Chicago, the proportion of Mexican families on relief declined from about 60 percent in 1933 to 32 percent by 1935. At the latter date an estimated 47 percent of African American, 22 percent of naturalized immigrant, 39.8 percent of European alien, and 14 percent of European American families received assistance. Relief agencies and social workers acknowledged that Mexicans received lower relief payments, claiming they could survive on less than U.S. citizens due to cultural factors. A St. Paul International Institute report asserted that "their lower standard of living made it possible for them to eke out an existence on seasonal earnings which would not have been sufficient for other families."[39]

Mexicans frequently struggled with welfare authorities, despite the risk, and many like Sra. Marcelina Urvina were ultimately denied relief. Born in Dallas in 1918, her family tried to settle in St. Paul in 1931 after beet topping ended around St. Clair, Minnesota, near Mankato: "we did not want to work or live on the farm, so, we came to the Twin Cities." They moved into a red brick apartment building on Fifth Street, near the old Holsum Bread Company, with another fifteen to twenty Mexican families. They were rejected for welfare, Sra. Urvina explained, because the authorities "did not want us here because they said we were not residents, and that they would not help us with anything; that we would have to go back where we came from." The family was frustrated:

we did not know what to do. We went to the relief office because we did not have anything, and we needed help. They did not want to help us. They came at night and put all of our things into a truck and took us back [to Mankato] and left us there. And then we came back. . . . My mother was angry and she said that we would be going back because we were born here [in the United States]. . . . My mother said that they had no right [to force us to leave St. Paul]. When she wanted to do something, she did it. She was not afraid. She did not speak English, but she could still make herself understood. We came to St. Paul at night and she insisted that we stay here so her children could go to school to learn to read and write. She did not want them to be like her.

Her mother was determined, Sra. Urvina explained, and "insisted that we come back, but this time she would not ask them to help us, and instead she went to work herself." Authorities also made welfare contingent on families dispossessing themselves of material goods, including washing machines, musical instruments, and even automobiles they used for work. A Lower West Side mother who worked with her son on a farm near Hopkins all summer returned home broke, but welfare authorities refused aid unless they sold the family car, which they needed to find employment in the city. As a result of such demands, many families refused welfare.[40]

Desire for greater stability convinced many, including Sra. Esther Avaloz and her family, to settle in St. Paul in 1935, after spending several years in the beet fields around Chaska. They did not expect conditions to be easier, yet they preferred the city, where although "we were poor . . . The difference was that we did not have to move around from town to town working like a tramp. Here I stayed in one place . . . [although life in the city was also hard] I had suffered a lot before." Sr. Luis Medina had a similar motivation for moving to the West Side. Born in 1907 in León, Guanajuato, he crossed the border with his family at Laredo in 1916 and for the next eight years worked in Texas, primarily in the cotton fields, before moving to Kansas City. In 1929 the family was recruited to Owatonna, in Southern Minnesota, to work in the sugar beets, and at the end of the season they moved to St. Paul to reside permanently. Sr. Medina, who soon married, recalled that "every year we would go back to the sugar beet fields, she and I. She is a good worker, a wonderful worker. Boy, she'd put rings around me any day. So it was every year back to the fields until 1935," when he got a job at the Twin City Railway. There he worked the year round, "so I didn't have to take the family out anymore. That was a heck of a job, to bring up children, when you go to the sugar beet fields. Terrible, I don't advise anybody to do it." Despite the lack of immediate opportunities, the hope of eventual employment in the city often was sufficient motivation. As Father Henry Dicks observed in 1940, "None of them expected to get rich. They hoped merely to make a living."[41]

Employment conditions for Mexicans in St. Paul deteriorated sharply from the previous decade. A 1936 survey of 326 employable Mexican men in St. Paul found that 34 percent had been unable to find any private work during the year. Of those employed, 70 percent had been beet workers during the summer of 1935, of whom only 7 percent had any private employment in the winter. The WPA offered temporary work relief to 18 percent of the group. Altogether, fewer than 20 percent had year-round employment, of whom 52 percent worked in meatpacking and 27 percent on the railroads. Of 215 women surveyed who were at least 21 years old, only four were reported working outside the home, two part-time in meatpacking, one translating for the WPA, and one in a WPA sewing unit. The vast majority of women had worked the previous summer in the beet fields alongside family members, and the survey also failed to account for many who worked in part-time or temporary jobs, particularly in domestic work. Many cared for families of widowed or divorced Mexican men, in settings where Mexican women were ill and hospitalized, or for middle-class European American families. Several women social workers considered themselves to be performing favors for the Mexican women they hired to clean their houses, scrub their floors, and care for their children. As in other cities throughout the country, Mexicanas in St. Paul were also engaged as seamstresses and embroiderers to augment family incomes during the Great Depression, often directed there by National

Youth Administration (NYA) and WPA projects. Furthermore, the flurry of legislation limiting the employment of children in urban industry had little impact on Mexicans, a report observed, for "child labor has been the accepted practice in the beet fields of Minnesota in spite of our child labor and compulsory school laws." [42]

As working conditions declined and housing deteriorated, a Neighborhood House report observed that "during the depression housing conditions in our district have fallen to an almost unbearable level." Mary Bishop, of the Guild of Catholic Women, lamented that "in most cases where they live can scarcely be called homes. The housing of Mexicans in our Northern states is a vexing problem, due largely to an unsympathetic attitude toward them." Social workers referred to the barrio as a "sordid patch of St. Paul" whose houses were typically "dark, stuffy hovels where ventilation is a matter to be balanced against a meager coal and wood budget." A University of Minnesota survey confirmed that the Lower West Side of St. Paul was the largest slum in the Twin Cities. [43]

Despite limited means, residents used available resources to improve their modest dwellings, including stringing curtains to create separate rooms and allow privacy; making tables, chairs, and beds from scrap wood; and hauling stoves from abandoned buildings and the nearby scrap yard to provide heat and cooking. A St. Paul report noted, "families seem to have no household furnishings except old quilts, a few cooking dishes, and occasionally a stove." It noted that one tiny four-room house had twenty-six inhabitants who shared a single cook stove and several battered dishes. Like many houses, it lacked running water or electricity, residents had to walk half a block to haul water, and the only light at night came from the open front and top holes of the cooking stove. For chairs, tables, and fuel, men used orange crates they obtained from the city market and local garbage dumps. Despite the meager furnishings, the house had been scrubbed clean. According to the St. Paul International Institute, Mexicans "living on the West Side appear to be relatively better off than those elsewhere in the city, perhaps because they have been here longer." [44]

Investigators uniformly alluded to health and safety concerns in midwestern barrios and rated housing for Mexicans as the worst of all groups. Sickels complained that the City of St. Paul "has had a blind spot about slum clearance. Mexicans still live in the worst housing in the city. They have had less opportunity than other nationalities." Another report observed that Mexicans were "living in hovels condemned years ago as unfit for human habitation and growing steadily worse," adding that "practically none have baths or inside toilets." One study reported that about

25 percent of their dwellings lacked running water, sewer connections, electricity, or gas, and almost 60 percent of units should have been torn down or were borderline cases. A 1937 survey by the state relief agency reported that 38 percent of the dwellings of St. Paul Mexicans were "unsuitable for human housing." Another report the previous year calculated that only 4 percent of housing units were in good condition, while 37 percent were fair, 45 percent poor, and 13 percent should have been condemned. In an effort to eliminate the worst dwellings, in 1940 the St. Paul fire, health, and building departments jointly conducted another inspection of Mexican housing. They stopped after three weeks because they had condemned so many buildings that they feared a housing shortage would result if they completed their task.[45]

Poor accommodations were exacerbated by rampant housing discrimination throughout the region, as Mexicans were systematically excluded from most neighborhoods or charged higher rents than others in the same units. Mary Faith Adams reported that in Chicago "it is taken for granted among the landlords of the district that rents for Negroes and Mexicans should be higher than for other tenants," while in South Chicago Mexicans were not permitted to rent west of Commercial Avenue. In St. Paul, a social worker for the International Institute, in response to a request from a family responding to a "For Rent" sign, phoned the Morris Real Estate Company "to consider leasing" to Mexicans, but was informed it had just been rented. An agent for Clapp and Thompson "said he would not rent to any other Mexicans families," asserting they were "irresponsible, not clean, and having too many children," and "was quite final in his attitude." One landlord agreed to rent to a Mexican family as a result of pressure from welfare authorities in St. Paul but complained that "our [European American] tenant of many years standing strenuously objected to sheltering colored folks adjacent to his business." In 1936 monthly rent on the Lower West Side, where Mexicans resided, averaged $2.90 per room, compared with $4 on the West Side Bluffs for rooms that were much larger, in better condition, and offered electricity and running water not available in the Mexican neighborhood. Social workers concluded that landlords were able to profit more from Mexicans because of "the scarcity of housing facilities" available to them.[46]

While housing quality deteriorated throughout the region during the Great Depression, trends in segregation were inconsistent. In Chicago, Edith Abbott reported, "the Mexicans are not the predominant nationality in any entire district," and despite tensions they had opportunities to move to adjacent neighborhoods. In Gary, Mexicans were moving out of company housing into the unplanned south side of town, but still congregated in the ethnically diverse "but hardly idyllic industrial slum." In Detroit, Father Peter Feixa in a talk before the Damas Católicas in 1939 observed: "for the Mexican to progress, he must not cling to a particular section of the city. I am glad that you Mexicans of Detroit are rapidly moving into all districts." [47] While Mexicans were spreading into certain industrial districts in Gary and Detroit, they were increasingly segregated in St. Paul.

Poor housing and poverty had particularly telling effects on children, and one St. Paul report found that they wore "clothes that were two short shreds from the ragman." Lacking sheets for beds, they often used old gunny sacks, "which scratch and itch and are very uncomfortable." One report noted that "the children do not get adequate rest and food," while another concluded that "the food problem is one of the most complex, food values being hard for them to grasp or act upon, with only a few cents a day to spend, or sometimes nothing." Malnutrition was reported as "endemic" among urban midwestern Mexicano children, while avoidable deaths due to starvation and illness were widespread. In Chicago in 1931 Cipriano Hernández wrote, "I have found homes where for lack of food or clothing, crying little children have fainted in the lap of anguish and suffering." [48]

Tuberculosis was the most feared disease, as it struck Mexicanos at particularly high rates. In Kansas City, Kansas, death rates for Mexicans in the period 1920–1939 were fifteen times higher than those for European Americans, while in St. Paul, Father Dicks estimated that the white plague was responsible for between 65 percent and 75 percent of deaths in the St. Paul barrio. A 1940 campaign to eliminate the disease found that 35 percent of *colonia* residents had been exposed to tuberculosis germs. It had become a public health concern, and laws were written requiring that individuals be treated at public expense, averaging about $1,000 per year per person. In St. Paul authorities established treatment facilities at Ancker Hospital. Although the treatment helped many people regain their health, some returned to the same settings where they had contracted the disease and were reinfected. It also lingered because some people left for the beet fields before the Health Department could administer x-ray examinations, and it remained an affliction into the 1940s. [49]

Despite the problems of unemployment, housing, and health, midwestern barrios were changing demographically, characterized by increasing stability. In a 1935 St. Paul study comparing adults and children, 87 percent of adult males and 74 percent of adult females were born in

Mexico, while 89 percent of their children were born in the United States. Practically all adults had lived in the United States continuously for at least five years, the minimum for legal residency and eligibility to apply for citizenship. Eighteen percent of adults had resided in the country between six and twelve years, another 60 percent between thirteen and twenty-four years; and 22 percent for more than twenty-five years.[50]

There were other indications of stability, including the presence in most households of nuclear families, with two parents and several children present, in contrast with a decade earlier when unmarried adult males predominated. In St. Paul, Mexican households reported an average of 4.7 persons and 3.2 children per household, while only 15 percent were composed of single men. The adult sex ratio of 53 men per 47 women contrasted with a ratio of almost 2:1 in St. Paul a decade earlier. In East Chicago, there were 76 men to 24 women in 1930, and the ratio declined to 58 men per 42 women in 1940. The average age of barrio populations also fell from the 1920s. In the St. Paul group, 62 percent were under age twenty-one, and only 4 percent more than fifty years old.[51] The rapid changes could be attributed partly to repatriation, which disproportionately removed single men; the migration of families employed in agriculture from rural sections to the city; and the birth of many children.

In contrast to the 1920s, the 1930s saw the Mexican population of Minnesota become more concentrated residentially in the West Side barrio. A "very careful survey" of March 1930 reported 495 Mexicano residents, roughly 8 percent of the total population of the neighborhood. It represented about 80 percent of the city's Mexican population of 628, based on the 1930 federal census, and about 25 percent of the state total of 3,525. The barrio population reached 600 by 1932 and, despite repatriation in the fall, increased to about 850 in early 1933. By 1936 it grew to about 1,100 of a total of 1,500 in the city. The Mexican population of St. Paul reached 1,560 by 1938 and more than 2,000 by 1940, thus more than trebling in a decade.[52]

A few small concentrations of Mexicans appeared elsewhere in the Twin Cities, including St. Paul north of the Seventh Street bridge, where residents occupied squatters' huts along Phalen Creek in the neighborhood once known as "Swede Hollow," and along Mississippi and Jackson Streets. A larger group was beginning to settle on the East Side, mostly in the Hoffman Avenue district, under the Third and Sixth Street bridges in dilapidated houses, and on the hillside below Mounds Boulevard. As the East Side Mexican population increased, a rivalry developed between its youth and those of the West Side, and concerned parents of the Comité de Reconstrucción urged in 1940 "not to maintain a rivalry between the Eastside and Westside but be united as Mexicanos." The only other significant clustering in the state was Minneapolis, where about 450 Mexicans resided in 1936. Elsewhere in Minnesota, the Mexican population had declined sharply, as it had in much of the Midwest, reaching its nadir in 1932. Mexicanos soon began to return to the urban and rural settings they had occupied in the 1920s, and later in the decade a new wave of migration from Texas added new complexity to the Mexican Midwest.[53]

The Tejano migration followed an earlier plan adopted by sugar beet companies in the nadir of the Great Depression to reduce the size of plots and offer work to more families, but with less employment and lower earnings for each. The corporate decision stimulated a surge of labor organizing among sugar beet workers in the Midwest and on the Great Plains. In 1937 and 1938 AFL and CIO organizers conducted drives among beet workers of the Twin Cities, with the former concentrating on St. Paul, the latter on Minneapolis. A hostile local report asserted that the drive was "largely sponsored by local leaders not of the Mexican group who aimed to organize agricultural workers," yet several Mexican organizers participated. The larger St. Paul drive quickly garnered the support of a majority of local *betabeleros*, primarily from the West Side, and the Minnesota State Federation of Labor chartered a local union. As part of the effort, the federation also sponsored investigations of working and housing conditions, wages, and child labor in the fields of the state and convinced superintendents of American Crystal to meet with workers and listen to their demands. Organized workers and their leaders faced widespread opposition, particularly in the corporate world, and the press it controlled "provoked a considerable public opinion against the organized workers."[54]

The urban farmworkers faced an even greater problem when American Crystal decided that rather than negotiating with the union, it would initiate a new round of recruitment in South Texas. As one unfriendly observer asserted, "sugar beet employers have been antagonized by the labor organizers among the resident Mexican groups and were therefore hiring families who had newly arrived from the South."[55] Thus corporate decisions early in the decade that encouraged beetworkers to concentrate in the St. Paul barrio made it easier for workers to organize than when they resided on widely scattered farms or in company housing under the watchful eye of growers and company agents. As the corporations squeezed workers to the point of rebellion and workers organized, the companies turned to an unorganized labor pool from South Texas. The farmworkers in St. Paul were as vulnerable as their rural counterparts who attempted to organize elsewhere during the Great Depression. Furthermore, the recent successes of corporations to thwart legislative reforms aimed at providing collective bargaining rights to agricultural workers made it easier for them to thwart organizing drives throughout beet country and to displace the Mexican immigrant workers who had dominated field work since the early 1920s.

Consequently, by 1939 an estimated five thousand Tejanos (Mexicans from Texas) were migrating annually to Minnesota's sugar beet fields. The average adult earned only about $185 for the five-month season, although one observer claimed, with unfounded optimism, that "ambitious ones find work at nearby farms during their own slack weeks."[56] The corporate decision to hire Tejanos further reduced costs and built up its reserve labor force, altered the relationship between agricultural employers and workers, and created a new division within the Mexican working class. The new arrivals from Texas soon joined their predecessors on St. Paul's West Side at season's end, adding another layer of complexity to the growing community.

## Agents of Americanization

In the Southwest, the Great Depression has been portrayed as a time of transition from an earlier Mexican immigrant consciousness to a Mexican American identity. The change was induced in large part by repatriation, as individuals with the closest ties to Mexico returned; a weakened Mexican consulate; and the increasing presence of children born and reared in the United States. In her study of Mexican Chicago, Louise Año Nuevo Kerr found that a similar shift had begun in the Midwest but was reversed in the 1940s with renewed migration from Mexico, coupled with rising prejudice and discrimination among European Americans. By the 1950s, she suggests, Mexican assimilation in Chicago had been aborted, demonstrating that it was not a simple linear process.[57]

The influence of institutional Americanization programs on Mexican identity appears problematic. Private and public efforts commonly turned to Mexicans in the 1910s and ceased with the onset of the Great Depression, only to intensify in the later 1930s and 1940s. Americanization programs in the Southwest and the Midwest were uniform in neither strategy nor desired outcome. Observers who suggest that they focused primarily on Mexican women err, for the most pervasive institution of Americanization, the public school system, directed its efforts at children. Americanization also took place on an organizational level within the working class. One reason for the great success of industrial unions in several large midwestern cities during the Great Depression was their ability to attract Mexicans by emphasizing common interests as workers and American neighbors. Yet many authors, including Richard Rodriguez, in *Hunger of Memory,* portray Americanization as an individual quest for middle-class status.[58] This section examines complexities and changing strategies of institutional Mexican Americanization through its agents in St. Paul, including the public schools, the Neighborhood House, the International Institute, and the Catholic Church.

The public school system had a long history of imposing the U.S. American way of life on the children of immigrants. A 1936 International Institute study acknowledged that Mexicans were less influenced than European children, for their school attendance was irregular and "only a very few go to High School." The childhood experience of Leonard López, arriving in Minnesota with his family from Kansas in 1933 to work in the beet fields around Lake Lillian, suggests how work impeded school achievement among Mexican children. He recalled that "in the winter we would come to St. Paul. . . . I'd go to school from November to April. In April we would go back to the farm and the next year we would probably go to Bird Island. Every year we would be at a different place, wherever we worked as migrants." Even when they settled in the city, children frequently missed classes, and St. Paul officials lamented that they received "very little school training." Furthermore, school officials acknowledged responsibility, as "school attendance of Mexican children is not strictly enforced."[59]

School officials were caught in a quandary between their obligation to follow the letter of the law and pressures from employers and European American parents to disallow public schooling for Mexicans. After a St. Paul investigation intent on resolving conflicting pressures, administrators decided that Mexican children should be "placed in a special ungraded school." They justified their decision by claims that the erratic attendance of Mexican children disrupted the schooling of European Americans, and in particular, "it is difficult to keep the older children in school," as they were self-conscious about being placed with much younger classmates. Officials asserted that the ungraded school "may be the best that can be done under the circumstances but it segregates the Mexicans." The plan did not address other factors they acknowledged as keeping Mexican children away, including the failure to enforce mandatory attendance laws, the lack of shoes and clothing, and failure to provide books. Although the schools were not responsible for ensuring that children had adequate clothing, they were compelled by law to ensure that all children had books, a requirement they considered a burden only for Mexican children.[60]

The policy of separation was not based on pedagogical theory seeking to provide the best education for children. Instead it catered to the demands of employers desiring child labor during school hours and the prejudices of a dominant culture whose parents did not want their children in the same classroom with Mexicans. The failure of school administrators and truant officers to prevent delinquency represented a willful violation of the state's own laws and an abrogation of their expressed educational policy of Americanizing Mexican youth, who with few exceptions were citizens of the United States.

Poor school attendance and lack of institutional support for Mexican children were widespread. In 1925 in the state of Kansas, where most Mexicans were segregated into separate classrooms or buildings, almost half of all Mexican children required by law to attend school did not do so. In Topeka, the Branner School Annex, opened for Mexicans in 1918, remained segregated until 1942, when parents, along with the Armed Services seeking the facilities, pressured public officials to close the school. In the Armourdale barrio of Kansas City, Kansas, Mexican elementary school children attended classes in the basement while White children had classrooms upstairs, and a white line separated Mexican and European American children's play areas. In Garden City, Kansas, where facilities were also segregated, during the period between 1925 and 1950 only 22 percent of Mexican children even graduated from grammar school.[61]

The attitudes and behavior of teachers and administrators influenced school attendance and performance. Miss Shea at Bowen High School in Chicago claimed that "compared with other students they [Mexicans] lack ambition and are not perseverant in their tasks." School administrators often displayed little regard, as in the case of a St. Paul boy with good grades who had to leave for the beet fields to work, forcing him to miss his examinations, and "the principal did not allow him to make this up so he quit." Children were sensitive to disparate treatment, as illustrated by a St. Paul girl who "said she felt teachers at St. Mary's did not like Mexican children and would not help them as much as others."[62]

Furthermore, standardized intelligence tests, increasingly common after World War I, became weapons to isolate Mexican children. St. Paul social workers used them to intrude into private family matters, claiming that because of low intelligence, parents could not care for their families, were likely to become a public charge, or should be deported. In addition to inherent class and cultural biases, the tests were commonly applied under highly dubious circumstances by untrained personnel and incompetent interpreters, casting further doubt on their validity. Yet social workers and teachers seldom questioned why few Mexicans obtained even average scores, or why individuals depicted as intelligent and articulate might be tested as a "moron" or "feeble minded." Where test results did raise serious doubts in the minds of case workers, they did not consistently take corrective steps. In May 1930, "selective tests were used through the aid of an interpreter," who spoke Spanish poorly, in which a Mexican woman with two baby girls born in the United States was determined to be a "moron." Welfare workers interpreted the results as meaning she was liable to become a public charge. They decided to allow her to "keep her children and deport her" and the girls, without considering how she might be better able to support them in Mexico than in Minnesota. In another case, a mental examiner for the Minnesota State Board of Control eagerly administered a test to a woman who "could neither talk nor write in English and is almost entirely deaf and an interpreter had to be used." One St. Paul social worker raised suspicions about testing in the case of a family that consistently refused to submit to them as a precondition for receiving public assistance. The tests were finally administered to the mother and her children when the father went to work in the beet fields, and he "particularly resented the mental tests which he felt were forced on the family during his absence." In another instance, an International Institute caseworker acknowledged, "it has been our experience that in cases where mental tests were given to families of limited backgrounds, in which a foreign language was spoken in the home, they were not entirely reliable. . . . The person who gave the mental test . . . was a somewhat inexperienced WPA worker."[63]

On other occasions local Mexicanas and Mexicanos challenged highly intrusive social workers. In one case a social worker accepted gossip and failure on a mental test as justifying a recommendation to separate a daughter from her father. An International Institute caseworker intervened in the hearing at the father's urging. She testified that the man's mental ability and expression was "much better than that of most of the Mexicans she knew, and she felt that the man was just as normal as he could be—just that he had no chance to learn English as well as the other immigrants." After the hearing, the "case was thrown out of Court and the Judge advised the social worker not to bring in a case like that again."[64]

Prejudice and discrimination extended from schools and social agencies to the media, which reinforced anti-Mexican attitudes. In a *Chicago Trib-*

*une* article, Dr. Benjamin Goldberg, chief physician of the Municipal Tuberculosis Sanitarium, complained that "the Mexican emigrants who cross the Rio Grande in numbers and who multiply very rapidly are not only undesirable but also constitute a menace to the health of the American people." In 1930 *The Chicago Daily News* reviewed the Mexican opera *Mariana*, presented by the Artistas Unidos Mexicanos of Chicago. Its identification of the performance site in the heart of the Mexican barrio on South Halsted Street as "tamaletown" angered many local Mexicanos and their press. Yet as Sra. Juanita Morán recalled, of all the obstacles Mexicans encountered, "probably the main one was prejudice."[65]

Attitudes paved the way for disparate treatment. Author Bertram Schrieke observed in 1936 that throughout the Midwest, "it is significant that Mexican farm laborers rarely eat at the table with the farmer's family, although it is customary for [European] American farmhands to do so." Schrieke himself did not portray Mexicans as Americans, or as Mexican-Americans, in the manner of the hyphenated identity of Europeans who were accepted into the dominant culture, and instead identified Mexicans as distinct from Americans. In many cities and towns, Mexicans were still segregated in public settings, including swimming pools, movie theaters, and restaurants. Even in the diverse city of Chicago, ordinances that prohibited Mexicans, Filipinos, and African Americans from using public beaches on Lake Michigan were only lifted in 1932 as a result of public protests. On the West Side of St. Paul, Sr. Federico Saucedo recalled that during his youth in the 1930s, there were no places for Mexicans to go swimming, and "they weren't allowed in some of the taverns, restaurants and hotels." A St. Paul report concluded that "with few exceptions, Mexicans are not found in any of the youth organizations of the city. They are as yet too unassimilated and under-privileged to normally find a place in the youth agencies which are functions of the American community. Many children have complained that they are not welcome in the playgrounds except West of the river."[66] Their barrio offered a refuge, the only urban space where their presence was not challenged.

Institutions on the West Side offered support, such as that provided by Neighborhood House, whose administrators represented their facilities as a "second home," and "haven" for poor Mexican children in particular. One Chicana recalled that it was considered "one of the better buildings" in the barrio and a place where on extremely cold days people who could not heat their homes sent children. Another St. Paul Chicana recalled that during her youth, "more importantly" than its Americanization classes, the Neighborhood House was a place where people could "take advantage" of WPA programs, hot lunches, nursery schools, and commodity foods. It was also a site for many youth and young adult groups peripherally concerned with Americanization, including the Mexican Eagles (a youth group), a Mexican *orquesta,* and Mexican choral groups. The Mexican Council, representing sixteen clubs in the barrio, also collectively organized social and cultural events, including national holidays, the *Pastorelas,* and the Harvest Festival. The last recognized the collective return of the community from the fields, a distinct "Homecoming" which "most of the Mexicans in and near the Twin Cities attend." It included a dance and festival celebrating an annual cycle of Mexican work and geography distinct from that of their Minnesota neighbors.[67]

Settlement houses also expressed a commitment to the Americanization of Mexicans, and the St. Paul Neighborhood House asserted that despite having lived many years in the United States, "they still had most of the characteristics of a foreign people." Its Americanization classes, which included English language training, cooking, sewing, and child care, were less concerned with changing identities than preparing workers for specific segments of the job market or performing their domestic roles more effectively. Food purchasing and buying habits were fair game for "education," evident in a 1930 discussion by social worker Agnes Fenton of a small Mexican store on the South Side of Milwaukee. She noted that on payday women purchased food for several weeks, eggs by the dozen, large bags of flour, cans of tomatoes by the half dozen, beans, garbanzos, cheese, and chile peppers, which "form the main diet of the Mexican. He does not eat a lot of meat." Fenton observed that "the women are learning" and increasingly shopping at the A&P, which pleased her because they purchased a wider range of "American" foods. She did not address the more questionable nutritional value of the largely processed "American" foods, increasingly laced with sugar, preservatives, and other additives, compared with the dietary mainstays of the Mexican store. Meanwhile, the Neighborhood House proudly trumpeted its success in Americanizing Mexicans in a brochure quoting a Mexican woman who asserted gratitude that it helped her husband find employment in a packinghouse, and it "teach he and I to speak American. . . . I learn to sew and cook American way. . . . Neighborhood House know American way."[68]

Elsewhere in the Midwest, settlement houses like the Byrd Memorial Center in South Chicago permitted Mexicans to use facilities for recreational, sports, music, art, and other activities not directly related to Americanization. Pervasive paternalism among directors and leaders of the settlement houses and churches slowed their Americanizing efforts, as the words of Chicago pastor Thomas M. Lineweaver confirmed: "they seem to be backward. I guess that is due to the lack of education and development," despite an "altruistic spirit in what concerns their groups. They lack experience in regards to the American life. . . . Economically they are not making it . . . they are a little slow in adapting themselves to the new American customs." Nevertheless, Americanization was advancing, and, as the newspaper *La Alianza* of Chicago revealed in 1936, during the Cinco de Mayo and Diez y Seis de Septiembre celebrations, "all sang the [United States] National Anthem in chorus."[69]

In St. Paul, the International Institute, which functioned as a service bureau and an informational and educational center offering Americanization classes in preparation for United States citizenship, became more involved with the growing Mexican *colonia* in the 1930s. In contrast with much popular and academic thought, it contended that Mexican assimilation was hindered by class factors, or being "itinerant agricultural labor caught in a depression," and by prejudice and discrimination, rather than Mexican culture. The International Institute proffered an optimistic future scenario because, "like many other immigrant groups the Mexicans were young, vigorous, and prolific." Arguing against heavy-handed Americanization, it suggested that while "it is desirable that people who live here adopt an American way of life and understand their American-born children, we strongly recommend the use of the mother tongue to convey American ideas to foreign-born adults. When a real idea is at stake, 'speak Spanish' is a good rule." It also urged bilingual instruction for children, so they "learn to read and write Spanish as well as to speak to their parents in the vernacular."[70]

Through volunteer teachers paid by the WPA, the International Institute conducted classes in community centers and in the homes of Mexican families, teaching "simple conversation," how to read newspapers and contracts, and basic arithmetic. The primary goal was to enable students to find employment "at a fair wage," and to protect themselves from being cheated by employers and owners of stores. Institute philosophy considered citizenship as necessary for survival, due to increasing discrimination against aliens in private and WPA employment and reception of social services.[71] Thus the Institute understood its educational efforts toward Americanization primarily in the context of socializing Mexicans as workers.

A still more influential institution, the Catholic Church, decided to permit a separate physical space for St. Paul Mexicans in 1930 following visits to the barrio by Mrs. J. B. O'Hara, an Americanization worker for the St. Paul Public Schools and a self-identified "Catholic on the trail for souls." She convinced members of the Guild of Catholic Women to initiate an Americanization project for Mexicans because they were "sadly in need of both material and spiritual help." Guild women found great interest among *colonia* residents in forming a Mexican parish, which began as a mission within the Department of Social Action of the Archdiocese.[72]

Guild director Mary Bishop explained that the organization had as its highest priority maintaining the "Catholic Kingdom" among Mexicans but first had to address concerns of physical survival. She noted that "the handicap of great poverty and shifting homes in a new and often not, to them, cordial country was very discouraging to both the foreign born mothers and to us, who desired to help them, especially during the cold winter." Among their early successes, according to one report, was that "irregular marriages have been corrected and sanctified." The educational program for Mexican women reflected Guild ideals: "Character building we blended with talks or instructions on home-making: obedience, cheerfulness, purity and truthfulness." Guild philosophy was replete with a sense of cultural and intellectual superiority toward Mexicans pervasive among Americanizers: "abstract truths, or statements are vague to them. They must *live* what they are taught. . . . As for example duty to parents would mean to them not only general, but explicitly obedience, tending the baby, washing the dishes, gathering wood for the fire, or keeping off the streets at night." Imbued with the values of middle-class European American society, the Guild accepted male superiority while criticizing machismo in Mexican culture. Mary Bishop finally emphasized that Guild women "knew and loved their Mexicans."[73]

With the assistance of guild women, the first Mass in the St. Paul barrio was conducted in February 1931 in a rented building on South Wabasha, and the chapel moved twice in subsequent years to sites on Fairfield street. Because of limited space, parishioners also built a four-room social center a block from the chapel to permit space for a clothing distribution center, recreational and social activities, and classrooms for instruction in religion for children and sewing, knitting, rug making, and other skills for women. The first priest, Father Joseph Guillemette, a professor of Spanish at St. Thomas College in St. Paul, served part-time until 1937. One woman recalled that she and Father Guillemette together "begged for clothing and coal supplies to keep people from freezing during those harsh winters." Sra. Guadalupe Cruz also recalls that the priest "had me give out food and clothing to the poor and needy families" which they begged "from the rich people. There are a lot of rich people in this state." Father

Guillemette was replaced by the Rev. Henry Dicks, a German, who had served previously in the Archdiocese of San Antonio, and in St. Louis at the Mexican Mission at Yorktown. Father Dicks, the first full-time priest in the barrio, had learned some Spanish but "does not speak it fluently." On his arrival, the newly-formed Comité de Reconstrucción conducted a fund-raising drive to purchase and renovate a building on East Fairfield, involving parishioners' labor. Sra. Juanita Morán recalled that "everyone in the community came to help out as much as they could." With pick and shovel, they dug a basement and converted the former bar into space for classrooms, a library, and meeting and recreation rooms.[74]

Catholic Church leaders were highly selective about what they considered appropriate Americanization activities. In St. Paul they sponsored a Mexican Girl Scout Division in 1936, adding a Boy Scout troop two years later. Segregation in this prototypical American institution suggests willingness by European Americans to expose Mexicans to the ideals of Americanism, but not in the company of their own children. In 1939 another group, the Society of Mexican Laborers, also sought use of Church facilities. It claimed as objectives "to study the means by which to benefit our future . . . to try for better understanding, so as to be useful and good American citizens, to try to help defend our rights as much as possible . . . to obey and respect the laws of the Constitution and of the United States." It declared that its members "as Catholics shall work hard for our Church and co-operate with its Priests." But a relief worker claimed to have been informed by a local grocer that the founder of the society was "a communistic individual who was likely to get his relief worker in 'hot water.'" Father Dicks refused to support the society, claiming that that it was a front for the Workers' Alliance, and that its founder was "communistic" and his family did not attend church. The priest discouraged people from joining and prohibited the society from using church facilities. A more sympathetic International Institute social worker recommended cooptation, suggesting that the Church cooperate with the Society of Mexican Laborers in seeking to resolve "the problems of the Mexicans so they would not turn to solutions which might be suggested by agitators."[75]

Despite the European and European American priests, parishioners maintained a degree of control through their voluntary labor in church construction, maintenance, and repair, as well as continuing financial support. Women sustained it particularly through the sodality of Nuestra Señora de Guadalupe, better known as the Guadalupanas, a devotional society that first appeared in St. Paul during the tenure of Father Guillemette. In its early years the Guadalupanas engaged mostly in charity work, but later they focused more on the upkeep of linens and church vestments, maintenance of church membership, and especially planning and conducting social functions. The new church building quickly became a community center offering religious instruction, emergency assistance, and cultural activities as home of the Guadalupe Men's Club, a Mexican Altar Boys group, and the Ballet Folklórico Guadalupano. As Sr. Federico Saucedo later observed, "most of the older people, of course, literally lived for the church. That was their whole life." [76]

The Catholic Church and Neighborhood House enhanced the cohesiveness of the *colonia* while it strengthened family and parental controls. As Sra. Morán recalls, they were acceptable places where parents permitted boys and girls to socialize: "as far as boyfriends were concerned, my father wouldn't let any of his girls go out to meet their sweethearts. He was very strict when it came to that affair." She and her future husband met at church functions or he would come to the house, but "not once did we go anywhere together" until they married in 1943. Sra. Morán recalled that her father was less strict with her younger sisters, suggesting that Americanization may have been weakening parental controls. Federico Saucedo recalled that during his youth in the 1930s and 1940s, "regardless of everything else we had, we always had the church. That was all there was at that time, besides the Neighborhood House. . . . Most of us didn't know anything over the Robert Street Bridge or the Wabasha Street Bridge. We were mostly confined down in this small area, this was our whole life." [77]

Another organizational effort in the Midwest involved the leadership of Mexican consular officials. In Chicago and Indiana Harbor, they assisted in the formation of a local Comité Pro-México, aimed at counteracting conservative clerical interests and anti-Mexican threats in the United States, including intervention. Consular officials also assisted in the creation of the Frente Popular, with five local affiliates in Cleveland and the Chicago–Indiana Harbor area. The Frente advanced its stated goal of "social and economic betterment of the working classes" by raising funds for scholarships to permit Mexicans in the United States to return to Mexico and train for businesses or the professions. It also sought to enlarge cultural horizons by offering classes in Spanish, Mexican history and culture, and the labor movement. [78] The influence of the consulate had declined sharply by the mid-1930s, for its strongest adherents usually were repatriates. Furthermore, it demonstrated a limited ability to protect Mexicans from abuse by federal, state, and local officials during the early years of the Great Depression. People who remained were more rooted in the United States and less interested in consular leadership, and children in particular had few expectations and little interest in politics in Mexico.

By the late 1930s, a distinct set of Mexican spaces had been created, particularly in settlement houses, churches, and other sites outwardly dedicated to Americanization, whose functions were more explicitly oriented toward families than single men. In Kansas City, the Guadalupe Center, a community house supported by the Catholic Diocese, Agnes Ward Amberg Club volunteers, and the federal government, constructed a new building in the heart of the barrio on West 23rd Street in 1936. Supported by the WPA, it offered language classes for adults, recreation, drama, dance, fiestas, and other cultural activities. According to director Dorothy Gallagher, its goal was "to adjust whole Mexican families rather than the individual to the American way of living," offering classes in Americanization and language and baby stations and attracting "clubs and groups of all ages and aims." Its folk dance group traveled widely, with notable tours to the Southwest Folk Festival in 1936 and to the National Folk Festivals in Chicago in 1937 and Washington D.C. in 1938 and 1939. When First Lady Eleanor Roosevelt visited Kansas City in 1939, she thought the Guadalupe Center's folk dance group was a professional organization and expressed surprise that most members worked in local packinghouses, on railroads and hotels, and "had succeeded in using their music in periods of unemployment as a means of support for their families." The Guadalupe Center also housed a parochial school with an enrollment of 230 Mexican youth in 1942. As one observer concluded, despite the population decline in Mexican barrios in Kansas during the Great Depression, "a new sense of mutual support and cultural pride was created."[79]

Community organizations in larger cities offered classes and other activities for youth to promote understanding of the Spanish language and Mexican culture. In 1936 La Alianza Fraternal Mexicana appointed local newspaper editor Sr. J. Xavier Mondragón to teach geography and Mexican history to Chicago children, and the newspaper *Mexico* editorialized: "under no circumstances shall we permit our children to forget our language." Even in places hardest hit by repatriation, like East Chicago, where one observer suggested that the Great Depression "destroyed most of the community-building institutions" of the 1920s, there was a resurgence of Mexican cultural activities. In Detroit, "fiestas were held nearly every Saturday night in the winter," when unemployment was high and hundreds of families who worked in the fields of Michigan and Ohio lived in the city.[80]

During the Great Depression, there was a sharp increase in commercial expressions of Mexican culture, including Spanish-language radio programming. In 1930 Chicago station WCFL initiated a weekly musical program featuring artists from Mexico, and the following year WGN, owned by the *Chicago Tribune,* began a biweekly program sponsored by the United Fruit Company, featuring the Orquesta Típica García. More than in other settings, Mexican audiences in Chicago were also able to view Mexican silent films at Hull House and other places where they were shown.[81]

Rising interest in Mexican sports clubs and teams also was evident during the Great Depression, especially in the Chicago area, where organizations like the Club Deportivo Yaquis, formed in 1932, engaged in basketball, football, soccer, and indoor ball. The case of the Monterrey Club in South Chicago indicates that sports activities often served as more than recreational outlets. Formed in 1932, the club was sponsored by the Wisconsin Steel Corporation, and although its stated purpose was to play baseball, it also functioned as a *mutualista,* with the employer contributing funds for workers suffering from illness or injury on the job. Wisconsin Steel thus maintained a paternalistic relationship and control through the club, discouraging independent worker organizing. As member Alberto Cuellar observed in 1936, no one from the club joined the industrial union (the Steel Workers Organizing Committee) because the employers "do not want them to join any union and of course the members do not want to endanger their jobs."[82]

Three groups of Mexicans repatriated from the Midwest during the Great Depression. The first departed voluntarily, often with the assistance of the Mexican consulate in conformity with its own revolutionary nationalist mission of encouraging its citizens to return. The second were deported by the U.S. Immigration Service, which conducted drives throughout the nation, beginning in Texas in 1928 and lasting until 1932. The Immigration Service engaged the media and other outlets to pressure individuals not meeting residency requirements, as well as legal residents and U.S. citizens, to leave. This effort was motivated largely by the U.S. Department of Labor, concerned about reversing the sharp decline in wages and oversupply of workers. The early repatriation drives in Texas were linked to overproduction and falling cotton prices, which had been plummeting since 1925. In the Midwest, the federal government drives of 1930–1932 were linked primarily to steel production, which declined from 90 percent to 50 percent of capacity during that period. The steel industry was the most important employer of Mexican urban workers in the Midwest. A third group departed as a result of drives initiated by local authorities in midwestern communities during the summer and fall of 1932, and this one has received the greatest attention. Local drives were uneven, and in some locations, like Chicago, they failed to coalesce due to pressure from organized Mexicans and their political allies. The high rates of repatriation in the region further dispelled any illusions of midwestern exceptionalism, for in its ethnically diverse cities with large foreign-born populations, the drives focused exclusively on Mexicans.

Repatriation tended to remove the least rooted, disproportionately male population, as families had more opportunities to continue working in the beet fields. Their experience indicates the capacity of a modern industry to adopt strategies of colonialist enterprises, including the creation of a racialized workforce isolated in residence hundreds of miles from work and forced to sustain itself for long periods outside the wage economy. Corporate employers did not separate production and reproduction between First and Third World settings, accepting instead a division between rural fields and the urban, inner-city *colonia*. The urban *betabeleros* quickly became rooted and made demands as residents and organized workers, and employers soon turned again to the Mexican border for a labor force.

Another consequence of repatriation was a greater gender balance and family stability among those who remained, and an increasing importance of children in Mexican communities. By 1933 local populations were stabilizing, and by the later 1930s they were again growing rapidly, as a result of both natural population increase and renewed migration from Texas and Mexico, including many who were "finding their way back" to the region.[83]

Demographic trends were not even, as demonstrated in Minnesota, where sugar beet industry efforts to maintain a labor pool of Mexicans "resulted in a build-up of workers remaining in the state."[84] Hundreds of families who had spent winters in the 1920s in rural sections moved to St. Paul's small *colonia*, which grew rapidly and continuously during the Great Depression. Families commonly worked several months in agriculture, returning to the city for the rest of the year despite few opportunities for wage employment. Mexican children formed an important segment of the agricultural labor force despite missing classes, another indication that they did not receive equal protection of laws mandating public schooling in the American way of life. Later in the decade, although working conditions had not improved, the sugar beet industry renewed efforts to import workers from Texas to prevent the threat of unionization. By 1940, with an industrial recovery on the horizon, the movement of Mexicans to large midwestern cities accelerated.

During the hard times, the mutual support network of the 1920s collapsed, and many individuals adopted noncapitalist relations of production and distribution. They often shared food and other resources. Being more rooted, they also established relations with local institutions to assist in their survival. Local social workers and other agencies viewed the support they provided to Mexicans as compatible with the goals of creating loyal citizens while socializing them as workers.

Among midwestern Mexicans, fear of deportation did not subside after 1932, and in St. Paul more than 93 percent of household heads were not citizens. One report asserted that the average Mexican did not understand the law and "is not sure that he is not deportable."[85] Factors related to work, namely threats of deportation, paucity of employment options beyond the sugar beet fields, seasonal unemployment, and dependency on emergency support from welfare agencies, intensified their sense of vulnerability and awareness of being Mexican. Demographic and institutional factors that tended to hasten Americanization, notably the rapid increase in the population of children and the wide reach of the Neighborhood House and the Catholic Church, were simultaneously and contradictorily used to enhance a somewhat altered, more vigorous Mexican cultural life and identity than had been the case a decade earlier. Greater crowds participated in national and religious holiday festivities and participated in local events like the Harvest Festival, replete with local *orquesta,* dance groups, and other activities. Hard times and the collective memory of hunger forged a stronger public identity among Mexican workers. The option of embarking on an individual journey into a middle-class American way of life sought by Richard Rodriguez a generation later was not open in the St. Paul of the Great Depression, and the agencies of Americanization made many accommodations to the Mexican community in their midst.

The growing popularity of national holiday celebrations offered opportunities for entrepreneurs in larger cities, who angered critics upset about individuals seeking profits through the commercialization of Mexican culture. Chicago newspaper editor F. P. Miranda, upset about the handling of monies by the sponsors of the 1929 Fiestas Patrias, demanded an investigation by the Mexican consul, whose office sanctioned the activities. Sr. Miranda asserted that profits should go to a worthy cause like the Cruz Azul, "rather than have them go to the pockets of the sharks of our colony." In 1932, the newspaper *El Nacional* complained that "in past years unscrupulous persons have promoted this celebration on a profit basis." Continued concern convinced members of several organizations to discuss mutual plans to celebrate the fiestas "and once and for all avoid the lucrative aims of our countrymen who, without any scruple, have utilized the name of our heroes in pursuing of their own selfish interests." In 1934 they formed a Pro-Fiestas Patrias committee, with representatives from each Mexican society in Chicago and the suburbs.[86] Such festivals proliferated amidst ongoing debates about seeking material profit from Mexican culture and the pernicious influence of Americanization.

1. Railroad boxcar residence of a Mexican family in Topeka. From Larry G. Rutter, "Mexican Americans in Kansas: A Survey and Social Mobility Study, 1900–1970," M.A. thesis, Kansas State University, 1972. Drawing originally appeared in *Topeka Capital Journal,* September 1, 1917.

2. *A Worker in the Steel Mills of Chicago.* Linoleum cut by William L. Ortiz. From Robert C. Jones and Louis R. Wilson, "The Mexican in Chicago" (Chicago: Chicago Congregational Union, 1931).

3. *The Mexican Boulevard (Halsted Street).* Linoleum cut by William L. Ortiz. From Robert C. Jones and Louis R. Wilson, "The Mexican in Chicago" (Chicago: Chicago Congregational Union, 1931).
4. *Chicago: End of the Trail.* Drawing by Morris Topchevsky. From Robert N. McLean, "Tightening the Mexican Border," *Survey* 64 (April 1, 1930): 28.

5. Theresa Araña, 21, working at a draw furnace at the Armor Plate Division, United States Steel, Gary, Indiana. Photograph by Margaret Bourke-White/LIFE Magazine © TIME Inc. From "Women in Steel: They Are Handling Tough Jobs in Heavy Industry," *Life* 15 (August 9, 1943): 79.

6. Dolores Macías, 26, working on a gang at United States Steel, Gary, Indiana. Photograph by Margaret Bourke-White/LIFE Magazine © TIME Inc. From "Women in Steel: They Are Handling Tough Jobs in Heavy Industry," *Life* 15 (August 9, 1943): 79.

7. Home of María Cruz Gonzales-Pas, who came to Minnesota as a migrant worker for a sugar beet company located on lowlands near airport, 1938. Photo by St. Paul Daily News, Minnesota Historical Society.

8. María Cruz Gonzales-Pas feeding her livestock, 1938. Photo by St. Paul Daily News, Minnesota Historical Society.

9. Guadalupe Society and the Holy Name Society, Our Lady of Guadalupe Church, St. Paul, at Harriet Island, 1946. Courtesy Minnesota Historical Society.

10. Young people from Our Lady of Guadalupe Church performing "Mexican Hat Dance," in observance of Pan-American Day, April 1948. Photo by St. Paul Daily News, Minnesota Historical Society.

11.  West Side, St. Paul, February 3, 1949. Courtesy Minnesota Historical Society.

12.  Procession on West Side, St. Paul, December 12, 1950, Our Lady of Guadalupe Church. Courtesy Minnesota Historical Society.

13. Flood at St. Paul, April 8, 1952. Courtesy Minnesota Historical Society.

14. Flood at St. Paul, April 8, 1952. Courtesy Minnesota Historical Society.

15. Flood at St. Paul, April 14, 1952. Courtesy Minnesota Historical Society.

16. Section of mural depicting the birth of Chicano studies at the University of Minnesota, by Armando Estrella, 1973. Located in Ford Hall, University of Minnesota, Minneapolis. From top right to bottom left: Nick Castillo; Ramona Arreguín, first president of the Latin Liberation Front; Ray Roybal; Alfredo González, first Chicano studies instructor at the University of Minnesota; and Manuel Guzmán. The mural is a stylized rendition of ancient Mexican codices depicting the birth of Aztlán.

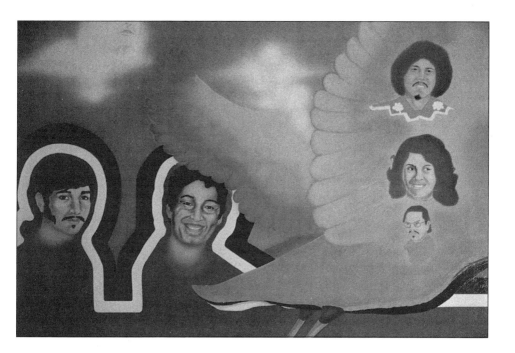

# 4 Good Solid Workers

The United States entry into World War II marked the heyday of monopoly capitalism, a generation-long era of economic growth and expanding production led by the major midwestern cities, which peaked in population in the early 1950s. Resolution of the struggles between capital and labor during the Great Depression allowed workers access to a greater share of the fruits of prosperity. Large industrial employers were able to adopt several Fordist strategies and had a relatively free hand in decisions relating to the production process, while making important concessions, including more stable employment, higher wages linked to increases in productivity, and a "safety net" of social and health benefits. The arrangement was predicated on the assumption that workers were also important consumers of industrial goods and were entitled to enjoy the material benefits of a middle-class lifestyle, their share of the fruits of the "American Dream."[1]

Midwestern Mexicans and their communities were profoundly influenced by the changes that marked the era. Thousands of long-established residents who had worked erratically since arriving earlier in the century found steadier employment on the railroads and in packing plants, steel mills, automobile factories, and other industrial settings, often joined by their children and recent arrivals from Texas and Mexico. In many older urban barrios, including the Lower West Side of St. Paul, Mexicans became a majority of the population, while new *colonias* appeared in smaller industrial cities and suburbs. By 1970 at least half a million people of Mexican birth and descent resided in the region between Ohio and Kansas, more than three times the numbers of 1940.[2]

In an era dominated by assimilationist thought in popular culture, many observers assumed that Mexicans in the Midwest would be absorbed into the dominant culture in the manner of European immigrants, leaving few traces. Contemporary union ideology also sought to include workers without regard to skill or ethnicity, suggesting that Mexicans would also assimilate into the region's industrial working class. Reflecting on the impact of repatriation and future expectations, Carey McWilliams wrote in 1948 that "it is a foregone conclusion that the northern Mexican settlements will have largely vanished in another generation."[3]

Assimilationist visions were not equally welcoming, and one tendency evident in the rising antiforeign sentiment stemming from World War II and the Cold War was a rigid conformity that made the Mexican presence unacceptable. Struggles over meanings of assimilation were further accompanied by conflicts over geographic space. During the 1950s and early 1960s, many barrios became sites of contention as they attracted the attention of politicians and entrepreneurs who had their own building, highway construction, and related urban renewal projects in mind. In the name of "progress," investors and local governments sought to apply the wrecking ball to many neighborhoods, leaving local residents to fend for themselves.

### An Urban Proletariat

Large-scale migration from Texas was renewed in the late 1930s as agricultural employers sought to break unionization efforts among resident midwestern farmworkers. Workers were willing to leave Texas, where they faced declining economic conditions, displacement from WPA employment, and the loss of thousands of jobs as the pecan industry remechanized operations following the 1938 strike in San Antonio. They also encountered "increasing discrimination by employers" and lost jobs they once held in packing and canning plants and in the garment and laundry industries. In 1940 South Texas union organizer Santos Vásquez observed that in earlier years "you rarely saw an Anglo in the sheds, now you rarely see a Mexican." The migration of Tejanos began to unhitch the link between midwestern urban *colonias* and beet fields, but it was a gradual uncoupling. A St. Paul report asserted that Mexican men "during the war years, with their wives and older children working too, . . . were able to earn some real money" in the beet fields. Increasingly they were also finding more permanent and higher-paying jobs in meatpacking, steel mills, defense plants, railroads, textile shops, and other urban industries in the region, often with the same employers where they had once engaged in seasonal or temporary work. Formerly an unstable labor reserve, they were becoming an increasingly permanent segment of the region's industrial proletariat.[4]

World War II profoundly influenced Mexicans, who entered the armed services at very high rates throughout the nation. The Neighborhood House reported that in many families from the St. Paul barrio, all the sons served and all the daughters were married to soldiers. Mexicans from Silvis, Illinois, were highly decorated as soldiers in World War II, and Second Street, the heart of the *colonia*, had the highest participation of any block in the United States. As a result of their exemplary military service during World War II, and later in Korea and Vietnam, it was renamed "Hero Street" in their honor.[5]

The high rates of induction into the armed forces reflected in part the success of social service agencies, churches, and other agents of Americanization in convincing them to fight on behalf of the country where most of them were born. Paratrooper Manuel Pérez, from Chicago, who won the Congressional Medal of Honor, stated, "we are proud of our Mexican heritage and loyal to the United States. There is no conflict between the two." Political and economic factors were also important, as they lacked influence on draft boards and opportunities to obtain employment in defense, farming, or other occupations that exempted them from military service. Limited employment options pushed fathers, sons, and grandsons into the armed forces to support their immediate relatives, who received a monthly allotment and hospitalization and insurance policies. Relatives nevertheless continued to face severe hardships, as young wives and children often returned to their parents' homes during spouses' military duty. Furthermore, many allotments were inadequate or not forthcoming. A St. Paul father drafted in 1944 had to leave his wife, their four children, and her widowed mother to fend for themselves. It was later discovered that they lacked clothing and shoes, the bed linens "had become threadbare," and the baby was suffering from severe malnutrition.[6]

Wartime labor demands convinced more midwestern employers to hire workers directly from Texas and Mexico. In agriculture Tejanos entered new fruit and vegetable crop areas and found jobs in canneries. They were also recruited from the Mexican border region to work in urban foundries, steel mills, and other factories. The International Labor Agreement between the United States and Mexico, popularly known as the Bracero Program, contracted thousands of men from Mexico for temporary employment in agriculture, on the tracks, and in some urban activities. Consequently, wartime Mexican migration and employment far surpassed the scale of the 1920s.

The braceros employed on the railroads were much less isolated from urban settings and merit specific attention. Like their agricultural counterparts, they experienced repeated and continuous violation of living and working conditions stipulated in their contracts. Inspectors regularly criticized bracero camps for abysmal conditions, unsanitary housing, a lack of proper toilet, laundry, and recreational facilities, spoiled and poorly prepared food, and illegal deductions from paychecks. At the Burlington Railroad camp at Hinsdale, near LaGrange, Illinois, an inspector found that workers were fed a monotonous fare of beans, "balogna sausage," "sickly looking spice cake," and "very weak" milk from soot-filled pitchers. Many bunks lacked mattresses, workers had not had hot water for almost forty days, and some had to travel to Chicago to bathe, which cost them a half-day of work, the price of rail fare, and a public bath. They also complained that the foreman treated them like "*bobos*" (stupid fools). Abuses of workers' rights, including medical treatment, were widespread, as railroad worker Julio de la Cruz Morales discovered in Toledo. In April 1945 he became severely ill after his crew was forced to work in pouring rain. For several days the company refused to heed "continuous requests to the foreman for medical attention," and a week after his first complaints he was finally taken to a nearby hospital, where he died of poliomyelitis.[7]

Braceros also encountered widespread public discrimination in violation of their contracts, including refusal of service in public places, abuses by local authorities, and frequent cases of police brutality. In Bucyrus, Ohio, the accident claims of Pennsylvania Railroad workers were treated in a "pathetic and shameful manner," and "practically every eating and drinking place" refused to sell to or serve them. When a group of braceros entered a local bar for a glass of beer after work, the bartender protested, "for Christ's sake, how many times do I have to tell you I don't want Mexicans in this place?" The bartender soon provoked an altercation with one of the men and "hit him with a terrific blow in the mouth," which bled profusely. They immediately departed, heading to the police station to press charges against the bartender for assault. Instead they were charged with intoxication, although none had consumed any alcoholic beverages; carrying a concealed weapon, in the form of a pocket knife; and assault, for which the police informed them they would be incarcerated for periods ranging from one to twenty years. When Mexican labor inspector Ricardo Pérez and two young, well-dressed workers went to several local eating places in Bucyrus to investigate the workers' complaints, they were threatened by police officers and railroad officials and refused service. Finally, the local Anglo administrator of the Bracero Program warned the arrested railroad braceros "that if they did not plead guilty to the charge of intoxication he would cancel their contracts and return them to Mexico. Since there was no other course they chose to plead guilty to the lesser charge" of intoxication.[8]

Braceros occasionally encountered violent law enforcement officers, including a group employed by the Erie Railroad in North Judson, Indiana.

They complained to Chicago consul Emilio Aldama about the conduct of police officer Walter Macejack, who "on several occasions, without any justification, has clubbed several Mexican workers, merely because he found them away from the camp late in the evening," and repeatedly threatened or fined them without cause. In September 1945, Gilberto Landa Morales "was brutally clubbed and then shot without any justification whatever" by Macejack, a large person, who claimed that he was attacked by the much smaller Landa Morales. Macejack was not charged with any crime or misdemeanor.[9]

Upset that the terms of their contracts were not being met and their rights as workers were not being protected, braceros often deserted their jobs and disappeared into nearby cities and towns to seek more agreeable jobs. Many other braceros completed their contracts and returned later, often with their families. Their experience as braceros and the employment network they had formed lured additional thousands of Mexicans to midwestern industries.[10]

To meet wartime labor demands, employers also induced thousands of women into urban industrial settings, and according to one observer, Mexicanas for the first time "cast aside their female role," presumably unpaid housework. Such an argument is oblivious to an earlier history, when most midwestern Mexicanas had worked in the fields and in shops and factories. Wage employment for women typically was erratic, as in the case of a Mexicana who crossed the border as an infant in 1907 and eventually settled in St. Paul after living in San Antonio, Chicago, Detroit, Dallas, and the Minnesota beet fields. Between the 1920s and 1940s she usually was identified as a housewife, despite holding a number of part-time and full-time jobs in addition to agricultural labor, including power machine operator in a cement company, pork trimmer at a Cudahy packing plant, and cutter and sewer at a textile company. The difference in the early 1940s was the scale and duration of women's participation in the industrial economy, including steel mills.[11]

The working roles and importance of Mexicanas during the war has been the subject of some differences of interpretation. Some have suggested that they worked in order to permit families to survive, while others indicate that they were motivated largely by a desire to purchase luxuries. Both motives attracted midwestern Mexicanas, who were able to purchase nonessential items but were more influenced by the need to contribute to family sustenance. Even women who were not engaged in wage labor were aware of the critical role of their contribution to the family economy, even when they remained "busy sewing on the machine" or caring for "quite a large victory garden with quite a lot of vegetables." Continued discrimination against their noncitizen fathers in employment and the entry of their brothers and husbands into the armed services commonly compelled young Mexicanas to enter the wage labor market to support their families.[12]

After the war, industrialists built new factories in suburbs and smaller cities, their decisions influenced by tax incentives and a public-funded highway construction program. They attracted returning soldiers, African Americans and European Americans from the South, Tejanos, and Mexican immigrants to settle outside the older urban barrios. Population growth and more dispersed settlement contributed to an increasing diversity of the region's Mexican population. A first generation of Mexican-born adults who had arrived before 1930 was being augmented by a second generation composed largely of their midwestern-born children who worked alongside them in shops and factories. Another group consisted of Tejanos, often farmworkers who decided to settle or individuals lured directly to factory employment. Lastly, a growing number of Mexican immigrants were heading directly to midwestern cities. It would be deceptive to consider this varied population a "Mexican American" generation, for it included longer established and more recent immigrants as well as their children. Even among those of the second generation, although they came into contact in various settings, were aware of differences. Sr. Frank Guzmán, who grew up in the neighborhood Mexicans called "El Pozo" (the Hole) in St. Paul during the 1930s and 1940s, spent several summers with his family in the fields around Maple Island, Minnesota, where he first came into contact with Tejanos. He recalled that when he was young he was quite conscious of the differences in their behavior and dress and the way they spoke Spanish, and "to us they were acting peculiar, as compared to people living around here. The difference between the people up here and the people living down in Texas doesn't seem as great anymore."[13]

In St. Paul, the West Side *colonia* continued to grow rapidly as new arrivals from the South Texas–Mexican border region settled. Sra. Teresa Muñoz was born in Piedras Negras, Coahuila, on the Mexican side of the Río Grande, although her mother had been born in Texas. She moved to neighboring Eagle Pass and married Sr. David Muñoz, a local Tejano. Shortly after marriage they went to work in the sugar beet fields around Sidney, Montana, but she emphasized, "I had never worked and I did not like it." In the fields they met several Minnesota Mexicans, who informed them of industrial employment opportunities in St. Paul, and at the end of the season they moved directly to the Lower West Side, into a duplex on Fairfield Street. As she recalled, "I had never seen a pair of overshoes.

I had never seen so much snow before, but I became accustomed to it because I wanted to stay. I did not want to go back to Texas. . . . I told my husband that if he wanted to keep working in the fields, that was fine, but that I was going to stay in St. Paul." They were fortunate, "because there were plenty of jobs," and both soon found packinghouse employment at Armour.[14]

It became difficult to find housing, as one report noted, and many families "have left [the Lower West Side] to go into sections where no Mexicans have lived before." By the 1940s, they were settling on the East Side along Jackson and Mississippi streets and in "El Pozo," once known as "Swede Hollow." Others moved into South St. Paul, an industrial suburb adjacent to the West Side, in order to live closer to local meat-packing plants. There were also clusters of Mexicans in Minneapolis, one on the North Side, centering on Plymouth between Washington and Lyndale avenues, another in South Minneapolis in the Seven Corners area. By the 1950s, families were also moving to the Concord Terrace neighborhood on the West Side of St. Paul and across the Mississippi River into the neighborhood immediately north and east of the state capitol building.[15]

As in most locations where they resided, the quality of housing on the Lower West Side was among the worst available in urban settings. Their houses and apartments were intermingled with shops, factories, ware-houses, and storage sites where junk and litter accumulated. The area also experienced heavy street traffic from automobiles, trucks, and trains and was the site of a city dump. Located on wetlands, a low-lying floodplain on the edge of the Mississippi River, it was subject to periodic flooding. As in most barrios, residents encountered a range of environmental, health, and safety problems they had not created.[16]

One report noted that Mexican neighborhoods in both Minneapolis and St. Paul "are labeled blighted areas by sociologists . . . there were very few houses that were in good condition." Another concluded that most residents "continue to live in circumstances that are appalling," including boxcars in the railroad yards. Most dwellings were small and crowded, in poor repair, and relied on kerosene- or coal-burning stoves instead of cen-tral heating, and many still lacked running water, private bathtubs, or showers. When Sra. Teresa Muñoz moved to St. Paul in 1946 she recalled that "the place where we lived was called 'Little Mexico' [and] had three floors . . . what they called a 'cold water flat.' No hot water. We only had a sink with cold water, a table, stove, two chairs, and a bed and one closet. And this is how most of the houses were." The demand for housing allowed landlords to permit conditions to deteriorate and charge rents substantially higher than comparable units elsewhere in the Twin Cities. Furthermore, heating bills often equaled rent because of poor insulation, warped doors, and cracked windows. One study concluded that "the housing of the Mexican community remains the worst in St. Paul," while another labeled it the worst in the Twin Cities metropolitan area.[17]

Yet the Lower West Side remained a vigorous neighborhood, and, as a St. Paul newspaper reporter observed, the nucleus of old-timers "liked it here and wrote home, urging relatives and *compadres* to join them." Although "the housing shortage has intensified the crowded conditions . . . probably the chief reason for the doubling of families is the desire of new arrivals to stay within the colony rather than seek housing somewhere else in the city." As one local resident mused, "if the colony grows much more, I don't know what we'll do. Most want to live in the colony."[18]

Throughout the Midwest, older barrios generally expanded while new *colonias* appeared in industrial suburbs and working-class districts of medium-sized and smaller cities. In Kansas, population growth was comparatively modest and due primarily to natural factors. Older *colonias* that had formed along the railroad tracks in the early twentieth century were augmented by railroad and sugar beet workers who continued to drift into Dodge City, Topeka, and other locations. Kansas City, however, suffered a devastating flood in 1951. High waters drowned thousands of cattle and hogs in the stockyards and compelled more than five thousand residents to evacuate their homes in the Argentine barrio and more than nine thousand from Armourdale. Despite the appearance of new restaurants and a local theater that showed Spanish-language movies, Argentine experienced physical deterioration and disruption. The West Side barrio in Kansas City was upset by employer departures, the construction of the Southwest Trafficway, and increasing noise. Meanwhile, local government and loan institutions discouraged new housing construction. The barrio's population declined from an estimated thirteen thousand to seven thousand between 1940 and 1970, while the overall population of the metropolitan area expanded only moderately.[19]

In Wisconsin, the Mexican population of Milwaukee reached about three thousand by the late 1940s and grew rapidly in subsequent decades. Mexicans concentrated overwhelmingly in the South Side barrio and became a majority in the district the following decade. Meanwhile, a smaller Latino *colonia* took form on the near northeast side of the city, comprised primarily of recently arrived Puerto Ricans, interspersed with Mexicans. By the mid-1960s, there were an estimated ten thousand Mexicans in the city, and tanneries remained their largest employer. A number of *colonias* formed in nearby industrial suburbs, led by Waukesha. In this suburb a neighborhood some called "Little Mexico" appeared in the northeast section of the city, along East Main and the Strand, where Mexicans were replacing a largely Italian population. Settling farmworkers, most from Texas, also were attracted to smaller cities in the industrialized eastern portion of the state, including Sheboygan, Green Bay, Kenosha, and Racine, whose Mexican population rose from less than one hundred in the early 1940s to about five thousand by 1970.[20]

In the Quad Cities area, the railroad community of Silvis, Illinois, was the heart of local Mexican life. But Second Street remained a muddy and rutted path, for despite the bravery of its youth and the willingness of parents to permit their children to die overseas, residents had gained little political influence. Their attitudinal assimilation was not accompanied by civic assimilation, as the barrio remained isolated, lacking in basic urban services.[21]

In Chicago, Mexicans continued to concentrate on the Near West Side, the Back of the Yards, or South Chicago. By the end of the 1940s the Mexican population in the metropolitan area had reached an estimated 35,000. It experienced modest growth in the 1950s and phenomenal expansion the following decade, and one informed estimate suggested a population of 250,000 by the end of the 1960s, the third largest urban Mexican concentration in the United States, following Los Angeles and San Antonio.[22]

On the Near West Side, in the 1940s Mexicans lived in "small islands" and were "still looked upon by the Italian-Americans as outsiders and intruders." They gradually moved west and south, displaced from sections to the north and east by African Americans and later by the construction of the Dan Ryan and Eisenhower expressways and the new Circle Campus of the University of Illinois. By the 1950s they were heading increasingly into the nearby Pilsen neighborhood, formerly inhabited by Czechs and other Eastern Europeans, and were trickling into adjacent Little Village, which would soon become a "Mexican suburb" of Pilsen. By the 1960s, they were the majority in many West Side neighborhoods and represented more than half the Mexican population in the city.[23]

In the Stockyards district, wartime employment of Mexicans in the meatpacking industry increased sharply and was estimated at around four thousand by 1945, although the industry stagnated afterward. They clustered in a few neighborhoods but were "not a majority in any particular area." A 1942 survey reported that local Mexicans were vividly aware of housing and rent discrimination but were afraid to complain for fear of not finding another place. They overwhelmingly agreed that their greatest problem was "the attitudes of prejudice toward them on the part of North Americans." Their historically tense relationship with the more numerous Slavic population had improved somewhat during the Great Depression as a result of their participation in the Unemployed Councils, CIO organizing efforts among packinghouse workers, and local "all-inclusive people's organizations," particularly the Back of the Yards Neighborhood Council. Mexicans in the Stockyards district tended to be more isolated than those in other parts of the city and often spent their entire lives in the neighborhood working in the packinghouses, attending union, church, and organizational meetings, and socializing.[24]

In South Chicago continued industrial expansion fueled a rapid population increase, and by 1945 there were already ten thousand Mexicans working in the steel industry, the largest employer in the area. Yet the district "could almost be said to be segregated without restrictive covenant," as neither Mexicans nor African Americans were permitted to reside west of Commercial Avenue, its "Mason-Dixon line." Even when they resided in close proximity, Mexican neighborhoods were largely isolated from both European Americans and African Americans.[25]

During the late 1940s and 1950s, the rapid influx of Puerto Ricans resulted in the appearance of a fourth large Spanish-speaking district, concentrated immediately to the north and northwest of the Loop. Chicago Puerto Ricans had working-class employment, principally in light manufacturing and restaurants or in the downtown business district as messengers, deliverymen, and janitors. Mexicans worked and resided mostly in districts where heavy manufacturing and agriculture were concentrated and rarely competed with Puerto Ricans for the same jobs. Yet Mexicans in Chicago were increasingly finding work in hotels and restaurants as kitchen help, bus boys, and similar occupations, anticipating their phenomenal increase in the service industries in later decades. Elsewhere in the Midwest, there were fewer Puerto Ricans, and in many states, like Minnesota, very few settled permanently during the period.[26]

*Colonias* expanded in the suburban industrial belt around Chicago, linked particularly to employment on the railroads, local industries, and agriculture. The Chicago area was "the focal point of relocation for a good many agricultural migrants." They were most numerous in the western suburbs of Aurora, Arlington Heights, Bensenville, and Joliet, and immediately to the south of the city around Blue Island, Harvey, South Holland, Lansing, and Chicago Heights, "with its fertile farm lands interspersed between subdivisions and industrial plants." Settling farmworkers formed a labor pool for local employers, particularly in nurseries and expanding suburban industries. By 1960 an estimated twenty-five hundred farmworkers had resettled in Chicago Heights, mostly in the southeast side of the city, where they attended St. Casimir Church. In the suburbs, Mexicans typically were more scattered than in the central city, yet their options were limited by realtors and residents who "openly refused to sell or rent housing" and by more subtle means of steering them into particular neighborhoods. Although job opportunities were expanding more rapidly in suburban locations, Mexicans were still "forced to drift in and out of the limited low-skill industrial jobs they had been able to find," often "living under extremely precarious circumstances."[27]

The Indiana steel industry continued to attract Mexicans to the northwestern part of the state, as reflected in the growth of barrios in East Chicago, Gary, and neighboring towns. Elsewhere in northern Indiana, several new *colonias* appeared, such as those in South Bend, Mishawaka, and towns along the Michigan border. Farmworkers were initially attracted to an expanding agricultural industry made possible by a reclamation of marshland in the early 1940s, when a few settled in St. Joseph County. Following a brief phase of slow growth, their numbers accelerated in the late 1950s and 1960s. In South Bend, men found jobs as common laborers in local industries, including soft drink bottling companies, farm machinery producers, and Kaiser Jeep. Women obtained employment in service occupations, particularly as kitchen helpers and workers in local restaurants and at the University of Notre Dame and St. Joseph's Hospital. In Indianapolis, a small Mexican community appeared during the late 1940s and 1950s on the near Eastside, composed largely of settling farmworkers who found jobs on the railroads and in construction. Throughout the state, Mexicans were still confined to a very narrow range of employment, and according to a mid 1960s East Chicago study, 90 percent were blue-collar workers.[28]

In Ohio, the early 1940s marked the beginning of a very rapid growth of the Mexican population in the northwestern section of the state, centering on Toledo and neighboring cities including Defiance and Fremont, where workers were attracted to industrial employment. Most were settled-out farmworkers, augmented by Mexican former braceros employed on the railroads and factories in the area during the war. Toledo was a midwestern city whose small Mexican community established in the 1920s was overwhelmed demographically by more recent arrivals from Texas. Migration surged during boom years like 1950, and by the end of the decade, just prior to an even more rapid spurt of growth, at least twenty-five hundred Mexicans resided in Toledo. A 1958 study found that among heads of household, 62 percent were born in Texas, 13 percent in Mexico, 15 percent in Toledo, and the rest in other states. Housing opportunities were limited by the refusal of most landlords to rent to Mexicans, and they clustered in three neighborhoods. The South End barrio became the heart of Mexican Toledo, replete with social, cultural, religious, and commercial activities. There were smaller clusters on the North End and the East Side. In Defiance, a new GMC plant opened in 1950 and was "begging for help," providing impetus for settlement that continued in subsequent years. In Fremont, several hundred families initially lured from Texas to work in agriculture settled in the 1950s and 1960s, finding "relatively unskilled labor" in food processing and other local industries. Reflecting a pattern evident throughout the region, recent settlers in Northwest Ohio continued to maintain strong ties with their kin through frequent trips to Texas and corresponding visits by Tejano relatives.[29]

The Mexican population of Michigan was scattered more widely than in neighboring states, a consequence of the dispersion of automobile factories, foundries, and parts plants. Growth was more rapid in the industrial suburbs than in Detroit, particularly its downriver neighbors of Ecorse, Wyandotte, and River Rouge, where foundries had begun recruiting workers directly from Texas during World War II. In Detroit, the aging barrio was disrupted by an expanding central business district and new warehouses, factories, and shops, and later it was divided by the John C. Lodge and Fisher Freeways. New construction destroyed hundreds of homes, caused a sharp increase in noise and air pollution, displaced thousands of residents, and shifted the heart of the barrio toward the Southwest, from Bagley and Porter to the Clark Street district.[30]

Impressive growth also took place in several medium-sized cities elsewhere in the state. In Adrian, a small *colonia* that appeared on the South Side in the late 1930s grew rapidly during and after the war. By 1958 an estimated twelve hundred Mexicanos lived in the city, including former farmworkers attracted by employment opportunities in local industries. Sr. Reymundo Cárdenas, who was part of the process, observed that "due to his folk culture and the prejudices which he encountered, the Mexicans moved next to each other. This resulted in the 'colonia.' In Adrian and in almost every town where there are Mexicans, the colonia came into existence in almost identical ways." It was typically located in a poor section of town or an unincorporated area on the urban fringe, often near factories and railroad yards. As Cárdenas noted, "this settlement was determined by low land values, cheap rent, an undesirable site, closeness to employment, and prejudice."[31]

In Pontiac, wartime labor demands influenced local industries, particularly the Wilson Foundry and Pontiac Motors, to recruit Mexicanos directly from Texas. In Flint, a company town dominated by the Buick and Chevrolet divisions of General Motors, the largely urban, Tejano workers dispersed into several industrial neighborhoods, particularly in the northeastern part of the city, while they quickly adjusted to the factory regime without attracting undue attention. In Port Huron, Mexicans settling out of farmwork found employment in foundries and factories in "the dirtiest jobs that there were. It was a word-of-mouth and family migration." Most were concentrated in the aging First Ward adjacent to downtown, an ethnically diverse working-class population.[32]

The barrio on the northeast side of Saginaw, the largest in the state outside Detroit, grew rapidly as settling farmworkers from Texas were attracted to booming local factories. The majority worked for General Motors and its suppliers; otherwise they found "poor job opportunities or job mobility" and limited opportunities to enter middle-class or professional positions. It became the most densely concentrated settlement in the state and the first to achieve a Mexican numerical majority, partly because of intense resistance by local landlords and residents and zoning policies specifically intent on restricting Blacks and other minorities from most urban neighborhoods. The Catholic Church promoted activities at the Guadalupe Center and St. Joseph's parish, with the support of the Social Mission Sisters of the Holy Ghost and Bishop William F. Murphy's "paternal interest in Mexicans."[33]

In Lansing a *colonia* did not emerge in the 1920s because the largest employers, including General Motors' Oldsmobile and Motor Wheel plants refused to hire Mexicans. But in the late 1930s the sugar beet factory constructed a camp on the north side of the city for farmworkers employed in nearby fields, which became the core of a new barrio. With the outbreak of war, employment opportunities expanded rapidly in Oldsmobile, Reo, Fisher Body, and several drop forge plants located around the city. Mexicans tended to cluster in a handful of locations, including the near north side, Town Gardens, and the South Logan–Maple Grove neighborhoods, in contrast to the more dispersed settlement in Flint.[34]

Western Michigan had offered few jobs for Mexicans prior to World War II, but in the 1940s hundreds found industrial employment in the Grand Rapids area. Modest growth in the 1950s accelerated in the 1960s, as opportunities increased at General Motors plants and in furniture and brass factories. The largest settlements appeared on the south side, in the Grandville Avenue area, and on the near west side of the city. With the outbreak of the war, foundries in Muskegon and Holland under war contract also began recruiting Mexican workers, setting the stage for employment in other industries. Canning and food processing plants also attracted settling farmworkers, who often formed the core of rapidly growing *colonias* of the area. In communities like Newaygo and Grant, as elsewhere in the region, small-town insularity and European American ethnic homogeneity often made initial settlement difficult for Mexicans.[35]

Somewhat distinct patterns of settlement characterized the Tejano and Mexican immigrant arrivals to the Midwest. A majority of Tejanos entered the region initially as seasonal workers in agriculture-related activities, often working for several seasons before they settled out permanently. A significant number also were lured to factories by direct recruitment or indirect networks established with recent settlers, often relatives and former neighbors. Tejanos were more likely to bypass established urban neighborhoods and settle in growing industrial suburbs and medium-sized towns, among recent arrivals from the Southern United States and the children of European immigrants. Workers from Mexico often came initially as agricultural braceros during the war to work in the more industrialized crops of the region, particularly sugar beets and pickling cucumbers, or as section workers on railroad lines. Those who decided to remain most often sought out established Mexican neighborhoods in the largest industrial cities, particularly Chicago, Detroit, and Milwaukee, where the Mexican population and related cultural and business activities were most densely concentrated.

Midwestern barrios in this period had more youth, contributing to greater proportions born in the United States, than during the 1920s. In St. Paul, by 1946 it was estimated that 77 percent of Mexicans were born in the United States, and almost 50 percent were under 18 years of age. A 1959 St. Paul study of two generations of adult Mexicanas revealed that family size was decreasing: among the older generation, 48 percent had between five and seven children, an additional 40 percent between eight and twelve children; and among the younger generation, 71 percent had three or fewer children. Smaller nuclear families and a greater tendency to form a single residential household reduced crowding in comparison with earlier years. Furthermore, gender balance comparable with the dominant population had been achieved. In 1960 among Mexicans in Michigan the sex ratio was 96 males per 100 females, in sharp contrast with the ratio in the 1920s. These changes reflected steadier employment, more permanent residence, and more stable households.[36]

Though they were largely a working-class population, midwestern Mexicans' employment experiences varied by gender and place of residence, evident in late-1940s studies of Minneapolis and St. Paul. In the former, among adult Mexican men, 11 percent did not have an occupation, 4 percent were unemployed, 49 percent were unskilled laborers (unspecified), 6 percent were skilled workers, 17 percent were foundry workers (largely unskilled), and the remaining 13 percent were scattered in a handful of occupations. According to the St. Paul report, 41 percent were employed in packinghouses, 11 percent on the railroads, 7 percent in textile mills, and 24 percent in sugar beets. Although the sugar beet industry remained an important employer for many West Side families through the 1940s, packinghouse work became more important. The report suggested that "in their employment with the packinghouses, the Mexicans for the first time had steady and lucrative work." Its notion of "steady" was fairly clear: "employment is considered permanent although dependent upon seasonal livestock receipts." A plant worker in the late 1940s could expect more than two thousand hours of employment per year, or a working week that averaged forty to forty-five hours over the entire year. The point of reference for "lucrative" was deceptively linked to the implicit alternative of the sugar beet fields, still represented as Mexican working space.[37]

Dominant bourgeois culture did not apply similar notions of lucre to itself, which could be attained as a result of inheritance, capital investments, land ownership, or having attained professions or entrepreneurial occupations, which were not realistic expectations for former beet workers. Despite their improved economic standing, expectations of wealth, success, and the American Dream continued to be posited in double standards for Mexicans and European Americans in the mid-twentieth-century Midwest.

During the war, many contemporaries expected that the entry of women into full-time wage labor would be permanent. As one St. Paul report suggested, younger Mexicanas "said they intended to continue working when their husbands returned." Their motives transcended economic factors, as Arturo Rosales and Daniel Simon concluded in their study of East Chicago, for the status of women who joined the military or worked in the steel mills increased within their own families. Yet assumptions of permanence were premature, as a 1947 survey of Minneapolis reported that 52 percent did not seek employment outside the home, 23 percent were unemployed, and only 25 percent were wage earners.[38] A majority of Mexicanas quickly left the factories once the war ended, although many remained. They were increasingly perceived as unnecessary once their male counterparts returned home, and the cult of domesticity again justified their exclusion from industrial employment, regardless of ethnic and class backgrounds.

For women who continued to work outside the home, a double wage standard prevailed. In 1947, entry-level wages for men at Swift in St. Paul were 96 cents per hour, but for women only 85.5 cents. Patterns of employment for women also varied by location, as confirmed by surveys of the Twin Cities in the late 1940s. In Minneapolis, 36 percent were employed in factories and shops, while 64 percent were laundry workers or domestic servants. In St. Paul, 56 percent of wage-earning Mexicanas worked in packinghouses, 20 percent in textile mills, with the remaining 24 percent in miscellaneous occupations.[39] Thus the packinghouses and textile factories of St. Paul offered Mexicanas greater opportunities for industrial employment than largely commercial Minneapolis, where they were more restricted to domestic tasks.

Formal surveys of the period typically underreported the extent of wage-earning employment among women because domestic work was often erratic or part-time, and typically considered temporary. Yet many Mexicanas discovered, even in industrial settings like St. Paul, that "housework was the only thing available." Such underreporting was likely because it contradicted a contemporary bourgeois domestic ideal reluctant to acknowledge that women had to work outside the home for survival. Francisco (Kiko) Rangel recalled growing up in St. Paul in the 1940s and 1950s: "I know my mother used to take care of the home, do the grocery shopping, scrub the floors, and clean the house for the Jewish families. A lot of people used to do that."[40] Such jobs were easier to reconcile with then-current dominant notions of women's proper places than was employment in shops and factories.

After the war ended, the cult of domesticity became more deeply entrenched, as the arrangement between labor and capital, accompanied by a lively economy, permitted a realistic expectation that wages for one factory worker could support a nuclear family above the poverty level. A 1958–1959 survey of Mexican families in Minneapolis and St. Paul found that only 25 percent of married women were employed outside the home, whether they were born in Mexico or the United States. Women of the second generation all reported having been employed for wages at some time after marriage, compared with only 44 percent of the older women. A 1971 survey found that 79 percent of adult Mexicanas were not employed for wages, although only 34 percent had never worked outside the home. The same year, a study of Waukesha, Wisconsin, reported that 85 percent of Mexicanas identified as housewives and not wage earners.

A notable difference between the two generations was that younger married women were not discouraged from working until their children were born. Yet it is also possible that older women failed to consider employment as *betabeleras* as wage labor, consistent with employer definitions that counted only their husbands. In comparison with the older generation, younger women were employed in a slightly greater range of jobs, particularly in higher-status factory employment. This suggests that the entrance of women into the wage labor force was not a linear process over the course of the twentieth century. Presumed assimilation into the U.S. American way of life and the acquisition of English language skills for the younger women did not necessarily bring them into the wage labor force permanently. Mexicanas did not stay out of wage labor because of "traditional" Mexican values, but rather because of a contemporary bourgeois ideal which transcended cultural, ethnic, and national boundaries, along with relatively higher wages and more stable employment of their husbands than in earlier or later generations.[41]

Women recognized phases in the life cycle when they could expect to work outside the home, as Sra. Irene Rivera clearly recalled. When her family moved from Texas to St. Paul, she quickly found employment in the nearby Cudahy packing plant, "but I had to quit when I got married, because he didn't like a working wife. At that time, he thought the wife had to stay home and take care of the children." In East Chicago, in the mid-1960s, Julián Samora and Richard Lamanna reported that 25 percent of adult females living in the densely concentrated Mexican neighborhoods engaged in wage employment, compared with 36 percent living outside of them. They concluded that "this pattern appears to reflect traditional cultural definitions of the role of women, as well as the paucity of employment opportunities for women in a community dominated by heavy industry." As Jesús Patlán, who grew up in Mexico City, recalled, in Mexico at the time, "it was unheard of for a married woman to work [outside the home]," a statement that did not hold up well among the very poor.[42] Yet as women's employment experience in those same factories during World War II attests, opportunities in the United States declined only after the war ended. Simultaneously, women in the home continued to engage in necessary domestic production and reproduction, as child care and similar facilities for working women were not widely available. In effect, the postwar U.S. American bourgeois dream meshed comfortably with ostensibly "traditional" Mexican middle-class values to discourage married women from wage employment.

Many Mexicanas, particularly the poorest, could not afford the luxury of removing themselves from wage labor, as Sra. Felicitas Herrera recalled. Migrating with her parents to Texas, she worked for many years in the cotton fields until recruited to the Minnesota beet fields. She settled with her family in St. Paul in 1932, and although her spouse died, she soon remarried. With her second husband she continued to work in the beet fields, departing St. Paul each spring and returning in the fall, until she found employment in 1945 at the Swift meatpacking plant, where she was employed until the operation closed in 1969. Despite her long residence in the United States, she never attended school, either in the United States or in Mexico, and did not learn English, asserting that "my father did not believe that girls should go to school." She was unaware that her employment in the cotton and sugar beet fields was also predicated on the unequal enforcement of mandatory school attendance laws in both Texas and Minnesota. Yet she was a versatile and highly skilled worker who learned a wide range of tasks in the packinghouse: "I cut meat, packed pigs feet in jars, turned smoked hams and worked with frozen meats without knowing any English. . . . I learned to operate some very complicated machinery. . . . What I did learn was to watch someone else do it and then I would be able to do it in my turn."[43] Working in factories thus did not necessarily require English language assimilation, even in cities like St. Paul.

Mexicanas were also restricted from several job categories dominated by European American women. A young Mexicana portrayed as very bright wanted to work as a waitress but was discouraged by her social worker, who felt she "should not train for waitress work because she would have such a slight chance for steady employment in that field" due to the abundance of "American waitresses. Worker felt that if she trained as a housemaid she would have more opportunities for employment." The dean of Mechanic Arts High School, which she attended, concurred that "it was a very poor arrangement to have Mexican girls train for waitresses as after they had finished their training, there would be no jobs for them." Another Mexicana graduate of Mechanic Arts enrolled in and graduated from a six-month course in typing and shorthand, and passed an exam for Minnesota State Employment with a very high score. For three years she tried to find employment in the field in which she had trained, but her social worker confirmed that "it was impossible for her to get office work," ostensibly because she lacked experience. Secretarial work, like waitressing, was a job classification reserved for White (articulated in dominant popular culture as American) and not Mexican women.[44]

Whether or not they worked in "public" settings, Mexicanas were perceived as making decisions in the "private" realm. There was little difference between generations, the 1958–1959 Twin Cities surveys found, as women were always responsible for domestic chores and their spouses were not. In both age groups, 80 percent of women reported making shared decisions with their husbands on matters pertaining to the family. Sra. Felicitas Herrera recalled that when she was first widowed, she took on the tasks of both male and female household head, until she remarried, when "I was again under the obligations of my husband" and responsible for cooking, cleaning the house, and washing his clothes. Although she and her second husband found employment in the same factory, she was expected to care for his household needs until he died, she recalled, "so I never really knew what it was like to be free until now."[45]

Improved employment conditions for Mexicans in the urban Midwest were the result of exceptional economic conditions during World War II and the postwar economic boom as well as the agreement between capitalists and workers that permitted more stable industrial employment for men. Yet their upward job mobility was confined almost entirely to semiskilled, unskilled and menial labor. In St. Paul, Mexican men continued to work mostly in shops, small factories, and warehouses, with their largest concentration still in the meatpacking plants. According to a 1971 survey of prior jobs held by adult male Mexicans, 6 percent were skilled, 13 percent semiskilled, and 80 percent unskilled. A miniscule number were employed as professionals, managers, technicians, and kindred workers. As sociologist Terry Caine reported, it was "best characterized as a working class community."[46]

Similarly, a Waukesha study found that between 1947 and 1971 there were only modest changes in Mexican male employment, as the number of laborers and operatives declined from 95 percent to 80 percent, while those in clerical-sales, foremen-craftsmen, and those in service positions increased from 4 percent to 15 percent. Yet as the study of Julián Samora and Richard Lamanna found, even Eastern Europeans, "who arrived only a little earlier than the Mexicans in East Chicago but who also had a language problem, have apparently done so much better in achieving higher status jobs." Limited opportunities for Mexicans were similarly confirmed by occupational clustering in most settings. The majority of men continued to work for the railroads of Kansas; the packinghouses of St. Paul and the Stockyards district of Chicago; the steel mills of South Chicago, East Chicago, and Gary; and the foundries and automobile plants of Michigan and northwest Ohio. As in St. Paul, they were universally underrepresented in technical, managerial, and clerical positions and overrepresented as unskilled operatives. Mexicans in the Midwest experienced a much slower assimilation into the industrial working class than Europeans.[47]

Within the middle classes, a detailed 1946 study found that the only Mexican professional in St. Paul was an engineer who had been trained in Mexico, and the only person independently engaged in business was a junk dealer. A single restaurant and tortillería, La Casa Coronado, operated for many years by Sra. Vera Coronado and her husband, Arturo, first opened in 1938. The person hired to prepare food, Sr. Bravo, reportedly "wasn't too good of a cook," and the operation soon folded. When it reopened six months later, Sra. Coronado was head cook and maintained it in the same location for more than two decades. Upward mobility was limited; a study of East Chicago in the 1960s confirmed, "a business class has been slow to develop, and it is still fairly novel to find Mexican-Americans even in the lower white-collar positions." The businesses were mostly "small, marginal family dominated affairs of rather limited economic significance," particularly grocery stores, meat markets, and similar businesses that faced severe competition from corporate-owned operations. Furthermore, the major early-twentieth-century businesses, *casas de asistencia* and pool rooms, geared toward single males, had practically vanished. A modest range of businesses appeared in Chicago, including bookstores with Mexican newspapers and magazines, radio and phonograph shops, butcher shops, tortilla factories, tailoring and cleaning shops, laundries, shoe repair shops, and barber and beauty shops, all operating "on a small scale" for local clientele. In several cities, a movie house or two began to show films in Spanish, although few had Mexican owners. Even in Chicago, Mexicans rarely entered the professions, and it was reported that "almost none are to be found in public services" as police officers, fire fighters, schoolteachers, or social workers.[48]

In St. Paul, European Americans controlled barrio businesses and professional activities. The grocery stores Sres. Zamora and Garzón owned in the 1920s had disappeared, and for many years, there was not a single Mexican-owned store in the barrio. As Francisco (Kiko) Rangel recalled, "we had Jewish stores. We didn't have any Mexican stores." Demographic factors could in part explain the decline in restaurants between the 1920s and 1950s, notably that earlier there had been a much higher proportion of single males less inclined to cook their own meals. A simple demographic argument might also suggest that the growing population would have created a demand for Mexican grocery stores, which did not occur. A contrary argument would suggest that demographic and occupational conditions were interrelated, and stable male employment in the 1950s was predicated on the presence of women who remained at home to prepare food. The restriction of midwestern Mexicans to working-class jobs was more extreme than in the Southwest. Sociologist Milton Gordon, a proponent of cultural pluralism, acknowledged that even in the Southwest, Mexicans achieved middle-class occupations very slowly, "an unmistakable sign of a retardation in the acculturation process." Yet the small midwestern Mexican middle class, much more than its African American counterpart, tended to live in European American sections of the city, apart from the working-class barrios. In Chicago, a higher proportion of Mexican males and a lower proportion of females worked than their European American counterparts. By 1969 labor force participation reached 81 percent for Latino males; compared with 76 percent for White males, 11 percent for Latinas, and 17 percent for White women. Median earnings for Latino males were 80 percent of those of White males, compared with 60 percent for White females and 51 percent for Latinas. As a Chicago study concluded, Mexicans' "relative economic position changed very little in the period 1930–1960."[49]

A widespread contemporary explanation for continuing inequality was that among Mexicans "the greater majority will continue their particularized culture of poverty for years to come." Midwestern scholars adopted "culture of poverty" arguments, aware of contradictory "demands for assimilation and conformity" by Anglos. A St. Paul report asserted that many young Mexican war veterans entered packinghouses because they preferred the immediate prospect of higher earnings in lieu of spending time to learn a trade. Consistent with cultural deficiency theories of the day, it blamed Mexicans for short-term planning while failing to consider systemic barriers to entering the trades, notably overt discrimination by employers and resistance by entrenched skilled tradesmen. Even the Cudahy packing plant at 91st and Baltimore, in the heart of the South Chicago barrio, did not have any Mexican employees. Frank X. Paz complained that Mexican employment in low-paying track maintenance "is where we seem to have the God-given right to employment in the railroad industry," while Mexicans were practically absent from higher-skilled jobs like those of engineers, brakemen, conductors, firemen, and switchmen. In steel, Mexicans were concentrated in the coke pits, blast furnaces, and scrap yards, and few could obtain skilled work as electricians, steam fitters, machinists, millwrights, or carpenters. When Paul Márquez, a Navy veteran and native of South Omaha, used the G.I. Bill to enter an apprenticeship to learn the skill of upholstery, the boss "continually yelled and tried to intimidate him, forcing him to quit," so he found employment in a local packinghouse. Paz asked rhetorically, "when a group of people are branded for employment only in one particular task there is something radically wrong. . . . Where is the equality of opportunity? Where is the American way of life?"[50]

Employment options for Mexicans in the urban Midwest during the middle of the twentieth century, while somewhat greater in range than earlier, remained quite limited. In Toledo, as a resident originally from Texas noted, "the jobs were jobs nobody wanted," clustered in occupations like railroads and foundries, where Mexicans were invisible. "You wouldn't dare drive a taxi. They wouldn't get in a car with you. . . . I don't ever remember seeing Mexicans in public." The "glass ceiling" restricting entry into the skilled trades, white-collar employment, and the professions was even more impenetrable than in the Southwest. In the latter the work experienced was more varied, and most communities had a small but visible Mexican population of small business operators, doctors, lawyers, other professionals, and in some locations, small farmers. An earlier Mexican presence in the Southwest, which included a landowning and professional class who were partly but not entirely dispossessed in the late nineteenth century, provided a base for organizing and modest upward social mobility in the twentieth century. By contrast, the earliest Mexicanos in the Midwest entered the region only to perform menial labor, lacking the collective experience or resources of established farmers, professionals, or politicians. Limited attitudinal assimilation by the majority population restricted their ascent into the middle class, and many talented midwestern Mexicanos, like Sr. Reymundo Cárdenas, of Adrian, Michigan, vividly recalled growing up in the 1940s and 1950s: "it was a terrible feeling for a youngster to experience. I was supposed to be different." Whether they were long-established residents, children born in the region, or more recent arrivals, their experience was limited to working-class life, and they were "given the hardest, lowest, and most unskilled jobs in the factory." Such employment did offer greater stability than before, and as Sr. Saucedo acknowledged, "they were good solid workers."[51]

## Dilemmas of Americanism

The lively academic and popular discourse on inequality and Americanism of the era included the work of sociologist Gunnar Myrdal, *An Ameri-*

*can Dilemma.* He emphasized structural bias, or unequal power, including ideology between White and non-White people that maintained inequality. The view challenged earlier liberal accounts including that of Paul Taylor, who predicted that in spite of prejudice and discrimination, Mexicans in the Midwest would assimilate. Consistent with Myrdal, a 1946 St. Paul International Institute study asserted that "the greatest problem of all lies within ourselves and will continue to do so as long as the dominant group clings to the stereotyped estimate of the 'dirty, lazy Mexican.'" The shift in focus represented a rift in liberal discourse. Meanwhile, conservatives maintained views of Mexicans as lazy and backward, often expressed less harshly, as in the words of University of Wisconsin Professor George W. Hill, who wrote in 1948 that the Mexican "knows he should work too . . . [but] their lives run at a much slower speed than do ours."[52]

This section will examine Americanization and Mexicans in the Midwest during the 1940s and 1950s, focusing first on Americanization rhetoric in popular culture. It then turns to institutional efforts to create midwestern Mexican Americans, particularly in the public schools, and institutional success in overcoming inequality. Finally, it explores Mexicans' own actions and institutional presence in the region.

Proponents of formal Americanization projects continued to debate meanings and methods to achieve their ends on somewhat different grounds than did their predecessors. Alice Sickels, head of the International Institute of St. Paul from 1931 to 1944, observed that agencies responsible for Americanization in the 1920s almost without exception believed that the sooner that an individual repudiated the native country, "the better 'American' he [*sic*] would become." She claimed that there were exceptions, including the International Institute, the Neighborhood House, "and a few individual seers," typically academics or artists, who "stood out alone for an entirely different conception of assimilation." She suggested that "the idea that the alien must be emptied inside and out of all vestiges of 'foreignness' and then filled up and dressed up with Early American patterns (adapted largely from England) gave way gradually to the melting pot idea. All the diverse peoples would be melted together into a mass and poured out into new molds." It would produce a unique country, "but with all the individuals looking and acting very much alike, a homogeneous nation. The melting pot idea, however, has not worked out too well either." She considered it necessary for immigrants to accept but also "[be] accepted by" residents and dominant institutions in the United States. Her vision "favored the idea of the symphony orchestra which recognizes great diversity in our backgrounds, encourages each group and individual to express what is best for himself [*sic*] but demands absolute loyalty to fundamental laws which will make for harmony in this nation." Challenging Anglo-conformist and melting-pot ideology, such a cultural pluralist approach permitted spaces for immigrants, particularly by encouraging them to promote their own folk arts and a revival of the "Old World." In practical terms, it allowed Mexicans to learn Mexican folk music and dancing, arts and crafts, and to participate in the Festival of Nations. There were arranged integrated settings, including YWCA day camps, where Mexican girls sang folk songs, offering them recognition, entertainment, and education.[53]

Yet Sickels's vision was anathema to more conservative midwestern teachers, social workers, and priests, who continued to express fear and disdain toward minorities and wished for an idealized society akin to "100 percent Americanisim." Anti-Mexican attitudes and hostility were deeply embedded in dominant culture, evident in a 1958 survey of Toledo teachers, one of whom stated that "whenever I see a group of Mexican people, I am rather afraid of them, and I am always glad to be at a distance from them." Another asserted, "I feel that they want to harm white people, in spite of the fact that I can't think of a time when I have read in the paper or heard in the news that they have harmed us in any way." Another teacher confirmed the prevalence of negative stereotypes: "we think of them as being inferior to us because of their color." Another stated: "I believe that generally when people in this area think of Mexican people, they think of lazy, dirty and quite irresponsible people." School officials blamed Mexican parents for having little regard for the education of their children, including a St. Paul principal who asserted, "unlike the mothers of other immigrant groups, they do not seem to appreciate the value of schooling for their children. Ignorant themselves, they care little whether their children learn anything." Investigators reported that in Grand Rapids, Michigan, "often teachers advise Mexican-American children to drop out of school because they believe that the Mexican-Americans cannot compete with other students." Such attitudes confirmed Mexican parents' complaints that their children often missed school "because they are not wanted."[54]

Mexican cultural spaces in institutional settings were dependent on the whims of the Europeans and European Americans who controlled them. Detroit Archbishop Edward Moody (1937–1958) initiated a conscious and public effort to repress Mexican culture. Early in his tenure, he presided over the closing of Nuestra Señora de Guadalupe, and despite frequent pleas he refused to permit parishioners to construct another national church or to engage in any Mexican religious or cultural functions under church auspices, claiming that such activities would impede Americanization. Furthermore, the archbishop demanded that "no racial or nationality distinction be made toward the Mexican. He absolutely forbids the priests giving any encouragement to the idea of a church especially for Mexicans, and this applies to other organizations, religious or otherwise." Saginaw priest Peter T. Feixa concurred: "churches for Mexicans would tend to segregate them."[55]

Yet suppression of Mexican cultural activities was not absolute, for there were differences of opinion among Americanizers over the best route to assimilation. Many church leaders disagreed with Archbishop Moody and suggested that if Mexicans were allowed to worship together and celebrate their own cultural activities, mutual tolerance would be enhanced, and they would identify more strongly with the United States. In Gary, after the Mexican Catholic Church burned in 1939, the new pastor worked vigorously to construct a new national church. In other places, including Toledo, church policy was inconsistent. Msgr. Gorman, Mexican parish priest from 1930 to 1951, was selectively sympathetic toward Mexican culture. He presided over the opening of the Guadalupe Center in the heart of the South Side barrio, holding masses and celebrating fiestas and Mexican dramas that Msgr. Gorman himself wrote. Simultaneously he encouraged assimilation by "regularizing" the Mexican folk Catholicism of the parishioners by adopting "universalistic" (in other words, European) practices. He was replaced by the "strongly assimilationist" Father James F. Southard, who held the post in the 1950s and 1960s. Asserting that "I just can't take the wildness," the new priest limited the fiesta cycle and secular activities to December 12 and July 26, the latter being the fiesta of St. James, his own Saint's Day. Contrasting his own "very tidy" behavior with the parishioners' ostensibly slovenly ways, he considered Mexicans as incapable of providing their own leadership. He dictated changes within the parish and "made it difficult for children growing up during his reign to learn appropriate sentiments when symbols of Mexican identity were presented to them."[56]

Parishioners often challenged efforts to eliminate Mexican cultural expressions within the church. In the case of Archbishop Moody, as professors Gumecindo Salas and Isabel Salas concluded, "the power of the Archbishop failed. It did not destroy the language and culture of a people determined to remain *mejicanos*." In other churches, where the hierarchy was more sympathetic, as in St. Paul, parishioners were permitted to use church facilities for social and cultural activities, and priests supported many activities that maintained and enriched the Mexican church and cultural traditions. Father Ward of St. Paul sought to maintain close relations, residing in a humble walk-up flat above the church, which he used as both his home and office, allowing him to mingle with parishioners. An obituary noted that he was "sensitive to the dignity of people. He was never condescending. He did not speak of 'his people.'"[57]

Differences between Alice Sickels or the St. Paul priests on the one hand and those like Archbishop Moody on the other obscured many essential similarities. The symphony of Sickels's imagery was no less a top-down imposition than Moody's closing of Detroit's Mexican parish. While the archbishop demanded conformity with Anglo practices, the progressives and liberals demanded "absolute loyalty" to the European traditions of the composers and conductors of their texts, while the Mexicans who produced the music were simply expected to play second fiddle. Neither Sickels nor Horace Kallen distinguished Europe from Mexico. Neither recognized that Mexicans had deep roots in the Americas, long before the composers, the conductors, and their ancestors who were trying to "Americanize" them had departed from their "Old World" in search of land, labor, souls, and other material and spiritual riches.

Assimilationists who expected Mexicans to make themselves into Europeans similarly failed to acknowledge the political and economic contexts that distinguished migration to the United States from Mexico and Europe. While the migrations originated in poorer countries, the scale of the mass movement from Europe dwindled as the economic gap narrowed and perceptions by Europeans of the United States as a land of opportunity declined. In contrast, the economic distance between Mexico and the United States widened during the course of the nineteenth century, and the political context of international relations ensured that Mexicans would be available to perform low-wage labor in the foreseeable future.

The reception of immigrants from the two continents also differed. The earliest Mexican arrivals to the Midwest were represented in dominant popular culture as poor, humble workers hired for temporary railroad or sugar beet field employment. Europeans also were portrayed as poor but were accepted as permanent residents, potential landowners, and ultimate citizens expected to participate in electoral democracy. Mexicans did establish roots in the region but were confined to a handful of the shabbiest and poorest neighborhoods, while European groups were not uniformly isolated in the slums and they quickly dispersed. Furthermore, portrayals of Mexicans as foreigners did not cease, unlike those of Europeans. As sociologist Norman Humphrey observed in Detroit, "the stereotype of the Mexican as non-citizen is popularly so strong that when a *naturalized* Mexican was recently laid off, the unquestioned assumption was that he was not a citizen." Even the children and grandchildren of Mexican immigrants, though born and reared in the United States, were commonly portrayed as foreigners.[58]

Class differences between the Americanizers and Americanizing Mexicans were also evident in treatment by the former of Mexicans as workers. The women who headed the settlement houses, the International Institute, Catholic Church groups, and the PTA, often under the guise of offering spiritual help, education, and assistance, individually and collectively exploited cheap Mexican labor. They hired Mexican women to perform cooking, cleaning, ironing, childcare, and other domestic tasks for them in public settings and their private homes. Mexicanas prepared and served meals for gatherings of women's groups, including the International Institute's Maintenance Committee. They cleaned houses and cooked for the chair of the Institute's Foreign-Born Women's club and for her relatives. The head of the Mexican Committee of the International Institute reported that the Mexicana she hired to clean her house and iron was doing "very satisfactory work." Another International Institute social worker sought out the "names of outstanding women" in the Roosevelt PTA and the West Side PTA, as she had "promised to try to help" find work for a young Mexicana to perform domestic chores. The middle-class agents of Americanization assumed that their Mexican clients had a future as unskilled and domestic workers and hired them for their own personal benefit.[59]

Meanwhile, agency staff and professionals rarely sought to include Mexicans among their own leadership. One exception was the Chicago Area Project (CAP), a nonprofit organization created in 1934 to promote grassroots voices and influence in poor urban neighborhoods. CAP efforts to encourage Mexican empowerment, including a leadership program it devised on the Near West Side, were often frustrated by "limited finances" and lack of support from other organizations. A more promising CAP project, the Mexican Civic Committee, appeared in 1943. With offices on Blue Island Avenue, it dealt with neighborhood concerns and offered a place for adult and youth groups to meet and engage in craft, recreational, and social activities. The committee stood apart from the settlement houses, agencies, and the Catholic Church by virtue of its community-based Mexican leadership, largely voluntary, and its self-help philosophy. According to Activities Director Rafael Pérez, "our work has become a community project, where we can draw from the best for an unselfish purpose." The committee also addressed emergency needs, including assistance to farmworkers in the area.[60]

In 1951 CAP formed the Mexican American Council, operating out of

Hull House, which represented the only citywide, self-directed, self-supported organization explicitly focusing on the betterment of Mexicans in Chicago. The council also addressed issues of discrimination and the lack of upward mobility of Mexicans in industry, and it became involved in civil rights cases, including the killing of two Mexican youth by Chicago police officer Mike Morietty. Its closest allies were the settlement houses, which, as Louise Año Nuevo Kerr notes, were "always more sympathetic to Chicanos than other Chicago institutions." Yet even settlement houses maintained paternalistic relations with Mexicans and excluded them from leadership positions, and, as Paz noted in 1949, no Chicago Mexicans had ever been members of their boards of directors.[61]

Criticism and challenges of the power wielded by the agents of Americanization came not only from visible community leaders but also from clients. A Mexicana from St. Paul, sixteen years old, defied social workers who tried to separate her mother from the children after her father died. The social workers claimed of the mother that "it might be beyond her capacities" to care for them because of low scores on mental tests. But the daughter felt herself capable, despite the opposition of social workers, who complained that her "impertinence and attitude was causing a great deal of trouble. . . . She has too much influence over her mother and is uncooperative . . . [and] she hates housework." In seeking to discredit her, they urged her school principal to issue a negative behavior report but were frustrated that he had "no complaints whatsoever" about her comportment or grades in school. While they tried to devise an alternative plan to involve her in recreational activities that would "distract her entire attention on her family," she successfully kept her mother and siblings together. St. Paul social workers particularly resented Mexicans who considered themselves equal, and one was angered by a Mexicana in her early twenties, "intelligent and well groomed, [who] carried with her a defiant attitude. She is a demonstrator and saleswoman for Park & Tilford cosmetics and seems inordinately proud of the fact. Worker found out later she distrusts the social workers and any others outside the Mexican group, characterizing as hypocritical and morbid curiosity any interest they may show in their welfare."[62]

Americanization programs involving midwestern Mexicans stood apart in some ways from those examined by historians of Mexicans in California and Texas. First, the midwestern programs began in the late nineteenth and early twentieth centuries originally for European immigrants, and they continued beyond the end of World War II. The southwestern projects typically started around the time of World War I, often focusing only on Mexicans. Many collapsed with the onset of the Great Depression, and some were later resuscitated. Second, the midwestern programs exhibited a range of philosophical positions, in part stemming from their long involvement with European immigrants, while those in the Southwest were more often predicated on a philosophy of Anglo-conformity. In the midwest, the concept of an American identity among European Americans was much more contested in theory and in practice, just as Anglo and Mexican American notions of being American were often at odds.[63]

Despite the impact of cultural pluralist institutional thought in the Midwest, demands for conformity to a unitary vision of the United States of America intensified during World War II and the Cold War. Furthermore, Americanization meant much more than resolving the ambiguities of individual identity and the angst of uncertainty. Conservatives shaped the Naturalization Act of 1940, the Immigration Act of 1952, and other laws that pressured Mexicans who were not U.S. citizens to take loyalty oaths, and they convinced private and public employers to demand citizenship as a condition of employment. Anglo-conformist pressures, legislation, and representations in popular culture narrowed employment options for Mexicans in comparison with those for European immigrants earlier in the century, while they cast suspicion on the citizenship status of all Mexicans.

Institutional Americanization in midwestern schools intensified as Mexican attendance increased. In St. Paul, it was reported that "the steady employment of the war years has made it possible for the children to remain throughout the school year." In the public schools of Dodge City, Kansas, Congressional Representative Clifford R. Hope proudly noted that Mexican boys and girls "keep right up with the white children and some of them are even in the high schools," acknowledging that despite similar capacities the two experienced different group outcomes. Among Mexicans, differences in school achievement by gender contradicted popular impressions and occasional individual cases that Mexican culture discouraged schooling for girls. In the mid 1940s in Detroit, few Mexicans had completed the equivalent of elementary school, and while boys averaged four years, girls averaged five years. In Chicago, Mexican girls graduated from high school more frequently than did boys. Paz attributed the differences not to culture but rather to job opportunities, for female high school graduates sometimes might find employment as office workers, but options for males did not improve on graduation.[64]

As Mexicans were aware of the limited rewards of schooling, their enrollment and graduation rates in Chicago declined in the 1940s and early

1950s despite the rapid growth of the school-age population. In 1946, 23 percent of the city's Mexican children of school age were not attending school, which indicated continued unequal enforcement of the law by truant officers and school officials. In general, most midwestern Mexican youth completed elementary school and dropped out during junior high. It was an improvement compared with an earlier generation and reflected steadier employment for parents as well as sugar beet company policies of recruiting workers from Texas, which "has made it possible for the children [in Minnesota] to remain throughout the school year." By 1960, European Americans in Milwaukee aged fourteen to twenty-four completed an average of 11.3 years of schooling, compared with 9.2 years for Mexican Americans. By 1970 Chicago Latinos had completed a median of 8.7 years of schooling, compared with non-Latinos, who still averaged 11.3 years. School attendance and grade completion rates increased in the late 1950s and 1960s, but a substantial gap with European Americans remained.[65]

Poor school records were also due in part to institutional factors, including a lack of role models in the classroom, the policy of student tracking, and curricular offerings that either neglected or explicitly denigrated Mexican culture. In Lansing, Michigan, a teacher chastised a youth's interpretation of the 1836 Battle of the Alamo as a Mexican victory. When the father protested to the teacher and the superintendent, the latter responded, "You know and I know what happened, but this is not what we teach in this school." In St. Paul, one of the few Mexican graduates of the West Side's Humboldt High in the 1940s, Sra. Dionisia Cárdenas Coates, recalled that "most of the Mexican kids who were my age went to Mechanic Arts High School (if they attended high school at all). So, I did feel isolated. I never went to any of the games or anything like that. . . . I felt that had there been more Mexican kids in my class, it would have been a little easier." She also observed that even when one tried to imitate the manners of Anglo youth and spoke English like them, "you are going to know that you are different. You aren't going to understand what makes you different. . . . the schools never taught us what the Mexican American contributed to the society. . . . We were ashamed to be different." Sr. Frank Guzmán, who also attended public schools in St. Paul, similarly acknowledged, "I was ashamed in my youth to be Mexican and I knew I was different but I didn't know why."[66]

School administrators and teachers adopted policies of tracking Mexican children into vocational schools and classes, but other factors also pushed them in that direction. In St. Paul, Sra. Juanita Morán, who completed junior high at Roosevelt, initially attended Humboldt, the nearest high school. It did not offer courses in Spanish as she desired, so she appealed for permission to attend Mechanic Arts, and she was pleased because it enrolled more Mexican students. When she later learned more about how the public schools functioned, Sra. Cárdenas Coates realized that Mexican parents, who were also taxpayers, "entrusted the school district with the education of their kids, and their kids were getting the worst education possible." Yet many educators blamed the low participation rates on "Mexican parents [who] are slow in taking part in school affairs." Isolation, tracking, low expectations, and teacher criticism of parents' values, an East Chicago report concluded, meant that Mexicans "faced a form of racial discrimination to which many Europeans were not subjected."[67]

Gaps between Mexicans and European Americans were much greater in higher education, and not a single person from the St. Paul colonia, with more than three thousand inhabitants, entered college until 1941. The first was a young woman who attended Duluth State Teacher's College (later the University of Minnesota–Duluth). To support herself while attending classes, she worked in domestic employment and in agricultural labor in the summer. A social worker considered her case critical to Americanization, asserting that she "has contributions to make necessary to the assimilations of Mexicans in the United States." Although she adjusted quickly to school, she wrote of a number of problems, including "having people pronounce my name." Her achievement was unusual. Beyond a handful of war veterans who took advantage of the G.I. Bill, few Mexicans attended the region's colleges or universities, and as Frank Paz noted, they were "engulfed by economic and social pressures." By 1960, more than 40 percent of all Michiganians between ages seventeen and twenty-four attended postsecondary educational institutions, compared with only 7 percent of its Mexicans. Low school achievement records limited opportunities among Mexicans to attain skilled positions, the professions, and employment in larger factories, which increasingly used written examinations in English to screen job applicants. Mexicans' continuation in school was further discouraged because occupational rewards for comparable achievement were less than those for European American youth.[68]

The public schools had a more limited impact on the assimilation of adults, a 1944 study reported: "There are very few Mexicans in Detroit who have the equivalent of an elementary school education, and fewer still with any secondary schooling. Complete illiteracy is common." A 1946 survey found that 40 percent of adult Mexicans in St. Paul were literate in Spanish, 31 percent in English, and 28 percent were illiterate. Almost all had been in the country more than twenty years, yet few ever attended its public schools, and their working experiences in the fields and factories offered few inducements to read or write in English.[69]

Mexican children retained the language of their parents "more than children of other foreign extractions," Norman Humphrey observed. As school attendance became the norm, they quickly acquired English reading and writing skills. Texas-born Manuel Beserra, who spoke only Spanish at home, moved with his parents to South Bend when he was very young, and enrolled in the public schools, recalled, "I learned English right away." A 1959 survey found that 88 percent of first-generation and 68 percent of second-generation Mexicans in St. Paul spoke Spanish at home, while 76 percent of the first generation and 48 percent of the second generation used Spanish at work. It also reported that 92 percent of parents of the second generation thought that Mexican children should learn Spanish, although opportunities for instruction outside the home were rare.[70]

The disciplinary record of the region's Mexicanos stood in sharp contrast to their scholastic achievement. A St. Paul school report observed that "Mexican children are respectful, amenable to discipline and cooperative," while another stated: "Mexican children present negligible disciplinary problems at any age. They are described as polite, co-operative and amenable to all helpful suggestion." While their conduct suggested ideal conditions for schooling, it was often misinterpreted by educators who adhered to contemporary cultural deficiency theories and preferred to suggest that they were ignorant and passive and deferred to others' authority.[71]

Mexicans' discipline and respect for the knowledge of elders was taught at home by parents, not in school, as Sra. Irene Rivera explained. Born in 1910 in Marathon, Texas, of parents born in Mexico, she accompanied her mother to Minnesota in 1925, after her father died, to join a sister who had already moved to St. Paul. Sra. Rivera emphasized that children "obeyed their parents. That's what good training did." She lamented changes taking place: "it's different now . . . [because youth] . . . go according to the American way. They do have dates and go to the prom. . . . You don't see the strict parents anymore." She suggested that such behavior reflected the breaking down of Mexican cultural patterns: "I'd say that the older generation is proud of its nationality, of being Mexicans. It's an honor for the old people that they did not force the Americans to show them appreciation. I had to figure out for myself how to survive in the United States and what was most useful was for me to teach my family that they were Mexicans blood and heart."[72]

Their classroom comportment suggests that Mexican children had not yet assimilated the individualistic and sometimes rude manners widespread among their European American classmates. Some critics have suggested that Mexicans were being trained to be polite, cooperative workers who followed directions without complaint rather than display imagination or individualism. Institutional expectations, they argue, differed for White middle-class youth, who were being prepared for higher education, careers in the professions, and other positions where they gave orders to compliant Mexicans.[73]

In their barrios, as Msgr. Clement Kern of Detroit observed, Mexican youth "didn't know about discrimination," but beyond those confines, they faced an array of problems, starting with school. Sr. Federico Saucedo, born on St. Paul's West Side in 1934, left his neighborhood to attend Central High School in the late 1940s and early 1950s to be closer to work after classes. He recalled: "while I was at Central, I became aware of the fact that there were different classifications of people. I found my first experience of being a minority, of being different. People dressed different, they had better clothes, they had cars, all the kids were better educated than from the area where I was from. It was difficult holding a conversation with them. . . . I didn't feel comfortable at all." Mexican children who moved to the East Side of St. Paul only rarely attended the nearby Capitol Community Center, where they felt "reluctant to participate in the activities because of the feeling of non-acceptance by earlier Italian residents." A young Mexican girl whose family had moved to the East Side in 1945, was initially "happy about going" to the Lincoln school, but "she was being tormented by one of her blond classmates, who pulled her hair, spat at her, and called her nigger." Mexican parents and children could not find friends among the Italians, who refused to associate with them. In many neighborhoods, according to St. Paul school counselor Mike Mansur, prejudiced attitudes and discriminatory actions of police officers further heightened tensions.[74]

Outside their established neighborhoods, Mexicans also faced problems in renting and buying homes. A 1941 Minatare, Nebraska, city ordinance barred "any person or persons of Mexican blood or race" from occupying or owning property outside a four-block area. In Dodge City, where a restrictive covenant effective until 1965 prohibited the sale or transfer of residence to Mexicans or Blacks, "Mexican Town" was confined to a small corridor located between the railroad lines and the Arkansas River. In several Illinois cities, Mexicans had difficulties because of restrictive zoning legislation "passed under stress from white constituents.

Financial institution loans are practically non-existent for buying or improving homes," and insurance companies marked districts inhabited by Mexicans as "high risk." While they were more constricted residentially than their European predecessors, urban Mexicans were less segregated than African Americans.[75]

Public discrimination continued into the 1950s and 1960s, when in East Chicago, it was observed, "Mexican-Americans are still not accepted by the dominant groups, as they were refused services by local businesses, blocked from renting and purchasing housing." They were denied service in many restaurants, barber shops, clothing stores, swimming pools, taverns, clubs, and even burial in graveyards. A Toledo man recalled that "you were afraid to go into the barber shop, afraid to go into the restaurant, because they were going to embarrass you" by refusing to offer service, being rude, and other actions aimed at discouraging Mexicans from entering public places. In Rochester, Minnesota, and other cities, signs reading "No Mexicans Allowed" continued to appear. Jesusa Ibarra recalls that in 1957 when she moved from Texas to Palmyra, Wisconsin, she was refused service in a restaurant although she only wanted to buy milk for her hungry baby.[76]

Restrictive practices were applied locally and enforced inconsistently, suggesting uncertainty within dominant society about civic assimilation for midwestern Mexicans, who understandably remained reluctant to identify with the United States of America. Low rates of naturalization echoed earlier years of the century, and it was reported in 1946 that more than 75 percent of Mexican-born adults in St. Paul were not citizens, "a startling figure," according to historian Susan Diebold, yet probably lower than that of several other cities in the region. She explained low naturalization as a function of the proximity of the Mexican border and "the fact that so many were unable to prove legal entry and continued residence in the United States and thus were afraid to apply for citizenship."[77] Yet most midwestern Mexicans had long met requirements for residency, and some had spent years seeking naturalization but ultimately quit in frustration.

Americanization was further hindered by increasing rates of immigration from Mexico and by the actions of immigration authorities. Once the war ended, INS agents began staging deportation raids throughout the region, which at first did not receive much media attention, but interest by local politicians in the early 1950s aroused public interest. Government agents could at any time capture several hundred industrial workers from a few days' efforts in Chicago, Detroit, Kansas City, and smaller midwestern cities. By 1952, even liberal Democratic Senator Paul Douglas of

Illinois warned that in his own state there were "tens of thousands of Mexicans who have illegally entered the country. The only time they are detected is when some of them get in trouble with the police." INS strategy included the Midwest in its nationwide "Operation Wetback," launched in 1954, and in Chicago alone it verified nearly fifteen hundred departures in less than six months.[78]

Within the dominant culture the distinction between foreign and native was fuzzy, and few Mexicans born and reared in the Midwest at this time can forget being the subject of bantering from classmates labeling them as a "wetback," "spic," or "greaser." Furthermore, words translated into actions, George Hernández recalled. A third-generation Chicano born during the Great Depression, he grew up in Joliet, Illinois. During his youth he and his cousins, upon returning from a fishing trip to Plainfield, were stopped by policemen who suspected that "these guys got to be wetbacks" and held the boys in jail overnight before they were released.[79]

The presence of Mexicans without legal residence in the United States divided organized labor. In 1952 Americanizers in the CIO asserted that "so long as the 'wetbacks' flock in they are a dangerous threat to American conditions in cities." Yet other labor groups, including a Spanish-Speaking Committee (SSC) composed primarily of Mexican members of the United Packinghouse Workers of America, sought to counter such attitudes. On behalf of the SSC, in 1954 Chicago UPWA member Hilario Alemán wrote to Mexican President Adolfo Ruiz Cortines during "Operation Wetback." Alemán criticized the INS campaign for "being conducted in a brutal manner and without consideration of the law. Unauthorized arrests are taking place and Mexicans are being jailed and deported like animals." He urged the Mexican government to take whatever actions necessary to ensure that the INS acted within the law.[80]

Although many Mexicans resisted U.S. citizenship, fewer were immune to the rampant consumerism of the period. Those with stable employment purchased washing machines, electric refrigerators, automobiles, and other items, indicating greater material resources than their predecessors had enjoyed, increasing needs related to employment, and the success of consumer advertising. Home ownership also increased modestly, and by the mid-1940s, about 13 percent of St. Paul West Side Mexican families had purchased homes, "most of them ramshackle affairs." According to one informed observer, "unscrupulous landlords had taken advantage of the housing shortages to unload their holdings at prices far beyond their worth" on the open market.[81]

The mixed messages of the era induced inconsistent individual expressions of ethnicity. As Reverend J. Jerome Boxleitner of St. Paul observed, decisions to assert a given identity might be strategic and situational, as "there was prejudice. Often a young person preferred to say he was Spanish rather than Mexican. Some feared giving a Lower West Side address to police or others because they knew this would compound their trouble or lessen their chance for employment." In a 1949 speech to a Mexican audience in Chicago, Gus García of the League of United Latin American Citizens (LULAC) observed, "some people in Colorado and New Mexico, I regret to say, want to be called Spanish-Americans. Now where they get the Spanish-American I don't know, because most of them have just as much Indian blood as you and I have. Others will want to call themselves Latin-Americans. I define a Latin-American as a Mexican who has become prosperous and joined the Rotary club." Norman Humphrey noted that Detroit Mexicans in the 1920s sometimes referred to themselves as Spaniards, but in the 1940s they identified overwhelmingly as Mexicans. He added that in response to discrimination, youth sometimes identified themselves as White and associated with Whites, while others more forcefully claimed pride in *la raza* and a Mexican identity.[82]

In a 1963 Toledo survey, adults born mostly in the United States identified overwhelmingly as "Mejicanos" or "Chicanos." In East Chicago, Julián Samora and Richard Lamanna reported, "we were struck by the intense nationalism" expressed by local residents, which "occasionally borders on chauvinism." Youth were increasingly sensitive about their Mexican identity, Humboldt High School Principal Krueger of St. Paul acknowledged in a 1962 report. "Mexican children are quite defensive and regard themselves as non-whites and fight 'whites' on the basis of ethnic background." During the middle years of the century, which several historians of the Southwest have dubbed "the Mexican American generation," the term Mexican American was rarely used anywhere in the Midwest, apart from occasional attempts to impose it from above by social workers, academics, and other middle-class agents of Americanization.[83]

Regional differences in expressions of identity were due in part to historical and demographic factors. In midwestern cities, people of very diverse but overwhelmingly recent European ethnic origins predominated numerically. Mexicans of the region retained a greater consciousness of differences among European groups, for in the Southwest the distinctions were less important. In relational terms, midwesterners identified as Mexicans to distinguish themselves from Germans, Swedes, Irish, Poles, Italians, Czechs, and the other nationalities represented in the area. From a World-Systems perspective, the adoption of a Mexican identity in the

Midwest also reflected consciousness of the continuing direct link with Mexico, the place of origin of practically all parents and grandparents, unlike the situation in many southwestern settings, where Mexican roots were often obscured by the passage of several generations. The Mexican identity of the Midwest also reflected a much smaller middle class, a class that was much quicker to identify with the United States of America and distance itself from Mexican roots.

Midwestern Mexicans had opportunities to assert their identities through fraternal, social, cultural, and labor organizations, some recently imported from the Southwest. While many older *mutualistas* collapsed, Sociedad Anahuac in St. Paul lasted until 1958, when it merged with the Comité Patriótico Mexicano. During its heyday in the late 1930s and 1940s, events it sponsored frequently attracted most Mexican residents of the Twin Cities area. Sociedad Anahuac members formed the Comité de Reconstrucción in 1938 to construct a church in the barrio, and the latter helped plan and coordinate community social and cultural activities until it merged with Anahuac in 1948. To support themselves or raise funds for local causes, organizations sponsored holiday celebrations, *bailes* and other musical events, boxing matches, and *jamaicas* (bazaars). The Comité de Reconstrucción, for example, sponsored a *baile* on October 31, 1940, in which a local *orquesta* provided music, charging 20 cents admission for men and 5 cents for women. Children under age twelve did not pay but were expected to work at the coat rack, sell soda pop, set up and take down tables and chairs, and run errands. To usher in calendar year 1941, the Comité invited all local Mexican clubs to participate in a *baile* "*al estilo mexicano,*" thus avoiding competition while sharing labor, expenses, and proceeds. It sponsored events at least monthly to ensure regular community social gatherings.[84]

In larger midwestern cities, the Mexican consul was titular head of the Comité Patriótico, responsible for organizing the Cinco de Mayo and the Diez y Seis de Septiembre celebrations. In St. Paul, Mexican Independence Day was held continuously after 1938. The two-day affair included a carnival at the Guadalupe Mexican Center and the Neighborhood House, events at the Pavilion on Harriet Island, and indoor social, cultural, and educational activities at Stem Hall in the Municipal Auditorium, highlighted by a parade through downtown St. Paul.

Women played critical roles in public activities, planning and setting up food booths; forming, training, and directing cultural and musical groups; and preparing the cuisine. To ensure a successful Independence Day celebration, a 1957 newspaper article reported, "women have been busy preparing fiesta foods all week." The winner of the Mexican festival queen competition sold the most tickets, while there were also awards for the best-dressed children as *chinas poblanas* (popular Puebla style) and *charros* (Mexican cowboys). Attendance fluctuated according to the weather, and despite a downpour in 1941, local newspapers estimated that about six hundred people participated in the outdoor events at Harriet Island, while in 1943, under more favorable conditions, more than five thousand people attended. Event organizers did not seek advertisers to support events, and as Sra. Crescencia Rangel recalled nostalgically, "it was so beautiful that it looked like Mexico."[85]

The Fiestas Patrias in St. Paul maintained a strong Mexican cultural nationalist emphasis in food, dancing, music, and an explicit educational focus highlighted by lectures on Mexican history and culture by community elders and live dramatizations of the struggle for independence against Spain. In one lecture, Professor Santiago Cuneo, one of the earliest Mexicano faculty members at the University of Minnesota, urged the audience to "be proud of your heritage. Teach your language to your children and let them learn Mexican history."[86] Because courses in Mexican history and culture were not part of public school curriculum and youth rarely attended colleges and universities, the Fiestas Patrias, along with oral traditions and occasional articles in newspapers or magazines, offered one of the few opportunities to learn about Mexico.

In many midwestern communities, parents organized cultural activities for youth, including Mexican folkloric dancers. One of the longest-surviving endeavors was the result of the labors of Sra. Juanita Morán in St. Paul, who taught folk dances from Mexico. Her daughter, María Morán, recalled that her father "put us up on stage and whether we liked it or not, we were there. We weren't in a position to say no. Both my brothers and sisters. It was hard to get me up there, but once I did it was hard to get me off, not for show, but pride of being 'Mexicana.'" When she was older, her parents sent her to Mexico to study with professionals and learn new dances and costuming techniques to bring back and enrich the culture in St. Paul. In the early 1960s, Father Ward encouraged her to establish the Ballet Folklórico Guadalupano (the Guadalupe Fiesta Dancers), using the facilities of the new Guadalupe Catholic School for practicing.[87] The dance tradition represented transmission of popular culture through collective folk memory, sustained and enriched by direct borrowing from Mexico, not the Southwest.

In addition to their ethnic organizations, midwestern Mexicans proved unexpectedly receptive to labor unionism. In the early 1930s many joined the Chicago Workers Committee on Unemployment and other unemployed councils, demanding that state and federal governments establish work projects and support legislation on behalf of unemployed workers regardless of nationality or citizenship. When the industrial union drives of the CIO began later in the decade, Mexicans quickly dispelled earlier negative stereotypes of strikebreakers. They were attracted to its inclusive, class-based strategy that downplayed ethnic and racial differences.[88]

In Chicago, the Steel Workers Organizing Committee (SWOC) actively recruited several hundred Mexicans into its membership during a four-month period in 1936, having had none up to that point. As CIO organizer John Riffe observed, although "it was a hard group to start," Mexicans became enthusiastic members who "responded to the union drive with body and soul." They raised money, organized auxiliary committees, and distributed handbills, posters, and brochures in Spanish to gain support for the union. Lizbeth Cohen notes that during the South Chicago drive against Carnegie Steel, Mexicans "became the first foreign-language group to organize 100 percent." They also joined SWOC drives against Inland Steel in Youngstown and East Chicago and were active in the "Little Steel" strikes of 1937.[89]

Mexican packinghouse workers were similarly responsive in the early days of the Packing House Workers Organizing Committee, (later UPWA-CIO) and helped write "a magnificent chapter" in its early successes in Chicago. They also "became a necessary component of the multi-ethnic coalition" in the Back-of-the-Yards Neighborhood Council, a grassroots organization focusing on conditions and local politics that were sympathetic to the union.[90]

As a result of their participation in the early SWOC organizing in South Chicago, where there had been a long history of tension and discord with their European neighbors, sociologist Edward Bauer noted "that open conflict has all but disappeared." Similarly, in the Chicago Stockyards district, Frank Paz observed, "the active participation of the Mexicans in the early days of the union gave them status and prestige. Here were the former strikebreakers participating as a vanguard group of the union." Their actions compelled union leaders to attack company exclusion and discrimination against Mexicans and African Americans and seek more effective grievance procedures in union contracts. Mexicans' participation in unions and grassroots community organizations also eased neighborhood tensions and brought them into a more central position the industrial working class of the urban Midwest.[91]

Union gains, however, did not translate into significant upward mobility for Mexican workers, particularly in steel, where rank-and-file participation was offset by the top-down organization of SWOC. Even after many years in the mills, they were confined overwhelmingly to unskilled positions in blast furnaces, coke plants, scrap yards, and chipping departments as chippers; in the foundries as moulders and punch press operators; or in the yards and paint departments. By 1951, only twenty-three of the more than three thousand Mexican employees at United States Steel, who made up 20 percent of its total workforce, were classified as semi-skilled, and similarly bleak figures obtained for the estimated fifteen thousand Mexicans at Inland Steel. They barely benefited from upgrading in the mills and learned that seniority "became somewhat of a farce." Frank Paz observed that they often turned "apathetic and even cynical" toward the steelworkers' union, which had no Mexican staff members or officers in the Chicago area. Nevertheless, when Inland Steel in Indiana Harbor recruited more than 250 Mexicans from Texas in April 1947, two days before a strike, "company plans back-fired. Not only did the Mexicans refuse to scab but they marched in the Inland Steel office in a body to demand the company pay their transportation back home and to add to the company's chagrin, signed up in the union as an indication of their solidarity." [92]

In Michigan foundries and automobile plants, Mexicans also participated in the union movement. At Wilson Foundry in Pontiac, they fought from within against unfair treatment. As Nick Migas, shop steward and later president of Steelworkers Local 1010 observed, "we had a lot of Mexican workers in my department where discrimination was practiced. They were constantly kept on small, menial jobs—scrap yard, labor gang, furnaces—dirty, menial, hard work. And no chance of promotion. That's why the union swept like a wildfire through the mills." Yet in union contracts with United States Steel, "the promotion or retention of 'superior men' [historically synonymous to White] was considered a business necessity." One Mexican observed, "I've seen departments where Mexican men have high seniority but the representation of the union doesn't do anything for them. They don't get the same chances for promotion." The "Steel Manual" weighted job classifications in favor of crafts and against the physical and hazardous jobs where Mexican and African Americans workers were concentrated. According to historian Jorge Hernández Fujigaki, between the late 1930s and the 1970s, wage differentials between skilled and unskilled workers in the steel industry widened because the union did not challenge company practices that "cemented an occupational hierarchy which kept Latinos at the bottom." [93]

In the packinghouses, the seniority system was somewhat less unfair, but Paz noted in 1948 that Mexicans "have not continued to play as prominent a role in the Union as they did during the early and trying days of its organization." They remained primarily unskilled workers concentrated in the freezers and yards, although their numbers as knifers, butchers and trimmers increased modestly. In general, they "were neglected by the union . . . their enthusiasm and interest diminish[ed] and practically vanished."[94]

In the railroad industry, dominated by various craft unions, efforts to organize Mexicans were "very weak as well as spasmodic," and they were relegated overwhelmingly to unskilled maintenance work. As Paz concluded, unions in general "have not paid the proper attention to them and their problems in their respective unions." Even in the CIO, which "claims to have a modern, radical, democratic program," Mexicans were rarely hired as union organizers, clerical staff, or even stenographers.[95]

Mexican packinghouse workers in St. Paul were active union members, and labor leaders, including Rodney Johnson, Minnesota's state CIO council secretary, regarded then as solid unionists and competent and loyal workers. Yet they often faced unresponsive local leadership, as in the 1953 case of a man employed twenty-three years who filed a grievance because he was still "shifted about from one department to another. He believes that he should have a steady assignment, and because of his seniority rights, he claims that he should have a better job than he has. He says that his fellow workers who have not been working there as long are better treated as far as promotions are concerned." The union responded to his grievance by claiming that under existing conditions, it could do nothing for him.[96]

Their vivid consciousness as workers convinced Mexicans to join and remain in unions while seeking to change policies from within. In South Bend, Manuel García responded to the failure of his employer, Kaiser Jeep, to hire more Mexicans, by becoming active in the United Auto Workers (UAW). The Corpus Christi native was elected shop steward and convinced his local to pressure the company to hire several dozen Chicanos. At the massive Great Lakes Steel Corporation plant in Ecorse, Michigan, the large contingent of Mexican employees responded to company and union leadership favoritism by organizing their own bargaining block, the Latin American Steelworkers, within the union. They were thereby able to elect Mexican committeemen, grievance men, and shop stewards and alter unfair practices. As Gus García of LULAC observed, "the labor unions might as well realize that all under-privileged and minority groups have to stick together. If we didn't help the labor unions, who is going to help them? . . . The Union movement must be a move-ment of crusades or it will die out."[97]

Midwestern Mexican organizational life was also influenced by imports from the Southwest, particularly LULAC and the American G.I. Forum, both of which consciously identified with Americanization efforts. The significance of these organizations, particularly in the Midwest, has been the subject of some debate. Sympathetic observers portray them primarily as civil rights groups concerned with the advancement of Mexican American interests. More unfavorable perspectives suggest that they were primarily accommodationist, served middle-class aspirations, and were more interested in social functions than engaging political and civil rights issues that pervaded working-class midwestern communities.[98]

LULAC, a social, cultural, and political organization established in Texas in 1929, spread to the Midwest in the 1940s and 1950s. While it gained a reputation as the most conservative of major national organizations representing Mexicans and catered explicitly to middle-class U.S. citizens, many members were neither citizens nor middle class. Furthermore, several national leaders enthusiastically endorsed working-class concerns, labor unions, and a civil rights agenda. LULAC accepted the thesis of Mexicans as the last of the immigrants and viewed itself as capable of providing leadership in assisting in their assimilation and improvement of their lives. It became active in St. Paul in 1958 when a national organizer from Chicago called and expressed interest in organizing a chapter composed largely of factory workers and their families. The LULAC local organization occasionally assisted individuals who had been subjected to discrimination, especially at work, by providing access to attorneys. Its impact was limited by the social structure of the local Mexican community, which lacked professionals or lawyers to engage in a civil rights agenda. Its most visible activities in St. Paul were parties, vaudeville shows, and *bailes,* the latter featuring well-known *orquestas* that drew large crowds. Many were fund-raisers that were considered "part of an 'operation bootstrap,'" to provide college scholarships for one or two upwardly mobile students each year.[99]

Many midwestern members were disappointed with LULAC, including Sr. Louis Medina of St. Paul, who said that it differed from other Mexican organizations to which he had belonged in one important respect: "the only thing about LULACS [*sic*] is that we went to big conventions and things like that." South Bend member Manuel García complained that "all they do is dance, and give out about $300 a year in scholarships. . . . they were afraid for their name." Another South Bend member, Concepción Niño, suggested that there were "other things we could be doing . . . (especially) to help the very needy." Despite the U.S. birth of most members and its enthusiastic acceptance of the importance of Americanization, the organization's agenda was further limited by dominant representations of Mexicans as foreigners. As a 1959 *St. Paul Dispatch* article asserted, "one of its aims in the broader field is to bring the Latin American into cultural and social contact with his adopted country."[100]

Many contemporary observers were enthusiastic about the organizational potential of the Mexican war veteran, for in comparison with his parents he was "young, more self-assured, speaks English fluently, is either American born or raised in the United States since childhood," characteristics consistent with the adoption of cultural pluralist perspectives. In many cities Mexican veterans formed independent ethnic organizations, while in others they joined the American Legion, the Veterans of Foreign Wars, or the American Veterans Committee. They were most active in the Texas-based American G.I. Forum, created in 1948 because Mexicans commonly were not welcomed into veterans' groups. It spread quickly to other parts of the country, and on one organizing tour President Héctor García established a chapter in St. Paul. The stated aims of this charitable organization were to serve the community, state, and nation; to defend the rights of Mexican Americans; to seek fair employment practices; to furnish scholarships; and to encourage Mexican Americans to vote. It was a family organization composed of active or former soldiers, with its greatest midwestern appeal in locations where large numbers of Tejanos had settled out. Joseph Anaya, who was active in the St. Paul chapter, explained that its function "was to try and help or provide services and do good for the community," and it held picnics and dances to raise funds for projects like assisting needy families and migrant workers. It had a more conscious working-class appeal than LULAC, and despite embracing cultural pluralism, even more than LULAC it downplayed ethnic distinctiveness. The ideology largely reflected its membership, made up of military veterans, and its formation in the early years of the Cold War, when a narrow vision of Americanism held sway within dominant public opinion. A critical assessment asserted that "its exaggerated conformity and overly dramatized patriotic posture did serious damage to the consciousness of the organization's membership."[101]

The histories and goals of organizations formed by Mexicans in St. Paul during the first and second generations differed in many ways. The former were created by immigrants not yet stable members of the industrial working class, who united for mutual protection against the cyclical effects of unemployment and the cultural shock of being newcomers to a region where they could expect little institutional support. The second generation faced a less compelling need for survival and placed greater emphasis on social and recreational activities. Unlike early organizations, which often were created to counteract the influence of the United States, groups like the American G.I. Forum and LULAC, imported to the Midwest from the outside, viewed themselves as a vanguard for Americanization among Mexicans.

In the late 1950s and the early 1960s, there was a major breakdown of Mexican organizations in St. Paul. One observer attributed the death of Sociedad Anahuac to its inability to recruit people from the younger generation: "Chicanos began forming their own organizations in response to the changing social and political conditions in Minnesota." Yet the organizing thrust of the Chicano Movement in Minnesota would not be evident for several years. Another explanation, according to former member Carlota Arellano, was that when the first generation was unable to continue, "there was no one to replace it." Simultaneously, however, organizations of the second generation in St. Paul also collapsed, for less evident reasons. As American G.I. Forum member Sr. Joseph Anaya recalled, "all of a sudden . . . it just died," despite sporadic efforts to resuscitate it. Such erratic local organizational histories were commonplace, including the formation of LULAC in Milwaukee in late 1957, when similar local councils were established in Racine, Waukesha, and Delavan. The Milwaukee council collapsed by 1963, as many of its members left the area. An effort to renew it, led by middle-class professionals, took place in 1978. Differing local histories of organizations reflect distinctive national, regional, and local rhythms of activity. Chapters flourished in some locations but foundered elsewhere, suggesting that examinations focusing exclusively on national leadership offer only a partial understanding of their impact.[102]

Beyond individual leadership, ethnic organizational activities were profoundly influenced by patterns of work. The presence of Mexicans in labor unions was consistent with current Keynesian economic ideas, which emphasized stability of employment and rising incomes as a necessary component of a healthy national economy. Steady employment made unnecessary some of the functions of earlier *mutualistas,* which offered short-term support for people who worked erratically and shifted jobs frequently. The need for *mutualistas* also diminished with the implementation of the New Deal and its social service network, which provided a partial buffer from hunger and unemployment. In addition, changing employment patterns among women affected organizational life. Sociedad Anahuac was able to survive into the early 1960s because of volunteer work of women displaced from the factories and permanent wage labor after the war. As women were again drawn increasingly into full-time wage-earning employment, they had less time to plan events, prepare food, and attend to the minute details that ensured the success of such organizations. Sra. Teresa Muñoz recalled the frustration in being unable to participate in planning and preparing for activities sponsored by Sociedad Anahuac "because I worked a lot and could not attend meetings."[103] Without volunteer labor the older ethnic organizations could not support an active community agenda and thus collapsed.

Meanwhile, the Catholic Church was also losing the central place it held in the lives of many midwestern Mexican communities. As Sr. Federico Saucedo recalled of the residents of St. Paul's Lower West Side in the 1930s and 1940s, "religion was the dominant force in their life. The second generation realized that there are other things, like sports and movies. . . . (But) the church wasn't doing anything. It never accomplished what it should have. That was to make the Mexican Americans more reliant on themselves."[104] Declining participation in organizations occurred at the precise moment when outsiders threatened to dismantle the barrio and further fragment the community.

### Dismantling the Barrio

Urban renewal projects in the 1950s and 1960s threatened the physical integrity of Mexican barrios and other poor neighborhoods throughout the country. Whether they involved construction of industrial parks, of new building complexes, or of elaborate urban highway systems, threatened barrios typically shared a number of common features, notably mixed residential, commercial, and industrial uses; physical deterioration; and the experience of several ethnic transitions during their history. Furthermore, planners and entrepreneurs typically chose them because local residents had less political influence in city hall to oppose them than did middle-class neighborhoods. The outcome of urban renewal schemes varied, for many neighborhoods were able to survive practically intact, some were physically scarred, and still others, including St. Paul's Lower West Side, were obliterated.

Popular accounts have portrayed the destruction of the St. Paul barrio as a necessary response to periodic Mississippi River floods, including those of 1943, 1951 and 1952. They refer in particular to the third inundation, when river waters reached eight feet above flood stage, and in many parts of the neighborhood "only boats could take residents to their homes." The waters destroyed personal belongings, including clothing, furniture, and tools; caused buckled floors, collapsed walls and foundations of dwellings; and required extensive repairs of furnaces and electrical items. Some owners of houses and buildings were fortunate to have pumps operating day and night, but even they faced the daunting task of cleaning up, clearing basements of water, and rooms of dirt and mud.[105]

St. Paul officials initiated the interpretation that the floods of 1951 and 1952 made the destruction of the barrio necessary, yet as early as 1937 city planners had been discussing urban redevelopment. At that time the neighborhood was not even "considered seriously for a proposed development simply due to adverse geographical conditions." In fact, geographic conditions had not changed since the 1930s, and flood control was neither more nor less feasible twenty years later. Nevertheless, observers including sociologist Terry Allen Caine accepted the city's claim that the destruction of the residential neighborhood "was done because of the spring flooding," adding as an afterthought that "the area, incidentally, is now an industrial park."[106]

In early 1959, almost seven years after the last floods, city officials announced inauspiciously that they had begun an urban renewal project starting with the construction of a levee to protect the district from floods. It would permit the creation of Riverview Industrial Park, "the largest single undertaking in St. Paul's urban renewal program." They quietly added that it would require the removal of all residential dwellings in the district.[107]

The project involved several agencies, including the U.S. Army Corps of Engineers, responsible for constructing the levee; the St. Paul Port Authority, charged with purchasing homes and removing residents; and the St. Paul Housing Authority, assigned with expediting the relocation of displaced residents. The Corps began construction of the levee in 1960, and the Port Authority began removing people in June 1961, at which time there were still 547 household units and 436 families in the neighborhood, comprising 2,147 residents, about four-fifths Mexican.[108]

The city either purchased homes or acquired them by condemnation, offering owners "fair market value," a skewed concept of capitalism when applied to units for which no market existed. City officials determined that "fair market value" would be based on "wet land" prices, which were far below residential costs and inadequate to permit barrio landowners to purchase homes anywhere else in the city. As further partial compensation, the Housing Authority paid a portion of moving costs, not to exceed one hundred dollars, for owners but not renters. It was widely agreed that "people were offered very little for their homes . . . and there was a feeling of hopelessness." A dejected resident, Sra. Ester Avaloz, observed, "if we wanted to fight so they would give us more money it would have all gone to a lawyer for his fees."[109]

Lacking organized political influence and with existing ethnic organizations on the verge of collapse, residential opposition to the urban renewal project developed slowly and remained largely unorganized. Many people directed their strongest feelings toward the Neighborhood House, which took upon itself a role as mediator between community residents and government authorities and permitted the Port and Housing Authorities to establish temporary offices in its library. Like the government agencies that initiated the project, it had not consulted with its constituents about whether they wanted it to serve as intermediary, and it accepted government rhetoric about progress and the need to demolish the neighborhood and remove its residents. It sought to ease the distress of urban removal by helping to establish the Old West Side Improvement Association, which provided temporary services and placement assistance for people displaced from their homes. Many residents, particularly renters, felt betrayed and united in opposition when the Port Authority reneged on its original agreement that they would be able to remain in their dwellings four months without paying rent to compensate for moving expenses and to permit time to find new homes. The renters' protests compelled the Port Authority to abide by its earlier promise. By the end of 1962, the city had moved almost all barrio residents, "to give room for industrial expansion," and its version of urban renewal and progress carried the day.[110]

A linear history of "urban renewal" in the barrio demonstrates that city officials consciously confused the story of the early 1950s floods, the flood control project, the Industrial Park, and the displacement of the Mexican *colonia*. Government officials did not make public their concern about barrio residents for seven years after the flood of 1952, and at no time in their deliberations did they seek input from them on the future of the neighborhood. Their version of local history successfully diverted attention from why they favored industrial interests over the residents of the barrio. It never addressed why they failed to consider either a project to improve the existing residential neighborhood or a less-costly and ecologically sound option of converting it into a public park to minimize the danger of future flooding elsewhere on the river floodplain. Instead, the city adopted a scheme to make the district safe for investors rather than residents.

Several observers assumed that midwestern Mexican communities would inevitably disappear after the upheavals of the Great Depression. A more careful examination would have concurred with the 1941 opinion of a St. Paul social worker that "they are here to stay."[111] The outbreak of World War II and the postwar economic boom induced record levels of migration and an expanding Mexican presence in the urban Midwest. At the time residential districts for African Americans were growing very rapidly, while ethnic neighborhoods were fading as European American residents and their children were dispersing into the suburbs.

Key to Mexican urban population growth was an improvement in employment options, which compared favorably with an earlier generation when even the highest-paying industrial jobs offered only seasonal or short-term employment and compelled individuals to shift employers and industries. The new economic regime offered thousands of factory workers a realistic expectation of comparatively stable employment for many years. Yet thousands of midwestern Mexicans continued to face the prospect of unstable and temporary work, including women who entered the wage labor force en mass during the war but departed as their husbands, fathers, and brothers returned from the armed services. Afterward, a substantial minority of Mexicanas continued to work in shops, factories, or domestic jobs to augment the family economy. Meanwhile, a new wave of labor migration, composed of women and men, was attracted to the region from Texas and Mexico, often for seasonal or temporary work in agriculture and increasingly for urban industries, and many settled permanently. Expanded employment options also contributed to the formation of new urban and suburban *colonias*. The children of immigrants and former farmworkers were most likely to enter these new neighborhoods, and they helped break down the narrow range of housing options of the previous generation.

Whether residing in the older or newer barrios, midwestern Mexicans were increasingly inundated by the influence of Americanization in political, social, and educational institutions, and through the increasing commercialization of culture. While their lives were more varied, options for significant occupational mobility were limited almost exclusively to the industrial working class. Even the most sympathetic agents of Americanization, the settlement houses and elements in the Catholic Church, reflected a dominant culture that offered little space for Mexican professionals, or for Mexican priests or nuns in the nationality parishes that barrio residents had constructed and continued to fund. Americanization helped deplete the vigor of Mexican organizational life while offering few alternatives to resolving the contradiction between the ideal of equality and the reality of ongoing prejudice and discrimination. Organized labor, despite its increasing emphasis on unity, was unable to overcome racism in its ranks. Even the most popular academic proponent of cultural pluralism of the era, Milton Gordon, acknowledged that assimilation did not apply for Mexicans, African Americans, and Puerto Ricans.[112]

Institutions of dominant culture further subordinated Mexicans by representing them as foreigners and outsiders, whether they were recent immigrants or U.S. citizens. Underlying such representations was the continued unequal political and economic relationship between the United States and Mexico, a legacy of colonialism. The homeland for Mexicans differed from that of European Americans in not only economic but also rhetorical terms. As Edward Said has observed, the capitalist maintained control over the colonized subject by ensuring that the latter was "talked about, analyzed, abused and worked," while simultaneously "covered with a discourse whose purpose was to keep him industrious and subordinate."[113] Meanwhile, rhetorical and material contradictions set the stage for the Chicano Movement, which offered its own explanations.

# 5 El Movimiento
## Becoming a Little More Militant

More than half the Mexican population of the Twin Cities area resided on the Lower West Side of St. Paul when the urban renewal project that razed their neighborhood began. The rigid segregation of earlier decades had already begun to break down, and some officials considered it likely that they would quickly disperse into working-class neighborhoods throughout the metropolitan area. Instead, most chose to follow a few neighbors who had earlier relocated to the adjacent Concord Terrace district on the West Side. Yet the prospect of a Mexican barrio in their midst led to vigorous opposition by local European American residents and pulled government officials into the fray. The struggle over urban space in St. Paul had already begun when the Chicano Movement burst onto the scene in the Southwest, and local Mexicans shared in the heady times.

Popular and scholarly analyses of the Chicano Movement have not paid much attention to the Midwest or to its links with the rest of the nation. In the 1970s, Chicanos in the Southwest who even considered the subject thought that the movement in the Midwest was derivative, lagged behind the Southwest chronologically, and accomplished very little. Some even asserted that midwestern Chicanos were "culturally deprived" or "don't know what it means to be a Chicano." European American observers added their own negative assessments and were quick to blame local leadership for shortcomings. As one Minneapolis newspaper asserted, "when different groups [of Chicanos] try to join forces, the efforts have broken down about who will be in charge." Others claimed that organizational possibilities in the Midwest were hampered by low numbers, which limited Chicano political influence, or by the unique diversity of the region's Latino population, which induced internal divisions.[1]

A closer examination of the movement indicates that the distinctiveness of the region was exaggerated and that like their counterparts elsewhere during this period, midwestern Chicanos engaged in unprecedented political, social, and cultural activism. They quickly established connections with Chicanos elsewhere, frequently responding to requests from Southwest-based organizations for support, just as they often turned to them for inspiration and guidance. They also joined coalitions with other organizations to address issues of the day, including the Vietnam War. Whether in the Midwest or the Southwest, Chicanos most often focused on struggles that were articulated locally, while they addressed several common themes.

One concern that captured their attention was the role of the state and its agencies, and as Donald Kurtz suggested in his analysis of Milwaukee, the Chicano Movement "views American institutions as oppressive. The goal of the Chicano Movement is to alleviate this oppression, by one means or another." The relationship between the state and the movement has been the subject of considerable debate. One interpretation suggests that liberal times and a sympathetic government permitted an opening for movement actions. A contrary view holds that the government itself was the oppressor and that the legislation and programs it enacted were motivated principally by fear of the movement and its potential to liberate the poor and oppressed. According to reporter Eli M. Baca, the Nixon administration "sought to manipulate Latino organizations and programs to its political advantage by using federal grants as bait."[2]

The Chicano Movement in Minnesota began as a local struggle over the destiny of a barrio and, as in many places, preceded the formal articulation of the movement in the Southwest. The individual and collective actions of its residents challenged visions of "progress" articulated by entrepreneurial interests and the state and contested the European Americans who coveted the Concord Terrace neighborhood.

## Reconstructing a Barrio

Several Mexican families from the Lower West Side moved into neighboring Concord Terrace before 1960, when the St. Paul Housing Authority announced a plan to build low-rent housing there for some barrio residents about to be displaced. European Americans in Concord Terrace immediately responded with "a flood of protests," seeking attention in the media and in political circles to prevent construction of the new dwellings. They forced the St. Paul City Council to hold an open meeting, where they articulated their opinions about the plan and the prospect of Mexicans in their midst. It was reported that "nearly all voice vigorous protests and many refer to the program as a 'slum relocation' plan." Concord Terrace resident John Nafus of Morton Street expressed a widespread opinion: "I feel that our property values will depreciate." Mrs. O. J. Olson, of Belvidere Street, complained that "we do not want the slums up here."

Another Concord Terrace householder was more explicit: "we do not wish to have the welfare of our children degraded by an influx of this type." They shared a fear that Mexicans from the Flats would ruin their neighborhood. Meanwhile, several social service agencies were more sympathetic, emphasizing the need for housing, and a Neighborhood House report claimed that the protests represented "evidences of discrimination." Yet the agencies could not counteract the European American householders, who convinced city officials to shelve the plan to assist Mexicans in relocating to Concord Terrace.[3]

Most residents of the old barrio would have preferred not to leave their former homes. One stated, "if you have ever lived on the West Side, you never want to live in any other part of St. Paul. This is home. It is friendly here." Another neighbor concurred, "down there around the old church we were like one family. We always had someone to talk with. There was always something happening."[4] They had positive memories of their old neighborhood, the comfort and convenience of residing within walking distance of relatives, friends, and nearby social and cultural activities. It was the only district in the Twin Cities area where people commonly used Spanish in daily conversations, and for many it was close to work, particularly the packing plants in South St. Paul.

Although European American residents of Concord Terrace convinced the city to shelve plans to construct new housing, Mexicans nevertheless rapidly moved into the neighborhood. There was little new construction, so they placed a great strain on existing housing, often doubling up on single units. Many landlords took the opportunity to divide older houses into duplexes and apartments. According to the St. Paul Port Authority, almost half the people displaced from the Flats had already found housing in the Concord Terrace district by early 1963, and more trickled in by the end of the year.[5] Despite opposition and without the support of local government agencies, they had successfully transplanted their barrio.

They also decided to continue to pressure agencies to construct new housing projects. They attended hearings, participated in meetings and mass demonstrations, and made individual demands on city government officials to proceed with plans to ease the crowding and permit former neighbors to rejoin them. They soon convinced the St. Paul Housing and Redevelopment Authority to complete Dunedin Terrace, which was ready for occupancy in 1966. The low-rent housing complex offered space for about fifteen hundred people, both families and elderly residents.[6]

Through civic, church, and school groups to which they belonged, St. Paul Mexicans initiated a more controversial effort in early 1968 aimed at convincing the City Council to approve the Concord Terrace Renewal Project (CTRP). It challenged the premises of many contemporary urban renewal projects, which focused on the demolition of residential dwellings and neighborhoods. CTRP instead sought to rehabilitate existing housing and to engage in neighborhood beautification, highlighted by the creation of Castillo Park. While the project eliminated some older housing, it also reduced commercial and industrial zoning to provide more space for new single and multifamily dwellings.[7]

Another contentious feature of the renewal effort was the Torre San Miguel project, a housing development named after the former Church of St. Michael's, constructed at the site in 1882. The church had been demolished, but the bell tower remained as the symbol of the development. Torre San Miguel had been under consideration for funding by the U.S. Housing and Urban Development Administration (HUD) as early as 1965 but was delayed by local opposition and bureaucratic negligence. A group of frustrated neighborhood residents organized to take action and by 1968 brought the issue to public attention by staging demonstrations and attending meetings of city and federal government officials, including the St. Paul Housing and Redevelopment Authority and the Federal Housing Administration (FHA). They gained visibility from a highly publicized trip to Chicago, where they met with and criticized HUD officials for delays. As a result of their efforts, the Rio Vista Citizens Planning Council was created to ensure neighborhood representation in planning and completing the project.[8]

Through the efforts of the St. Paul Housing Authority and several federal agencies, it was ready for occupancy in 1972. The multileveled rough cedar buildings, consisting of 142 private family homes, represented the state's first cooperatively owned low-cost housing development. Reporter Peter Vaughan observed that "it is generally agreed that the Torre project is of immense importance to the community" and a victory in their effort to create new housing in an old urban neighborhood. Although the plan to make the homes resident owned failed, due largely to mismanagement and miscalculations by the planners, in 1981 the Catholic Archdiocese took over the project through its Community Development Corporation. It formed a new elected board of directors, the majority of whom were local residents, and renovated and repaired the housing that had been badly neglected since its construction. As local resident Rubén Ruiz observed, "the Torre gave me a new sense of pride in the community."[9]

As individuals, residents also constructed new houses and apartments and refurbished older ones, their efforts made easier by changes in zoning laws and loan policies. As a result, the Concord Terrace neighborhood was more residential than the Lower West Side had been in the 1950s, and its housing stock was sturdier and more comfortable. The individual and collective efforts to regroup had enabled almost 70 percent of the former residents of the Flats to find housing in the new barrio, and by 1970 the Concord Terrace district was about 60 percent Mexican, with a greater concentration in the area between the Church and Castillo Park.[10]

The new neighborhood served as the principal port of entry for Mexican immigrants and Mexican Americans settling in the Twin Cities. The growing population was simultaneously dispersing into neighborhoods elsewhere in the metropolitan area, lured by employment in urban and suburban shops and factories. By 1974, according to one estimate, about twenty-eight thousand of the thirty-two thousand Latinos in Minnesota were Mexicans, of whom 72 percent resided in the Twin Cities metropolitan area. An estimated six thousand lived in Minneapolis and another twelve thousand in St. Paul, of whom ten thousand resided on the West Side.[11] While the majority of Minnesota Mexicans continued to reside in the Twin Cities, the West Side contained slightly less than a third of the state's total, as the growing barrio could not keep pace with the more rapid expansion beyond. The informal apartheid of an earlier generation had clearly broken down.

Based on representations in the media and by police, the neighborhood was becoming more dangerous and violent, yet as David Ramírez, editor of *La Voz*, observed, such portrayals were highly exaggerated. He reported a case in which St. Paul police beat up a group of Chicanos on the West Side which the mainstream press of both St. Paul and Minneapolis labeled a riot, basing their stories on police reports. After a detailed investigation, including thirty-eight eyewitness interviews, Ramírez concluded, "it was a completely different picture than the police stated." In another highly publicized incident, Sr. Luis Trejo, owner of the Casa del Sol restaurant on Concord Street, was charged with interference when he attempted to calm tensions between police and patrons outside the nearby Cozy Cantina. Rather than accept his assistance, police turned on him and beat him, breaking his arm and sending him to the hospital. He charged them with brutality, but despite the testimony of several witnesses who confirmed his version of the events, the municipal court declared the police officers not guilty. Such incidents suggest that the West Side was becoming more typical of barrios elsewhere, and local residents had to be increasingly wary of a frequently uncontrolled police force. Although crime had risen over earlier years, an informed police sergeant in 1980 characterized the neighborhood as "one of the lowest crime areas in the city."[12]

As in St. Paul, residents of many midwestern Mexican barrios faced threats of displacement because of highway construction and urban renewal projects, but outcomes were inconsistent. In the largest barrio in the region, Chicago's Near West Side, thousands of Mexicans were displaced from the northern and eastern sections of their neighborhood in the late 1950s as a result of the construction of the Dan Ryan and Eisenhower Freeways. Even more were forced to relocate in the early 1960s, particularly as a result of construction of the Chicago Circle Campus of the University of Illinois. The combined projects forced more than half the residents of the district to move, and a majority found new homes in neighboring Pilsen, which centered along 18th Street. Rents were comparatively low in a neighborhood that was already largely abandoned by Czechs and other Eastern Europeans and their children, who were moving west into suburban Cicero and Berwyn. The Mexican population of Pilsen expanded so rapidly that by 1970 more than half its residents were Mexican and totaled more than 40 percent of the Chicano population in the city. It was also a port of entry for the very poor, and the formal educational attainment of Pilsen residents ranked eighty-fourth of eighty-five Chicago neighborhoods. Despite Pilsen's location near the bottom of most other indices of material well-being, it was the first major district in the city with a majority of Mexican residents and quickly became the largest and most dynamic barrio in the Midwest. Pilsen residents soon began to flock into neighboring districts, particularly Little Village, which they renamed La Villita, centering on 26th Street, and the West Side of Chicago was becoming Mexican turf as well.[13]

In Southwest Detroit, a haphazard urban renewal effort accompanied by the construction of the Fisher Freeway removed hundreds of dwellings. Unlike St. Paul, however, little new housing appeared, and the heart of the barrio moved westward from the Bagely Street area toward Clark Street. On the West Side of Kansas City, the construction of the Southwest Trafficway forced many barrio residents out of the neighborhood. Furthermore, private investors and public officials, including HUD, declared the Mexican district "no longer a viable residential community," which further expedited the decline of the barrio. Their designation of the neighborhood as "a bad risk" made it difficult for residents to obtain loans for home improvement and hindered the construction of new housing. Kansas City officials and investors were more interested in luring industrial projects, but barrio residents fought back with public demonstrations and other forms of pressure. The pattern of urban renewal in Detroit and Kansas was commonplace: city officials and their entrepreneurial allies depleted housing stock, fragmented neighborhoods, and weakened the integrity of established barrios but did not destroy them entirely.[14]

Uneven residential patterns unfolded in smaller midwestern communities. In Dodge City, Kansas, *la colonia* appeared in the first decade of the twentieth century as a company town of the Atchison, Topeka and Santa Fe Railroad. Located between the railroad tracks and the Arkansas River, the small, noisy, segregated neighborhood was the home of Mexican railroad employees and settled agricultural workers. In the name of urban renewal, bulldozers razed *la colonia* in the late 1940s, and most residents then moved to the Eastside barrio. Their options were limited by a restrictive covenant prohibiting the sales of houses elsewhere to Blacks or Mexicans, a practice that was eliminated only after legal challenges based on the federal Civil Rights Act of 1965. In the early 1980s, about 1,450 Mexicans, or 85 percent of the total in this city of about 18,000 inhabitants, remained clustered in the barrio. Thus the destruction of the first Dodge City barrio did not substantially eliminate segregated housing. In Port Huron, Michigan, Mexicans concentrated in the ethnically diverse working-class neighborhood in the 1st Ward, on the edge of downtown. The neighborhood was razed in 1957 by city fathers "who considered it an eyesore," and Mexicans scattered more widely through the South Side of the city.[15] While the fate of barrios that faced the threat of the wrecking ball varied, struggles to maintain coherent neighborhoods made local residents in many locations more receptive to the unfolding Chicano Movement.

### *El Movimiento* and the Community

The Concord Street neighborhood of St. Paul had few visible markings of a barrio when the Mexican influx began in the early 1960s. At one end of Concord, the principal commercial street, the Church of Our Lady of Guadalupe was constructed in 1961, and at the other, the Astor Theater, located on the corner of Robert Street, had already begun showing Mexican movies. As late as 1970, it lacked Mexican businesses and restaurants, and the only establishment where one could purchase anything that resembled Mexican food was the Dairy Queen, where, as one critic observed, Anglo cooks prepared what they referred to as tacos. The Mexican restaurant located on the edge of the neighborhood, a European American observer astutely noted, "seems to be rather Americanized," its clientele composed principally of "middle-class Anglos relating to each other how much they know about Mexico and Mexican food." Despite its meager physical markings, it was observed that "on the Lower Westside it is only the Mexicans who have retained the physical and symbolic evidence of their national origins." The West Side remained a magnet for Mexicanos to attend church and other social and cultural functions and for local residents who wanted to rebuild the barrio. In keeping with the times, many important changes were already taking place.[16]

The reconstruction of the barrio on the West Side of St. Paul began shortly before the Chicano Movement burst onto the national scene, and it was intimately linked to the movement. The common experiences of Mexicans at work, in school, and in public and private settings throughout the country permitted recognized Chicano leaders to come to the Midwest to find receptive audiences. César Chávez and the movement that became the United Farm Workers (UFW) first gained national attention in the months following the outbreak of the grape strike in Delano, California, in September 1965. As the union and its supporters brought their struggle to other parts of the country, they provided an inspiration for Chicanos elsewhere. They sought out thousands of volunteer supporters, disproportionately Chicanos, to join grape boycott committees in cities and on campuses throughout the country. The UFW provided entry into Chicano Movement activities for thousands of Chicanos in the Southwest and the Midwest, a training ground that inspired them to create their own local organizations. While midwestern Chicanos supported the UFW in its victories in California, the union directly influenced the appearance of independent farmworker organizing efforts, particularly Obreros Unidos (OU) in Wisconsin and the Farm Labor Organizing Committee (FLOC) in Ohio, whose volunteers were also active in Michigan, Indiana, and Illinois.

When UFW representatives visited Minnesota, they struck a responsive chord among local Chicanos already involved in battles of their own. Local residents heeded advice from Chávez and other movement leaders that they were responsible for making the world a better place and that such efforts should begin in their own community. Many were experienced in recent collective activities in their own barrio and as workers in the fields, shops, and factories. They faced a more difficult problem with "allies" who were accustomed to taking leadership positions on their behalf, including social service agencies, the Catholic Church, and other organizations long involved in their community.

The problem of establishing an independent voice was further complicated by the War on Poverty and related programs that first appeared in the middle and later 1960s. Governmental moneys made possible the formation of what authors Ricardo Parra, Víctor Ríos, and Armando Gutiérrez referred to as parallel organizations.[17] In contrast with alternative organizations like the UFW, which challenged the status quo, parallel organizations typically sought to mimic European American institutions and thus were perceived as less threatening by those holding power. They were typically reformist, aimed at achieving gains within the universalist goals of equal opportunity for upward mobility and amelioration of the most blatant forms of public discrimination. Funds from the War on Poverty and related programs of the era permitted Chicanos opportunities for personal advancement but often lured them into local struggles with the expectation of improving life in the barrios. The government programs exposed the profound contradictions between the assimilationist rhetoric that had been bandied about for several generations and the material reality of continued inequality in Chicano communities throughout the nation. If Mexicans had been the last of the immigrants and experienced similar access to institutions and opportunities for schooling and personal advancement as European Americans, there would have been no need for such programs and organizations. Their very existence acknowledged ongoing inequality long after the barrios were first formed, and they challenged notions that treatment had been equal for all.

Some parallel organizations had very specific goals, including the provision of barrio health clinics. Extant health services for many neighborhoods were limited in quantity and quality, typically provided by paternalistic and uncaring doctors in distant locations. In St. Paul, a group of Chicana and Chicano volunteers organized to establish a neighborhood clinic, engaging in a gradualist approach. They first found available space and then convinced administrators of area hospitals to provide equipment. Finally they sought and found a number of willing young volunteer doctors. Their efforts made possible the creation in 1970 of the West Side People's Health Center, popularly called La Clínica, which quickly demonstrated its viability and need. La Clínica was soon able to hire its own full-time professionals to replace the volunteers. Its bilingual staff provided regular and emergency treatment to deal with a range of family services, chronic and terminal illnesses, and prenatal and dental care. Because the task was clear and specific and the project could sustain itself once established, the volunteer organization had no further reason to exist. It was a reformist and parallel organization, as it sought simply to ensure that services already available in most neighborhoods would also be offered for barrio residents. Similar concern resulted in local volunteer efforts to create clinics in many midwestern barrios around the same time, including the Alivio Medical Center in the Pilsen barrio of Chicago, La Clínica Latina on the near South Side of Milwaukee, and the Community Health and Social Service Center in Southwest Detroit.[18]

Community-based organizing often involved more militant approaches inspired by the grassroots tactics of Saul Alinsky's Back-of-the-Yards Neighborhood Council in Chicago, which combined features of both parallel and alternative organizations. Alinsky had been directly instrumental in the formation of the Community Services Organization (CSO), active in California Mexican communities since 1947 and a training ground for many organizers who formed the UFW. The model also influenced organizations around Chicago and the Calumet area, including the Calumet Community Congress and the Concerned Latins Organization in East Chicago, and the United Neighborhood Organization (UNO) in Chicago. UNO addressed issues pertinent to the Latino neighborhoods and its residents in the city, including immigrant protection, dealing with the INS, seeking public school accountability, construction of new schools in the rapidly growing Latino barrios, and addressing census bureau population undercounting.[19]

Community-based midwestern organizations that appeared elsewhere included the Latin American Union for Civil Rights (LAUCR) in Milwaukee, the Latin Americans United for Political Action (LAUPA) in the Detroit area, the Hispanic Action Council in Toledo, and United Mexican Americans in South Bend. With a primary concern for civil rights, they addressed issues of education, social change, justice, and increasing Chicano political power by pressuring policy makers and office holders to adopt positions more responsive to local Mexican working-class populations. LAUCR, formed in 1968, addressed discriminatory hiring practices by public and private employers, police brutality, harassment by immigration authorities, educational policies in public schools and universities, and the treatment of Chicanos by social service agencies. It also joined other Milwaukee organizations to assist in the creation of a bilingual/bicultural school for Chicano and Puerto Rican youth, a free health clinic, local recreational facilities, and the formation of the Spanish-Speaking Outreach Institute at the University of Wisconsin–Milwaukee. The tactics of these organizations often appeared more threatening than their objectives, as they organized street demonstrations, sat in on the offices of public officials, and attended city council and other meetings en masse.

Their longer-range goal of empowerment through ongoing organizing, raising the consciousness of working-class Mexicans, gaining greater influence in political life, and curbing abuses did suggest a profound challenge to the status quo. Yet most objectives were reformist and did not seek to change the structures of power or relations in society and thus could be viewed as adopting alternative methods to achieve largely parallel goals.[20]

Midwestern Chicanos also joined organizations transplanted directly from the Southwest. The most explicitly political, the Texas-based Raza Unida Party, established chapters in twenty-five states and the District of Columbia. It was influential throughout the Midwest, with greatest activity in Illinois and northern Indiana. Aware of limited possibilities for electoral politics in the region, party members primarily addressed broader issues, including immigration and the establishment of a unified Chicano political voice throughout the nation.[21]

Another transplant, the Brown Berets, formed in California during the heyday of the Chicano Movement in 1967, spread to most midwestern barrios in the late 1960s and early 1970s. A chapter appeared on the West Side of St. Paul in 1969 that maintained an erratic presence until 1973, and as in other cities it attracted working-class and the poorest youth in the barrio, many of whom had police records and were targets of repression. Because the Brown Berets lacked a centralized organizational structure, as former member Rudolph Saucedo observed, "we didn't know who belonged to the national organization." At its peak the chapter had about fifty active members, ranging in age between twelve and twenty-seven years, including females, in contrast to some of the organizations of their parents and grandparents, which often permitted only auxiliary status for women. While primarily oriented toward youth, it had a number of associates who were older "but did not want to become known as official members" because they were not willing to openly associate with a group that dominant society and "respectable" Mexican American and Latino organizations held in low esteem.[22]

During its most active phase, the St. Paul Berets held weekly meetings during which members addressed community and youth issues, including recreation, better housing, and employment. They disavowed the use of narcotics and alcohol and encouraged members to remain in school or maintain gainful employment, although, as Saucedo noted, they "didn't know about higher education. They didn't know it was available to them."[23] Their access to schooling was limited not only by racism but also by class background, as most came from the poorest families, attended schools with the lowest scholastic achievement records, and had few positive contacts with collegiate role models.

St. Paul Brown Berets members participated in many volunteer activities, support for the UFW grape boycott and other Chicano groups, fundraising, dances and paper drives to aid West Side youth, and assistance in local rallies. The also performed personal good works, including chaperoning children for Christmas parties and weekend camping trips. Members claim to have originated the idea for the Neighborhood House annual arts and crafts festival that began in 1973.[24]

Brown Berets members understood many of their own strengths and limitations; as Saucedo observed, "the streets we knew about, and we could deal with it. Political areas we didn't know." They helped make the streets safer by calming rowdy people and parties and convinced the city to place street lighting in key neighborhood locations. They also kept the streets safe from drugs. According to Saucedo, "at that time, we didn't know the people who were pushing the drugs. They were informed to stay out of the West Side with those drugs. Those were measures we could deal with ourselves." In protecting their neighborhood, they were performing a function they had learned from their parents, that an organized community could prevent problems and reduce tensions. The distinctiveness of local chapters was evident in a comparison of the St. Paul Brown Berets with the chapter in East Chicago, which addressed many similar issues, including support for the grape boycott, schooling, recreation, and safety in the streets. Many East Chicago Berets members were more solidly working class and employed in local steel mills. They organized also to secure better representation and employment opportunities for Chicanos "willing to challenge anyone on issues pertaining to the socioeconomic situation of the Latino" and "to coalesce with almost anyone" interested in participating in the betterment "of the Latin people of East Chicago." In seeking to gain respect and justice for Chicanos of the working class and the very poor, the Brown Berets represented a threat to dominant society and its biases. Dominant local institutions consistently tried to discredit them and their efforts: "they didn't want to recognize us," Saucedo observed. He added, "teachers knew about us and tried to warn the kids about us. Even many parents who had internalized the attitudes of the dominant institutions "were working against us. They would have their children stay away from our group."[25]

In part because of their class backgrounds, youth, and loose organizational structure, the Brown Berets were misunderstood and had difficulty countering misrepresentations of them as street toughs, gang members, and delinquents. As Saucedo noted, "most organizations didn't recognize us. They for sure, didn't respect us. They thought we were loud-mouth punks." Societal racism and class biases made it easier for police to engage in open repression, and as Saucedo ruefully noted, "one of the reasons why we became less active in the community was police harassment." Members were stopped consistently for police checks of cars and licenses, and because their vehicles usually were old, "we almost always got tickets for faulty equipment on our car." He added, "it was mostly physical abuse that occurred during the time the guy should have just given us the ticket. Instead we'd either get our hair pulled or get yanked out of the car, we'd get clubbed and end up going to jail for disorderly conduct." Law enforcement officers also sought to discredit members to other influential people in the community, "letting them know about our police records." Despite efforts to improve their own images and to clean up the community, member Gilbert de lao acknowledged, "we have a bad image," which Saucedo asserted "was our downfall." The Brown Berets were most feared because they sought to alter the class biases of dominant society through eliminating discrimination against the poorest residents of the community, assuming they could be treated with respect. Although they often failed to articulate that vision, a midwestern study concluded, they "did serve, however, to realign the positions of other organizations to a more militant and compatible position in terms of *la causa*." [26]

## Agency and Agencies

The activities of the poor, particularly Blacks, Chicanos, Puerto Ricans, and American Indians, were profoundly influenced by a shift in government philosophy that accompanied the War on Poverty. Its programs accepted an assumption that private initiative alone had failed to resolve long-standing problems of poverty and discrimination and that government intervention was necessary. Initiated during the presidency of Lyndon B. Johnson, it focused on schooling, job training, and placement programs that offered opportunities for individuals to overcome economic inequality, which historically had never been a systematic concern in assimilationist thought. The job training and placement efforts were highlighted by the Economic Opportunity Act of 1964, which created the Office of Economic Opportunity. To address more general deficits in schooling, Title I of the Elementary and Secondary Education Act of 1964 provided funds for programs aimed at the needs of culturally and educationally disadvantaged children, with later amendments to address the needs of their parents. The programs permitted local agencies to use federal funds to create courses in basic education and job training, as well as services including emergency housing, transportation, advocacy counseling, and job referrals. The OEO was modified on several occasions after its creation and then replaced by the Comprehensive Employment and Training Act (CETA) in 1973, which in turn was superseded by the Jobs Training Partnership Act (JTPA) in 1983.[27]

To deal with related concerns of unfair legal treatment, the Civil Rights Act of 1964, particularly Title VII, explicitly prohibited discrimination on the basis of gender, creed, race, or ethnic background, "to achieve equality of employment opportunities and remove barriers that have operated in the past." To deal with employment discrimination, the Equal Employment Opportunity Commission (EEOC) monitored cases to ensure compliance with the law. Under the OEO, legal aid offices were established in many barrios, including the Centro Legal in St. Paul and Justicia in Topeka. By removing barriers to education and employment and providing legal aid, it was argued, minorities would have equal opportunities to overcome inequality through their own individual efforts.[28]

The broader goals of the War on Poverty programs have been the subject of ongoing debate. A central issue is whether the government sought to create conditions that would permit greater agency among Chicanos, or simply created agencies intent on coopting dissent and quieting militants. In its early years, as Juan García has noted in East Chicago, the government programs "prompted Mexican American associations to become more clearly oriented toward social action." Furthermore, as Harvey Choldin and Grafton Trout concluded in their study of Mexicans in Michigan, as a result of the programs, "some new organizational activity has been generated and new leadership has been developing."[29]

By design, the legislation permitted a windfall for established social service agencies and Catholic and Protestant church groups to expand their community-based activities. Local organizations could apply for government funding to operate the programs. In the Twin Cities, the two institutions with the longest involvement in the barrio, the Catholic Archdiocese and Neighborhood House, sponsored the earliest proposals. In other cities, ethnic organizations including the American G.I. Forum and LULAC also got an early start. In some cases organizations that had been floundering received a new lease on life. Thus the first beneficiaries of the poverty programs were parallel organizations able to create new agencies, funded by the federal government, aimed at creating opportunities for hard-working Mexicans to attain the middle-class respectability that had long eluded them.

Chicanos were particularly visible in establishing and maintaining leadership positions in job training programs, highlighted by the combined efforts of the American G.I. Forum and LULAC, which in 1965 created SER, a nonprofit corporation that focused on job training, counseling, and placement. Funded by the U.S. Department of Labor (USDL), the OEO, and the Department of Health, Education, and Welfare, SER established offices for the Spanish-speaking throughout the nation, including the midwestern states of Illinois, Kansas, Wisconsin, Indiana, Nebraska, and Michigan. Similar programs were created by other organizations, particularly the Catholic Church, through regional offices of the National Catholic Conference of Bishops. In Northwest Ohio, the Toledo Diocesan Opportunity Commission used OEO antipoverty grant money for a program at the Guadalupe Center in the South End barrio that offered education, counseling, family services, and recreational activities.[30]

The ability of established institutions to take advantage of federal funds was also evident in Milwaukee, where the Catholic Archdiocese initiated its first project, the Spanish Center, in 1963, concerned about its waning influence in the barrio. As the Center's executive officer reported in a board meeting the following year, "the Protestant churches and the YMCA were making bids for the Latin races, a challenge was there to be met." It received early OEO and state grants to establish pre-school, adult basic education, consumer education, work training and job placement programs, a credit union, and a medical and dental clinic. As with other programs funded by the OEO, relationships of empowerment and control were not addressed, as one critic noted, for the church was not concerned with "self-determination." During a heated debate over naming a director, "the board decided on having an Anglo in charge so neither Puerto Ricans nor Mexican-Americans could charge favoritism." As the Chicano insurgency intensified in Milwaukee in the late 1960s, Catholic Church hierarchy was forced to respond to such criticism. Its Anglo director claimed it was a successful center because of its ability "to attract the older, more conservative Latins who might object to confrontation politics" that challenged its domination.[31]

Chicano concerns extended to schooling, where sharp inequality with the majority population continued. In the mid 1960s, Julián Samora and Richard Lamanna found that one of eight Mexican American adults in East Chicago had never attended school, only one of five finished high school, and one in fifty graduated from college. They concluded that in the 1920s Paul Taylor "was somewhat too optimistic about the educational opportunities" for midwestern Mexican youth, as his assumption that educational gaps would be readily overcome remained a distant dream forty years later. In St. Paul, a 1971 study also found that only 20 percent of adult Chicanos had graduated from high school, and a report five years later revealed that among those still attending the city's public schools, 82 percent were reading far below their grade level. According to an Illinois report, dropout rates for Latino students in 1970–1971 were between 55 percent and 60 percent. Yet the distressing findings compiled by school districts were unduly optimistic according to a number of independent authors who concluded that school officials commonly manipulated statistics deliberately in order to cover up their own failures. As a 1974 U.S. Civil Rights Commission report for Illinois determined, there was "a systemic denial of the rights of Latino students to an education." [32]

Many interested parties turned to bilingual education as a remedy, often premised on an assumption that since Chicano students "stand far behind their Anglo counterparts in English-language ability," as a St. Paul report observed, they could fare better in Spanish.[33] Advocates promoted two types of programs based on different premises. One considered bilingual education a panacea for problems that Chicano children encountered and expected them to serve as a vehicle for regaining a language and culture they were losing. A second considered it simply as a temporary tool to hasten English-language assimilation for nonnative English speakers. In practice, only a small number of bilingual programs focused on improving Spanish or teaching history and culture, and such programs often were adopted in settings where children already had adequate English language skills. Some of their participants were Chicanos, but a greater number were European Americans whose parents hoped to keep them abreast of the changing world economy and the internationalization of culture. The vast majority of bilingual programs focused on individuals with weak English language skills, particularly immigrants and their young children, and their goal was to gain competency and total immersion in English-language instruction as soon as possible.

Despite the modest expectations of most programs, a core of staunch opponents quickly rose to challenge any form of bilingual instruction, claiming that it threatened the unity of the nation. They consciously distorted goals of advocates of bilingual education, who consistently agreed that Americanization and fluency in English were ultimate goals of the educational system. Opposition groups succeeded in preventing full implementation of comprehensive bilingual education programs in most locations, but they could not prevent increased demands for bilingual instruction or English as a Second Language (ESL) classes, because foreign-born populations were growing rapidly.

The largest program in the region, conducted by the Chicago Department of Cultural and Language Education, by 1992 offered bilingual classes at the elementary, secondary, and community college levels to almost fifty thousand students, overwhelmingly immigrants and their children, about 80 percent Spanish-speaking. Elsewhere in the Midwest bilingual programs were implemented most frequently amidst dense concentrations of immigrant children. In most settings, like Garden City, Kansas, administrators "somewhat reluctantly" agreed to them but lacked a clear understanding of their role, goals, and functions, thereby limiting their effectiveness. Despite confusion and criticism, "serious research increasingly points toward a consensus: children learn English faster and are more likely to excel academically if they are given several years of instruction in their native language first." A 1995 Chicago study found that dropout rates for students enrolled in bilingual programs were 30 percent, compared with 60 percent for students in the regular program.[34]

In St. Paul and many other midwestern cities with smaller Mexican-born populations, the earliest bilingual centers and schools for Latino children often survived only a few years. Federal funding permitted the formation of the Mexican-American Cultural and Educational Center within the St. Paul School District in 1971. It met Minnesota State Board of Education guidelines of complementing "existing school curriculum" by enhancing Mexican American education and cultural and historical awareness. The center offered a bilingual education program and classes in Spanish, as well as regional Mexican dancing, driver's training, and music for children. Located in the former Garfield Elementary School building, during its brief history it also housed the office of the Mexican Consulate, the Migrant Tutorial Program, the Mexican Dance Troupe, the Minnesota Migrant Council, the Mexican-American Boxing Club, and the Guadalupe Credit Union. As a creation of the state, it was also dependent on its largesse, and in 1975 the St. Paul School District ordered the building torn down after it had been condemned as a firetrap. The decision coincided with the success of bilingual education opponents to reduce Title VII funding. The school district was unwilling to provide its own money, so after four years, the Center ceased to function. In many other midwestern cities and towns, opposition groups successfully prevented the implementation of even minimalist remedial programs aimed at students with limited English-language proficiency, often despite the laws.[35]

Funding for education during the early years of the War on Poverty also offered opportunities for local institutions, including churches, to establish new programs. In St. Paul, the Roman Catholic Archdiocese initiated a schooling program through the Guadalupe Area Project (GAP), a multiservice center which "operates as a combined Catholic welfare agency and a community neighborhood house," and an alternative education center for local youth and adults. Directed by Sister Giovanni, herself a native of the West Side of St. Paul and a teacher at the Catholic Youth Center, the GAP began as a summer project offering craft and recreational activities for youth in 1964 and its first adult basic education classes in 1966. Federal funding permitted it to expand into preschool Head Start classes, continuing adult education, ESL, basic literacy training, employment assistance and job counseling, arts and crafts courses, special tutorial programs, and courses in Mexican art and history. It also had an emergency food pantry, clothing, counseling for parents and teens, assistance, and referral.[36]

Funded in its early years by the OEO and private donations, the GAP relied heavily on volunteers and student teachers from area colleges and universities. After disagreements with the federal government over regulations, it eventually turned to the United Way to augment its own money-generating efforts. In 1976 it started an alternative school for youth who had dropped out of high school, focusing mostly on practical courses like basic education; remedial reading, writing, arithmetic, and current events; money management; homemaking and child care; preparation for the GED equivalency diploma; and counseling. By 1984, more than nine hundred teenagers had attended the school.[37] With its top-down approach and control within the church hierarchy, the GAP was a parallel institution that accepted a "bootstrap" philosophy consistent with the War on Poverty.

The Catholic Archdiocese also established two projects for St. Paul Mexican children through Our Lady of Guadalupe Church. It opened the Guadalupe Elementary School in 1962, fulfilling desires articulated by local parishioners and Father James Ward since the late 1940s. They hoped that by offering a culturally sensitive curriculum and a familiar and comfortable environment that encouraged learning, it would be an improvement over the public schools, where Chicano youth had fared so poorly. It could not, however, attract a critical mass of students, and the small parish lacked funds to maintain the effort. It ceased operations in 1968, and the dream of a Mexican school in the barrio again went into abeyance. In 1971 the church established a preschool, Mi Cultura Day Care Center, the first bilingual Mexican American licensed child care center in Minnesota. It also offered classes in Spanish language, Mexican customs, culture, dance, and other traditions.[38] Reflecting the rapid increase in full-time female employment outside the home, it served to hasten the assimilation of women with young children into the workforce.

A more successful school appeared in Milwaukee in 1969, when Mexican parents gained control of Holy Trinity's parochial school, renamed the Bruce-Guadalupe community school. It developed a rigorous academic program with mandatory bilingual education; every teacher was bilingual and all classes were conducted in both languages. It was predicated on close involvement with the working-class parents of students, and high school dropout rates approached zero. Elsewhere, a few Catholic schools made smooth adjustments to changing demographics, including St. Agnes in Chicago, which became overwhelmingly Mexican. Through dedicated faculty and parental involvement, it continued to thrive, although 87 percent of its student body came from families below the poverty line.[39]

Church leaders justified educational projects as a necessary alternative to public schools, which they justly criticized for neglecting Mexican children. Yet they challenged neither dominant society nor power relations within the Catholic Church, and their curriculum offered a limited alternative vision of society. The hierarchy of archbishops, bishops, priests, nuns, and teachers remained overwhelmingly European and European American. The programs focused principally on providing Mexican children and adults survival skills that permitted them to function as a working class, employed by and serving the demands of dominant society. Parishioners like South Bend resident María Hernández of the Guadalupanas in South Bend were concerned about control. She observed, "we would like a Mexican priest but it seems to be impossible." Even at the level of the teaching faculty, power relations had changed only slightly. By the early 1990s, the Latino population represented more than one third of the Catholic population of the United States, but Latinas were only 2 percent of the nation's nuns.[40] While the Catholic Church responded to concerns of the Chicano Movement by establishing educational programs for parishioners, changes in power relations were little more than symbolic.

The War on Poverty had a special focus on the farmworker population, overwhelmingly Chicano, which was settling out increasingly in midwestern cities and towns. Earlier programs attending to migrant workers and their children in the region had been established in the 1930s and 1940s by volunteers of the Migrant Ministry, a coalition of Protestant churches, and the Catholic Church quickly created its own programs in response to that challenge. Their influence was limited, and in the 1960s governments passed legislation providing a range of educational, health, and legal services specifically on behalf of migrant and seasonal farmworkers. The same groups, along with independent organizations, took advantage of the legislation to establish local programs to encourage settlement and assist recently settled farmworkers. In St. Paul, the Migrant Tutorial Program, established in 1971, offered courses in reading, math, and spelling, mostly for elementary school children of farmworkers and recent settlers. Teachers found that student test scores improved very rapidly, often because it was the first time they had received systematic attention from teachers and tutors, and because of close communication with parents.[41]

Migrant agencies in Minnesota began in 1965 when local volunteers supported by the Catholic Church established the organization that became Migrants, Incorporated, in St. Paul and elsewhere in Minnesota and North Dakota. A second agency, the Twin Cities Resettlement Center, which soon changed its name to Migrants in Action, formed in 1969 at Neighborhood House, also focusing on settling former farmworkers. It soon folded, but some of its staff organized another Migrants in Action in 1971. Both groups identified as advocates for farmworkers, offering counseling programs, health care, and basic education and skills training programs to enhance job preparedness and rehabilitate housing. They competed for funds for several years until they eventually split along geographic lines, with the Minnesota Migrant Council operating in central, southern, and western Minnesota, and a resurrected Migrants in Action developing an "all encompassing community resettlement program for migrants who choose to live in St. Paul." It later expanded its mission and changed its name to Hispanos en Minnesota.[42]

The erratic and often turbulent history of migrant agencies in Minnesota was replicated elsewhere, popularly attributed to lack of experience with paperwork, overextension, internal competition, and opposition by farmers and small-town neighbors. Yet state agencies responsible for approving funding were a source of greater difficulties, according to Peter Moreno, a coordinator of migrant programs in the Office of Economic Opportunity in Minnesota. Moreno stated that bureaucrats were slow to acknowledge that "the cultural shock that comes with changing from one cultural environment to another, is rather severe," and in comparison to other states, he charged, migrant programs were a disgrace to Minnesota. The nature of funding enhanced factionalism and discord, while frequent changes in funding agencies, competition over soft-money grants, and whims of local administrators helped ensure program instability and ineffectiveness.[43]

The difficulties community-based organizing efforts faced in taking advantage of War on Poverty funds were evident on several levels. The programs most likely to be funded were affiliated with churches and, as a Milwaukee activist complained, were "controlled by Anglo administrators who were not concerned with the farm workers." In Chicago Heights, an effort to establish an independent antipoverty agency by the Community Effort Organization resulted in the Centro de Oportunidad in 1967, using soft money from the OEO and USDL. As historian Juan García observed, when funding crises occurred, "people operating such programs were often blamed for the lack of results." Still another problem was that the competitive nature of funding ensured friction between competing interests, between Chicanos and African Americans, and even among different factions of Chicanos. Most importantly, the agencies responsible for funding had other priorities. In Kansas City, the Economic Opportunity Foundation was challenged for being racist and bigoted and for refusing to listen to Chicanos despite petitions, public hearings, board meetings, and demonstrations. By design the government-funded programs created dependency, ineffectiveness, and destructive competition—as García noted, "a built-in mechanism that practically guaranteed failure."[44]

In response to criticism, statewide coordinating agencies appeared, including the Office for Spanish Speaking People in Minnesota in 1977, which changed its name to the Spanish Speaking Affairs Council in 1978, and to the Chicano/Latino Affairs Council in 1995. Its purpose was "to promote the social, economic and political development" of the Spanish-speaking people of the state, to serve as a conduit for Latinos to the state government, and to act as a referral agency. This advisory body was also charged with investigating complaints from Spanish-speaking people about state services, researching their concerns, and making recommendations to the state on policy and legislation. Similar agencies eventually appeared in more than twenty states in the nation, including Kansas, Nebraska, Iowa, Michigan, Wisconsin, Ohio, and Illinois.[45]

Among their first research projects was to examine Latino employment in state governments, and they consistently found severe underrepresentation, particularly at top administrative levels. Most states promptly reduced their funding, limited their investigative powers; and dismissed staff, apparently for being unduly diligent in research and investigation. As one critic noted, the Spanish Speaking Affairs Council "has little power and . . . functions more as a token Chicano in the governor's office." With only two full-time staff responsible for researching, investigating, and representing the interests of both migrants and permanent Spanish-speaking residents to the state government, it could accomplish little. Yet its high visibility attracted attention, and critics could claim that such state agencies had been created principally to co-opt criticism and direct attention away from structural inequalities within state government itself. Criticisms were strongest among youth, where expectations were highest. As the Chicano Youth Commission complained in a 1970 Kansas City meeting, such agencies and programs "have given little or no opportunities for Mexican-American students to study their history and culture." The state was reluctant to allow intrusions into established bases of knowledge, setting the stage for another challenge.[46]

### The Struggle for Knowledge: Chicano Studies

The activities surrounding Chicano studies complicate distinctions between parallel and alternative organizations. In form, as a department or program, Chicano studies could be considered a parallel institution. Its role in the production and transmission of knowledge, in particular in creating distinct paradigms for understanding, challenged the hegemony of European-based knowledge at its foundations. While the struggle over Chicano studies achieved its greatest successes in California, with important victories elsewhere in the Southwest, Chicano youth also participated in high school blowouts and university demonstrations in cities and on campuses throughout the Midwest. High school blowouts in Topeka in April 1970 protested against the lack of Chicano studies in the curriculum, while in Milwaukee the Centro Cultural Educativo Chicano-Boricua created an alternative high school with a curriculum that included courses on Mexican and Puerto Rican history and culture.[47]

In the region's universities, Chicano students often began their ethnic research by seeking to uncover student enrollments. A 1972–1973 study found that at Michigan State University, with more than 41,000 students, there were fewer than 100 Latinos enrolled, while at Notre Dame, with more than 8,000 total, there were less than fifty Mexicans and Puerto Ricans. Conditions were similarly bleak at the University of Wisconsin–Madison, with more than 35,000 students in 1973–1974, of whom only 219 were Latinos. The numbers of Chicanas, Chicanos, and Puerto Ricans often were not made public, "due to the lack of full cooperation" from University administrators. In 1973, Latino students at the Chicago Circle Campus of the University of Illinois (later UIC) staged a peaceful sit-in. They sought to alter "Circle's refusal to end its discriminatory admissions quota against Latins," who represented only 2 percent of university enrollment, although the campus was located "in a largely Black and Latin setting," and for its failure to offer Latino curricular content. Adopting a pattern more popular in Illinois than neighboring states, the administration responded not by addressing the issues but instead by attempting to smother the publicity by arresting thirty-nine protesters. Nevertheless, the public pressure helped create the Rafael Cintrón-Ortiz Latino Cultural Center.[48]

Chicano enrollment was one of the earliest student concerns on the Minneapolis campus of the University of Minnesota, the flagship institution of higher education in the state. In 1970 it was reported that there were fewer than 100 Mexican Americans out of more than 40,000 students matriculated on campus. As a result of student demonstrations and demands, an embarrassed university administration permitted students to serve as volunteer recruiters and later hired recruiters to increase Chicano enrollment to about 300 by 1974. Although the state's Chicano population continued to increase rapidly, enrollment figures appeared to stagnate, and university officials devised a number of ways to provide the appearance of linear progress. The most successful involved a strategy of counting Spanish-surnamed or "Hispanic" students instead of Chicanos, consistent with federal practices. By 1976, official figures indicated 376 Spanish-surnamed students at the Twin Cities campus.[49]

The reason for the collapsing of groups was not difficult to understand, for although Chicanos represented between 65 percent and 80 percent of the identified Latino population in midwestern states, they were a minority of "Hispanic" students enrolled on university campuses. Because Chicanos were much more severely underrepresented than other Latinos, administrators used the broader "Hispanic" identifier to cover up their disastrous recruitment efforts. At the University of Minnesota and some other campuses, administrators sometimes tried to augment figures by including international students and faculty. In the case of Minnesota, Chicana and Chicano students, staff, and faculty engaged in a twenty-five-year struggle for full disclosure. University officials stonewalled, offering a number of excuses, including deceptive assertions that it was illegal to divulge personal enrollment information of students that distinguished the various components of the "Hispanic" group. They also argued that there were few Chicanos in the pool of qualified students, staff, or faculty, in effect updating cultural deficiency theories that had been in abeyance and were largely discredited in academic circles. In 1994 the university finally acknowledged that it was possible to distinguish and reveal enrollment data by national origin. The figures revealed, not surprisingly, that less than one third of recently enrolled Latino students at the university were Chicanas and Chicanos, although about 80 percent of Latinos identified by ethnic origin in the state were of Mexican descent.[50] The data revealed glaring contradictions between a public higher education system that promoted equality of opportunity and the lack of assimilation into institutions of higher learning by Chicanos as a group. It also revealed administrative strategies aimed at obfuscation rather than enlightenment.

Struggles over Chicano representation in the institution also extended to the creation of representations, namely in the production and teaching of knowledge on Chicanos and its legitimacy in academia. It was much more contentious than issues of student enrollments or the numbers of staff and faculty, for it challenged the long-established base of power within the faculty and its ability to define the paradigms of knowledge, which had long been overwhelmingly European American, male creations. In Minnesota the struggle was initiated by a coalition of Chicana and Chicano students from the University of Minnesota and Macalester College who in the fall of 1969 formed the Latin Liberation Front, later the Chicano Liberation Front (CLF), under the auspices of the Dr. Martin Luther King Scholarship Program. According to Ramona Arreguín, the organization's first president, a key concern was the low number of Chicano students, and much early effort involved voluntary recruitment efforts by those already enrolled. Front members simultaneously addressed the lack of Chicana and Chicano staff and faculty or support programs and the absence of curriculum focusing on Chicanos. They exerted influence beyond their own small numbers because of unswerving support from parents and from Chicano organizations elsewhere in the Midwest.[51]

In its search for curricular materials and teaching models, the Chicano Liberation Front became involved in a field study highlighted by participation in the March 1970 symposium sponsored by the Crusade for Justice in Denver. It addressed a wide range of issues, including teaching, knowledge, and the recently announced Plan de Santa Bárbara proposed by the Chicano Coordinating Council on Higher Education. It inspired members who attended the symposium as well as their faculty mentor, Sr. Alfredo González, to demand a Chicano Studies Department based on the Plan. Members continued to meet with University of Minnesota administrators, who proved unresponsive until the Front coordinated a public demonstration in front of Morrill Hall on September 15, 1970, timed to coincide with the Fiestas Patrias and garner community-wide support. As CLF member Adam Chavarría recalled, "basically nothing was done. They only budged when we yelled at them." [52]

The public demonstrations by students and growing support from their community-based allies convinced the university to sponsor a Chicano symposium in December, in which academics and students from throughout the Midwest addressed Chicano studies curricular issues. The group chose the University of Minnesota as the site for the creation of a Chicano Studies Department in the Midwest. It would serve "the purposes and needs of the community within the state of Minnesota and . . . students in the surrounding areas as well as interested Anglo students." Strong support came from African American and American Indian student and community constituencies, as well as from a handful of sympathetic faculty and administrators who agreed to permit the formation of a Chicano Studies Curriculum Committee, which submitted a proposal for a department in May 1971. The administration procrastinated until faced with more public demonstrations, including another general strike and occupation of Morrill Hall, and promises of continued unrest, as had been necessary for the formation of the African and Afro-American Studies Department. In February 1972, the University Regents voted to establish the Department of Chicano Studies in the College of Liberal Arts, "for the purpose of providing a course of study designed to acquaint students with the historical and contemporary experience of Chicanos." While they justified the new department primarily as serving the academic needs and interests of Chicano students, and secondarily as providing a more general intellectual and academic function within the university setting, the administration fully realized its public relations value among minority populations of the Twin Cities and academic institutions throughout the nation. [53]

The department considered its mission as "the product of collective effort dedicated to quality instruction and creative scholarship," while serving as a resource base for Chicano-related programs conducted in cooperation with local Chicano constituencies. The first acting chair was appointed in August 1972, and the department offered its first courses during the 1972–1973 academic year, although Chicano studies courses had appeared on campus first during the 1969–1970 academic year. By August

1974, the department had a permanent chair, four additional full-time faculty members, plus part-time teaching and research assistants. It was committed to three distinct academic areas: education, including Spanish for Spanish-speaking people and bilingual education for elementary and secondary teachers; the humanities; and the social sciences.[54]

Early department faculty reflected diverse currents in the Chicano Movement, including those seeking reform (equity), in which Chicano studies would augment and parallel existing curricula; a second element willing to collaborate with efforts to suppress the department for individual ends; and a third group that challenged the academic status quo. The first considered Chicano curriculum essentially as filling a gap in information, as articulated in a Chicano Studies Department planning document of 1975. The document stated that "the central issue of establishing Chicano studies in institutions of higher learning is the question of assimilation versus cultural pluralism," one voice or many parallel voices in the nation. Historian Albert Camarillo of Stanford University concurred that the central purpose of Chicano studies has been to ensure that a story previously unavailable be brought to light. Similarly, Professor Rolando Hinojosa, chair of the department at the University of Minnesota in the late 1970s, in his rich litany of novels and short stories portrayed a Chicano reality that existed alongside an English-speaking world.[55]

Those who collaborated with efforts to suppress Chicano studies typically lacked the intellectual rigor or imagination to engage in creative scholarship and often turned to administrative positions when they were available. Commonly removed from Chicano constituencies, they were willing to accept the reward of employment over others more highly qualified. As administrators, they failed to address critical issues within the department, including class enrollments, which plummeted in the late 1970s after initial student interest largely because of their own lack of administrative leadership and incompetent teaching. Once they performed their function for the university, they were likely to be ousted, often on the grounds of failure to publish.

Individuals who viewed Chicano studies as a challenge to dominant academic paradigms did not share a single vision. One faculty member who focused principally on the European American hegemony in scholarship, anthropologist Gilberto López y Rivas, made a mark in academia through his writings on Chicanos as a national minority. His political sympathies, according to oral traditions, forced him to leave the department abruptly and flee the country, later appearing as a professor at the Universidad Autónoma Metropolitana in Mexico City and a politician for the Partido Revolucionario Democrático (PRD), where he supported the Zapatista movement. The late Marcela Lucero Trujillo, a scholar, teacher, and community activist and a department member for much of the 1970s, served as an inspirational role model to students while her early poetry addressed concerns of Chicanas and machismo and illuminated historical experiences of individual and collective struggles.[56]

Although Chicano studies academics did not speak with a single voice, their presence was sufficiently threatening to conservative and reactionary academics, who quickly sought to undo their modest accomplishments. Riding a political backlash that gained strength in the 1980s, they challenged the department's existence on three distinct premises: the need for priorities during a time of budget cuts, intellectual integrity, and cost-effectiveness. Their first argument found favor within the administration, which reduced the faculty by two thirds, entirely eliminating the curriculum in education and Spanish for the Spanish-speaking, a cut disproportionate to any conceivable notion of sharing the burden of shrinking funds. They were unable to make convincing arguments on other grounds. Academic interest in ethnic studies and minority populations continued to increase, and several highly productive scholars in the department brought recognition to the university and to the discipline. Furthermore, by the mid 1980s the department had demonstrated rising student interest as one of the most cost-effective budget units in the university. The strongest support for the department came from students, who engaged in ongoing demonstrations and appeared at public meetings of the Board of Governors and hearings before various university and faculty groups. They convinced the administration to curtail its open attacks and accept the political, intellectual, and pedagogical value of a curriculum based on Chicana and Chicano studies. The department survived as a small but viable unit, producing a coherent undergraduate curriculum and attracting graduate students who were making their own mark in academia.[57]

A second successful academic program to emerge from the early phase of the Chicano struggles in the Midwest was the Center for Chicano-Boricua Studies at Wayne State University in Detroit. Initiated by the Latin American Steelworkers caucus at Great Lakes Steel Corporation in Ecorse, it quickly gained allies from within local Mexican and Puerto Rican communities. They convinced the Chicano Caucus of the State Democratic Convention to support their proposal to establish the Latino en Marcha Scholarship Program, a step in the formation of Chicano-Boricua Studies in the university's Monteith College in 1971. Funded by

Wayne State University, its primary mission was the recruitment and retention of Chicano and Puerto Rican students.

Influenced directly by Carlos Arce, a former member of the Chicano Studies Department at California State University at Northridge, the largest in the nation, the center emphasized the direct link between an effective retention program and a culturally relevant curriculum. It had independent control over recruitment and retention, which involved instruction in reading and writing skills and personal counseling. The key component was academic, as faculty offered courses on Chicano, Mexican, and Puerto Rican history, literature, and culture, leading to a co-major in Chicano-Boricua Studies. It was based on a premise that poor student retention was not the result of students' own culture; instead, it held dominant assimilationist models as responsible. It devised a curriculum that enhanced students' own self-awareness and identity. In other words, Chicano and Puerto Rican history, culture, and literature were sources of knowledge and power rather than ignorance and impotence. In contrast to academia in general, and even to the solely academic criteria of Chicano studies departments generally, which catered largely to middle-class students, Chicano-Boricua Studies was committed to a working-class constituency and accountable to the Latino community responsible for its creation.

Chicano-Boricua Studies quickly confirmed that alternative form and content, focusing on the needs and interests of Chicano and Puerto Rican students, would result in success. The students it enrolled consistently maintained retention rates sharply higher than those of the general student population, although most had been branded as "high risk" students on entering the university. It further demonstrated that minority students from the worst schools in the city could flourish amidst the academic rigor of a major university under proper conditions. Academics, educators, and psychologists who continued to blame the culture of Chicanos and other working-class minority students were offered compelling evidence that dominant teaching and curricular paradigms and practices, rather than the cultural and class backgrounds of students, were responsible for failure.[58]

On many other midwestern campuses, students struggled for years to gain an institutionalized presence, but with less success than in Minneapolis and Detroit, and they were often repressed, sidetracked, or co-opted by university administrators and faculty. Many struggles that began in the late 1960s and early 1970s continued into the 1980s and 1990s, as a new generation of students came of age. The later efforts differed from their predecessors in two important ways. First, they were characterized by more visible leadership of women, who typically were more active and assertive than their male counterparts. On several campuses women formed distinct organizations, including La Fuerza at the University of Illinois and LUNA (Latinas Unidas Avanzando) at the University of Minnesota, which functioned as cultural and support groups while dealing with ongoing sexism in their midst. Second, they had to confront a sharp increase in open bigotry against non–European American students beginning in the late 1980s, which spread even to the public schools. As Leonard Zeskin of the Center for Democratic Renewal observed, "as a society, we don't have the commitment to racial justice we once had. That lack of commitment has been noticed and transferred to our young people." Students in many locations challenged racism, as in the memorable 1988 demonstrations at Roberto Clemente High School in Chicago, where students protested the lack of disciplinary actions against faculty who openly demeaned Mexicans, Puerto Ricans, and other Latino students in the classroom. On university campuses protests by Chicano and Latino students and their allies often gained national attention, including those at the University of Wisconsin, the University of Michigan, and the University of Illinois at Urbana-Champaign. The protests were accompanied by renewed demands for curricular reform.[59]

At the University of Wisconsin, students in Milwaukee made demands for a Chicano studies curriculum in 1969, while those in Madison called for a department beginning in 1970. Their efforts resulted in the formation of a Chicano Advisory Committee, which recommended a department on the Madison campus. University administrators bluntly rejected committee recommendations and other efforts to establish Chicano studies at the flagship campus at Madison or at the campus near the state's largest concentration of Chicanos in Milwaukee, despite ongoing student pressure. Meanwhile, efforts initiated by support staff at the small Whitewater campus, with strong support from a broadly based community throughout the state and a sympathetic administration, led to the formation of a viable Chicano studies academic program. For a period in the early and mid 1980s, the University of Wisconsin–Whitewater had the largest number and broadest range of Chicano studies course offerings in the region. Interest in Chicano studies curriculum was rekindled at Madison in the late 1980s, stimulated in part by racist incidents on campus and community pressure on the state legislature. Those efforts forced administrators in the early 1990s to hire faculty to offer a curriculum leading to a certificate in Chicano studies, but the lack of community pressure and inability to control hiring and tenure decisions precluded all but old-fashioned academic approaches.[60]

In several settings, administrators responded to student demands by providing modest course offerings under the rubrics of Latino, Latin American, or Hispanic Studies. The University of Michigan in Ann Arbor successfully kept students at bay until the early 1980s, when it sought to deflect their influence by announcing plans to create a Hispanic Studies Program, which student pressure changed to Latino Studies. Housed in the American Culture Program, it maintained a top-down focus with little student influence, permitting traditional departments to control crucial facets of hiring and governance, which severely limited program autonomy and ensured the hiring of compliant faculty. On several Illinois campuses, including Northern Illinois University and the University of Illinois at Chicago, administrators responded to student pressures by attaching Latino Studies to already-existing offerings on Latin America. The established Latin Americanists, seldom nurtured in traditions of student activism or Chicano studies, maintained control of curriculum and program agendas, and Latino curricula occupied a distinctly inferior position. Occasional student pressure, including protests at UIC in 1992, led to statements of renewed commitment, which administrators tried to forget once student unrest subsided.[61]

In other locations, administrators adopted strategies of establishing research centers to deflect curricular issues. At DePaul University in Chicago, the Hispanic Studies Institute was established in 1984 to promote research rather than teaching. Michigan State University permitted the formation of the Julián Samora Research Institute in 1989, contingent on support from outside funding. Although it acknowledged a broad-based commitment, research came first, as the administration proved unwilling to invest in curriculum until convinced by renewed waves of highly publicized student protests in the early 1990s.[62]

A more popular and callous strategy of midwestern administrations was to divert student demands for education by supporting cultural centers, which provided a place on campus for students to study, socialize, and celebrate culture through Mexican food, dance, and holidays. When controlled by committed students, as in the case of the Raza Student Cultural Center of the University of Minnesota, they could offer an impressive range of cultural and educational programs, movies, speakers, and conferences that attracted widespread interest from the university, urban, and regional communities. More often they functioned as little more than places for students to socialize while they served the greater administrative end of calming students in lieu of more costly and intellectually challenging investments in Chicano studies.[63]

Perhaps the most successful case of combining the cultural center strategy with blatant repression occurred at the University of Illinois at Urbana-Champaign, where ongoing student unrest and demands for curriculum in the early 1970s were initially calmed by administrators who established La Casa Cultural Latina in 1974. La Casa offered a setting for students to socialize, hold occasional cultural activities, and invite guest speakers, and the administration hoped it would placate their demands for knowledge. A renewed wave of student activism broke out in 1989, when a broad front of students including Mexicans, Puerto Ricans, and African Americans staged several demonstrations in response to racial incidents on campus. Their efforts forced the administration to acquiesce to their demands and create a committee to deal with the student dissatisfaction and concern for curriculum. After three additional years of waiting in vain, students intensified their pressure on the administration in the spring of 1992, when a surge of protests rocked the campus. Students demanded more than "insensitive" and "token" efforts to recruit more Latino students, offer greater autonomy for La Casa Cultural Latina, and hire more Latina and Latino faculty to provide a coherent curriculum. Their efforts were highlighted by a Cinco de Mayo rally and sit-in, which shut down the Henry Administration Building.[64]

University administrators responded with force, calling in local police attired in riot gear and carrying stun guns to quell the protest. Agents of the law treated the nonviolent protesters roughly, forcibly removing fifty-six individuals from the building, while administrators placed disciplinary letters in student files. University Chancellor Morton Weir officially criticized the students for "insensitive and confrontational behavior," which he claimed justified the administration's violence. He even canceled a meeting with the Latino Alumni Association that had been scheduled to discuss student concerns.[65] His actions further convinced students that the administration had little regard for the legitimacy of their demands or even the concerns of alumni. It appeared that the administration again covered its own failure in student recruitment and retention, hiring of Latina and Latino faculty, and demands for a timely curriculum by dragging out a new "Mexican problem."

Another set of allies intervened to thwart the administration. While most faculty on the Urbana-Champaign campus maintained a low profile during the heavy-handed administration behavior, Juliet Walker, the first African American woman on campus to be promoted to Full Professor, asserted, "this is a crisis of ethnic and racial intolerance." Law Professor Francis Boyle more bluntly complained that the chancellor and other administrators were "fit to run a prison. It was clearly racist. I have never seen white students treated this way." Simultaneously, ringing criticism poured in from prominent Latino leaders in Chicago and neighboring communities, who reminded the administration and the state of Illinois that its largest university had not complied with a long-standing commitment to represent all its citizens. The chancellor who had tried to demean the students and belittle their efforts was forced to backpedal, and three days after the sit-in, he released a report calling for sweeping changes at the university, including the hiring of additional faculty to institute curricular offerings in Latino studies.[66]

Even on smaller campuses, student pressure frequently yielded positive results. At Saint Cloud State University in Minnesota, after several years of amicable but fruitless discussions with university administrators, student members of the Movimiento Estudiantil Chicano de Aztlán (MEChA) and a diverse group of allies initiated a dramatic hunger strike on Cinco de Mayo, 1995. They demanded a Chicano student cultural center, a Chicano studies curriculum, cultural awareness training for all students, and the elimination of the offensive "Hispanic" classification by the university. They found support from allies elsewhere in the state, the region, and the nation, and after nine days the surprised university administration agreed to accept the modest student demands. Their efforts demonstrated that even small numbers of highly committed students, armed with information and a vision, could generate support and influence university policy that challenged its own narrowly based paradigms of knowledge.[67]

The efforts to establish Chicano and Latino studies programs, part of the struggle against bigotry and racism on campus, were spearheaded by students who were forced to the forefront to challenge hostile administrators and faculty who continued to deny the academic validity of the discipline of Chicano studies. The midwestern case studies confirm that faculty and administrative initiative had not resulted in the creation of a single academic program, while students' efforts were initially demeaned and consistently belittled and could not have succeeded without support from a larger community. Even on large campuses and in communities with a large demographic base, academia showed little respect for knowledge that challenged Eurocentric dominance.

The Chicano Movement in the Midwest paralleled that of the Southwest, and early activities in both regions preceded the articulation of a consciously Chicano Movement. Many midwestern efforts, including the creation of Chicano studies, found inspiration from the Plan de Santa Bárbara and southwestern models. Simultaneously, organizations like the United Farm Workers established boycott committees and attracted volunteers from cities throughout the Midwest and other parts of the country. As César Chávez and other leaders made tours, offering inspiration and advice, they also gained critical financial, institutional, and personnel support which made possible many of their important victories. The local and regional movements drew inspiration, strength, and assistance from each other, allowing youth to discover that Chicanos constituted a nationwide minority, as their elders had long understood.

The state itself became a battleground for political, educational, social, and cultural influence and was understood simultaneously as a tool of oppression and a source of liberation. As the demolition of the St. Paul barrio demonstrates, residents were unable to prevent a decision by the state to displace them, but local urban renewal and poverty projects taught them important lessons about how governments and their agencies functioned. Their ability to regroup in Concord Terrace also demonstrates that working-class White resistance was not sufficient to block their entry, as had been demonstrated earlier in other midwestern settings. While the state was not neutral in its actions, Chicanos could sometimes influence insensitive bureaucrats and government policies, if they would organize, as St. Paul resident Federico Saucedo observed, and "become a little more militant."[68]

Claims that the movement was a failure because of short-lived organizations or divisions over leadership are unduly simplistic. The brief histories of many organizations did not necessarily indicate failure, particularly when they had formed for a specific purpose, such as the volunteers who made La Clínica possible or students from the Latin Liberation Front, who created Chicano studies. They had not organized to perpetuate needless organization, and short lives for Mexican groups and agencies continued to be the norm. A 1987 report indicated that most of the thirty-four Latino-affiliated agencies and organizations in the Twin Cities area had been created in the previous ten years. Pressure from below during the War on Poverty resulted in efforts that improved physical conditions on the West Side of St. Paul and created community institutions and cultural markers. Furthermore, the struggles helped narrow gaps between Chicanos and the dominant population, reducing inequality in education and income to their lowest levels of the twentieth century.[69]

While the movement often suffered from individualism and petty infighting, divisions often reflected diversity in a population that continued to be stereotyped as monolithic. Tension also stemmed from new government programs, which often were designed to create dependency, instability, and competition over resources and not to empower constituents. The state in effect took over a role that had earlier been performed by institutions, including the Catholic Church and settlement houses, that often hindered autonomous Mexican organization. The greater presence of the state also changed leadership from that of earlier generations, when most leaders were men with relatively low levels of formal schooling who resided in and maintained close ties to the barrios and were rooted in the working class. The new agency directors were products of leadership-training programs, increasingly university-trained men and a few women, often from Latin American middle- and upper-middle-class backgrounds, having little prior contact with the working-class communities they were hired to represent or the agencies that paid their salaries. The state and private funders preferred the latter because, as one report explicitly stated, they could "more easily interact" with mainstream European Americans and dominant institutions.[70] The programs of the War on Poverty could calm potential constituents while coopting discontent, molding both agencies and their agents in their own image. It would stretch one's imagination to consider them alternative institutions.

Yet the movement was not entirely co-opted, as local struggles permitted the articulation of alternative visions, particularly in higher education, where Chicanas and Chicanos challenged insensitive bureaucrats, shoddy research, and an intense recalcitrance toward a Chicano-based curriculum. Although the struggles of the late 1960s and early 1970s established significant academic programs on only a few campuses, they were an inspiration to midwestern students of a later generation. The successful programs were not simply a function of demographics, for although the Department of Chicano Studies at Minnesota was created in the heart of a major metropolitan area, other cities in the region with greater Chicano populations lacked similar academic programs. Nor was a diverse Latino population necessarily an impediment, as demonstrated by Chicano-Boricua Studies in Detroit. The greatest hindrance to the creation and survival of Chicano studies in the academy was the resistance of university administrators and faculty who belittled efforts to establish such units and kept them under constant siege by changing criteria, agendas, and priorities that had little relationship to the quest for knowledge. The successes were the result of struggles of students and allies in the communities where they resided, creating a political base outside the university. As a University of Minnesota administrator acknowledged in 1972, "Chicano students had to sacrifice themselves to get Chicano Studies. . . . They had to force the establishment to listen to them. I would hope that in the future . . . Chicano Studies students wouldn't have to sacrifice to do that."[71] Since neither university administrators nor government agents were willing to concede defeat, struggles continued for programs to survive.

# 6 Completing a Circle

Profound changes in the world economy in the final decades of the twentieth century inaugurated another cycle in the history of midwestern Mexicanos. Rearranged labor markets, altered patterns of work, and accelerated migration from Mexico contributed to the growth of established barrios, the appearance of new *colonias,* and a more diverse population. The changes also stimulated a complex range of reactions within dominant political and popular culture and among Mexicans. This examination of the late-twentieth-century urban Midwest is informed by two broad questions—first, how have recent changes served to distinguish the recent past from earlier periods, and second, how do current conditions of midwestern Mexicans conform to popular perspectives and theories of inequality?

Assimilationist expectations remained a standard point of reference in popular culture and among academics. Its adherents continued to portray Mexicans in the Midwest as the last of the immigrants who were becoming increasingly similar to European Americans, attributing continued inequality to the rapid influx of poor immigrants. They adopted push-pull models of migration, suggesting that long-standing economic problems and depressed conditions pushed people out of Texas and Mexico and pulled them to northern states, including Minnesota, to a better quality of life, often replacing European Americans who were pulled to still more attractive opportunities elsewhere. As Arthur Campa reported in Garden City, Kansas, Anglos' expectations "are widespread" that Mexicans and Southeast Asians will assimilate as Europeans did in the past. Similarly, in seeking to account for changes in urban geography, Minneapolis newspaper reporter Don Hayner suggested that Mexicans "are behaving much like other immigrant groups in the past. They move to the suburbs."[1]

Race-based approaches countered that inequality was increasing, consistent with the prediction of the Kern Commission Report in 1968 that the United States was dividing into two societies—one largely White, suburban, and relatively well off; the other poor, urban, and significantly non-White. University of Michigan demographer William Frey stated: "I see America becoming more polarized. We will have a couple of states that are very diverse, and others where the population is older, more staid, with slightly higher income." European Americans engaged in "the flight from diversity" were moving to the latter, seeking homogeneous communities in the nation's heartland and elsewhere.[2]

Interpretations stressing class suggested that among midwestern Mexicans some individuals improved their occupational status, but a much larger proportion experienced downward mobility. The changing economy created some opportunities in high-end occupations but a much larger number of unstable, low-wage jobs in manufacturing and services. Labor market conditions also explained suburbanization, according to sociologist Doug Massey. In his study of metropolitan Chicago, he observed that Mexicans "tend to work mainly in the service and manufacturing sectors. And increasingly [the suburbs] are where those kinds of jobs have gone."[3]

World-Systems variants of class analysis emphasized that "capital mobility has created new conditions for the mobility of labor," or a world labor market, according to economist Saskia Sassen. They challenged popular views that the Midwest would consistently lose jobs in favor of low-wage countries, suggesting instead a more complex interplay of capital and labor on the international, interregional, and local levels. While some industries fled to the Third World, others remained or shifted operations to nearby settings while they restructured production and labor processes. The new industrial order upset the Fordist tendencies of an earlier era that favored large factories with stable workforces, tending instead to offer unstable, low-wage employment in smaller operations, a view consistent with the deskilling thesis of Harry Braverman. Economic restructuring influenced urban systems unevenly, as some became global cities with a specialized niche in the world economy while others could not adjust as easily and declined sharply. Along with the economic transformation, a profound change in dominant popular culture and its ideology also occurred. It was characterized by "a process through which the business class has been institutionalized as the *universal class*."[4]

## Migration and Settlement

In the final decades of the twentieth century, the European American population of the Midwest stagnated and the numbers of African Americans grew only modestly, while the Mexican population increased very rapidly but unevenly. During the generalized recession of the 1970s, detractors characterized the region as "The Rust Belt," and with the exception of Illinois, even the rate of Mexican population growth was slow. As economic restructuring accelerated during the 1980s, the number of Mexicans grew by more than 40 percent, representing more than half the total increase in the region. During the boom of the 1990s, the regional Mexican population grew at record levels, and by the end of the decade it approached two million inhabitants.[5]

Several trends characterized Mexican work and settlement in the late-twentieth-century Midwest, including modest occupational dispersion despite continued concentration in a relatively narrow range of poorly paid jobs. The sharp decline of heavy industry displaced thousands of long-established workers in large, unionized factories. Some found high-wage employment, but most worked in low-paying and unstable jobs in smaller factories, shops, and service industries, including domestics and building cleaners, restaurant workers, refuse haulers, lawn crews, and nursery workers. As a group, Mexicans experienced declining incomes, particularly among the poorest. The legal minimum wage, an important income benchmark for the working poor, declined sharply, from 98 percent of poverty level for a family of three in the 1950s to 78 percent by the late 1980s.[6]

Second, employers intensified efforts to attract workers from Mexico, who soon exceeded Texas as a source of labor migrants to the Midwest. Academic literature on relations between capital and labor reflected this change, shifting from earlier nation-based perspectives, including internal colonialism, to international and World-Systems analyses. While the majority of Mexican migration came from sending communities with long histories of links to the Midwest, it also extended farther into central and southern Mexico. The accelerated migration could be understood in the context of international pressures, particularly the Mexican recession of the 1980s, in which a sharp decline in wages, estimated at approximately 60 percent, combined with economic restructuring that made employment less stable. It forced more family members, including children, to work at poorly remunerated jobs, induced more stringent family economic measures, and compelled many individuals and families to migrate for the first time to the United States.[7]

The recently arrived Midwesterners were increasingly undocumented and vulnerable to employer efforts to drive down wages, block unionization drives, and break unions. Capitalists' behavior was reminiscent of the early twentieth century, when employers lured Mexicans to reduce wages, divide workers, and break strikes in foundries, packinghouses, tanneries, and other settings. In the late twentieth century, employers benefited from workers' vulnerable legal status and the greater intrusion of government agencies, particularly the INS, to subdue worker challenges. Chicago employer Sure-Tan, Inc., a leather processing company, for years employed a largely undocumented Mexican workforce at wages slightly above the legal minimum, offering few benefits. When employees voted to join a union in 1983, Sure-Tan promptly notified the INS of their legal status to have them deported. But workers challenged the case in court and protected their right to organize without regard to residency status.[8]

Third, Mexican settlement accelerated in established barrios and "away from traditional ports of entry."[9] New *colonias* appeared in industrial suburbs, medium-sized cities, and smaller towns. Workers from Mexico, who were hired increasingly in services and agriculture, were likely to settle out in suburbs, medium-sized cities, and smaller towns as well as in older neighborhoods, further extending the geography of Mexican settlements in the region.

Fourth, the trend toward increasing ethnic diversity within the midwestern Latino population was reversed. In the 1970s and 1980s several observers alluded to an emerging Latino identity in the Midwest, particularly Chicago, reflecting the rapid post–World War II growth of Puerto Ricans, Cubans, and Central and South Americans. But another shift soon became evident, as the Mexican population "showed explosive growth in the cities and suburbs in the 1980s, while other minorities lagged." In the Chicago metropolitan area between 1970 and 1990, the Mexican population increased by more than 50 percent, but Puerto Ricans grew by only 7 percent, while the Cuban population declined. The 1990 census reported that in Minnesota, Mexicans were more than ten times the number of Puerto Ricans, the second largest Latino group, and twenty-five times the number of Cubans, who were third. Throughout the Midwest, the growth of the Mexican population was greater than that of all other groups of Latin American origin combined. Simultaneously, self-reference to pan-ethnic identifiers like "Hispanic" and "Latino" declined in the 1990s except "in limited or restricted contexts," particularly by self-identified community leaders.[10]

Migration and settlement continued to center on Chicago, from which a "geyser" spread out in several directions, including its western suburbs, to its south and southeast into Indiana, and northward into Wisconsin beyond Milwaukee to Sheboygan and Green Bay. The home of more than half the Mexican population between Ohio and the Rocky Mountain States, the Chicago area saw the regional dominance of its Chicano communities increase as its size quadrupled between 1970 and the late 1990s.

By the latter date the city had the third largest Mexican population in the United States, surpassed only by Los Angeles and San Antonio.[11]

In 1990 Mexicans were more than two thirds of the Latino population of Chicago, who approached 20 percent of the city's total, compared with 38 percent for European Americans and 39 percent for African Americans. While Chicago's total population declined by 7.4 percent during the 1980s, its Mexican population rose by more than two hundred thousand, while Puerto Rican numbers increased by only fifteen thousand and those of Cubans declined by nine hundred. Latinos in Illinois remained highly concentrated, as 93 percent of the state total resided in the six-county metropolitan area. Future continued growth seemed likely as an estimated 30 percent of children enrolled in the Chicago public schools were Latinos, compared with less than 10 percent in 1970. As they approached 25 percent of Chicago's population by the mid-1990s, demographer Pierre de Vise predicted that they would exceed both African Americans and European Americans by the year 2005.[12]

Within Chicago, Mexicans were highly concentrated in three sections—the Near Southwest Side, the Southeast Side, and the Near Northwest Side—which combined were home to 83 percent of the city's total. Latinos were nearly one half the total population in those districts, compared with one twentieth in the rest of the city. The Near Southwest Side districts of Pilsen and Little Village were more than 90 percent Latino, overwhelmingly Mexican neighborhoods. Pilsen, a port of entry for newcomers for more than a century, was initially inhabited in the 1860s and 1870s by Germans, Irish, and Swedes before it gained a reputation as the major neighborhood of Bohemians. The last group, along with Slovaks, Lithuanians, Poles, and other Central Europeans, came to predominate in the late nineteenth century, remaining until their descendants abandoned it after World War II. While a few Mexicans had entered Pilsen as early as the 1920s, their rapid influx dates only from the 1950s and 1960s, as they were displaced from the neighboring Hull House district by urban renewal and the construction of the Circle Campus of the University of Illinois. Soon Pilsen replaced Hull House as the principal and poorest large Mexican barrio in the Midwest. As of 1990, slightly more than one quarter of its adult population completed high school, and median family income declined by 8 percent during the 1980s. Population growth in Pilsen did not occur in direct response to immediate employment opportunities, as in earlier generations, for most residents worked elsewhere in the city. Rather, it was due to the availability of housing and conscious decisions regarding settlement.[13]

Pilsen was also the heart of Mexican Chicago, with distinctive stores, shops, and street vendors; institutions including the Casa Aztlán and the Rudy Lozano Library; and few corporate chain stores or businesses. It gained a reputation as a cultural haven with a flourishing art community and home to the region's largest concentration of Mexican artists, art organizations, and opportunities to paint murals and exhibit in studios, galleries, and the Mexican Fine Arts Museum.[14]

Neighboring Little Village, "La Villita" (formerly South Lawndale), became one of Chicago's "most densely inhabited and fastest-growing [Mexican] neighborhoods." La Villita was home to many second- and third-generation Mexican residents, who often moved from Pilsen. They were revitalizing a neighborhood that had been in decline as its German, Polish, and Bohemian residents and their children were moving into nearby suburbs to the west after World War II. Mexicans began trickling into the deteriorating neighborhood in the 1950s, and their settlement accelerated in the 1960s and 1970s. By the 1990s the retail business district centering on 26th Street had more than 850 stores, *panaderías* (bakeries), shops, restaurants, and other small businesses and was considered the city's "most prosperous Hispanic commercial strip," an attraction that lured more tourist money than the City's Gold Coast.[15]

Southeast Chicago, whose Latino population was also almost entirely Mexican, was more diverse ethnically than Pilsen and La Villita. According to the 1990 census, Latinos were 34 percent of the total, while African Americans were 45 percent and European Americans 20 percent, each residing in largely segregated neighborhoods. For many decades it had a stable and solidly working-class population, and of the three major Latino districts in the city, it had the highest per capita income and the largest proportion of property owners. As late as 1980, it was home to about 20 percent of the nation's steelworkers but was soon devastated by steel mill closings. In a decade it lost almost 30 percent of its jobs, and by the early 1990s only one small steel factory remained. Its South Chicago section, composed mostly of African Americans and Mexicans, suffered the worst, losing 46 percent of its jobs. The huge mills of USX and Wisconsin Steel that once employed thousands of workers closed, and the newer, smaller enterprises that appeared in their stead averaged only twenty-five to fifty employees.[16]

The third major Mexican district in the city, the Northwest Side, once had been a middle-class area but became more diverse as a working-class population moved into several sections. Puerto Ricans were the first important Latino group to establish themselves, settling in the 1950s and

1960s in response to employment downtown. They were the predominant Latino group until the 1980s, when they were outnumbered by Mexicans, who by 1990 represented 19 percent of its total, while Puerto Ricans were 16 percent. Latinos combined to form 41 percent of its population, European Americans were 40 percent, and African Americans were 12 percent. Latinos were the majority in several Northwest Side neighborhoods, including West Town and Hermosa, both 69 percent, and Logan Square, 62 percent of the total inhabitants. Elsewhere in the city, there were several rapidly growing neighborhoods, including Bridgeport, which was 26 percent Latino, and Uptown on the far north side, which was 23 percent Latino.[17]

In the sprawling Chicago suburbs, the number of Mexicans more than doubled in the 1980s, and while they were entering suburban communities more rapidly than African Americans, a majority still lived in the city, unlike European Americans. In the six-county metropolitan area, Latinos were 15 percent of the total and its fastest-growing segment. The African American population fell by 113,000 in Chicago and increased by 103,000 in the suburbs, while the Latino population increased by 124,000 in the city and 133,000 in the suburbs. In the Chicago Consolidated Metropolitan Statistical Area (CMSA) in 1990, 34 percent of European Americans and 81 percent of African Americans lived in Chicago, compared with 62 percent of Mexicans, 85 percent of Puerto Ricans, and 61 percent of Cubans. The suburban Mexicans continued to concentrate in a handful of communities.[18]

Suburban *colonia* formation was the result of the departure of individuals from older urban neighborhoods and migration directly from other places, including Mexico. Most of the fastest-growing suburban barrios were small but long-established Mexican *colonias* typically located in older industrial cities or declining inner-ring suburbs rather than the newer "bedroom communities" comprised mostly of middle-class families seeking the amenities of suburban living. The phenomenal growth of the Mexican population in older suburban communities sent thousands of European American families "packing and fleeing" to more distant suburbs, repeating patterns of outward flight of earlier generations. Despite hostility, reactions by longer-established European American populations toward Mexicans tended to be less visceral and involved less violence than those against African Americans who sought homes in the suburbs.[19]

In metropolitan Chicago, growth was most concentrated in about a dozen school districts in the western suburbs. It included inner-ring Cicero, located immediately to the west of the large Mexican concentrations of Pilsen and La Villita on the southwest side of Chicago. Long a European American enclave and one-time residence of gangster Al Capone, it had been the site of violent White resistance to African Americans seeking to move in during the 1960s. Whites were successful in keeping out most Blacks, who numbered only 74 according to the 1980 census. In the 1960s Mexicans also began to move into Cicero, and their reception was not warm. As one early Mexican resident recalled, European Americans stared at her family on the street, and the first time they attended church, the "priest went dumbstruck in mid-mass." Yet organized White resistance to Mexicans failed to prevent a more than five-fold increase in the city's Latino population in the 1980s to more than twenty-five thousand, or 37 percent of the total, approaching a majority in the late 1990s.[20]

Aurora, an older industrial city being absorbed by suburban growth, had a long-established Mexican barrio on the East Side, where Mexicans continued to concentrate. During the 1980s the city's Latino population increased nearly 60 percent to almost twenty-three thousand, a quarter of its total. The barrio boasted a "distinctive Latin flavor," with Mexican restaurants, bars, record stores, and offices for professionals and social service organizations. Like several industrial suburbs, it received many arrivals directly from rural areas in Mexico and the Southwest, particularly people not accustomed to big-city life, who were attracted to employment opportunities, larger houses for families, and space for gardens.[21]

A number of suburbs of Chicago also experienced rapid Mexican population growth. In the industrial city of Waukegan, home of a long-established Mexican community, the Latino population reached 24 percent of the total in the 1990 census, or more than sixteen thousand people. Joliet, with almost ten thousand Latinos, or 13 percent of the total, also experienced a large influx of migration directly from Mexico. As in many industrial suburbs, it was divided geographically, and the East Side barrio, centering on North Collins Street, was avoided by many European Americans from the West Side. The city of Elgin also had had a small established Mexican population since the early years of the century, attracted to work on the railroads and in foundries and dairies. Its East Side Latino community, overwhelmingly Mexican, increased by 121 percent during the 1980s to almost fifteen thousand, or 18 percent of the total. West Chicago, an old railroad town and site of a Campbell Soup Company mushroom farm where Mexicans had worked for several decades, attained a population more than 30 percent Mexican by the mid 1990s. The tiny inner-ring suburb of Stone Park, from which Italians, Poles, Lithuanians, and their children were departing rapidly, was the first city in the metropolitan area to attain a Latino majority, almost entirely Mexican, reaching 58 percent of the total by 1990. By the mid 1990s Mexicanos were also at least 25 percent of the total population in the suburbs of Blue Island, Chicago Ridge, Melrose Park, Hodgkins, and Summit, where barrios appeared and Mexican groceries, *panaderías*, and services proliferated. By the end of the 1980s, Mexicans were more numerous than African Americans or any White ethnic group in the metropolitan Chicago area, suggesting that suburban employers were more willing to hire them than African Americans in low-paying manufacturing and service jobs.[22]

Immediately to the east of Chicago in neighboring northwest Indiana, the long-established industrial suburbs of East Chicago and Gary suffered economically as the steel industry declined, but the Mexican population of the area approached 100,000 by the mid 1990s, still concentrated mostly in Lake County. A majority of children in East Chicago public schools were Mexican, as were a third of the population of the northern Indiana town of Ligonier. Elsewhere in the state, in Indianapolis, which lacked a clearly defined barrio, Mexicans were most numerous in the working-class neighborhood on the near Eastside. They were lured by employment opportunities in local hotels and other services and manufacturing firms, and by the mid 1990s the Latino population of Marion County reached an estimated 13,000. Elsewhere in the state, hog slaughterhouses acquired by the IBP Corporation (formerly Iowa Beef Packers) in Logansport and Japan's Mitsubishi Corporation in Delphi also attracted Mexican workers in the early and mid 1990s, while modest growth occurred in several other northern Indiana cities and towns.[23]

To the north of Chicago, the Mexican population extended into southeastern and eastern Wisconsin, principally in the industrial belt from Kenosha to Green Bay. Although Milwaukee's population declined by 12 percent between 1970 and 1980, its Latino population grew by 60 percent, while Blacks increased their numbers by 40 percent and that of Whites declined by 23 percent. More than 40 percent of Mexicanos in the state resided in Milwaukee in 1990, suggesting urban concentration closer to Chicago and the rest of Illinois than other midwestern states. Defying patterns evident in other cities in the region, during the 1980s Mexicans became more concentrated in the largest district, the near South Side, where they increased from 48 percent to 56 percent of Milwaukee's Latinos. Several South Side neighborhoods exceeded 75 percent Latino, particularly around Sixth and National, while Puerto Ricans, who had earlier been concentrated on the North Side, also moved into the district. The

Mexican population also grew rapidly in several industrial cities in the eastern part of the state, particularly Waukesha, Racine, Green Bay, and Kenosha, where factory employment in textiles, meatpacking plants, and canneries predominated, and new work was available in many smaller enterprises, including restaurants, laundries, and nurseries.[24]

The second largest zone of Mexican concentration in the Midwest was a somewhat more disperse area fanning out from Detroit southward into Northwestern Ohio, north to the Saginaw Bay area, and west through Mid-Michigan and the Lake Michigan coast. The most dynamic growth in this zone occurred in Western Michigan, where a diverse population of former farmworkers, urban residents of Detroit and Chicago, and recent arrivals from Texas and Mexico was attracted to a vibrant industrial economy. Less rapid growth characterized the longer-settled band of Mexican communities extending from northwestern Ohio, centering on Toledo, northward through Detroit, Pontiac, Saginaw, Bay City, and westward to Lansing. The decline of heavy industry, the major lure for Mexican workers, was particularly pronounced in Detroit, where the number of factory jobs decreased by 72 percent between 1947 and 1982 and was not adequately offset by smaller industrial or service employment.[25]

Despite surface parallels between the two largest cities in the Midwest, particularly the decline of heavy industry on which their economies were based, the Mexican history of Chicago and Detroit in the final years of the twentieth century took sharply different trajectories. During the 1980s the population of Illinois increased by .04 percent, compared with .4 percent for Michigan. Between 1970 and 1990, Chicago fell from the second to the third-largest city in the nation, while Detroit slid from fourth to ninth. By 1990, European Americans were only 39 percent of the total in Chicago and less than 20 percent in Detroit. Furthermore, although African Americans had become the majority in Detroit by 1970 and the largest group in Chicago by the mid 1990s, their numbers were stagnating in both cities.[26]

There were also significant differences between the two cities and the states in which they were located. The decline of industry was more notable in Chicago, and during the period from 1970 to 1988 manufacturing employment in Illinois fell by 28 percent, compared with only 11 percent in Michigan. Yet Detroit suffered more because it lacked a diverse economic base beyond autos and steel, and its employment stagnated. In Chicago the industrial restructuring was accompanied by a proliferation of jobs in small shops, factories, and service industries paying minimum or slightly higher wages, which attracted tens of thousands of Mexicans.

Meanwhile, for much of the 1970s and 1980s, Michigan had the highest unemployment rate in the region. Local urban geography also differed, as neighborhoods in Detroit with a few exceptions continued to decline, while in Chicago many business and residential districts experienced a sharp economic boom, reflecting increased employment in construction and the retail trades and services. Chicago had become a global city, in large part due to the influx of low-wage factory and service workers from Mexico, while Detroit languished.[27]

Earlier in the twentieth century, patterns of migration, employment, and settlement in Detroit and Chicago had followed similar trajectories, characterized by a predominantly Mexican-born population attracted to employment in heavy industry. Between the 1910s and the 1960s, the cities experienced parallel rates of migration, and the Mexican population of metropolitan Detroit generally hovered around 50 to 60 percent that of Chicago. Differences between the two included a larger number and proportion of settled farmworkers in Michigan, where there was a greater tendency to disperse into industrial suburbs and medium-sized cities. The wider scattering of Mexicans in Michigan continued, and according to the 1990 census, Chicago was home to 57 percent of Mexicans in Illinois, Detroit of only 13 percent of Mexicans in Michigan. Finally, the Mexican population of Detroit grew modestly in comparison with that of Chicago, as employers in the Motor City did not find replacements for the automobile and steel plants, mainstays for Mexican workers throughout the industrial Midwest.[28]

The most notable demographic contrast between the two states and their largest cities was the pace of Mexicano population growth. In the 1970s, the Latino population of Illinois increased by 62 percent, while that of Michigan rose by only 7.5 percent. In Chicago, the increase of Mexicans practically offset the decline of European Americans and African Americans, while it had little impact on the continued precipitous demographic decline in Detroit. Chicago's major Mexican neighborhoods on the Near Westside, Southeast, and Near Northwest sides expanded phenomenally, while the barrio in Southwest Detroit grew only modestly. Increase in the Detroit neighborhood was further limited by condemnation and removal of houses for freeway construction and demands for space around the Ambassador Bridge, which crossed the Detroit River into Windsor, Ontario. By the late 1990s Mexicans were only 3 percent of Detroit's population, while they exceeded 25 percent in Chicago, representing the most dynamic population in its emergence as a global city.[29]

A third important concentration, in Minnesota and the Twin Cities, experienced the fastest rate of Mexican population growth in the region during the 1980s and early 1990s. The established barrio on the West Side increased in density, and Mexicans spilled over into surrounding neighborhoods and adjacent suburbs including South St. Paul and Inver Grove Heights. The St. Paul growth rate of 30 percent during the 1980s lagged behind that of Minneapolis, which soon surpassed its neighbor as home of the largest Mexican population in the state. In the early 1990s a *colonia* appeared in south Minneapolis in the vicinity of Lake Street and Nicollet Avenues, and late in the decade a Mexican district appeared in northeast Minneapolis around Central Avenue and Lowry.[30]

Although the sharp segregation of the 1930s had broken down, Mexicans in the Twin Cities dispersed into the suburbs much more slowly than European Americans and Asian Americans, but more rapidly than Blacks. A 1990 Urban Coalition study found that about 80 percent of the African American population of the metropolitan area resided in Minneapolis or St. Paul. It compared with 49 percent of Latinos, 46 percent of Asians, and only 15 percent of European Americans. Furthermore, Mexicans were more concentrated in the city than the other major Latino groups. As in other urban settings, their movement out from established barrios was selective and often resulted in the appearance of new concentrations elsewhere.[31]

After increasing on a "barely perceptible scale for years," the Mexican population of southern and western Minnesota increased at a phenomenal rate beginning in the 1980s. Armando Cuellar, a rural Minnesota jobs counselor, observed in 1990 that "more have relocated to the area in the last three years than in the [previous] 50 years." Some growth could be attributed to settling farmworkers attracted by a healthy rural economy as sugar beet production in the Red River Valley increased sharply in the 1970s and 1980s and many employers outside of agriculture were willing to hire Mexicans for the first time. As in other parts of the country, Minnesota farmworkers were increasingly Mexican, and employers reached deeper into the interior of Mexico to find workers. In several Minnesota cities and towns, including East Grand Forks, Moorhead, Crookston, and Oslo, farmworker settlement represented a major share of Mexican population increase. Some who lacked immediate employment opportunities or continued to work in agriculture were influenced by local factors, such as schools, low land values, and opportunities to purchase old houses very cheaply and on more favorable terms than in South Texas *colonias*, as sufficient inducements to settle.[32]

A greater number were lured directly by employment in food processing, led by Hormel subsidiary Jennie-O, which required workers for its rapidly expanding turkey processing operations in Willmar and Pelican Rapids. *Colonias* appeared near sites of other meat- and poultry-packing plants, including Tony Downs in Madelia and Montfort in Worthington, while Mexicans also settled in Rochester, Albert Lea, Northfield, Marshall, Blooming Prairie, and St. James. The unprecedented and unanticipated appearance and growth of Mexican *colonias* in rural Minnesota in the 1980s and 1990s contributed to a Mexican population that approached 100,000 in the state at seasonal peak by the final years of the decade.[33]

The sudden appearance and spectacular growth of Mexican *colonias* in medium-sized cities and smaller towns that occurred elsewhere in Prairie and Great Plains states were linked largely to the meatpacking industry. Steve Kay, editor of *Cattle Buyer's Weekly*, attributed a great wave of migration to the industry's "voracious appetite for recruits to work the production lines" and to high annual turnover, estimated at 84 percent in 1992. In Nebraska, plants attracted Mexicans to Lexington, Grand Island, Dakota City, Columbus, Schuyler, Madison, Omaha, and neighboring cities, and in the early 1990s the fastest growth in the state occurred in counties where meatpacking plants were located. In Lexington, the Latino population rose from 3.3 percent of the total in 1990 to more than 30 percent by 1996 as a result of the opening of an IBP beef-packing plant, and an estimated 75 percent to 80 percent of the workers were from Texas and Mexico. In South Omaha the Mexican population reached an estimated twenty thousand by the mid 1990s as packing plants lured a new wave of arrivals, crowded into small barrio houses.[34] In Iowa, scores of beef, pork, and turkey processing operations lured Mexicans to cities such as Des Moines, Sioux City, Marshalltown, Columbus Junction, Council Bluffs, Waterloo, Charles City, and Storm Lake.

In the Kansas City metropolitan area, despite an overall decline in meatpacking, the Latino population, overwhelmingly Mexican, reached an estimated sixty thousand by the mid 1990s. Elsewhere in Kansas, media and scholarly attention focused on the construction of several huge meatpacking plants, including those of Wichita, Dodge City, Liberal, and Garden City, and accompanying social and demographic changes. In Garden City, Mexicans had established themselves in the early years of the century as workers on the railroads, cattle ranches, and sugar beet fields. They had a visible presence in the small Western Kansas city and by 1980 comprised about 16 percent of its residents, of whom only 2 percent were foreign born. Sudden change accompanied the opening of huge factories by IBP and Montfort in Garden City and nearby Holcomb, which required forty-five thousand workers between them. In the dozen years after IBP opened in 1980, the city's population increased by 42 percent, while Finney became the fastest-growing county in the state. Employers were unable to recruit enough workers locally, a former city commissioner asserted: "the simple fact is that this is hard, tough work, and farm boys just didn't want it." The corporations lured people from Mexico and Texas, and smaller numbers from El Salvador and Southeast Asia, to work as carcass bleeders, tail rippers, flankers, head droppers, gutters, and horn sawers. They resided in aging rental homes, older apartments including run-down former motels, hastily constructed new apartments, and mobile home parks like the East Garden Village and Wagon Wheel trailer courts. By 1990, the non–European American population reached almost nine thousand, of whom about 80 percent were Mexican, and among the adults, those born in Mexico far exceeded Tejanos. As one recent arrival commented, "I hadn't seen so many Mexicans since I left Mexico in 1976." Yet they remained overwhelmingly a working-class population, whether longtime residents or recent arrivals. Consistent with century-long midwestern trends, only a few achieved middle-class occupations in the professions or established businesses. In 1993 there was only one full-time Latino teacher in the high school and no Latino officers on the police force.[35]

In Missouri, Mexicans in St. Louis were still "hiding within the melting pot," according to anthropologist Ann Rynearson. They were scattered throughout the city and county and without a visible barrio. In 1990 the average household incomes of Latinos [overwhelmingly Mexican] in St. Louis County exceeded those of European Americans and ranked ninth among Latinos in the United States. Yet even in St. Louis, indications of possible future change were evident, as a healthy economy attracted a rapid influx of immigrants. The Mexican population of the city, estimated at fourteen thousand by 1995, was the most numerous in a group of immigrants who were revitalizing South St. Louis. Although still depicted as "perhaps the most invisible of all foreign populations," Mexicans were lured to low-wage industrial and service employment and were establishing visible cultural symbols, including Spanish-speaking churches, restaurants, and a cultural center. Mexicans in St. Louis had never achieved the semblance of an urban village, as on the West Side of St. Paul or the Argentine district in Kansas City, nor had they formed a major urban barrio. Among the large cities of the Midwest, their twentieth-century experience most closely approximated the assimilationist model commonly applied to European immigrants.[36]

Elsewhere in Missouri, which had long served as little more than a temporary stop for workers headed farther north, Mexican immigrants were lured to poultry plants and started settling in towns in the southwestern part of the state in the early 1990s. Many had experience in poultry work in Mexico City and the state of Veracruz, suggesting widening recruitment networks into Mexico. Lacking an established barrio, they found dwellings where available, including cheap rental houses, vacant tourist motels, and cabins that had fallen into disrepair. The Elk River Court in Noel, quickly dubbed "Little Mexico" by European Americans, was an abandoned motor court and typical of worker housing at an early stage of Mexican settlement in the region.[37]

Mexicans were an integral part of the late-twentieth-century restructuring of the beef, pork, and poultry processing industries, highlighted by centralization of ownership, changes in production and the work process, and widening markets for meat products. The plants were located in the midst of farm production and convenient to markets. In meatpacking, a phase of industrial concentration had taken place early in the century when five major firms—Cudahy, Swift, Armour, Wilson, and Morris—came to dominate. The Federal Trade Commission, through the Sherman Anti-Trust Act, gradually weakened corporate control. Union struggles and labor legislation in the 1930s and 1940s, furthermore, helped create somewhat safer working conditions, comparatively stable higher-paying jobs, and a greater balance in power between workers and employers.[38]

In the 1960s another phase of consolidation began, and by the mid 1990s three firms had gained control of almost 80 percent of the nation's commercial slaughter of cattle. All had operations in the Midwest, with IBP Inc. headquartered in Dakota City, Nebraska; Excel Corporation in Wichita, a division of Cargill, Inc., of Minneapolis; and Montfort in Greeley, Colorado, a division of ConAgra, of Omaha. Similar concentration was taking place in pork, lamb, and poultry processing. By 1994 the Midwest packed 51.4 percent of the nation's beef and 58.5 percent of its pork. The corporations shifted processing operations from larger cities in major industrial districts, including the Back of the Yards in Chicago, South St. Paul, South Omaha, and Armourdale in Kansas City, to smaller cities and towns closer to farm production. They dangled the lure of jobs to gain tax breaks, releases from water treatment and other environmental regulations, and additional incentives, often confidential, from city, county, and state governmental bodies. Weakened regulations permitted them to discharge increasing amounts of waste materials, including sludge, ammonia, and other chemicals, animal hairs, blood, and fecal coliform bacteria into the water, causing noxious odors that endangered air and water quality and fish, plant, and human life downstream.[39]

The corporations constructed fewer huge plants, each of which employed much larger numbers of workers, with an overall decline in employment. The new factories in the fields typically were located close to increasingly ubiquitous feedlots, which restrained animals for long periods to permit more rapid weight gain. Speedup in production also involved injecting hormones to accelerate animal growth and drugs to reduce the spread of infectious diseases, practices criticized on health and medical grounds. Another feature of the restructuring involved specialization by species—pork, cattle, lamb, and poultry. Established corporations thereby had to change to survive, and Hormel, which became a leader in poultry, reduced reliance on fresh meat from 70 percent to 30 percent of total sales between the early 1980s and the early 1990s while increasing dependence on processed foods. The second largest turkey processor in the United States, Hormel saw its profits triple between 1980 and 1991.[40]

Highlights of the altered work and production process included eliminating the distinction between meat cutters and meat packers and creating a more "disposable" workforce composed increasingly of Mexicanos. As supermarkets became more mechanized, they relinquished the tasks long performed by the retail trades of cutting and preparing meat for the buyer in the store. Instead they became part of the standardized manufacturing processes in the new meatpacking plants, which packaged and sealed meat before it reached the supermarket, thus eliminating the skilled butcher. The new production process also eliminated the earlier practice of transporting live animals, as they "deteriorate in value through shrinkage, bruising, and crippling while being shipped long distances." Companies instead transported boxed meat and specialty cuts without fat and bones, and they introduced "value-added" foods, including prepackaged catfish, chicken, "Hispanic" and "Oriental" meals, precooked bacon, prepared luncheon meats, frozen foods, and microwaveable or pre-oven-roasted items. These changes yielded greater profit margins and more stable prices.[41]

Within the new plants, companies also aimed at "recapturing initiative over wages and regulations," highlighted by a direct speedup on the production line. The increase for an IBP plant in Dakota City was calculated at 125 percent between 1969 and 1994, and an additional 17 percent from 1994 to 1996, with greater repetition of tasks. This classic deskilling permitted employers to hire new workers for lower wages while achieving sharp increases in output. They simultaneously reduced safety standards, and meatpacking became the nation's "most hazardous industry," with increasing work stress, illnesses, and injuries on the job, particularly cuts as well as back and repetitive motion injuries, including carpal tunnel syndrome. Corporations benefited from declining government regulations, reduced inspections (down by 43 percent between 1994 and 1996), and failure of safety regulations to keep up with rapid changes in production methods that did not adequately screen contaminants such as *E. coli* and salmonella. In rare cases like a 1993 quick-hit inspection by the USDA, fifty-two of ninety plants in the nation that killed cattle for hamburger violated federal standards, and thirty had to be closed immediately to correct for problems including carcasses contaminated with fecal matter, hairs, and grease. The inspectors confirmed charges by critics who asserted that in the new plants meat was often "packed with breakneck speed, under filthy conditions, or with insufficient care to remove diseased parts." Companies balked at taking corrective measures, which required slowing down production and resulted in lowered profits. They preferred to treat health risks either by avoidance and denial or through additional high-tech procedures like irradiation, which had the added feature of eliminating nuclear waste by feeding it to consumers. The workers and their union challenged such remedies, arguing that feces sanitized by radiation is not palatable to people.[42]

Another feature of corporate restructuring targeted wages, "labor unions and expensive benefit plans." The attacks on organized labor took place throughout the private sector, where according to one account the unionized segment of the nation's workforce declined from almost 30 percent in 1970 to 10.4 percent by 1996. In the meatpacking industry, base wages in the late 1970s were slightly under $11.00 when corporate leaders initiated a concerted attack against the United Food and Commercial Workers (UFCW) involving wage reductions, plant closings, transfer of ownership, and new plant construction aimed at destabilizing the union. By 1982, the corporations had reduced base wages in many settings to between $8 and $8.40. When IBP, which had recently purchased and remodeled a plant at Storm Lake, Iowa, cut wages again to $6.50 per hour, the quickly followed suit.[43]

Lower incomes, more dangerous working conditions, and other changes in the labor process invited worker challenges. A key labor-management struggle took place in Austin, Minnesota, where Hormel had just opened a new meatpacking plant in 1982. In 1984, following reports of very hefty profits, the company announced wage reductions of more than 20 percent and a cutback in benefits of more than 30 percent. UFCW Local P-9 initiated a campaign to challenge Hormel involving a systematic stage of planning and education before it called for a strike vote in the summer of 1985. Local leaders gained broad support but ran into difficulties with hesitant national union leadership and corporate influence over the government, highlighted by a decision by Democratic Governor Rudy Perpich to call in the National Guard in an incident in which twenty-four strikers were arrested. The action further placed the union on the defensive, and by the following spring, Hormel claimed victory. As Historian Peter Rachleff observed, members of P-9 not only lost the strike, but many could not afford mortgage payments and had to give up their homes and leave town without prospects of employment elsewhere. It marked one of the most concerted worker efforts to stem wage reductions among the nation's meatpackers. Average wages in the industry fell an estimated 38 percent, adjusted for inflation, between 1979 and 1992.[44]

Efforts to weaken unions were critical to another feature of the industrial restructuring, the replacement of long-established European American workers. As *Food Processing* magazine editor Steve Bjerklie wrote in 1990, "it's an issue no one thought about 10 or 15 years ago when forces bringing about consolidation in the meat and poultry industries got going. Those very large plants require a hell of a lot of volume, and you've got to have a hell of a lot of people." In the older operations, European American workers earned "enough to buy houses, cars and boats, and raise families." As wages and benefits were reduced and work became harder and more dangerous, "the job lost its primary appeal."[45] Departing workers were not "pulled" by "greener" pastures in the cities but rather left disheartened because the work no longer offered the illusion or comforts of the middle-class lifestyle to which they had become accustomed.

Employers found replacements principally among Mexicans, along with smaller numbers of other Latino and Asian workers, whom they initially lured to the small towns on the prairies and plains through employment agents and contractors in larger Texas cities and in communities along the United States–Mexican border. They also placed advertisements in Spanish-language newspapers in both countries and offered bonuses to their Mexican employees to use informal networks to attract relatives and friends. The new workers came because they lacked more attractive alternatives in the international labor markets in which they moved. By 1985 officials at IBP, the largest employer, estimated that about half its workforce nationwide was European American and one-third was Latino, overwhelmingly Mexicanos, who became a majority in the industry by the 1990s. As anthropologist Mark Grey observed, work in the new plants "is sort of like slave labor. They have a lot of leverage over the workers."[46]

The case of the meatpacking industry challenges popular interpretations that the transformation of the world economy will result in the destruction of midwestern industry, which is unable to compete with runaway shops in low-wage regions of the Third World. It also challenges those World-Systems analyses that depict a fragmentation of production and the end of Fordist production methods. Many features of Fordism have greater applicability in the transformed meat industry, particularly a greater concentration of ownership, production in larger factories, and increasing mechanization of the work process, which eliminated the longstanding division between packers and butchers. Despite industrial concentration, the corporations weakened but did not eliminate organized labor, and at IBP, seven of twenty-four plants were unionized in 1996, representing thirteen thousand of the corporation's thirty-four thousand employees. The transformation of the packing industries suggests that capitalists are not following a single trajectory and are engaged in constant change. In Mexico since the early 1980s, industries similarly have been compelled to adjust. In its major cities, the largest factories tended to suffer most, while medium and small industries more often adapted. Meanwhile, many urban operations were shifted to plants and shops in smaller cities and towns and increasingly turned to home-based production. In both Mexico and the United States, capitalists simultaneously employed various strategies, including moving sites of production and changing the labor process and hiring cheaper labor from rural settings, thus reducing the influence of unions. In some cases they turned to smaller, dispersed units of production, but in others, including the food processing industry, they concentrated operations.[47]

Casting an even wider net than meatpacking, the construction industry recruited Mexicans to work at sites as distant as Richmond, Virginia; Raleigh, North Carolina; Providence, Rhode Island; Overland Park, Kansas; Philadelphia, Chicago, Indianapolis, Minneapolis, Nashville, and hundreds of other cities. They were often hired for projects of short duration, reflecting the increasing tendency of employers to create and maintain a mobile labor force, which for workers meant greater instability. It involved subcontracting specific tasks, which had a long history among agricultural workers. Unlike agriculture, however, construction had a reputation for offering "middle-class" wage rates sustained by influential building trade unions. In many locations union representatives, following their short-term interests, successfully convinced public opinion and government authorities that Mexican construction workers threatened living standards and even informed immigration officials, resulting in frequent raids at construction sites. As Richard Henshaw, INS supervisor of the Kansas City, Missouri, district office, observed, "we're definitely not going to get involved very much in the harvest. It's not that cost effective. . . . The primary purpose of area control is to open up high-paying jobs. This is why it is going on and this is why it will continue in the future." Yet INS critic James Johnson of the ACLU maintained, "on the face of it, it would sound like it's selective enforcement." [48]

While employment in the construction industry reflected increasing geographic mobility among Mexican workers, it did not necessarily indicate upward occupational mobility. Positions for which they were hired were clustered at the bottom, principally as unskilled carpenters or carpenters' helpers. Yet critics observed that Mexicans often performed tasks of skilled carpenters, electricians, plumbers, and cement finishers, though at unskilled wage rates. In effect, the strategy was another aspect of industrial restructuring, deskilling tasks by reclassification of skilled and highly paid work to unskilled and temporary, using Mexican workers. The craft unions fared poorly trying to counter employer strategies of using Mexican workers to reduce wages, deskill tasks, create less stable employment, and divide workers. [49]

Mexicans attracted to work in eastern cities also settled, and in New York City they became "one of the newest and fastest-growing immigrant groups." According to the 1970 census, there were 7,400 in the city, including a substantial contingent of professionals scattered in different neighborhoods. As they became a "preferred labor source" for employers in light industry, restaurants, and other services, their population increased eight times over the next two decades and was estimated at more than 120,000 by the mid 1990s. Their regional origins differed from those of longer-established Mexican communities in the Midwest, nearly half coming from the Mixteca Baja of Puebla, where many retained close attachments with their home villages and towns, while the next most important sending locations were Mexico City, Guerrero, Oaxaca, Michoacán, and Jalisco. While they were not yet heavily concentrated residentially, they were most visible in Brooklyn, Jackson Heights, Washington Heights, El Barrio of the South Bronx, Bushwick, and Staten Island. Elsewhere in New York State they also established *colonias* in several smaller communities, including New Rochelle, where they found work in construction, gardening, and lawn care. [50]

Mexicans also were spreading to other states in the East, particularly

Georgia and the Carolinas. In Atlanta, Georgia, the Mexican population increased by more than 80,000 between 1980 and 1992, while in Dalton, they increased from a handful in 1980 to more than 10 percent of the city's 23,000 residents by the mid 1990s. They also increased very rapidly in North Carolina, led by Charlotte, where more than 35,000 resided in the early 1990s, exceeding 5 percent of the city's population. They were also attracted to smaller towns, including Huntersville, Silver City, Chapel Hill, Greensboro, Guilford, Kernersville, and Haw River. North Carolina's Latino population, primarily Mexican, was estimated at 200,000 by the middle of the decade, almost doubling from 1990. In these southern cities and towns they were lured to jobs in poultry processing plants, textile and carpet mills, and construction. Others were settled-out farmworkers engaged in the cultivation and harvest of tobacco, peaches, sweet potatoes, cucumbers, and apples and in nursery work. Jerry Brown, a sock manufacturer in Haw River, claimed that "if it hadn't been for the Mexicans I'd be shut down long ago." Meanwhile, Mexican entrepreneurs quickly established stores, restaurants, and a Spanish-language radio chain.[51]

The surge in Mexican migration and settlement in the urban and rural Midwest, as well as in the East, belies popular portrayals of a relentless flight of industry and jobs to Mexico and other Third-World settings. The world economic restructuring of the late twentieth century was more complex, as industries could deskill operations whether moving production sites to the Third World or to the Prairies and the Plains or remaining in the largest cities. They increasingly relied on a Third-World labor force, the largest segment of which was composed of Mexican workers. Low-wage operations in the Midwest often could compete with more distant locations due to the high costs of transferring operations and building new infrastructure, shipping expenses, and time. Major employers, whether in meat and poultry processing plants, shops, hotels, restaurants, or construction, tended to offer unstable, low-paying jobs with few benefits, where turnover was high. Although conditions were less attractive than in urban work at midcentury, employers were able to lure tens of thousands of Mexicans seeking more permanent employment and more stable lives.

### Chasing the Dream

Mexicans can be considered the last of the immigrants to the Midwest only through a selective and partial reading of the region's past. While immigration continues from many countries, Mexican experiences in the region encompass the entire twentieth century. It is appropriate to examine how midwestern Mexicans as a group have shared the wealth, participated in the region's institutional life, and in general come to terms with the American Dream. This section will examine material indicators, including patterns of employment, wealth, and poverty, and civic assimilation through participation in the institutions of government, namely the schools, social services, and the electoral system.

The initial presence of Mexicans in the region was linked to selective employer demands for labor, and permanent settlement was conditional on many factors. It contrasted with the present-day Southwest, where Mexicans were rooted in the land and until the mid-nineteenth century also came as settlers. The land base, although greatly diminished after the conquest of 1848, offered a foundation for an entrepreneurial and professional class, which primarily met demands of a local Spanish-speaking population. In the Midwest, conditions were less conducive for such a middle class, for in addition to lacking a land base, immigrants brought relatively few resources and had fewer inducements for upward mobility. In fact, a self-conscious professional class developed largely as a result of the expanded government and private agencies in the wake of the Chicano and other civil rights movements of the 1960s and 1970s. Yet the social and educational programs created to serve urban and rural Mexicans were largely staffed by European Americans, and Chicanos initially had to fight to gain representation within them. Later program directors and staff followed trends of the 1970s and 1980s by identifying as Latino or Hispanic, reflecting less a changing clientele than a recognition that they were serving as hired agents of government and corporate entities threatened by the Chicano Movement. Even among Latinos, who had a weak overall presence in management and the professions, Mexicans were underrepresented. Furthermore, as a 1993 Illinois study confirmed, slashes in social service programs resulting from anti–affirmative action politics during the previous decade resulted in a decline in the numbers of Mexicans and other minorities in state government, which "frankly surprised" the Republican governor, who had promoted the cutbacks. At the time Latinos represented about 8 percent of the state's population but held only 2.5 percent of state jobs, and these were overwhelmingly concentrated in lower-paying social service agencies being cut. Even highly visible institutions like the police force had changed very slowly. In Chicago, officially 39 percent African American, 38 percent European American, and 20 percent Latino in 1990, only 3 African Americans and 2 Latinos were included among the 114 police officers promoted during the first nine months of that year. At the time the city's post office employees were 80 percent African American and 4.5 percent Latino. Scottsbluff, Nebraska, with a population 20 percent Mexican, had none on its thirty-member police force. Despite public protests and lawsuits seeking to increase numbers in many cities, pressure by White police officers successfully halted efforts, long before the forces achieved even a semblance of diversity. Politicians were also quick to respond with legislation including the so-called "Civil Rights Restoration Act" of 1991, which banned "race norming," thus heightening already wide disparities.[52]

Upward mobility into the corporate world was even more bleak, a 1994 Minnesota study concluded, for although the term "diversity" had been a corporate "buzzword" since the 1980s, none of the state's largest industries "has made more than microscopic gains in the number of minority employees hired." It reported that during the period from 1981 to 1992, the number of officials and managers in the state increased by 10 percent for White women, but only 0.5 percent for minorities, a rate one-third that of the increase in the state's minority population. Thus the number of Mexican professionals remained minuscule and the gap increased, even prior to the legislative onslaught against affirmative action.[53]

In contrast to leadership in the professions and corporations, in cities including Chicago, Detroit, Kansas City, St. Louis, and Minneapolis, there was a more visible increase in the number of independent Mexican entrepreneurs, which some observers considered proof of upward mobility and attainment of the American Dream. A closer examination of the *tortillería* (tortilla factory), a prototypical Mexican small business producing one of the most rapidly expanding food items of the 1990s, suggests that such claims are not so easily measured. On the one hand, the number of local tortilla factories increased sharply in direct response to entrepreneurial initiative, the rapid expansion of Mexican barrios, and the growing popularity of Mexican foods. On the other, the survival of *tortillerías* was jeopardized by the New World Order, namely transnational corporations often headquartered in the Midwest, the heart of the grain belt. Midwestern corporations that dominated the production and processing of flour, bread, and other baked goods for the world economy increasingly were producing tortillas. Independent, family-owned operations like La Michoacana in Detroit, which had served local clientele for many years, were threatened when corporations like St. Louis–based Wonder Bread offered tortillas in direct competition. Some local Mexican producers decided to join the crowd rather than fight, as in the case of El Rey, which had begun as a family-owned operation in Milwaukee, initially attracting customers from the South Side who wanted fresh, homemade tortillas. Its owners responded to opportunities to reach a larger market by changing its production methods, including developing more sophisticated preservation and freezing techniques that enabled it to expand its operations and distribute its products throughout the region.[54]

The greatest tortilla success story in the Midwest, touted by several observers as a case of the "American Dream" come true, was the Chicago-based Azteca brand. In a characteristically U.S. American manner, its Mexican American founder turned to non-Hispanic consumers, who by 1993 accounted for an estimated 60 percent of commercially produced Mexican food items in the nation. In order to reach them, Azteca altered the production process and perfected techniques of preparing and packaging tortillas. Through preservatives and refrigeration, the company claimed it could extend the shelf life of flour tortillas to a month and a half, a concept that attracted the attention of Minneapolis-based Pillsbury, a subsidiary of Grand Metropolitan, which purchased the company in 1985. But enterprising company founder Art Velásquez regained ownership in 1989, and Pillsbury soon purchased Old El Paso, which produced its own tortillas. Meanwhile, by the mid 1990s Velásquez had expanded Azteca distribution to supermarkets in thirty-five states. It adopted imaginative strategies for the production, preservation, marketing, and shipment of tortillas (including "Kid size" and "Burrito size"), chips, salsa, and other Mexican foods. While they sacrificed flavor, quality, and nutrition, the restructured operations brought a new exoticism to European American palates. Azteca success could be understood as a conquest of the world system by Mexican foods, appropriately altered, treated, and commercialized to meet the demands of a market composed mostly of non-Mexicans.[55]

Despite success stories like Azteca, Mexican businesses in the Midwest were overwhelmingly small establishments. They typically catered to rapidly growing local populations in urban barrios and the inner-ring suburbs whose rising demand made possible the appearance of Mexican groceries, video stores, bakeries, tortilla factories, and other services, typically located in districts abandoned by older businesses moving to newer malls in more distant suburbs. They formed local business organizations and Hispanic Chambers of Commerce in cities throughout the region. Despite their increased numbers, according to a 1986 study by the Chicago Department of Economic Development, the increase in local Latino businesses sharply lagged behind the expansion of the city's Latino population. Furthermore, it disproportionately concentrated in retail activities that catered to local markets, with little investment in manufacturing. Another Chicago study in 1987 similarly found that Latino businesses were very small, with under 18 percent hiring paid employees, and their growth was inhibited, owners complained, by racist lending practices by banks. Even in comparison with Mexican and Latino communities elsewhere in the nation, the business class in the Midwest remained disproportionately small. Chicago had the fifth largest Latino population in the United States but ranked tenth in number of Latino businesses. The boom in Mexican businesses in the late 1980s and 1990s did not approach parity with that of Anglos or even Latino communities elsewhere in the nation, yet it offered improvements for the palates of midwestern Mexicans. [56]

Mexicans in the late-twentieth-century Midwest still were concentrated heavily in low-paying industrial jobs. A 1993 study of Latinos in the Chicago area found almost 40 percent employed in manufacturing, more than double the average for the city, while 21 percent worked in durable goods, double the national rate. Mexicans were largely concentrated in smaller manufacturing operations, including the production of fabrics and textiles, electronics, rubber and plastics, foundries, warehouses, and in meat, poultry, and other food processing operations. As workers they were favorably received by employers; as one Chicago-area manufacturer stated, "they like to work. They work hard and they show up on time, they work overtime, they don't get into fights and they're relatively docile." [57]

More impressive increases were evident in the service industries, including restaurants, hotels, nurseries, horticulture, and landscape gardening. In larger cities, Mexican restaurant workers even attracted the attention of former INS Commissioner Leonard Chapman, who commented, "I'm almost afraid to go out to dinner. I'm a law enforcement officer and I'd be surrounded by illegal aliens." Employment in nurseries and landscaping companies resulted in the appearance of Mexican *colonias* in communities beyond Chicago's metropolitan fringe, like Harvard, Illinois. Increased service employment was a direct consequence of suburban sprawl, or the geographic extension of cities into formerly rural areas far in excess of the rate of population growth. In metropolitan Chicago, the total population grew by 4 percent between 1970 and 1990, but land use increased by 50 percent. The vast spaces were filled by large yards in the newer subdivisions, office parks, shopping malls, and golf courses, and Mexicans were hired to plant and manicure trees, bushes, and plants, to cut and tend lawns, and to work in restaurants and clean buildings. María Enchautegui of the Urban Institute observed that land use patterns represented "an extension of the stratification of the cities. The nation's wealthy hire Hispanics" to care for them and their properties. Whether they found jobs in services or manufacturing, Mexicans in midwestern cities were largely part of the "working poor."[58]

Another dramatic change was the sharp increase in Mexican women working for wages. In 1992 labor force participation nationwide for non-Latino males was 75.2 percent, substantially below the rate of 82.1 percent among Mexican men. Among women, the rate of wage employment in the nation for non-Latinas was 58.2 percent, compared to 52.4 percent for Mexicanas. Changes were more dramatic in the Midwest, where for many decades Latina labor force participation had been lower than that of either White or Black women. By 1990 it reached 59.9 percent, compared with 47.1 percent for African American women and 57.3 percent for White women, suggesting that the restructuring of the world economy had a more profound effect on them than on White or Black women, or on Latinas elsewhere in the nation. Yet economic rewards were not even, and nationwide among full-time workers over age sixteen, median annual incomes for non-Latina women were 76 percent those of non-Latino men, compared with 63 percent for Mexican men and 55 percent for Mexican women. Low wages drove Mexican women and men into the labor force at higher rates than their European American and African American counterparts.[59]

In sum, the transformation of the world economy in the late twentieth century led to a substantial decline in wages and conditions of employment for working people, particularly in sectors where Mexicans were most heavily clustered. In the industry where employment expansion was most notable, meatpacking, wages declined sharply during the 1980s, coupled with a speedup on the production line, less rigorous enforcement of safety standards, more dangerous and less healthy working conditions, increased rates of injury, and declining influence of labor unions. At Long Prairie Packing in St. Paul, where more than half the workforce was Mexican, reporter Don Jacobson concluded, "it's a job only the most desperate would take." Mexicans at the IBP packing plants in Emporia and Garden City, Kansas, complained of a hostile work environment and more systematic discrimination than European American and Asian workers did. They received the hardest and most dangerous job assignments on the killing floor, encountered name-calling, were denied requests to go to the restroom, and were stalled when seeking medical attention when injured. In a study of Mexican factory workers in Chicago, Joseph Kinney found that economic changes were creating "a fairly vicious economic situation where employers are chasing lower costs, which leads them to

Hispanic workers. Part of the dictum of lower costs is to squeeze the people on wages, benefits and safety. Their expectations are low, so abuse is invited."[60]

While employment statistics suggest that Mexicans as a group did not narrow the gap with the majority population, parents often accepted a deferred dream of better conditions for their children. Many individual and family decisions to move to or remain in the Midwest were motivated by the promise of schooling. Esmeralda Mendoza, whose family left Texas to settle in Willmar, Minnesota, said that their most important reason for remaining was because "we want to get an education." Another Willmar resident, Oralia Ceniceros, like many others, had a favorable first impression: "The minute I walked into the high school here, it felt like a breath of fresh air." Yet in the aggregate, whether measured by standardized tests, achievement scores, or graduation or dropout rates, Mexican and other Latino children fared poorly. On the national level, dropout rates in 1991 were 35 percent for Latinos, compared with 14 percent for African Americans and 9 percent for European Americans. In Illinois, a 1987 study reported dropout rates for students entering high school at 47 percent for Latinos, 35 percent for Blacks, and 17 percent for Whites. In Minnesota, between 1972 and 1991, high school dropout rates for individuals ages sixteen to twenty-four fell from 12 percent to 9 percent among European Americans and from 21 percent to 14 percent among African Americans, but they increased from 34 percent to 35 percent for Latinos. Furthermore, even the bleak data in official reports were often manipulated, Chicago School Board member Raúl Villalobos complained, because "some administrators don't want accurate reporting," and the actual figures were worse.[61]

The story of higher education was similarly bleak, and between 1970 and 1994 both the absolute and proportionate gaps between Latinos and non-Latinos earning bachelor's degrees widened, clearly contradicting complaints by conservatives about the negative impact of affirmative action on the dominant population. Mexicans and other students of color who enrolled were disproportionately concentrated in community colleges, which on the national level enrolled 46 percent of European American students, 56 percent of African Americans, and 68 percent of Latinos who attended colleges or universities. Transfer rates were abysmally low; Illinois data from 1989 reported 27,435 African Americans and 7,926 Latinos enrolled in community colleges but only 777 African Americans and 249 Latinos transferred that year to public universities. In the state's public universities between 1980 and 1985, four-year graduation rates were 30 percent for European Americans, 9 percent for Latinos, and 5 percent for African Americans. According to 1989 data Latinos were 12 percent of students at Northeastern Illinois University, 10 percent at University of Illinois-Chicago, less than 4 percent at the University of Illinois at Urbana-Champaign, 3 percent at the University of Chicago, and less than 2 percent at Northwestern University. The worst statistics thus obtained at the most elitist schools, with even more severe underrepresentation in graduate and professional schools. Yet such bleak statistics were deceptive and consciously manipulated, as Illinois state Senator Miguel del Valle observed, because they counted students in courses like adult basic education, English as a Second Language, GED high school credit, and other programs that were precollegiate. Any increase in enrollments, he observed, "is nowhere near proportionate to the over-all growth of the Latino population." On a nationwide level, between 1970 and 1994, the gap in rates of college graduation between non-Latinos and Latinos increased from 2.32 times to 2.67 times, despite affirmative action. The data indicated that opportunities for students of color, particularly from low-income families, declined substantially and that the likelihood of attaining upward mobility through schooling remained a distant dream.[62]

Another pernicious and deceptive means of covering up severe under-enrollments of Mexicans was the widespread practice of including them in pan-ethnic designations, such as Hispanic. Mexicans were more than two thirds of the Latino population in all midwestern states but barely approached one third of Latinos enrolled in the region's colleges and universities. In 1990 Latinos were 8 percent of the population of Illinois but 3.8 percent of total enrollment at the University of Illinois at Urbana-Champaign, or 48.5 percent of proportionate representation. Mexicans, with 5.6 percent of the state's population, were only 1.2 percent of university enrollment, or 21.4 percent of proportionate, democratic representation based on assimilationist expectations.[63]

Meanwhile, explanations for the bleak scholastic attainment of Mexicanos and other minority students continued to be the source of raging debate. Biological and cultural arguments long in abeyance were updated by academics and educational psychologists who attributed lower achievement scores primarily to hereditary factors. Educators more frequently reverted to cultural bias theories. For example, the principal of the Moorhead, Minnesota, school district asserted that "because of their migratory nature, many Hispanic students don't have the background to compete educationally. Many are several grade levels behind. There are isolated cases of success."[64]

Other educators focused on class factors and racism, including conscious educational policies causing rising school segregation, as responsible for increasing inequality. In the middle of the twentieth century, many liberals had argued that the most appropriate route to successful assimilation and equality was school integration. Their efforts led to important legal victories, capped by the 1954 United States Supreme Court decision *Brown v. School Board of Topeka,* mandating integrated school systems. Sympathizers heralded *Brown* as the "call to arms" for the Civil Rights Movement and an important prelude to the 1964 Civil Rights Act, whose Title VI allowed the federal government to withhold funds from districts that failed to desegregate schools. The presidential administrations of Nixon, Ford, and Reagan "were openly hostile to urban desegregation orders," while Carter "took few initiatives," and court rulings caused more highly segregated schools throughout the country. Attacks on integration reached such a level of acceptance in dominant popular culture by the 1990s that neither liberals nor conservatives supported busing, and school districts throughout the nation scrapped plans to integrate and permitted rates of school segregation to rise sharply. Among Black students, attendance rates in schools more than half non–European American fell from 77 percent in 1968 to 63 percent in 1980, the year Reagan was elected, but by 1991–1992 they had risen again to 66 percent. For Latinos, attendance in schools with predominantly non–European American enrollments increased steadily, from 54.8 percent in 1968 to 73.4 percent by 1991–1992, thus exceeding the rates of Blacks.[65]

According to the U.S. Office of Civil Rights, the six Great Lakes states of Ohio, Michigan, Indiana, Illinois, Wisconsin, and Minnesota had the most segregated schools in the nation. In 1990, Latinos were about 3 percent of all students enrolled in midwestern schools, in comparison with 11 percent for African Americans. Yet even with relatively small percentages, a majority of each was concentrated in two systems. More than 50 percent of African Americans were enrolled either in the Detroit school system, which in 1993 was 10 percent White, 88 percent Black, and 2 percent Latino; or Chicago, which was 12 percent White, 56 percent Black, and 30 percent Latino. For Latinos in those states, 44 percent attended the Chicago public schools, and an additional 6 percent were enrolled in Milwaukee. The majority of Latino students in Minnesota attended either the St. Paul or Minneapolis public school systems. Blacks and Latinos, unlike Asians, who usually attended schools with White students and performed much better as a group, attended "less challenging" schools with high dropout rates, low test scores, and the worst facilities, curricula, and faculty. In the Great Lakes states, the number of Latinos who attended schools more than 90 percent non-White increased from 6.8 percent in 1968 to 23.5 percent in 1986. Furthermore, unlike African Americans, there was "no major governmental or civil rights group effort to desegregate Mexicans and other Latinos, who "have been becoming steadily more isolated in virtually all parts of the country." [66]

Most public debates on busing and affirmative action deceptively ignored the question of how one could expect equality of performance when minority children were born increasingly into poverty and attended increasingly segregated schools with unequal and declining facilities. An exception, educator Gary Orfield, observed that "segregation by race is strongly related to segregation by poverty. Much of the educational damage of racial segregation probably grows out of this relationship," including dominant stereotypes about minority schools, where students encountered greater health, social, and neighborhood problems, reinforced by discrimination. He concluded that "you can predict with terrifying accuracy how bad a school's performance will be just by knowing the race and income level of its students." Yet poor schooling alone could not account for the relative lack of economic and occupational mobility. In a Chicago-based study, economist Barry Chiswick concluded that for Latinos "the whole earnings pattern is 15 percent to 20 percent lower than it is for the general population, over three generations, even when you correct for educational deficits." Schooling was not the great equalizer. [67]

Another factor influencing student performance, according to many educators, was the paucity of role models in public schools, colleges, and universities. In 1985, Latino enrollment in Illinois public schools was about 8 percent statewide, yet less than 1 percent of certified high school and 2 percent of elementary teachers were Latinos, almost all concentrated in Chicago, where more than 21 percent of students but only 3 percent of teachers were Mexican. In the "collar counties" of Chicago, Latino students were more than 8 percent of enrollment, but only 1.1 percent of teachers, and during the 1980s, while the number of minority students increased by 62 percent, that of minority teachers increased by only 39 percent. In Michigan in 1990, the ratio of students to teachers in the public schools was 16:1 for European Americans, 35:1 for African Americans, 58:1 for American Indians, 63:1 for Asian Americans, and 76:1 for Latinos. In St. Paul, 49 percent of students were non–European Americans, but only 11 percent of teachers were. An informed observer noted that because of the lack of Latino faculty, teachers in Garden City had lower expectations for immigrant Mexicans than for any other group, as they were "the most powerless and impotent students in the school." At the community college and university levels, underrepresentation was substantially worse, but administrators' success at obscuring information made it more difficult to uncover precise data.[68]

Beyond the paucity of role models, the severe underrepresentation of Mexican teachers raised other concerns. One was that colleges and universities were not matriculating enough future teachers to maintain even the dismal proportions necessary to keep pace with increasing student enrollments. Another involved power relations, evident in the deceptive strategy of maintaining system-wide statistics, which masked sharp occupational segregation among the ranks of teachers. In the Chicago schools, more than 81 percent of Latinos were employed in bilingual education programs, which were geared toward a select group of Latino students, for which relatively small numbers of European American teachers could claim competence. A large portion of the remainder taught in Spanish language classes, which were numerically dominated by non-Latino faculty.[69] It meant that few Mexican teachers could be found anywhere in the school system outside classes for which special proficiency in the Spanish language was required. Politically, it also meant that the increasingly strident attacks on bilingual education would result in driving out the small but highly segregated Latino professional class in the public schools and eliminating their only important sphere of influence.

Another explanation for poor school performance of Mexicans, Blacks, and American Indians introduced a structural interpretation that combined elements of internal colonialism, caste, class, and World-Systems approaches. Popularized by John Ogbu, it suggested that although all immigrants and minority groups in the United States encountered prejudice, Mexicans, Blacks, and American Indians suffered more. They shared in common the experience of conquest and/or enslavement, which relegated them ideologically to a castelike status and systematically influenced relations of economic and political power. Economically, minority children were disproportionately limited by being born into grinding poverty. Politically, teachers created a self-fulfilling prophecy of failure by lowering expectations in comparison to those they held for European American children. Later in life, employers stereotyped them, further imposing a ceiling on upward mobility. Ogbu suggests that similar conditions occurred in other parts of the world as a result of colonialism, where children were taught to internalize the oppression of their conquerors, which contributed to lower scores on achievement and I.Q. tests. Among equally talented children, those from the subordinated caste "see doing well in school and getting a high-status job as selling out. You see the same dynamic among Mexican-American children; they identify achievement with betraying their roots." To eliminate inequality, according to Ogbu, would require acknowledging the role of ideology and societal prejudice and making major financial investments to eliminate bad teaching, low expectations, and inferior schools attended by minority children.[70]

In the late twentieth century, such investment was declining while discrimination was becoming even more subtle and pernicious. In the Rockford, Illinois, school system, Federal Magistrate P. Michael Mahoney found that school officials engaged in systematic efforts to segregate European American from African American and Latino children that "raise discrimination to an art form." Rockford officials succeeded in creating schools that were much more sharply separated racially, although housing segregation had declined during the 1980s.[71]

Meanwhile, alternatives to school busing, including magnet schools and school choice, ignored the conclusion on which the *Brown* decision originally was based, that separate schools were inherently unequal. Magnet schools, which offered a specialized curriculum, attracted only small numbers of European American students because their parents were unwilling to send them to inner-city schools, which in turn prevented greater numbers of African Americans and Latinos from enrolling because of a requirement that they achieve a racial balance. When successful, they accelerated the decline of neighborhood schools by drawing away the best students and their parents, who were most likely to contribute time, energy, and effort to improve schools their children attended.

School choice, which encouraged urban students to attend in the suburbs, assumed that urban minority students would enroll in the overwhelmingly European American suburban schools. The results quickly demonstrated otherwise. In Iowa, where school choice was enacted in 1989, Des Moines, the state's largest city, had an enrollment 30 percent minority. In the first two years of school choice, 402 European Americans but only 11 students of color left the city for the suburbs, causing concern among school officials. When the school board sought to discourage even greater numbers of European American students from leaving the city, their parents complained of reverse discrimination. Educator Jonathan Kozol argued that the Des Moines case "confirms the worst fears of urban districts," and "these parents are not fleeing ugly schools with leaky roofs, classes of 45 students," concern over funding, or gangs. Rather, he observed, "all these white parents once passionately opposed to busing for integration because it was unfair to keep children on a bus for an hour are now putting their children on two-hour bus rides to get away from Black and Hispanic children. The bus ride was never the issue. The destination was the issue." One White Des Moines parent passionately argued that she did not want her children enrolled in a school that was only 70 percent White: "I want my kids to go to school with kids that look like them." Her European American Dream was laden with class biases and racism that helped derail the original intent of the Brown decision, magnet schools, and school choice. As educator William H. Freivogel concluded, actions of European American citizenry and courts further confirmed that the constitutional guarantee of equal education for children of formerly conquered and enslaved populations "has been an arid abstraction."[72]

## Mexican Menace

In the late twentieth century, a "public backlash against immigrants," particularly Mexicans, occurred in political and popular culture throughout the nation. Anti-Mexican discourse initiated by politicians and dutifully reported in the commercial media entered the daily lives of European Americans. It reached even the smallest midwestern communities where few foreign-born people lived. Politicians assumed that Mexicans do not vote and that a majority of voters would be more likely to support candidates favoring tougher immigration laws. By the mid-1990s, opinion polls reported "anti-immigration sentiment now as high as it's been at anytime since World War II." The backlash was based on three central premises, often operating in tandem: that Mexicans had reached a critical mass to merit concern, that they were not assimilable like Europeans, and that their presence threatened the American way of life and the security of its citizens.[73]

Waves of anti-Mexican actions by the dominant population had flared up erratically in the Southwest in the nineteenth and early twentieth centuries. As Mexican workers arrived in the Midwest and *colonias* appeared in the first decades of the twentieth century, European American observers portrayed them as temporary or their numbers too small to be significant. In the late 1920s and early years of the Great Depression, popular fears materialized quickly, only to subside later in the decade. In 1944, sociologist Norman Humphrey again ventured a hypothesis of population density as a precondition for systematic distinction, suggesting that in the Midwest "germinal elements for a Mexican caste are present." Unlike the Southwest, he reasoned, it had not developed because of "the small size of the Mexican group, which prevents the Mexicans from being defined by the dominant American group as threatening its economic position."[74] Based on such reasoning, one might hypothesize that midwestern Mexicans achieved sufficient critical mass in the late twentieth century to explain heightened animosity. Yet population density alone might not explain the backlash, particularly in light of sharply varying Mexican population densities and uneven reactions in time and place.

Assumptions that Mexicans were inferior and incapable of assimilation were not unanimously accepted in the 1930s and 1940s, when academics challenged and largely discredited eugenics, Nazism, and related deficiency theories. Yet variants of those theories remained among segments of popular culture and resurfaced more openly among politicians and academicians in the final decades of the century. Organizations supporting such beliefs established midwestern roots, including the Posse Comitatus. Its national director for counterinsurgency, James Wikstrom, who resided in Tigertown, Wisconsin, asserted, "I know some Negroes who are fine individuals but I don't like niggers. I've got some Mexican friends but I don't like spics." He accepted the notion that Mexicans had reached a dangerous critical mass and claimed that the growth of the Posse in several states, including Colorado, Texas, and Kansas, occurred "because of the massive invasion of Mexicans into those states. They're preparing to defend themselves from the Mexicans." Although denying ties to the Ku Klux Klan, he acknowledged, "We've taken in a lot of Klansmen." Klan members and sympathizers dispersed widely in midwestern settings, including Ada, Minnesota, a town in the Red River Valley, where Mexican settlement increased rapidly. Along with neo-Nazis, skinheads, and other groups who openly claimed that Whites were a superior race, they contributed to a sharp rise in bias crimes against Mexicans and other non-Aryans.[75]

Proponents of deficiency theories found many venues for expression in the media, including radio and television talk shows and newspaper and magazine articles and editorials. On occasion they used highly offensive stereotyping rationalized as humor, as in the case of Jackson, Michigan, radio station WJXQ, which held a "promotion" for the Cinco de Mayo, "giving away real live Mexicans. . . . They'll wash your car, clean your house, pick your crops—anything you want because if they don't you'll have them deported. . . . Bathing and delousing of Mexicans is the winner's responsibility [as the station] assumes no liability for infectious diseases carried by Mexicans." Despite criticism by Esther Rentería of the National Hispanic Media Coalition for "totally outrageous behavior," the station manager "refused to try to correct the racist behavior of his

employees, or to make amends for offending an entire community."
Meanwhile, newspaper articles and editorials presented vicious deficiency
theories, including letters to the editor by Mary Johnson of Moorhead,
Minnesota, who wrote disparagingly about "MEXANS [*sic*]" who, she
claimed, had already "ruined" Texas and threatened to do the same to
Minnesota unless they were barred. She argued that the state should
tighten up welfare benefits. She also supported a publicity campaign, urging that "for every bumper sticker handed out in Austin, Texas, reading,
HEAD TO MINNESOTA FOR A FREE RIDE, there should be two
bumper stickers handed out in St. Paul, reading, THERE IS NO SUCH
THING AS AN HONEST MEXAN [*sic*]." Despite their offensive and
provocative nature and debilitating impact, editors and station managers
accepted them as legitimate expressions of free speech.[76]
   A third feature of the anti-Mexican popular discourse was that their
growing number threatened the security of European Americans. Even
President Ronald Reagan, who grew up in Dixon, Illinois, claimed that
"this country has lost control of its own borders," a theme repeated in
the press, on radio and television, and particularly by politicians "competing to fashion reform legislation." Their complaints, often reported without comment by a compliant media, influenced public opinion, including
a University of Chicago survey, which found that Latinos were stereotyped by 60 percent of European Americans as less intelligent and more
lazy, violence-prone, and welfare-dependent than European Americans.
Crookston, Minnesota, public officials expressed concern that "the whole
fabric of life in the city" was being upset by the presence of Mexicans,
while Nebraska farmer John Kovac complained that as a result of the rapid
growth of the Mexican population of Lexington, "this place is going to
hell. All I hear is Spanish. All I see are these people in their rusty old cars.
We got too many in our schools. We got too much crime and I don't care
if they have jobs, it is costing us taxpayers."[77]
   Concern for security had an economic dimension, as many blamed
Mexicans for their own failure to achieve the European American Dream.
Such attitudes were fed by popular images that Mexicans and other minorities were favored by affirmative action in job hiring and school admissions policies. Critics popularized the term "reverse racism," an assumption that affirmative action programs discriminated against Whites by
permitting large numbers of non-Whites to claim jobs instead of "more
deserving" European Americans. The notion gained great currency in the
aftermath of *Regents of the University of California v. Bakke* (1978), in
which the U.S. Supreme Court determined that a policy of admitting a

specific number of minority students into institutions of higher learning was inherently unconstitutional. The decision set the stage for bolder challenges to efforts by non-Whites to achieve proportional representation in institutions of the state and private industry, an index of civic assimilation. The foundations of reverse discrimination beliefs were belied in many studies. Joleen Kirschenman and Kathryn Neckerman found that Chicago employers acted on their own strong prejudices to create and maintain a racially segmented workforce, accepting stereotypes that Latinos lacked motivation as well as "environment and background" in contrast to European and European American workers. One Chicago employer advertised for skilled workers in Polish and German ethnic newspapers but obtained unskilled workers, who were 97 percent Latinos, through word of mouth referrals from employees. Other studies demonstrated that even with equal resumes, Black and Latino job candidates trailed European Americans at every stage of the job-seeking process. Furthermore, employers' prior beliefs, or prejudice, sustained wage differences over time. Even the supposed beneficiaries of affirmative action had less to gain, as the great equalizer, the university education, was losing its clout. In 1987 Latino college graduates in the United States earned only 88 percent as much as European Americans, down from 99 percent in 1975.[78]

Meanwhile, popular expressions of economic dissatisfaction against Mexican workers increased. Charlene Stevens, director of the Casa Latino in Sioux City, Iowa, observed that when Mexicans started arriving in the 1980s to work in meatpacking jobs, "there was a lot of resentment" from longtime residents, many of whom had once worked in the plants. The discontent in part reflected frustrated rising expectations, for between 1979 and 1989 European American median family incomes in the Midwest fell by $833. During the same time span, incomes of Latinos slipped by $1,050 and those of African Americans by $2,102, and in the latter year the per capita income of African Americans in the region was only 61 percent and of Latinos 59 percent of average incomes of European Americans. In the Chicago metropolitan area, family incomes during the 1970 to 1990 period for Asian Americans increased from 85 percent of European Americans' to 91 percent, while for African Americans they declined from 63 percent to 50 percent; for Latinos from 69 percent to 59 percent. Because of larger Mexican families, per capita income disparities were greater. In Chicago, African American workers earned 42 percent of the average of European Americans, compared with only 40 percent for Latinos. As groups, Latinos and African Americans had suffered more, and they were not taking good jobs away from European Americans. The data also contradict assimilationist interpretations attributing declining Mexican incomes to high rates of immigration, for they fail to explain either the simultaneous income declines among African Americans, who were not immigrants, or the rising incomes of Asian Americans, whose immigration rates exceeded those of Mexicans.[79]

The class source of anti-Mexican and anti-minority fears has long been the subject of debate, whether it was primarily from a frustrated White working class or the capitalist and middle classes. Midwestern employers have long contended that the first interpretation was accurate, often asserting that they could not hire Mexicans because of resistance by European American employees. Their claims are consistent with the disproportionate presence of Mexican farmworkers, domestics, nursery workers, restaurant workers, and unskilled factory workers, all jobs typically not in great demand by White workers. The argument does not explain the highly selective pattern of Mexican employment in the region, even within a single industry. Nor does it account for the late-twentieth-century trend toward dominance by Mexicans in midwestern packing plants, which European American workers did not want to leave. A hostile White working class appears to have been most successful in limiting the numbers of Mexicans entering skilled occupations. In white-collar and professional positions, where Mexican underrepresentation was most severe, the White working class had negligible influence. Rather, European American employers and professionals adopted hiring practices and trained their successors through their power to determine admissions practices and societal attitudes as administrators and instructors in schools, colleges, and universities. Furthermore, employer decisions made possible the rapid increase of Mexicans in small-scale production and service occupations, more to their benefit than that of the White working class. Even the notion of "reverse discrimination" had a largely class dimension, for it most often involved hiring, promotion, and admissions policies that trained students for professions and other middle-class occupations.[80]

Critics' arguments that reverse discrimination enabled Mexicans to steal jobs from European Americans have flimsy statistical foundations. In Minnesota in 1977, Chicanos held only 107 jobs in a state bureaucracy with approximately 30,000 employees, or less than 0.4 percent of the total. In Illinois, Latinos were 8 percent of the population in 1990 but held only 2 percent of public sector jobs, clustered overwhelmingly in the lowest pay categories. In Milwaukee, Black and Latino workers were hired for only 1.2 percent of management jobs in new businesses opened in the downtown area between 1982 and 1994. Furthermore, a weakened EEOC in the

1980s reduced workers' opportunities to file discrimination claims, particularly when based on race and ethnicity, and few were successful.[81]

Negative dominant representations of Mexicans commonly had a class bias. European Americans and the press often applied the terms *Mexican* and *migrant* interchangeably, even to Chicanos born and reared in the region. One European American complained that apartments in South Moorhead, Minnesota, "become run down while the migrants are living in them. They leave bedding hanging out their windows, leave beer cans and garbage all over the yards and parking lots, throw dirty water and garbage out of the windows, and leave broken-down cars sitting in the parking lots." According to state laws, migrants and other individuals who had not established permanent residency were not eligible for many legal and social services and could not vote.[82]

Another increasingly popular stereotype was the welfare cheat, or an assumption that Mexicans were settling in the region to take advantage of welfare. A Moorhead resident, concerned about an "increase in welfare costs," complained that "on numerous occasions migrants deliver babies in our community hospitals which taxpayers and hospitals end up paying for." Another town dweller expressed concern about "increased expenditures for a variety of social service programs. . . . One reality is that food stamp use increases in those counties that host migrants." Residents of Blooming Prairie, Minnesota, became "embroiled in a not-so-private debate over a new wave of Hispanic [Mexican] families moving into the city" and held public hearings where they aired complaints that "Blooming Prairie has become the welfare capital of Steele County." Local politicians jumped on the bandwagon, including Minnesota State Representative Bob Berthelsen of Albert Lea. Aware of the voting potential of his European American constituents, he charged that overly generous welfare benefits had created a "Minnesota Monster." The stereotype accompanied other misconceptions, including one that "Minnesota welfare benefits are for Minnesotans, and migrant farm workers are not Minnesotans."[83]

Some Wisconsin politicians offered a distinct twist, blaming Illinois for the state's welfare costs. Beloit City Council representative Bill Walton acknowledged that voter fears about welfare costs helped his successful reelection. He was certainly eager to fan the flames, claiming that "people here are pretty upset about seeing these new people sitting around, collecting AFDC checks and not doing anything about getting a job." Yet a University of Wisconsin Institute on Poverty study by Bernard Stumbras belied such claims, finding that only 1.02 percent of AFDC recipients in the state were not permanent residents.[84]

In contrast to such claims, serious studies consistently revealed that Mexican immigrants with and without documents paid more in taxes than they received in benefits. Politicians and agency administrators, nonetheless, sought to adopt new policies and pass "welfare reform" legislation at the state and national levels. Congress enacted legislation eliminating food stamps and Social Security to alien adult legal residents, while the 1996 Republican Party platform endorsed a constitutional amendment to deny citizenship to children born in the United States if their parents were undocumented. In Minnesota, Steele and Polk county officials adopted overt and passive mechanisms to block welfare payments for settled residents of Mexican birth and descent. In Madison, Wisconsin, agency workers reported applications for welfare by U.S.-born residents of Mexican descent to immigration officials to investigate their residency status, until the illegal practice was publicized. Meanwhile, local politicians introduced bills to stiffen residency requirements in hopes of "saving" communities. A 1993 Minnesota law "based on questionable data and a growing anti-immigrant sentiment in the United States" denied undocumented foreign-born adult residents of the state the right to public health care or general assistance.[85]

The rhetoric of opposition to Mexicans settling in formerly all-White communities included class-coded concern about "a decrease in property values." In Cicero, a Chicago suburb where the Mexican population was approaching the majority, the city council passed a "density law" reminiscent of restrictive housing covenants banned by the 1968 Fair Housing Act. The ordinance sought to prohibit large families by establishing space requirements per resident and by eliminating "mother-in-law apartments" from the calculations. In response, the U.S. Department of Justice filed a lawsuit charging that the ordinance discriminated because it was aimed at "stemming the influx of Hispanic families into town" and that it singled out working-class Mexicans from buying the small homes they could afford. Furthermore, it was selectively enforced, for "all or nearly all" of prospective home buyers denied housing were Mexican, while longer-established European American owners were not inspected.[86]

In Waukegan, Illinois, a housing code restricted single-family dwellings to a single family, defined as husband, wife, and children with no more than two additional relatives. It was accompanied by a highly publicized enforcement campaign which set up a telephone "hot line" allowing neighbors to report cases of suspected overcrowding to city authorities. As Margaret Carrasco of the Waukegan Hispanic Organization noted, it targeted houses in predominantly White neighborhoods because "the underlying objective is not concern for overcrowding, but how can [they] keep Hispanics out of all white areas." Meanwhile, in suburban Crystal Lake, a vigilante-type group called FAIR (Families Against Ignoring Regulations), ostensibly concerned about declining housing values, reported suspected code violations to the city's Building Department. In the suburbs of Hodgkins, Addison, West Chicago, and Prospect Heights, officials systematically targeted apartment complexes with the highest density of Mexican families for demolition, on the grounds that they were blighted. The Addison plan would have razed housing for the majority of the town's Mexican residents, which Deval L. Patrick, at the time assistant attorney general for civil rights under President Clinton, called a "textbook case" of discrimination. He charged that it was "not urban renewal; it is urban destruction motivated by the national origin of the residents." Local Mexican residents filed a lawsuit successfully halting the Addison plan. In Franklin Park, another inner-ring Chicago suburb, the city passed an ordinance prohibiting more than two residents from occupying any one-bedroom apartment, seeking to prevent Mexicans from taking over a complex in the West Manneheim Residential Area. A longtime Franklin Park resident born in France stated that the increase of Mexicans and other Latinos in the community "makes people afraid," logic based on an assumption that European immigrants but not Mexicans merited inclusion as "people."[87]

Fear of Mexicans moving into new neighborhoods was not confined to working-class districts, evident in the affluent Chicago North Shore suburb of Highwood, where the Latino population doubled between the mid-1980s and mid-1990s. Mexicans found work in local restaurants and other establishments that provided services for nearby residents. When they appeared on the steps of their apartments, on the streets, and in other public settings after school or work, European Americans accustomed to the racial and class homogeneity of their community "are prodding police to disperse them." Fear of a planned Mexican Independence Day celebration in 1993 prompted Highwood's "city fathers" to halt the event by a hastily written ordinance prohibiting the consumption of alcoholic beverages in public. As Highwood Mayor John Sirotti observed, "whether it is real or not, the perception is that [Mexicans are] a threat. . . . I don't know what customs are in Mexico as far as public drinking or loitering. More than throwing laws at them, it's to educate them about how to fit into society with us." To fit in, Mexicans mostly born and reared in the United States were forced to accept a standard of behavior that had not been applied to imagined immigrant European and European American communities of an earlier era.[88]

Sophisticated resistance to Mexicans entering certain neighborhoods was a long-standing practice among banking and real estate interests, institutions not controlled by the White working class. The National Fair Housing Alliance, using paired teams of Anglo and Latino investigators, in a 1994 study found that 95 percent of Latinos seeking insurance coverage in the Chicago area were victims of discriminatory practices. Insurance agents consistently failed to return phone calls and offered lower-quality coverage, but their "most pervasive" action was to charge higher rates than to European Americans for comparable houses and neighborhoods. A Milwaukee study found Latinos three times as likely to be rejected for mortgage loans as European Americans of similar socioeconomic standing. Yet as in many aspects of their daily lives, midwestern Mexicans were not directly aware of such discrimination or the "festering intolerance they face from people in power."[89]

More overt expressions of fear about Mexicans in unaccustomed places occurred in rural and small-town settings, including Harvard, Illinois, located northwest of Chicago near the Wisconsin border. Mexicans were settling as a result of employment on local farms and nurseries, but longer-established residents had difficulty "coping with growing diversity," and they provoked numerous unpleasant incidents in schools, on the streets, and elsewhere in town. At public hearings they claimed that they "feared for their families" and they sought to convince local officials to prohibit converting single-family homes into two-family flats. In a curious twist on dominant representations about fears of dishonesty, a Harvard bank established a policy of not cashing checks for Mexicans without accounts, in response to an incident in which fifty workers employed at a local nursery were paid on checks written from a closed account. Six of them had cashed their paychecks, totaling about $1,000, before the local bank discovered the problem. Bank officials protected themselves from future victimization by what they considered Mexicans' "dishonesty" for not returning the cash. Yet neither bank nor town authorities expressed concern about the forty-four workers unable to collect more than $10,000 in unpaid wages from the dishonest European American employer who had written the bad checks.[90]

In another Harvard incident, two European American girls claimed that a dozen local Mexican workers had assaulted them. In retaliation, European American men formed an ad hoc vigilante group, which gathered in front of the workers' residences and showered them with chunks of asphalt, bottles, and racial epithets, breaking windows and injuring one inhabitant. When a Mexican victim reported the assault to police, he was immediately arrested and jailed, only to be released after authorities discovered that the girls' accusations were false. In contrast, public officials did not punish or reprimand the European American vigilantes for destruction of property, assault, or other crimes and misdemeanors. At Harvard High, Mexicans and European Americans "formed their own groups and didn't socialize," and María Ortiz, an honors student, expressed the hope that Mexicans could walk the halls without being "called obscene names." Diane González, the 1991 high school valedictorian, asserted that migrant families "are viewed as trash. They get dirty looks at stores. They feel they are not wanted. They see your last name and wonder, 'what are you doing here?' I would like to see a day when Mexicans are not stereotyped."[91]

Hostility and ill treatment, moreover, were widespread in small midwestern cities and towns where Mexicans had settled. In response to complaints, the Minnesota Human Rights Commission conducted statewide hearings in 1994, finding "widespread discrimination" in rural and small-town locations at work, in public settings, and in housing. Workers in virtually every community were inadequately trained for their jobs on the production line, making tasks more difficult and dangerous. Injured workers frequently were denied medical treatment and instead advised and assisted by employers to return to Texas unattended. Employers and public employment services tracked skilled workers into farm labor or processing-plant jobs.[92]

Mexicans in small towns also encountered systematic harassment by police and ridicule from European American students in public schools. In Moorhead, Mexican students were accustomed to seeing such graffiti as "Beaners Go Home" and "Mexicans Suck," and well as swastikas painted on walls and on their school lockers. The Minnesota hearings found that "racial prejudice exists in the housing market," as managers and owners of motels, apartments, and houses refused to rent to Mexicans based on skin color, surnames, and accents. In Detroit Lakes, Minnesota, a prospective tenant was informed on the phone by the landlord that an apartment was available but on arriving to inspect the premises was bluntly informed, "I'm not going to rent to your kind." Antonio Hernández and his family, who had recently moved to Minnesota from Texas, reported that many landlords "have told us to our face that they don't want to rent to Mexican people." They finally scraped enough money together to buy a trailer in Elm Lane trailer park in Willmar, but European American neighbors continued to taunt, threaten, and harass them, engaging in name-calling and throwing rotten eggs and firecrackers at the family trailer. City officials in Willmar were so distraught over the formation of the Elm Lane barrio that in 1995 they ordered it closed, hoping to eliminate the "Mexican menace" in their midst. Instead, most Elm Lane residents simply moved nearby, many to another Willmar trailer park where conditions were better. Yet the Minnesota report concluded that "many violations go unreported for fear of reprisal either through job loss or inability to obtain housing."[93]

In a more highly publicized effort to remove the Mexican menace, the INS sharply escalated its activities in the 1980s and 1990s. In schemes with names like "Project Jobs" and "Operation Jobs," agents selectively raided business and industrial establishments, factories, and shops, particularly meat, chicken, and turkey processing plants. They extended their searches to coin laundries and drivers' license bureaus, public parks and underneath bridges. The number of undocumented returned to Mexico from Nebraska and Iowa nearly tripled between fiscal 1994 and 1996 alone. Critics emphasized the discriminatory nature of the searches, as did a Minnesota Chicano who complained that the INS never directly sought out Europeans and Canadians, who represented the majority of the state's undocumented population, but instead, "100 percent of the raids are targeted at Mexicans." He barely exaggerated, as INS data for thirteen central states reporting on raids in July and August, 1996, acknowledged that 97.6 percent of 3,679 undocumented persons apprehended were from Mexico, 2.3 percent from elsewhere in Latin America (mostly El Salvador and Guatemala), and 0.1 percent from Europe and Africa. While INS raids were directed at workers without proper documentation, they often detained legal residents and even citizens of Mexican descent without probable cause, simply on the basis of their appearance. One Chicago area employer noted that the INS "stopped everybody that was dark-skinned . . . it was a racist kind of thing." Even former INS commissioner Leonel Castillo acknowledged the irony of the agency's efforts: "we always find that the jobs that are opened up are filled eight months later by noncitizens." A Mexican IBP employee in Storm Lake stated more bluntly, "everyone knows they are never going to arrest all of us. Who would do this shitty work for them?"[94]

Some INS high-profile actions attracted attention and criticism, including cases of agents descending upon, harassing, and threatening people attending church. Following Easter Sunday Mass in 1979, agents waiting outside the Holy Trinity–Our Lady of Guadalupe Church in Milwaukee alighted upon several parishioners as services ended, demanding residency papers as they left the building. One of the detainees, Sra. Ponce Rentería of Milwaukee, complained, "I still don't feel you have the right to stop me just because I have the same color of skin as someone who may be an illegal alien." Yet Chicago INS Director Alva Pilliod emphatically disagreed, claiming that "the courts say we do." Government agents even disrupted the lives of youth in schools, including Ambrosio López, aged seventeen, and Agustín Atúñez, fifteen, who were arrested while attending South Omaha High in 1992 and then shipped across the border. Neither government agents nor school administrators notified their parents, and López's mother feared that her son had been kidnapped. Regional INS Director Cole justified the action: "It's legally appropriate. It's ethical. The morality, well, you can argue the propriety of immigration laws, but they are decided by Congress." [95]

The language of fear for security within dominant popular culture also turned to criminality, reigniting images dating from the nineteenth century, before visible Mexican communities became established in the Midwest. Representations of Mexicans as prone to crime increased sharply, and even the St. Paul barrio, long portrayed as peaceful, became "a place of knives, guns and violence." Popular media associated Mexicans with assorted crimes and misdemeanors, including fighting, drug dealing, and gang activity, widely exaggerated and often unfounded. Rochester, Minnesota, journalist Mychal Wilmes claimed that "the influx of Hispanics has created tension in many small towns. Some natives [European Americans] blame the migrants for increased crime." In Moorhead, Mexicans were held responsible for an "increase of drug trafficking in our community, [and an] increase in arrests for drugs and DUIs (driving under the influence)." During a trial in Cook County, Illinois, Circuit Judge James G. Smith, in a case in which a man shot a gun indoors, claimed, "Of course, this is a common practice among Hispanics. I'm speaking as a criminal judge now. Every New Year's I had to dismiss cases because it was common for them to shoot at anything that was out there. You're not telling me anything. . . . I can tell the kids that live in that quote unquote multiple housing entity adjacent to us. In that environment, they do not learn . . . and they come with knives and guns . . . and we can't keep them out of our school." Local Mexicans staged highly publicized protests against Judge Smith and forced court officials to transfer him to the pretrial mediation section, where they were less likely to face his wrath. Hostile judges typically were more discreet than Judge Smith and not likely to be reprimanded for biased actions. [96]

In many communities, police seeking crimes and misdemeanors singled out and harassed people of Mexican appearance, confirming stereotypes they learned and promoted. In Chicago, where Latinos were about 22 percent of the city's population in 1994, they accounted for more than 38 percent of individuals arrested. In 1992 they were about 19 percent of the total in Elgin but received 64 percent of citations for driving under the influence, 91 percent of those for lacking a valid driver's license, and 71 percent for lacking valid insurance. An unidentified Chicago police officer acknowledged that "some policemen know it's an easy ticket," because Mexicans want "to avoid a long and costly court process."[97]

Eager to demonstrate its enthusiastic application of law and order toward Mexicans, the Elgin Police Department joined a program permitting INS agents to accompany city youth officers in search of undocumented gangbangers cruising the city's streets. In pursuit of their mission, they apprehended a Mustang convertible occupied by four young men on the probable cause of Mexican appearance, demanding green cards of its occupants. All were United States citizens, including the driver, Juan Velásquez, a twenty-five-year resident of Elgin. While detaining people augmented police statistics, on a personal level, Velásquez observed that it was a "degrading and racist experience [that] was definitely harassment." Similar cases of police abuse, persecution, and even beatings took place throughout the region. In Moorhead, Minnesota, police detained and handcuffed a woman motorist without cause, other than the automobile's Texas license. As one Mexican resident of Willmar observed, "around here, you don't play with the law. You get pulled over for the hell of it."[98]

Popular representations of Mexicans as criminals had tragic consequences for some individuals, including Francisco Rentería, a resident of Lincoln, Nebraska, who was stopped by police in 1994 while walking down a major street. They were seeking "a Hispanic male" reportedly for causing a disturbance by beating on doors and being loud. They questioned him in English, although he only spoke Spanish and did not understand their orders. The family attorney later stated that there was "no evidence in this case that the suspect did anything wrong but walk away." Yet the officers repeatedly struck, kneed, and choked him, pulled his hair, and pushed his head into the ground, causing profuse bleeding and vomiting before and after they handcuffed and hogtied him. He was already unconscious by the time a Spanish-speaking police officer arrived on the scene, and he died the next day.

Police later acknowledged that Rentería did not even resemble the suspect, who if tried and convicted, would have been guilty only of a misdemeanor. During his trial for third-degree assault (a misdemeanor), police officer Luke Wilkie testified that he had applied two different neck holds on Rentería because other attempts to restrain him, including blows to the neck and leg, had failed. Wilkie's testimony resulted in his acquittal. Misdemeanor trials of police officer Stephen Schellpeper for assault and Fire Captain Danny Wright, charged with falsifying the official report, also brought not-guilty verdicts. Meanwhile an indictment against Police Chief Tom Casady, charged with withholding information from investigators probing the death, was dismissed on grounds that the grand jury could investigate only the circumstances of his death while in police custody, but not the cause of the death. All the trials revealed abundant evidence of contradictory testimony, witnesses not allowed to testify or whose testimony was curtailed, information being intentionally withheld, and unexplained medical procedures. The verdicts prompted protests from a coalition of Latino, African American, Native American, and European American citizens in Lincoln, and as one stated, "they can't seem to get it through their heads that any minority person walking down the streets is not a criminal. And that's essentially what happened to Francisco Rentería." Yet police faced no repercussions because they convinced juries they had followed proper procedures, although they had resulted in the murder of an innocent man.[99]

Another case involved Manuel Salazar, of Joliet, Illinois, who was accused of murdering a policeman in 1984 at age nineteen. Because of an outstanding warrant against him, Joliet officer Martin Murrin started chasing Salazar on foot when he saw him on a street and cornered him in an alley, where the youth tried to surrender. Murrin had a reputation for harassing Latinos, who referred to him as "Wyatt Earp," and instead of handcuffing Salazar, he repeatedly punched him in the face and then placed a .38 revolver to his head. Fearing for his life, Salazar tried to gain possession of the gun, and in the ensuing struggle he shot and killed Murrin. Beaten so badly that he was difficult to recognize, the frightened Salazar decided to flee to Mexico, for he had dual citizenship. The following year Mexican officials arrested him on a farm near Monterrey, Nuevo León, and he was returned to Illinois, where he was tried, convicted, and sentenced to death.

In 1994 the Illinois Supreme Court overturned the conviction because improper jury instruction had prevented him from being convicted of a lesser offense of second-degree murder (involuntary manslaughter), which carried a maximum prison sentence of five years. A second trial in 1996 further revealed that the prosecution had engaged in destruction of documents and fabrication of evidence. The extradition records, as well as paperwork of his arrest warrant, blood samples from the slain officer

showing alcohol in his blood system, and records of police radio commu-
nications on the day of the shooting, had all mysteriously disappeared
from the files. It was difficult to escape the conclusion of a conspiracy by
county, state, and federal officials against Salazar, who was convicted of
involuntary manslaughter and released from prison after serving twelve
years.[100]

The trials involving Rolando Cruz and Alejandro Hernández, both
from the East Side of Aurora, revealed that on occasions police so intent
on criminalizing Mexicans resorted to high-level conspiracy and corruption. Both were accused of kidnapping, raping, and murdering ten-year-
old Jeanine Nicarico of neighboring Naperville in 1983. Police dismissed
the account of a non-Mexican resident of Aurora who admitted being the
sole killer before their first trial. Then in 1985 an all-White jury found
Hernández and Cruz guilty and sentenced them to death. On appeal the
Illinois Supreme Court ruled that they were denied a fair trial by being
tried together. A second Hernández trial ended with a hung jury, and a
third trial imposed an eighty-year prison sentence, overturned in 1995 by
the Illinois Appellate court. Cruz was retried in 1990 and again sentenced
to death. In a 1995 Cruz retrial, no reliable physical evidence and not a
single eyewitness could link Cruz to the crime. The court ruled that the
case was based on fabricated testimony, and Cruz was released after
spending eleven years in prison. Chicago attorney Jeremy Margolis, con-
templating a federal civil rights lawsuit on behalf of Hernández, contended that the case set "the low-water mark for corruption in public office
and the perversion of the ethics and goals of the criminal justice system."
It involved perjury, subordination of perjury, official misconduct, and ob-
struction of justice "committed by criminals employed as DuPage County
prosecutors, police officers and jailers." Shortly afterward, three former
prosecutors and four sheriff's officers were indicted, charged with crimes
including fabricating evidence and official misconduct.[101]

Midwestern Mexicans challenged negative stereotyping, INS raids,
and police actions in many ways. They complained constantly about the
widespread and pernicious police practice of stopping motorists on the
basis of appearance and without probable cause, in violation of Fourth
Amendment guarantees against unreasonable search and seizure and the
1964 Civil Rights Act. Individual citizens and groups filed several lawsuits,
including a 1994 action initiated by the American Civil Liberties Union
(ACLU) against the Illinois State Highway Patrol for illegally detaining
Black and Latino drivers without cause. To confirm its complaint, the
ACLU hired attorney and politician Peso Chávez, a former city council

member of Santa Fe, New Mexico, as a decoy, to drive through a notorious section of Interstate 80 in northern Illinois. On Chávez's third pass, the patrol stopped and detained him for ninety minutes, and as he sat in the rear seat of a police cruiser, four officers and a dog searched and sniffed the car for its contents. During the detention an officer told Chávez that the dog appeared to detect drugs, which were never unveiled. Chávez eventually was ticketed for failure to signal a lane change and allowed to depart. Unknown to the police, an ACLU paralegal monitored the entire incident and in court testified that Chávez had signaled the lane change. Meanwhile, Blacks and Latinos continued to struggle over freedom to travel the open spaces of the Midwest that often were coveted "For Whites Only." [102]

Mexicano challenges against the INS were overwhelmingly the efforts of working people seeking to defend their rights. Omaha employment attorney Joseph López-Wilson complained that the INS raids were aimed at reinforcing employers' control, permitting them to say to employees, "you work the way we want you to work—long hours, under terrible conditions—or we'll just jot down your number and eventually call immigration." In Marshall, Minnesota, in response to successive INS roundups of undocumented workers at Heartland Foods, suspiciously timed shortly before employer payments of semi-annual bonuses, UFCW members staged a series of public protests to end the practice. In other communities they formed independent civic groups, including the Joliet-based Community Organization for Justice, the Hispanic Council in Bensenville, the Waukegan Hispanic Organization, and Latinos Organizados Luchando por Avanzar in Wheeling, Illinois. The groups held educational forums and news conferences, pressured local officials, and staged demonstrations protesting the conduct of police and immigration officials. As a result, INS raids subsided and police attended sensitivity training, cultural awareness and language training seminars, although the long-term results were questionable. Mexicano pressure was most successful in Chicago, compelling immigration officials to operate with more discretion and a lower profile than elsewhere in the Midwest. [103]

In the electoral arena, efforts by Mexicans to establish a presence materialized slowly. Before the 1970s, only a handful of individuals ran for political office, with victories occurring at several levels, including the mayoral elections in Hutchinson, Kansas, and Stone Park, Illinois. A more systematic thrust began with the appearance of the Midwest Voter Registration Project, an extension of the earlier Southwest Voter Registration Project, and found a more responsive audience as anti-immigrant rhetoric intensified in the 1980s. Yet even in Chicago, many elected officials showed little concern, including some who represented districts with large Mexican populations. Alderman Vito Marzullo of the 25th Ward, which was 65 percent Latino in 1983, expressed open contempt when complaining in public, "for God's sake, these people better learn something about America or go back to Mexico where they belong." A more visible catalyst for Latino electoral politics in Chicago was the 1983 Democratic Primary, when Harold Washington stood a chance to become the city's first African American mayor. In a city noted for voting by ethnic and racial blocs, African Americans and European Americans were closely balanced, and a Latino block could cast a swing vote. Aware of that possibility, Washington consciously courted Latinos, who proved decisive in his victory. During his first term as mayor, Washington made more Latino appointments than any predecessors, and in 1986 he supported a redistricting plan that permitted the election of three Latino aldermen who soon came to his support in "the Council Wars," his struggle with the City Council for control. The alliance was stronger than ever in his successful bid for reelection in 1987, but his untimely death later that year weakened the fragile Black-Brown coalition.[104]

By 1989 candidate Richard M. Daley, son of the late mayor Richard J. Daley, actively wooed Latinos and gained their support. Henceforth both White ethnic and Black politicians sought to establish alliances, suggesting the coming of age of Latino politics in Chicago. The younger Daley supported redistricting which combined the Near Southwest and the Near Northwest Sides to form the first Spanish-speaking congressional district in the Midwest, which elected Luis Gutiérrez, a Chicago-born Puerto Rican, in 1992. As a result of the new electoral presence, influential politicians, including Mayors Washington and Daley and even Republican Governor James Edgar, showed greater sympathy toward Latinos, refrained from immigrant-bashing, and occasionally criticized arbitrary INS actions. Meanwhile, community groups, including the United Neighborhood Organization (UNO), took advantage of electoral influence to participate in the Chicago school reform movement, aimed at greater parental control. It involved electing sympathetic Latino school board members, strengthening preschool and bilingual programs, and constructing new schools in rapidly expanding Mexican neighborhoods.[105]

Despite their increased presence, Mexicanos' participation in electoral politics remained far below the general average. It was thus easier for politicians to attack Mexicans who were not likely to vote against them, while it raised the cost of being Mexican and lowered costs for employers.[106] Yet individuals who advanced their careers by portraying Mexicans as a menace realized that Mexican civic assimilation did not threaten dominant political culture.

### Contradictions of Culture

The rapidly growing working-class midwestern Mexican communities of the late twentieth century made possible increasingly visible cultural markers, particularly because of greater commercialization than in earlier generations. Mexican immigrants in the early twentieth century and their descendants during the peak of the Chicano Movement sharply criticized and thereby restricted the appropriation of Mexican culture and its symbols by private interests. Deeply entrenched resistance within Mexican communities against exploiting culture for the pursuit of profit faced a much greater challenge in the final decades of the century as entrepreneurs recognized commercial possibilities.[107]

Barrios throughout the region were marked by a profusion of Mexican commercial enterprises, including grocery stores, *panaderías, tortillerías,* restaurants, record and video stores, theaters, and other businesses. These were made possible by demographic growth and changes in the world economy, which reduced the cost of imported foods and pulled Mexicanas into wage employment and out of their kitchens. Several Mexican commercial districts attracted tourists, suggesting the contradiction of intensified anti-Mexican sentiment in dominant society and its simultaneous greater attraction to Mexican culture and cuisine.

Throughout the Midwest, Spanish language use among Mexicans increased, in part because of the presence of more native Spanish-speaking people, but also because of the cultural awakening associated with the Chicano Movement. It was more acceptable among midwestern youth who might otherwise have little reason to use the language, particularly in light of the experiences of their parents and grandparents, who were often ridiculed or punished for speaking Spanish. More people used the language on the streets, in community meetings, at Mass, and in private homes. In Minnesota, the number of people speaking Spanish at home doubled during the 1980s, a rate of growth greater than demographics would suggest. Simultaneously, interest in culture for its own sake and for commercial purposes was increasing sharply through Spanish-language programming on radio and television. On a national level, the number of full-time Spanish-language radio stations increased from about 35 in 1975 to about 250 by the end of the 1980s. By the early 1990s, four full-time Spanish-language radio and two Spanish-language television stations served Chicago, with a wide range of programming that catered to more assimilated or working-class immigrant audiences. Several other cities operated full-time Spanish-language radio stations, while throughout the region there was a vast increase in the number of "brokered" programs on established commercial and public radio stations. In metropolitan settings and small cities alike, individuals could listen to and watch at least several hours of Spanish-language programs each week. They typically offered music, news, and talk show formats while consciously avoiding any political agenda.[108]

The increase of distinctly Mexican space on the airwaves was accompanied by a decline in the appearance of Mexicans on mainstream television, according to a 1994 study released by the Center for Media and Public Affairs. During the 1992 season, it found that Latinos represented only 1 percent of speaking characters in prime-time entertainment programs, down from 3 percent in 1955. Thus for mainstream audiences images of Mexicans were increasingly reduced to soundbites in which politicians and editors announced reform legislation reducing access to social services, newspaper articles and television news segments reporting workplace raids, and television programs focusing on crime.[109]

Simultaneously, small Spanish-language newspapers proliferated, led by the Chicago metropolitan area, with more than thirty biweekly, weekly, bimonthly, and monthly publications, including tabloids and broadsheets, in the mid-1990s. Most cities with even modest Mexican populations had at least one newspaper which provided information about local events and often offered national and international newsbriefs, along with advertising. In Minnesota, *La Voz, Visiones de la Raza, La Prensa, La Gente,* and *Carajo* were among local offerings, but as in earlier decades, they most typically survived only a few years. The profusion of Spanish-language newspapers, television, and radio indicated declining incentives for monolingualism in English, a most popular index of assimilation in conservative circles. Yet their commercial focus, except for some advertised products, was practically indistinguishable from mainstream media.[110]

Another established institution, the Catholic Church, responded inconsistently to the rapid growth of Mexican populations in its midst. On first encounter, some churches expressed open hostility, while others offered warm welcomes, and eventually most made accommodations. By 1983, in Chicago alone seventy-three Catholic parishes offered at least one weekly mass in Spanish. In St. Paul, attendance for Mass at Nuestra Señora de Guadalupe tripled between the early 1980s and the early 1990s, yet only about 20 percent to 30 percent of Mexican Catholics in the area regularly attended church. In the late twentieth century, church-based groups tended to adopt a narrower focus than their predecessors and were less involved in the social and cultural life of the larger, more dispersed, and heterogeneous communities. Within the Catholic Church, social services were increasingly regularized through the Secretariat for Hispanic Affairs of the United States Catholic Conference, through local Offices of Hispanic Affairs. Its programs tended to have specific ends, like Hispanic Outreach, or Guadalupe CARES (Central American Resettlement Services), which aimed at assisting immigrants in settling in the Twin Cities area. Directed by local archdiocesan or diocesan offices, they were run increasingly by professional staff rather than volunteers.[111]

Spanish-speaking Protestant churches also increased, and by the 1990s there were at least a dozen congregations in the Twin Cities alone, a majority *evangélicos,* or fundamentalist, sects. Many catered to recent immigrants from Mexico and other Latin American countries, attracting individuals who had already converted or were likely to convert soon after arriving in the United States. Even in places like St. Louis, with its highly dispersed Mexican population, the number of Spanish-speaking Protestant churches increased from three to ten between 1992 and 1995. Despite the increased Protestant presence, an estimated 80 to 85 percent of Mexicans in the Midwest still identified as Catholics.[112]

Beyond churches, formal Mexican cultural activities flourished, particularly in major cities like Chicago, which had an annual Latino Film Festival, lectures, art shows, and related functions at the Casa Aztlán, the Mexican Fine Arts Museum, and other settings. Omaha established the first museum of its kind in the Midwest, El Museo Latino, which also served as a cultural center for the Midlands. Painting murals, as had occurred during the heyday of the Chicano Movement throughout the Midwest, often directly inspired by the muralist movement of the Mexican Revolution, continued as local artists adapted Chicano, Mexicano, and Latin American themes to local settings. Mural painting declined somewhat in the early 1980s, but soon a new crop of artists took "to the streets alongside seasoned veterans." In Chicago alone more than three hundred murals and mosaics survived in the early 1990s, many the result of collective efforts by cultural groups and artists' alliances.[113]

Recreation and social activities also flourished, including Mexican soccer and baseball leagues, bowling clubs, and boxing tournaments. Sponsors included churches, local businesses, and employers, and participants numbered in the tens of thousands. As in other locations, some traditions of debatable origin gained popularity, including the *Quinceañera,* a celebration of the fifteenth birthday, symbolizing approaching adulthood for young women; and November 1 and 2, *el Día de los Muertos* (the Day of the Dead), which had long been popular in Mexico.[114]

While many cultural forms originated in Mexico, others had distinctly southwestern roots. The sway of Texas was evident in the spread of *conjunto* music, particularly in locations where Tejanos had settled out, established restaurants, created artwork, and celebrated the annual Midwest Conjunto Awards Festival. California influence was less immediate, but evident in the 1993 formation of the Midwest Lowriders Club in Chicago. One Chicano member expressed its inherent contradictions: "many people don't even think there's Mexicans in the Midwest. That's why we're doing this in Chicago. We've been underground for a long time and we're going through some growing pains. This is all part of the American dream. Cars have always been associated with the United States and I don't think we're any different. But we add a different cultural experience and come up with lowriders, which aren't particularly associated with Latinos anymore. African-Americans have some awesome lowriders. What it boils down to is freedom of expression. We're all living the myth."[115] Lowriders were becoming increasingly popular throughout the region, often congregating at local popular restaurants or drive-ins, like Porky's in St. Paul.

Midwestern theater groups also proliferated, influenced by broader political tendencies and pressures to assimilate in order to obtain funding from mainstream foundations and commissions. In the previous generation, theatrical efforts often were directly inspired by the Teatro Campesino, which identified consciously with the Chicano Movement. The actors originally were nonprofessional, the productions of modest scale, and the messages consciously oriented toward political and social activism. Groups like Teatro del Barrio, formed in 1970 in Chicago, explicitly accepted their primary mission as "education of our Raza" and addressed the "conditions of the urban Chicano." In later years, consistent with the Teatro Campesino, troupes became increasingly concerned with "professionalism" in terms largely defined by mainstream theater organizations, evident in Chicago-based groups like La Barraca, Vista, and Aguijón II Theater Company. Tension between professionalism and politics animated many organizations, including the Minnesota-based Teatro Latino de Minnesota and the Teatro del Pueblo. A source of ongoing debate, it pointed to the contradictory pressures within cultural groups over whether to assimilate middle-class values and perspectives of mainstream theater and operate as commercial enterprises, or to offer alternative critiques that challenged the dominant order.[116]

Professionalization of many sectors of organizational life in the late twentieth century meant increasing dependence on government or non-profit charitable institutions. It also reflected economic and social changes resulting from the decline of leisure time, which sharply reduced opportunities for time-consuming volunteer activities. Yet professionalization was evident in hegemonic popular culture, which increasingly abandoned the inclusive rhetoric of equality, democracy, and rewards for nonmaterial incentives. As St. Paul resident Sra. Irene Rivera lamented, "all the old timers were poor, but they helped each other more than they do now. . . . this generation is proud. They don't get together, because everybody thinks they have more than the rest"[117] As Mexicans of a younger generation assimilated the hedonism and individualism of dominant popular culture, they also showed less interest in voluntary activities that did not accrue direct material benefits.

Changed attitudes were evident in community-based celebrations, including national holidays like the Diez y Seis de Septiembre and Cinco de Mayo. The activities were both larger and more numerous while more commercialized and mainstream, attracting dominant politicians and investors seeking to sell their wares. Politicians recognized the Fiestas Patrias with the presidential proclamation of National Hispanic Heritage Week, expanded to Hispanic Heritage Month in 1989. Celebrations independent of national holidays included the Mexican Fiesta in Milwaukee in August, the Mexicantown Fiesta in Detroit in June, the Festival de México in several Indiana cities in March, and Fiesta del Sol in Chicago in August, advertised as "the largest free festival of its kind in the Midwest." There were performances by dance groups, musicians, and comedians, as well as *charreadas* (Mexican rodeos), sales of food, and arts and crafts. Local businesses viewed the celebrations as a "strategic marketing tool."[118]

Initiatives by Chicano students had made the Cinco de Mayo the largest Mexican celebration in many communities, despite its declining importance in Mexico. Some observers suggest that its popularity in the United States could be attributed to the Texas birthplace of the hero of the 1863 Battle of Puebla, Ignacio Zaragoza. A more likely reason, according to historians Luís Arroyo and Antonio Ríos-Bustamante, was the Chicano Movement itself. Youth had found an opportunity to celebrate their Mexican heritage, "to overcome the division between Mexican immigrants and Mexican-Americans that had existed for many years, and to publicize their struggle for justice in the United States."[119]

In the Twin Cities, students at the University of Minnesota reinvigorated the Cinco de Mayo in the early 1970s as part of Chicano Week celebrations. Planners envisioned linking students on campus with the barrio and beyond and initially worked closely with volunteers at Our Lady of Guadalupe Parish, where many activities took place. They had an explicit educational and political agenda, as workshops, slide shows, movies, and public lectures addressed Chicanos and Mexicanos and their struggles, farmworker issues, and topics relating to indigenous heritage, particularly that of the Aztecs. Cultural activities included local, regional, and national dance troupes, art shows, musical performances, dinners, and public *bailes*. Student organizations throughout the Midwest had their own celebrations, and in larger cities like Chicago, many joined the citywide, month-long celebration that included art exhibits, film and music festivals, lectures, and dance performances.[120]

In keeping with the times, business interests soon joined, seeking an "opportunity" to capitalize on the growing Mexican and Mexican American market. In the Twin Cities the celebration took a distinct twist in 1985, when the Concord Street Business Association approached the Chicano Student Cultural Center of the University of Minnesota to include a parade along Concord Street, the heart of the West Side barrio. According to the *St. Paul Pioneer Press*, the business association considered as its model the Grand Old Day Parade, set in the city's upper-middle-class Grand Avenue neighborhood. The parade, initially cosponsored by the Chicano Student Cultural Center and the Concord Street Business Association, quickly became the largest single Mexican event in the state. It attracted about four thousand people its first year and ten thousand two years later, almost all Mexicanos and other Latinos. But the business association, in its quest for profit, sold space to any group with the money to participate in the parade or sell goods. Vendors could advertise whatever they wished, whether it had any cultural, educational, or social value or relationship to the national holiday, and by the early 1990s it retained only modest Mexican cultural content. Partly in reaction to the commercialization, Mexicans in Minneapolis staged alternative Cinco de Mayo celebrations focusing on cultural and educational activities. Elsewhere in the region, in central cities, suburbs, and small towns, Cinco de Mayo celebrations proliferated in commercial districts, neighborhood parks, community centers, and on college and university campuses.[121]

Meanwhile, the older Diez y Seis de Septiembre celebration had a more erratic history, barely surviving in the Twin Cities while flourishing in Chicago. In St. Paul, the Comité Patriótico Mexicano, which had sponsored the event since 1937, was reorganized in 1969 as the Mexican Independence Celebration Committee, a nonprofit organization. It coordinated activities, including a parade that attracted thousands as it wound through the West Side over the Robert Street Bridge to Downtown. It included *bailes típicos* (regional dances), crowning of the Mexican Queen (awarded to the person who sold the most buttons for the evening *baile*), and music provided by local artists. As the volunteers retired, a vacuum in leadership ensued and the committee dissolved in 1973, replaced by the short-lived New Mexican Independence Celebration Committee. Sporadic and smallscale celebrations followed, and an all-volunteer El Grito Committee resuscitated the event in 1991, offering an art exhibit and lectures. The following year it held a traditional parade in the St. Anthony main business district in Minneapolis, with food, entertainment, folkloric music, arts and crafts, a mass, a symposium, and a flower flotilla down the Mississippi River. Identifying itself simultaneously as a Chicano and Mexicano event, in its early years it successfully avoided the rampant commercialism of the Concord Street Cinco de Mayo.[122]

Throughout the region, celebrations of the Fiestas Patrias expanded exponentially, spreading to small towns and suburban communities. In cities like Waukegan, a contest for control erupted between business groups and "a gaggle of politicians" vying for publicity, votes, and profit. A disgruntled Waukegan businesswoman complained, "I put my heart and soul into this parade, spent thousands of my own money, brought the Hispanic people together, and now they took it away from me."[123] While lamenting her lack of proprietary rights, she proposed to sponsor an alternative celebration of her own, eyes open to opportunities.

The proliferation of such ethnic celebrations reflect the simultaneous impact of local forces and the world economy, as sponsors simultaneously attracted Mexicans of different generations and places of birth, as well as onlookers. The content of such events varied widely, as sponsors debated whether they should advance educational, political, and social concerns, or simply offer opportunities to convert cultural icons into cash.

The late-twentieth-century restructuring of the world economy had a profound impact on midwestern Mexicans, whose presence increased in older as well as new work settings. Established networks and formal recruitment enhanced labor migration from Texas and Mexico, which reached the highest levels of the century, evidence that popular portrayals of inevitable and massive deindustrialization in the region were greatly oversimplified. As many employers discovered, lower wages in Mexico could not always offset the higher costs of building an infrastructure, educating a workforce, importing unfinished goods, and shipping to major markets in the United States.

Contemporary demographics, combined with the impact of economic, political, and cultural reforms of the previous generation, contributed to an increase in Mexican professionals and entrepreneurs, whose numbers nevertheless remained small compared with the European American, African American, and Asian American populations. As in earlier years, a majority of urban Mexicans worked in factories and shops, but increasingly they were employed in low-wage service industries as well. Midwestern Mexicanas, whether born in Mexico or in the United States, defied old stereotypes and entered wage work at rates higher than women of other major ethnic and racial backgrounds. Their working experiences, which contributed to increasing diversity among Mexicans, could not obscure rising levels of inequality or their employment primarily in poorly paid jobs.

In the 1980s Mexicans emerged as the most rapidly increasing major population group in the region. The European American population stagnated as it moved increasingly to more distant suburbs, and the African American population increased very modestly while slowly moving into a handful of inner-ring suburban neighborhoods. Mexican urban barrios in the largest cities expanded sharply while new *colonias* emerged in suburban and rural settings, following the direction of employment. Asian Americans, whose numbers increased very rapidly from a much smaller base, were less concentrated in central cities than African Americans or Mexicans, and dispersed widely in suburban communities and small towns.

As Mexicans gained greater visibility, they attracted the attention of dominant politicians and the media, which emphasized difference and contributed to a backlash and rising tensions based on race, national origins, and culture. Stereotypes of Mexicans as immigrants pervaded dominant popular culture, as anthropologist Mark Grey found in Garden City, noting that although immigrant and nonimmigrant Mexican youth had significantly different self-perceptions and identities, most Anglos were not aware of the differences, lumped both together, and referred to them as "Mexicans." As economist Nigel Harris observed, "there are few areas of political life where opinions at variance with the known facts are advanced with confidence and by people supposedly in authority," but through constant repetition, "a majority of people are persuaded that immigration is a serious problem." Portrayals of Mexicans as welfare loafers and prone to criminality were also bandied about, despite widespread evidence to the contrary.[124]

The political backlash was also influenced by disillusionment over declining opportunities for upward mobility among European Americans and by the long-standing stereotype that Mexicans in the region were "migrants" and consequently not entitled to the rights of "permanent" residents. Dominant popular culture maintained a racialized American Dream and treated many spaces as the exclusive domain of Whites, while some Mexicans spoke positively about separation. The racialization of Mexicans helped resolve a contradiction in dominant political culture that simultaneously demanded theoretical equality and material inequality, playing on mentalities of Mexicans and non-Mexicans alike.

As a political phenomenon, the anti-Mexican menace gained strength even in sections of the Midwest with relatively few Mexicans, who thus posed little threat to local politicians. Its strongest expressions occurred in Republican and rural strongholds, while it was weaker in settings where a Mexican presence was recognized. In Chicago, politicians soon learned not to upset a whimsical voting public or alienate the Mexican population, a growing segment of potential swing voters. Although rhetoric about Mexicans' unwillingness to assimilate helped justify exclusionary legislation in many places, the commercialization of culture and increased participation in electoral politics suggested inclusion. Meanwhile, the century-long debates between assimilationists and their detractors continued, independent of academics ensconced in ivory towers.

# Retrospective

The Mexican presence in the twentieth-century Midwest belonged to the third major cycle of migration and settlement from the former Mexica heartland that accompanied the articulation of the modern world system. The first, marked by the Spanish conquest in the sixteenth and seventeenth centuries, was stimulated by a search for accumulated riches and the establishment of a colonial empire. It was based on the forced labor of native peoples and African slaves. During this cycle, conquering soldiers and settlers identified as Españoles, mestizos, and Indians from central Mexico extended their sway as far north as the province of Nuevo México.

The second cycle, associated with the industrial revolution of the eighteenth and nineteenth centuries, took place in the context of European imperial competition over colonial territories, resources, and the labor of native peoples. In the far Mexican north, settlers identified as mestizos, mulattos, Indios, and Españoles extended the Spanish colonial empire to Texas and Alta California. These territories contributed mineral, ranching, and agricultural wealth to the world economy that permitted an expansion of industrial production, while they simultaneously offered markets for finished goods. The Mexicans who remained in the far northern provinces after 1848 became a regional minority in the southwestern United States. They enjoyed some of the rights of citizens, reflecting inequalities that were articulated in the unfolding neocolonial relationship between the former conquering and conquered nations.

A third cycle of migration and settlement, which took place in the twentieth century, was characterized by the elaboration of industrial capitalist efforts to expand their labor pool as production and distribution of goods in the world economy became more complicated. Capitalists lured Mexican workers increasingly beyond "Greater Mexico" to the Midwest, the Pacific Northwest, the Southeast, and the eastern United States. The workers' place in the political and economic order was influenced by unequal relations between the United States and Mexico, which distinguished them from Europeans, European Americans, Africans, and African Americans. In an earlier cycle of the world economy, hundreds of thousands of Europeans came to the United States as laborers, but as economic inequality between their homelands and their adopted nation diminished, capitalist employers found them less attractive as cheap labor. Earlier experiences of Africans were based on legal notions informed by slavery rather than wage labor. As Frantz Fanon observed, the master-slave dialectic was based on reciprocity, which recognized the legal personality of the slave. In contrast, under wage relations, the capitalist sought "not recognition but work."[1] The descendants of slaves gained a distinct place in midwestern urban society and culture during the twentieth century. Initially recruited as unskilled industrial, domestic, and service workers, over time they became more diverse in occupation but increasingly segregated in space residentially. Mexicans in the Midwest, by contrast, worked in unskilled menial jobs of low visibility, they were not given recognition, and their low profiles were reinforced by dominant cultural representations of race relations in bipolar, black-and-white terms.

The twentieth-century history of midwestern Mexicans encompassed three shorter cycles of migration, work, and settlement. In the early decades, especially as the industrial economy heated up during World War I and continued to expand in the early 1920s, employers lured Mexican immigrants for unstable employment in sectors of the industrial urban and agricultural economy. The workers established a tenuous residential presence on the farms, adjacent to railroad lines or near the shops, factories, and mills where they worked. Their first *colonias* were unstable and, like employment, determined and shaped by their interaction with employers, landlords, and neighbors. Urban barrios were composed overwhelmingly of young adult males, with few very young or elderly individuals, while the more scattered rural populations had greater gender balance and larger numbers of children. The urban and rural settlements, not unlike those of migrants from some parts of the rural South, typically were closely intertwined. Employers and the governments of Mexico and the United States portrayed midwestern Mexicans as temporary workers who were expected to depart once the discontinuous or seasonal demand for their labor abated. In keeping with dominant societal expectations, Mexicanos typically viewed their sojourn in the United States as transitory.

Countervailing forces simultaneously induced midwestern Mexicans to remain and establish a more permanent presence. In agriculture, sugar beet companies seeking to reduce the expense and inconvenience of annual recruitment encouraged them to remain throughout the winter. Seeking to create a residential agricultural proletariat, the companies hired families rather than individuals, provided housing, and offered bonuses and higher wage rates to workers who could appear in the spring unassisted. In the urban settings, thousands of Mexicans also decided to remain and take up roots, despite the instability of work.

Individual decisions to settle in both countryside and city hinged on a number of factors in which the influence of conscious actions by women and children weighed heavily. Agricultural employers quickly discovered that working units with women and children reduced their costs. Women who initially came north as *betabeleras* frequently found employment outside their homes in shops or factories or as domestic workers. While men constantly looked back to Mexico with nostalgia, women often found relative freedom and material advantages in the Midwest, and children commonly had few or no memories of the land where their parents were born. Contesting patriarchy, pressure from children and their mothers ensured that the early urban midwestern *colonias* would not disappear.

Mexicans in the urban Midwest commonly learned English and adopted material features of dominant popular culture more rapidly than their counterparts in the rural Southwest. Yet they discovered that adopting the language and other cultural accoutrements did not automatically lead to equality, as they had been led to believe, and they were afforded only partial inclusion in mainstream society. Mexican children born and reared in the Midwest did not have equal access to institutions of the dominant society and were not afforded the same treatment when attending school. School officials tolerated their absence because they accepted arguments that children should contribute to family production when their parents were paid so poorly and worked erratically. Truant officers complied with the imperatives of capitalism rather than the letter of the law, while they compelled European and European American children to remain in school. Vividly aware of difference, Mexican youth adopted dominant material culture selectively. Even young "sheiks" emulating Hollywood movie star Rudolph Valentino accepted a commercialized but Latin representation that challenged normative images of hegemonic Anglo American culture. They served as a prelude to their younger brethren and children who adopted zoot suits a generation later.

The onset of the Great Depression confirmed that Mexicans were different from immigrants from Europe or migrants from the southern United States. It aroused the most intense anti-Mexican rhetoric and the most significant reverse migration of the century. Politicians and other agents of the state singled out Mexicans for deportation and repatriation based on representations of Mexico as inferior and Mexicanos as less deserving than other workers who resided in the United States, consistent with the inequality inherent in the world economy. Midwestern Mexicans were overwhelmingly legal residents or citizens of the United States but were treated differently than Europeans of similar legal standing. Federal immigration agents and local officials removed Mexicans at much higher rates than in other parts of the country and convinced many informed observers that midwestern Mexican communities would disappear. Departures from the Midwest were uneven across space, as barrios in East Chicago, Gary, and Detroit were badly weakened while Mexican populations in many communities farther east disappeared. Those of Chicago were somewhat less severely affected, while the St. Paul *colonia* expanded rapidly throughout the 1930s.

Attitudinal changes during the Great Depression came from many directions, often countervailing. The combined impact of the deportation and repatriation campaigns had weakened Mexicans' attitudinal links with their homeland. As living conditions fell in absolute terms and in relationship to those of the European and European American populations, conditions of work and residence of Mexicans in Minnesota tended toward apartheid. Yet their own shared employment and residential experiences, reinforced by dominant societal racism, contributed to a stronger sense of Mexican identity in the United States and promoted an awareness that enhanced collective cultural expressions.[2]

A second cycle of midwestern Chicano history, marked by the dominance of monopoly capital, had similarly antagonistic tendencies. Thousands of Mexican workers found employment in the region's factories, foundries, and shops, joined labor unions, and were accepted into the industrial working class. They benefited from an ideology, shared by capital and labor, that workers were simultaneously important as consumers and entitled to earnings permitting them access to the material comforts of a middle-class lifestyle. Their employment, residential conditions, and families stabilized markedly in comparison with their Mexican predecessors of the early twentieth century. Mexicanas entered factories during World War II, but like women of other ethnic backgrounds, most were pushed out after the war ended. They were expected to accept shifting versions of an American Dream, increasingly consistent with patriarchal notions current in Mexico, in which they could expect to find happiness and satisfaction in the domestic sphere and caring for their families.

Meanwhile, workers from Texas and Mexico formed new labor reserves and were portrayed and treated much differently. Thousands of Tejanos were recruited to work in an expanding number of crops and agricultural sections of the Midwest. Workers from Mexico came initially under the contract provisions of the Bracero Program during World War II for agricultural and railroad enterprises. Both groups resided in isolated settings, worked in dead-end jobs, and were portrayed as migratory people who moved with the seasons and never established roots, stereotypes that commonly were applied to Mexicans in the Midwest without distinction. Yet workers from Texas and Mexico often found employment opportunities elsewhere, and as they settled they contributed to the growth and diversity of established midwestern barrios and *colonias.*

A third cycle of midwestern Chicano history occurred in the final decades of the century and signaled the breakdown of nation-based monopoly capital, as the economy took on increasingly international dimensions. Changes in production and distribution induced a record scale of labor migration from Mexico, which helped stem industrial flight from the Midwest and permitted expansion in a number of industries and services. Throughout the region, the new wave of migration contributed to very rapid growth of barrios in older cities, industrial suburbs, small towns, and rural communities. The growing midwestern Mexican presence confirms that industrialists have engaged in strategies much more sophisticated than simple flight from northern cities to the Sun Belt or the Third World. While some industries separated the work process into component parts to be completed in different parts of the world, others restructured by setting up new operations in the Midwest. They often discovered that established transportation networks and infrastructure offered competitive advantages, while they saved on labor costs by tapping a new reserve of women, young adults, and immigrants. They found Mexicanos readily available and particularly vulnerable. Popular representations singled out Mexicans as illegal immigrants subject to INS and police harassment, though equally numerous undocumented Europeans were permitted to pursue their lives without such disturbance. Meanwhile, the Mexican government was unable or unwilling to compel the U.S. government to permit more open travel for its citizens and in other ways mitigate continued unequal treatment.

Midwestern Mexicans, still overwhelmingly workers, also entered the ranks of professionals and entrepreneurs in much larger numbers than before. While there were some businesses in the earliest *colonias* that catered largely to the needs of the local population, there had been few professionals. In the 1960s and 1970s the latter increased largely in response to the expansion of government social and public service programs. That growth was accompanied by an even more rapid expansion of businesses oriented primarily to the growing Spanish-speaking population. Changing patterns of work, particularly the very rapid entry of Mexicanas into the workforce, created additional demands for services and businesses. Midwestern Mexicanas became wage earners at rates even higher than their European American, Asian American, or African American counterparts while working for lower wages. Meanwhile, labor migration of single Mexicanas and Tejanas accelerated, and entrepreneurs quickly demonstrated the ability to commodify many tasks earlier performed by women in the domestic realm.

The concept of Chicanas and Chicanos as a regional southwestern minority became increasingly problematic in the twentieth century. From the beginning, important differences characterized those of the Midwest from the Southwest, notably weaker ties to the land and the lack of an immediate memory of conquest and forced incorporation. A more complicated class formation had long been in place in the Southwest, in contrast with the overwhelmingly unstable and unskilled wage labor that characterized midwestern Mexicanos. During the course of the century, common experiences became more numerous, including the deportation and repatriation movements of the Great Depression. The Midwest also developed an increasingly complex class formation as a stabler industrial working class appeared, augmenting its less stable laboring population. In the final years of the century, the more visible and growing business and professional class segments formed symbiotic links with still larger industrial and service sectors. As a nation-wide minority, the occupational, economic, and educational profiles of Mexicans in different regions became increasingly similar. Furthermore, rapid population growth, increasing occupational segmentation, and spatial segregation in the Midwest contributed to rising social, political, and cultural tensions, partly reflecting the incapacity of dominant popular culture and academia to adjust to racial paradigms not predicated in simple terms of black and white.

Perspectives on inequality between Mexicanos in the Midwest and Southwest have also experienced increasing convergence. In the former, from the early years of the century academics and other observers discussed whether Mexicans were assimilable. They addressed the issue implicitly and explicitly in comparison with the large European-born population, which was less a factor in southwestern settings where Mexicans were more numerous. Many observers predicted a linear trend toward assimilation in the Midwest, and even Paul Taylor cited diversity within the European population and its common experience with Mexican workers as factors likely to enhance Mexican adjustment and acceptance. Yet other contemporary industrialists, journalists, academicians, and politicians disagreed, and their ideas formed the justification for deportation and repatriation programs.

With the coming of World War II, further Mexican assimilation was limited by European American prejudice and discrimination, fueled by events of World War II and new waves of immigration and migration to the region. Nevertheless, during the mid twentieth century the rhetoric of assimilation was more consistently articulated and deeply embedded in midwestern popular and academic thought than at any other time in the century. It was predicated on the increasing stability of Mexican communities, the approaching adulthood of a generation of Mexicans reared in the Midwest, and the *Pax Americana*, laden with the rhetoric of democracy and equality on the homefront in the worldwide struggle against communism. Meanwhile in the Southwest, informal apartheid, though under attack, became a basis for the articulation among academics of internal colonial models in the 1960s and 1970s. Both assimilationist and internal colonial theories were predicated on spaces within the United States.

Mexicano organizational activities, often motivated by persistent inequality and lack of structural assimilation, followed distinct trajectories in different cycles during the century. In the early years, many Mexican *mutualistas* and patriotic societies appeared, sometimes through the initiative or support of the Mexican consulate. They offered mutual aid and other temporary assistance to individuals in distress, recognizing a different standard of public and private support for Mexicans than for Europeans. Meanwhile, settlement houses and Church organizations tended to recognize the need to socialize Mexicans as workers and parishioners.

During the second cycle of the twentieth century, explicit national links developed organizationally, as chapters of LULAC and the American G.I. Forum were directly transplanted from their base in Texas, although older groups and established institutions continued to offer a base for local activities. During the peak of the Chicano Movement, national links were evident in the creation of the Midwest Council for La Raza and the Brown Berets. Other midwestern groups were directly inspired by southwestern models, including the Latin Liberation Front, which created the Department of Chicano Studies at Minnesota, inspired by the Crusade for Justice; and the Farm Labor Organizing Committee in Ohio and Obreros Unidos in Wisconsin, influenced by the United Farm Workers. Midwestern organizations commonly worked closely with those in the Southwest, and groups from different places supported each other as they confronted inequality in local settings.

The reorganization of production in the late twentieth century revealed even more clearly the inadequacies of assimilationist and internal colonial perspectives on inequality. The New World Order was predicated on increasing foreign investment and echoing of the political will of the United States across the international divide. The economic transformation was not patterned on formal colonial relationships or on the export of raw or partially finished materials using subordinated labor in the colony. Rather, it involved the production and movement of goods and the transfer of labor between core and periphery. Whether employed in Mexico or in the United States, Mexican workers experienced unequal conditions as they produced and serviced an international market based in the United States. The growth of barrios in the core represented Mexicans' increasingly important role, based ideologically on a racialized division of labor between core and periphery. Their subordination was further reinforced by popular and political representations of Mexicans as inferior, whether as illegal immigrants, welfare abusers, criminals, or carriers of drugs. The images helped dominant culture justify increasing segregation in schools and residence and rising inequality in the application of the law, earnings, and other material indicators. Meanwhile, accelerating migration, expanding barrios, and the spread of a common culture contributed to increasing similarities between Mexicans in the Midwest and the Southwest over the course of the century. The political border has less immediate meaning to workers who fly directly to Houston, Los Angeles, Minneapolis, St. Paul, Chicago, New York, and other cities where employers seek their labor.

# Notes

## Introduction

1. Edson, "Minneapolis and St. Paul."
2. Among the exceptions in the published literature are Año Nuevo Kerr, "Mexican Chicago"; Rogers, "The Role"; and Allsup, "Concerned Latins." De León, *Ethnicity*, is the only Chicano urban history approaching complete coverage of the century. Criticism of linearity has been justly leveled, for example, in Broyles-González, *Teatro*.
3. Wolf, "Perilous Ideas"; Hobsbawm, "Afterword," in Hoerder, *Labor Migration*, 446.
4. See especially, Anderson, *Imagined*; and Roediger, *Wages*.
5. See, for example, Sánchez, *Becoming*, 38–62. In the Midwest, Humphrey, "Integration," 161–162; Leininger, "South Bend."
6. For more recent usage, see, for example, Salazar, "What is a Chicano?"; "The Spiritual Plan of Aztlán," in Servín, *Awakened*, 207; Macklin and Teniente de Costilla, "La Virgen," 138, n. 1. Hernández's story is based on an interview in Gamio, *Mexican Immigrant*, 104–106. See also the corrido "*El Lavaplatos*," probably written in the late 1920s. A recent debate on terminology appears in *Latin American Perspectives*, 19 (Fall 1992).
7. Some suggest the earliest use of Latino identity in Chicago for strategic purposes. See Padilla, *Latino*.

## 1. Mexican Inequality and the Midwest

1. For Chicano social science theory, see especially Barrera, *Race and Class*; Mirandé, *Chicano Experience*; Martínez and McCaughan, "Chicanas and Mexicanas."
2. St. John de Crèvecoeur, *Letters*, 66–90; Gordon, *Assimilation*, 120 ff.
3. Bevans, *Treaties*, IX: 791–806; McCall, *New Mexico*, 86–87.
4. Stoddard, *Re-Forging*, 38; Barrera, *Race and Class*, 2, 174–182; Edwards, *Campaign*, 50. For racism of the late nineteenth century, see also Weber, *Foreigners*; and De León, *Greasers*.
5. Testimony of A. H. Naftzger, U.S. Industrial Commission, *Report*, 957; McWilliams, *North*, 35–41; De León, *In Re Rodríguez*.
6. Sullenger, "Ethnic Assimilation," 549; Nordahl, *Weaving*; Beijbom, *Swedes in Chicago*; interview with Ulf Beijbom.

7. Takaki, *Strangers,* 109–112.

8. Turner, *Frontier;* Roy L. Garis, "Review," 116; Stoddard, *Re-Forging,* 91–132; Handlin, *Immigration,* 3–4. The vicious racism prevalent in European popular culture was widespread, as demonstrated by the Swedish film *The Emigrant* (1911). On contemporary Europe, see Olsson, "Labor Migration."

9. U.S. Congress, House, *Seasonal,* 295; U.S. Congress, House, *Western Hemisphere,* 111, 118.

10. U.S. Congress, House, "Our Present," 1104; Stoddard, *Re-Forging,* 216, 257; Garis, "Review," 121; U.S. Congress, House, *Western Hemisphere,* 426.

11. See Winant, *Racial Conditions,* 1–4, on more recent discussions.

12. Kallen, "Democracy," 190–194, 220; Gordon, *Assimilation,* 4, 71, 108, 129, 201.

13. Mirandé, *Chicano Experience,* 186–188.

14. Myrdal, *American Dilemma;* Fanon, *Wretched;* Memmi, *Colonizer;* Gosse, *Where the Boys Are.*

15. See especially, Blauner, *Racial Oppression;* Barrera et al., "The Barrio," 465–498.

16. Slavín Ruiz and Moreau, *Latino-americanos,* 3–6; Tennayuca and Brooks, "Mexican Question," 257–268.

17. McWilliams, *North;* Acuña, *Occupied America,* 25–26, 135–137; Barrera, *Race and Class,* 212–218.

18. Córdova et al., *Chicana Voices;* Glenn, "From Servitude," 1–43; Sánchez, "History of Chicanas," 1–25; Baca Zinn, "Sociological Theory," 257.

19. Nostrand, *Hispano Homeland,* 3–25; Deutsch, *No Separate.* A more fruitful approach to the notion of homelands appears in Alonso, *Tejano Legacy,* 105, 141, which suggests regional variations in "homelands" experiences.

20. Classics in the Spanish borderlands tradition include Bolton, *Spanish Borderlands;* Bannon, *Borderlands Frontier;* and Weber, *Spanish Frontier.*

21. McWilliams, "Mexican Problem," 14; Rosales, "Indiana Harbor," 88; Rosales and Simon, "East Chicago," 333; Cárdenas, "Desarraigados," 159–160.

22. Diebold, "Mexicans"; Alice L. Sickels, "International Institute"; MHS; McCulley, "Spanish-speaking," 25; Hernández Alvarez, "Demographic," 490; interview with María J. Bosquez, MHS, OH.

23. Taylor, *Chicago,* 35; Ford, "Toledo's Spanish"; Fr. Michael Bradley to Most Rev. Leo Binz, April 23, 1970, ASPM, folder: St. Paul—Our Lady of Guadalupe (1), "A Butcher Shop."

24. Goldner, "Profile," 102–103, 106. See also Skendzel, *Detroit's Pioneer,* 68–73; Matthews, "Migrants Battled." Feminist critiques include Glenn, "From Servitude"; Blackwelder, *Women,* 120–122.

25. Rosales, "Interethnic Violence," 67; Macklin and Teniente, "La Virgen," 119.

26. Humphrey, "Ethnic Images," 306; Humphrey, "Detroit Mexican Im-

migrant," 332; Barrera, *Race and Class,* 62; Reisler, "Mexican Immigrant," 155, 158; Escobar, "Forging," 9–13.

27. Humphrey, "Migration and Settlement," 358; Edson, "North Central"; García and Cal, "El círculo," 95.

28. On aspects of the world system, see Wallerstein, *Capitalist Agriculture, Historical Capitalism,* and "Culture as the Ideological Battleground." On culture, see especially Said, *Culture and Imperialism.* A valuable critique of global models is Baca Zinn, "Sociological Theory," 255–272.

## 2. Reckoning with Winter

1. Statement of Roy O. Woodruff, U.S. Congress, House, *Western Hemisphere,* 621.

2. On post–civil war industrial cycles, see in particular Gómez-Quiñones, *Mexican American,* 11; and Gordon et al., *Segmented Work.*

3. Vargas, *Proletarians,* 4; Taylor, *Chicago,* 1; Smith, "Kansas City, 33; Edson, "Summary."

4. On Europe, see Strikwerda and Guerín-Gonzales, *Politics;* and Hoerder, *Labor Migration,* 17. On Mexican railroads, see Coatsworth, *Growth.*

5. Rosales, "Regional Origins," 187–201; Taylor, "Notes," 287–288; Zamora, *Mexican Worker,* 15–16; Smith, *Oklahoma.*

6. Smith, "Kansas City," 30–32; Laird, "Argentine," 42–55; Cardoso, "Labor Emigration," 400–416; Humphrey, "Mexican Peasant," 55; Valdés, "Perspiring Capitalists," 229–230; Rosales, "Indiana Harbor," 89; Jones, "Mexican Colonies," 586; Cohen, *New Deal,* 165–167; Edson, "Lorain"; Taylor, *Bethlehem;* West, "Cinco Chacuacos," 63, 68–69.

7. Taylor, *Chicago,* 1; Jones, "Mexican Colonies," 586–591; Edson, "North Central"; Edson, "Summary."

8. Taylor, *Chicago,* 48; Rosales, "Regional Origins," 187–201; Camblon, "Mexicans in Chicago," 208; Smith, "Kansas City," 30; Statement of James Ward, n.d., MHS, MAC, folder: Our Lady of Guadalupe; Taylor, *Arandas,* 12, 36; Alvarado, "Mexican Immigration," 479; Brading and Wu, "Population Growth," 35–36; Sánchez, *Becoming,* 54.

9. Taylor, *Chicago,* 183; Paz, "Survey," 4; Edson, "Summary"; Fenton, "The Mexicans," 22.

10. Taylor, *Chicago,* 73. On the urban Midwest, see Cárdenas, "Desarraigados," 159–160; Hernández Alvarez, "Demographic Profile," 489; Edson, "Central West."

11. U.S. Bureau of the Census, *1930 Census,* vol. 4; Edson, "Detroit."

12. Many Southwestern mining, ranching, and agricultural entrepreneurs had operations earlier established in Mexico. In file of Immigrants Protective League, May 31, 1916—Notes of N. R. on visit re: complaint of Mexicans, BL, PT, folder: Chicago—General.

13. Taylor, *Arandas*, 35–36; Smith, "Beyond," 239–251; Martínez, "Dodge City"; Edson, "Omaha"; Edson, "Des Moines"; Edson, "Fort Madison"; Edson, "Sioux City"; Edson, "Aurora"; Edson, "Joliet"; Betten and Mohl, "Discrimination," 162; Edson, "Summary"; Edson, "Central West." Rutledge quote from Jasso and Tejeda, "Chicano in Kansas."

14. Edson, "Summary"; Taylor, *Chicago*, 268; Hernández-Fujigaki, "Mexican Steelworkers," 29.

15. Halpern, *Killing Floor*, 77–78, 80–82; Edson, "Sioux City"; Sullenger, "Mexican Population," 289–293; Rutter, "Mexican Americans," 66.

16. McLean, *Northern Mexican*, 14.

17. Oppenheimer, "Acculturation," 431–432; Informe de protección, Kansas City, SRE, IV/241 (04) (73-25) "33"/1; Alfredo C. Vásquez a consulado, New Orleans, May 22, 1929, SRE, IV/823 (73-25)/1; C. M. Gaxiola to Secretario de Relaciones Exteriores, December 15, 1930, SRE, IV/241 (04) (73-25)/1; Arthur Campa, "Immigrant Latinos," 350.

18. Laird, "Argentine," 2–3, 44, 46, 80, 168, 178–179; Rutter, "Mexican Americans," 132–133; Smith, "Kansas City," 30–36; Lamar, "Identity," 17–21.

19. Edson, "Central West"; "Kansas City Urged"; Duncan and Alanzo, *Guadalupe Center*, 8, 28, 69; U.S. Chamber of Commerce, "Mexican Immigration," 23; Laird, "Argentine," 47–49, 52.

20. Jasso and Tejeda, "Chicano in Kansas"; Rutter, "Mexican Americans," 45, 66–67, 72, 132–133; Laird, "Argentine," 178; Smith, "Kansas City," 32; Oppenheimer, "Acculturation," 432–436.

21. Boellstorff, "Conflicting Emotions"; Sullenger, "Mexican Population"; Edson, "Omaha."

22. Sullenger, "Mexican Population," 289; Stapp, "Melting Pot"; Edson, "Omaha."

23. Quoted from Edson, "Mason City." See also Edson, "Sioux City"; Edson, "Des Moines"; Edson, "Fort Madison"; Edson, "Davenport."

24. Edson, "Chicago"; Rosales, "Interethnic Violence," 61; Informe de los ciudadanos Mexicanos residentes en la jurisdicción del consulado de México en Chicago, Illinois, BL, MG, Box 3, folder 14; Notes from vice consul Bustamante, BL, PT, Box 3, folder 16; Edson, "Pittsburgh"; Edson, "Philadelphia"; Edson, "New York City." McConnell, "Poor Man's Paradise," made much higher estimates of Mexican population, suggesting 55,000 for Michigan alone, compared with consular estimates of 25,000 for Michigan and Ohio combined in 1927. See also comments below on census undercounting.

25. Jones and Wilson, "Mexican in Chicago," 4–5; Jones, "Mexican Colonies," 64; Camblon, "Mexicans in Chicago," 210; F. L. Larned to Anthony Caminetti, June 2, 1919, NA, RG 85, 55261/202-1; M. R. Ibáñez, Report of Mexican Work at the University of Chicago Settlement for the year 1930–31, UIC, UCSP, Box 21, folder: Mexican Work.

26. Jones, "Mexican Colonies," 589, 596; Robert C. Jones, "Protestant Mexican Work in the Near West Side," PHS, HMC.

27. Grant, "Little Mexico"; Jones, "Mexican Colonies," 589, 596; Jones and Wilson, "Mexican in Chicago," 5–6; Año Nuevo, "Chicano Settlements," 22, 24; "The Foreign Born," CHS, MED, folder 12; Barrio inmediato a Hull House, BL, MG, Box 3, folder 11; "Arte Mexicano"; Edson, "Chicago."

28. Jones, "Mexican Colonies," 586, 590; Cohen, *New Deal,* 41; Jones and Wilson, "Mexican Immigrant," 4–5; Abbott, *Tenements,* 136.

29. Edson, "Chicago"; Taylor, *Chicago,* 57; Raymond E. Nelson, "The Mexican in South Chicago," BL, PT, folder: "Mexican in South Chicago"; interview with Alberto Cuellar, December 11, 1936, IHRC, CFLPS, Reel 62; interview with Padre Catatina, December 10, 1936, IHRC, CFLPS, Reel 63. Company support of churches and other institutions to maintain worker loyalty and prevent unionization was applied to others, including Blacks in Chicago's stockyards; see Street, "Logic and Limits," 659–681.

30. Edson, "Chicago"; Abbott, *Tenements,* 147–148; Año Nuevo, "Chicano Settlements," 24; Jones, "Mexican Colonies," 587; Edson, "Chicago"; Nelson, "Mexican in South Chicago"; Interview with Sr. Galindo, BL, MG, Box 2, folder 2.

31. Jones, "Mexican Colonies," 587–588; Abbott, *Tenements,* 80–83; Camblon, "Mexicans in Chicago," 211; Taylor, *Chicago,* 181; Britton and Constable, "Mexican Patients," 453.

32. Taylor, *Chicago,* 220–226; Abbott, *Tenements,* 136; "Act of Barbarism"; "Assaulted Mexican"; "Compatriot Assaulted"; "Impudence of Policemen"; "More Mexicans."

33. García, "Mexican American People," 13–14; Edson, "Waukegan."

34. Edson, "Joliet"; Grant, "Spanish Center."

35. Campos Carr, "Mexican Workers," 31–52; Edson, "Aurora"; Dardick, "Hispanic Police"; Palmer, "Building Ethnic Communities"; McDowell, "A Study," 15.

36. García, "Mexican American People," 24.

37. García, "Chicanos in Chicago Heights," 291–296; Taylor, *Chicago,* 1, 25; interview with D. P. Thompson, May 31, 1928, PT, Box 1, folder: Indiana Harbor.

38. Sepúlveda, "Research Note," 329–330; Sepúlveda, "Origins," 105–106; Rosales, "Indiana Harbor," 90; Edson, "Indiana Harbor"; Rosales and Simon, "Mexican Immigrant," 337.

39. Rosales, "Indiana Harbor," 88; Edson, "Indiana Harbor"; Leitman, "Exile," 50–52; interview with J. M. Uvina, BL, MG, Box 3, folder 11.

40. Edson, "Gary"; Betten and Mohl, "Discrimination," 373, 387; Beth Bissell, "The Mexican Colony 1921–1926 inclusive," BL, PT, Box 1, folder: Gary, Indiana; Crocker, "Gary Mexicans," 120–121, 125–126.

41. Jones, "Mexican Colonies," 588–589; Reisler, "Mexican Immigrant," 152; Edson, "Chicago."

42. Edson, "Milwaukee"; Fenton, "The Mexicans," 20; Pabst, "Illegal Aliens"; Garza, "So American"; U.S. Chamber of Commerce, "Mexican Immigration," 23.

43. Skendzel, *Detroit's Pioneer,* 58; Edson, "Detroit"; interview with Javier Tovar, August 10, 1926, BL, MG, Box 3, folder 16; Valdés, "Perspiring Capitalists," 227–239.

44. Humphrey, "Mexican Peasant," 62; Edson, "Detroit."

45. Edson, "Detroit"; U.S. Congress, Senate, *Agricultural Labor Supply,* 115.

46. Humphrey, "Mexican Peasant," 56; Edson, "Detroit"; interview with Joaquín Terrazas, August 10, 1926, BL, MG, Box 3, folder 16.

47. Humphrey, "Mexican Peasant," 56, 144–145; Skendzel, *Detroit's Pioneer,* 20; Edson, "Detroit"; Taylor, *Chicago,* 246.

48. Vargas, *Proletarians,* 52, 94, 100–101, 123, 158, 166; Gramsci, "Americanism and Fordism," 275–299; Edson, "Detroit."

49. George L. Cady, "Report of the Commission on International and Interracial Factors in the Problem of Mexicans in the United States," 24, 29, BL; McDowell, "Study," 12; interview with Sra. Rose Aguilar; interviews with Mr. Fitzgerald, Miss Hutzel, Sr. Martínez, and Father Castillo, BL, PT, Carton 1, folder: Martínez.

50. Interview with José Alfaro; interview with Miss Hutzel, BL, PT, Carton 1, folder: Jones, Robert C., case studies.

51. Vargas, *Proletarians,* 116–120; Edson, "Detroit"; Humphrey, "Employment Patterns," 913.

52. T. A. Meehan to George Edson, October 6, 1926, in Edson, "Pontiac."

53. Edson, "Flint"; Albig, "Opinions," 62.

54. Edson, "Saginaw"; U.S. Congress, Senate, *Farm Labor Supply,* 534; interviews with Ramiro González and María Castellanos.

55. "Go to School"; Edson, "Toledo."

56. Edson, "Lorain."

57. "Mexican Laborers for Bethlehem," 103; "Mexican Journeys," 103–104; West, "Cinco *Chacuacos,*" 63–82; Taylor, *Bethlehem,* 1–19; Edson, "Philadelphia"; Edson, "New York City."

58. Interview with C. M. Brading, BL, PT, folder: Chicago; Edson, "Davenport"; Edson, "Pittsburgh"; Taylor, *Chicago,* 81.

59. International Institute, "Mexican Nationality," 8; Mary A. Bishop, Notes on Mexican Community in St. Paul, 1933, MHS, GCW, Box 3, folder: Mission House of Our Lady of Guadalupe.

60. Reisler, *By the Sweat,* 51; Taylor, *Chicago,* 2; Rutter, "Mexican Americans," 102; William T. Kemper to Alvaro Obregon, June 2, 1921, SRE, 822–

M-1; Johnson, "Detroit Out," 106–107; Commissioner Montreal to Caminetti, NA, RG85, 11212/28; "497 Mexicans."

61. Matthews, "Migrants Battled"; Valdés, "Mexican Revolutionary," 5; International Institute, "Mexican Nationality," 8; Edson, "North Central."

62. U.S. Congress, House, *Western Hemisphere*, 486; Edson, "North Central."

63. Interviews with Manuel Contreras, Esiquia S. Monita, Guadalupe Cruz, and Marcelino and Irene Rivera, MHS, OH.

64. Interviews with Jesse and Ramona Méndez, MHS, OH.

65. Interview with Manuel Contreras Prieto, MHS, OH.

66. Interview with Alfonso de León, MHS, OH.

67. Edson, "North Central"; Edson, "Minneapolis and St. Paul"; International Institute, "Mexican Nationality," 4.

68. Edson, "North Central"; Edson, "Minneapolis and St. Paul."

69. Taylor, *Chicago*, 276; interview with Felicitas Herrera, MHS, OH.

70. Interview with Sebastián R. Jara, MHS, OH.

71. Fenton, "The Mexicans," 27; Goldner, "Profile," 102–103, 106; Taylor, *Chicago*, 193, 194.

72. Taylor, *Chicago*, 267; Jones, "Mexican Colonies," 597; Taylor, *Bethlehem*, 21.

73. Sánchez, *Telling Identities*, 202–203, 211–217; Dysart, "Mexican Women," 365–375.

74. Edson, "Minneapolis and St. Paul"; Edson, "Northern Sugar."

75. Pierce, "St. Paul's," 5; Diebold, "Mexicans," 92; U.S. Bureau of the Census, *1920 Census of Population*.

76. Smith, "Kansas City," 36; McLean, *Northern Mexican*, 18; Edson, "Gary"; Edson, "Minneapolis and St. Paul"; IHRC, II, Box 34, file 518; Stapp, "Melting Pot"; "497 Mexicans"; U.S. Congress, Senate, *Agricultural Labor Supply*, 115.

77. Macklin and Teniente, "La Virgen," 117; Teodosia Moreno, "History of the Mexican Colony," in Edson, "Gary"; Edson, "Pittsburgh"; Cárdenas Coates, *Nuestra Señora*, 3–4; "Mexican Colony Enlisted in War on Tuberculosis," in Scrapbook of Robert C. Jones, IHRC, CFLPS, reel 62; Edson, "North Central."

78. Edson, "Milwaukee"; Edson, "Chicago"; Beth Bissell, "The Mexican Colony (Gary) 1921–1926," in Edson, "Indiana Harbor"; E. P. Kirby Hade a Sociedad M. R. Hispano Azteca, March 13, 1931, SRE, IV/241 (73-59)/4; Abbott, *Tenements*, 297, 303, 317; Taylor, *Chicago*, 220–221; Ibáñez, "Report of Mexican Work," UIC, UCSP, Box 21, folder: Mexican work; Edson, "Pittsburgh."

79. Interview with Mr. McKeany, August 3, 1926, BL, MG, Box 3, folder 11; McDowell, "Study," 23; Britton and Constable, "Mexican Patients," 456; Hughes, "Living Conditions," 21–22; Hoyt, *Hundred Years*, 314–315.

80. Edson, "Summary"; Albig, "Opinions," 62–72; Taylor, *Chicago*, 235.

81. Rosales, "Interethnic Violence," 68–69; Edson, "Manly"; Edson, "Pittsburgh"; Warnshius, "Crime," 267; Taylor, *Chicago*, 145; Sullenger, "Mexican Population," 292.

82. Warnshius, "Crime," 276, 282–286; Sullenger, "Mexican Population," 292; Rosales, "Interethnic Violence," 68.

83. *In Re Camille* (1880) involves an instance in which a court determined that people of non-European backgrounds are treated as non-White for immigration purposes—yet another example of courts applying different standards to people defined as non-White. Taylor, *Chicago*, 151, 154; Warnshius, "Crime," 276–292.

84. Warnshius, "Crime," 279; McLean, "Mexican Workers," 537; Edson, "Detroit"; Edson, "Summary."

85. Minnesota Governor, *Mexican in Minnesota*, 37; International Institute, "Mexican Nationality," 21; Sickels, *Around the World*, 19–20; Interviews with Ramedo J. and Catalina Saucedo and Manuel Contreras, MHS, OH.

86. Edson, "Gary"; Edson, "North Central"; Camblon, "Mexicans in Chicago," 208; Interview with Luis García, BL, PT, folder: Chicago.

87. Oppenheimer, "Acculturation," 432; Gaxiola to Secretario de Relaciones Exteriores, December 15, 1930, SRE, IV/241 (04) (73-25)/1; Smith, "Kansas City," 39; Rutter, "Mexican Americans," 109–113; Martínez, "Historical Development," 7; Betten and Mohl, "Discrimination," 167; Cohen, *New Deal*, 123–124; Edson, "North Central."

88. Smith, "Kansas City," 40; Badillo, "Catholic Church," 249; International Institute, "Mexican Nationality," 16; Taylor, *Chicago*, 172; U.S. Congress, Senate, *Agricultural Labor Supply*, 115.

89. Taylor, *Chicago*, 180; Reports of April 30, 1929, and Summer 1931, UIC, UCSP, Box 21, folder: Mexican Work; Fenton, "The Mexicans," 22; Edson, "Omaha."

90. Interview with Rose Aguilar; Taylor, *Chicago*, 112; interview with Carlos Pérez López, BL, MG, Box 2, folder 13.

91. Andrews, *Shoulder*, 10–11; Edson, "Waukegan"; Taylor, *Chicago*, 116; Questionnaire, Mexican Labor in Illinois, BL, PT, folder: Illinois Federation of Labor.

92. West, *Mexican Aztec*, 94; Taylor, *Chicago*, 94; Cohen, *New Deal*, 165–167; Interview with W. H. Baird, BL, PT, folder: Chicago.

93. Bauer, "Delinquency," 23; Rutter, "Mexican Americans," 111; Laird, "Argentine," 139–140; Immigrants Protective League, May 31, 1916, BL, PT, folder: Chicago.

94. Taylor, *Chicago*, 115–116; Untitled clipping, *Gary Post-Tribune*, January 25, 1927, BL, MG, Box 3, folder 12.

95. González, *Labor and Community*, 99–134; Esquivel, "Immigrant," 131; "Mexican Invaders," 54; Vargas, *Proletarians*, 74.

96. Bell, "Americanization"; Sullenger, "Mexican Population," 289; Cohen, *New Deal,* 165.

97. Hill, "Americanization," 609–642; Aronovici, "Assimilation," 134; Bromley, "Mexican in Los Angeles," 130; Crocker, "Gary Mexicans," 116; Edson, "Indiana Harbor"; Edson, "Detroit"; Edson, "Lorain."

98. Neighborhood House, Board of Directors, *Minutes,* November 29, 1954, MHS, NH, folder: 1953–1956.

99. Notes from Secretary's Minutes, December 13, 1923, and February 14, 1924, MHS, NH, Box 1, folder: History and Purpose, General; Interview with Crescencia Rangel, MHS, OH; Neighborhood House, Board of Directors, *Minutes,* March 8, 1934, MHS, NH, folder: Board Minutes, 1933–1939.

100. Humphrey, "Mexican Peasant," 145–146.

101. "Dolores Awaits"; Edson, "Chicago"; Edson, "Omaha"; Edson, "Mason City"; Guerin-Gonzales, *Mexican Workers,* 51–76.

102. Talk by his Eminence John Cardinal Cody, November 8, 1974, UND, MCLR, Box 58, folder: Chicago; Reisler, "Mexican Immigrant," 151–152; García, "Midwest Mexicanos," 96.

103. Edson, "Lorain"; Crocker, "Gary Mexicans," 125–127; Robert C. Jones, "Protestant Mexican Work in the Near West Side," PHS, HMC; McLean, *Northern Mexican,* 22; Taylor, *Chicago,* 220–241.

104. Interview with Padre Catatina, December 10, 1936, IHRC, CFLPS, reel 63; Humphrey, "Integration," 164.

105. Cárdenas Coates, *Nuestra Señora,* 2.

106. Edson, "North Central."

107. Edson, "North Central"; Crocker, "Gary Mexicans," 127; untitled clipping from *Gary Post-Tribune,* January 25, 1927, BL, PT, Box 3, folder 12.

108. Oppenheimer, "Acculturation," 431; McLean, *Northern Mexican,* 18; quoted from Gamio, *Immigration,* 119; Edson, "Detroit"; Edson, "Waukegan"; Edson, "Lorain"; Taylor, *Bethlehem,* 17; Taylor, *Chicago,* 175, 179, 220.

109. Taylor, *Chicago,* 129–134; J. Jesús Cortez to George Edson, in Edson, "Indiana Harbor."

110. Smith, "Kansas City," 41–42; Gustavo del Río a Eduardo Hernández Charazo, April 14, 1930, AGN, POR, expediente 49, folder 104; Edson, "Indiana Harbor"; Edson, "Milwaukee."

111. Sullenger, "Mexican Population," 293; interview with Sebastián Jara, MHS, OH; Edson, "North Central."

112. Taylor, *Chicago,* 131–137; Humphrey, "Mexican Peasant," 204–214.

113. Paz, "Survey," 14; García, "Midwest Mexicanos," 89, 93; Nelson, "Mexican in South Chicago"; Smith, "20,000 Mexicans"; Taylor, *Chicago,* 124, 126.

114. Reglamento de la Sociedad Mutua Beneficia Recreativa Anahuac, St. Paul, Minnesota, 1935, MHS, MAC, Box 1, folder: Research; "St. Paul Is City of Charity"; "Dolores Awaits"; Interview Crescencia Rangel, MHS, OH; Nelson, "Mexican in South Chicago."

115. García, "Midwest Mexicanos," 94; Taylor, *Chicago*, 132–139; interview with Sebastián R. Jara, MHS, OH.

116. García and Cal, "El círculo," 95–114; interview with Crescencia Rangel, MHS, OH; "Dolores Awaits."

117. "2-Day Fiesta Begins Here Today," unidentified clipping, September 15, 1957, MHS, MAC, Box 1, folder: Mexican Independence—1; Comité de reconstrucción, *Minutes*, September 9, October 14, and November 4, 1940, MHS, MAC, Box 1, folder: Research; Interviews Antonio Zepeda and Petra Treviño Zepeda, Carlota Arellano, and Esiquia S. Monita, MHS, OH; interview with Juan Gómez; Parra, Ríos, and Gutiérrez, "Chicano Organizations," 248–249.

118. Interviews with Crescencia Rangel and Juanita Morán, MHS, OH; Edson, "North Central."

119. Interview with Crescencia Rangel, MHS, OH; "Reglamento de la Sociedad Mutua Beneficia Recreativa Anahuac," 1935, MHS, MAC, Box 1, folder: Research.

120. García, "Midwest Mexicanos," 93–94; Rosales, "Indiana Harbor," 90; Leitman, "Exile," 52–53; García and Cal, "El círculo," 95; Smith, "Kansas City"; Humphrey, "Mexican Peasant," 205, 208.

121. Grant, "Little Mexico"; "Celebration"; interview with J. M. Uvina, BL, MG, Box 3, folder 11; "S. M. Carmen"; interview with Javier Tovar, BL, MG, Box 3, folder 16; Gaxiola to Secretario de Relaciones Exteriores, December 15, 1930, SRE, IV/241 (04) (73-25)/1; Bolton, "Socio-Cultural," 9; Neighborhood House, Board of Directors, *Minutes*, March 8, 1934, MHS, NH, Box 1, folder: 1933–1939; Edson, "Davenport."

122. Gramsci, "The Intellectuals," 5–23; "Dolores Awaits"; Bichler, "Jewish, Italians," 62; Edson, "Northern Sugar"; interview with José Alfaro; Leitman, "Exile"; Edson, "Indiana Harbor"; Stapp, "Melting Pot."

123. Chambers, "Mutual Cooperation," 22–28; interview with Juanita Morán, MHS, OH.

124. Interviews with Crescencia Rangel and Juanita Morán, MHS, OH.

125. "Edson, "North Central"; Humphrey, "Mexican Peasant," 204–214; Taylor, *Chicago*, 131–137.

126. Informe sobre los ciudadanos Mexicanos residentes en la jurisdicción del consulado de México en Chicago Illinois, 20 septiembre 1926, BL, MG, Box 3, folder: 14; Nelson, "Mexican in South Chicago"; Edson, "Summary."

127. Edson, "Omaha"; Edson, "North Central"; Britton and Constable, "Mexican Patients," 456; interview with Mrs. Kembell, June 11, 1928, BL, PT, folder: Chicago.

128. Informe sobre sanidad en las fundiciones en Saginaw, SRE, IV/592 (73-14)/2; Edson, "Pittsburgh"; Taylor, *Chicago*, 36–37, 101–102, 159; Taylor, *Bethlehem*, 13, 15–16.

129. McDowell, *Study*, 13; Edson, "North Central"; interview with Luis García, June 2, 1928, BL, PT, folder: Chicago.

130. McLean, *Northern Mexican,* 13; Edson, "North Central"; Edson, "Omaha"; Edson, "Detroit"; Rutter, "Mexican Americans," 110–111; Taylor, *Chicago,* 77–79; interview with Roberto Cortina; interview with Javier Tovar, BL, MG, Box 3, folder 16.

131. Taylor, *Chicago,* 79; Edson, "Gary"; Edson, "Detroit."

132. Taylor, *Chicago,* 166–167, 170; Edson, "Chicago"; Edson, "North Central"; Edson, "Indiana Harbor."

133. Interview with Trini, August 10, 1926, BL, MG, Box 3, folder 16; Edson, "Pittsburgh"; Informe de protección, Pittsburgh, September 1931, SRE, IV/241 (04) (73-38)/1; Lambert, "Tank Town," 29; interview with Inspector Knauth, July 11, 1928, BL, PT, folder: Robert C. Jones case studies; interview with J. M. Uvina, BL, MG, Box 3, folder 11; Edson, "North Central"; Edson, "Indiana Harbor"; Warnshius, "Crime," 280–281. On the role of the informal economy, see Portes and Sassen-Koob, "Making It," 30–61.

134. Fenton, "The Mexicans," 20; Bogardus, "Segregation," 74; Smith, "Kansas City," 40, 74; Humphrey, "Naturalization," 334–335; Taylor, *Chicago,* 214–218.

135. McLean, *Northern Mexican,* 8.


## 3. Memory of Hunger

1. Laird, "Argentine," 203; International Institute, "Mexican Nationality," 12.

2. Taylor, "More Bars," 26–27; Taylor, *Chicago,* 152; Ryan, "Who Shall," 29.

3. R. E. Wood to Ralph Budd, April 24, 1929, MHS, GNPSF, 7648; Thomson, "The Man," 275.

4. McLean, "Tightening," 29; Rutter, "Mexican Americans," 73; IHRC, II, Box 34, folder 518.

5. Betten and Mohl, "Discrimination," 381; Edson, "North Central"; McKay, "Federal Deportation," 95–97.

6. Mexican Work, October 1930, UIC, UCSP Box 21, folder: Mexican Work; Humphrey, "Employment Patterns," 913–914; Dean, "Detroit's Melting Pot," 187; Ignacio Batiza a Secretario de Relaciones Exteriores, December 12, 1932, SRE, IV/524.5/(73-14)/8; Rafael Avelina a Consul de México, December 30, 1930, SRE, IV/524.5 (73-10)/4.

7. Interview with Rev. Thomas M. Lineweaver, December 12, 1936, IHRC, CFLPS, reel 63; "Relief Efforts"; "Festival"; "Dance"; González, "The Problem."

8. IHRC, II, Box 24, folder 707; Sotero Arriaga a Secretario de Relaciones Exteriores, December 1, 1931, and Ignacio Batiza a Secretario de Relaciones Exteriores, December 14, 1932, SRE, IV/524.5/(73-14)/8; Rodolfo R. Benavides et al. a Pascual Ortiz Rubio, AGN, POR, expediente 49, folder: 104; "Open Grants"; "Message from"; González Navarro, "Efectos," 542–543.

9. Vargas, *Proletarians,* 190–194; Badillo, "Catholic Church," 269; McLean, "Mexican Return," 165–166; "Mexican Workers Victimized."

10. Laird, "Argentine," 204.

11. Report on Investigation of Lake County, HHL, RG 73, Series 10, State Files, folder: Indiana; Lane, "Extranjeros," 29.

12. American Legion Post #266, untitled report on repatriation program, ECHS, RF.

13. Rosales and Simon, "Mexican Immigrant," 344–350; Simon, "Mexican Repatriation," 14–19; quotation from Escobar, "Forging," 13; Paul E. Kelly to William Doak, March 4, 1932, and M. E. Crites to Paul V. McNutt, March 24, 1933, ECHS, RF.

14. "Mexican Population Here."

15. Oppenheimer, "Deportation," 231–234; Informe de deportados, consulado de Detroit, julio 1931, SRE, IV/524.4 (73-14) "32"/1; "Train Carries"; "Detroit Opens"; interview with Carmen Cortina; Valdés, "Mexican Revolutionary," 11–23; Gilbert, "Field Study," 106–109; Humphrey, "Repatriation," 497; Ignacio Batiza a Secretario de Relaciones Exteriores, September 10, 1931, and November 1932, SRE, IV/524.5/(73-14)/8; Batiza, Informe de protección, January 11, 1933, SRE, IV/241.04/(73-14)/12.

16. Año Nuevo, "Chicano Experience," 73; Edson, "Detroit"; Badillo, "Catholic Church," 276; "Back to," 39; Paz, "Survey," 3–4; Rafael Aveleyra to Pascual Ortiz Rubio, March 14, 1930, AGN, POR, expediente 49, folder 104; Comité Organizador de Repatriación to Secretaría de Relaciones Exteriores, June 3, 1931, SRE, IV/524.5 (73-10)/4; "Message from"; "Open Grants"; "Return of Mexicans."

17. Mrs. Kenneth Rich, Memorandum on the U.S. Deportation Drive of October–November, 1931, Chicago, UIC, IPL, Supplement 2, folder 54A; "Mexican Family Insulted."

18. Sra. H. Sahagún de la Mora a Secretario de Relaciones Exteriores, September 25, 1931, SRE, IV/524.5 (02)/64; Weber, "Anglo Views," 213–214, 258, 264–265; Año Nuevo, "Chicano Settlements," 25; "A Repatriation Program"; Año Nuevo, "Chicano Experience," 75.

19. "Back to," 39; Miss Currie's Report, 1932, and Notes from Secretary's Minutes, November 10, 1932, MHS, NH, Box 1, folder: History and Purpose, General; Neighborhood House, Board of Directors Minutes, November 10, 1932, MHS, NH, folder: Board Minutes, 1928–1933.

20. Story from interview of Francisco and Dolores Guzmán, MHS, OH.

21. Humphrey, "Employment Patterns," 915–916.

22. IHRC, Box 25, folder 734; Minnesota Governor, *Mexican in Minnesota,* 41; "1,500 Mexicans"; IHRC, II, Box 24, folder 1286; IHRC, II Box 25, folder 734; IHRC, II Box 24, folder 1286.

23. Taylor, *Chicago,* 218–219; Diebold, "Mexicans," 94; McKay, "Texas Mexican," 532; Gilbert, "Field Study," 32; Simon, "Mexican Repatriation," 18.

24. Taylor, *Migration Statistics,* 48; McKay, "Texas Mexican," 225.

25. International Institute, "Mexican Nationality," 24.

26. Minnesota Governor, *Mexican in Minnesota*, 9; Informe de protección, Chicago, June 1935, SRE, IV/241.1 (73-10)/90; International Institute, "Mexican Nationality," 8; interviews with Alfonso de León and Francisco Gómez, MHS, OH; Neighborhood House, *1939 Annual Report*, MHS, NH, Box 1, folder: History.

27. Neighborhood House, Board of Directors Minutes, April 14, 1932; MHS, NH, Box 1, folder: Minutes 1928–1933; International Institute, "Mexican Nationality," 7; interview with Esiquia S. Monita, MHS, OH.

28. U.S. Congress, House, *Destitute Citizens*, III, 835–836; Minnesota Governor, *Mexican in Minnesota*, 41–42; Humphrey, "Employment Patterns," 921–922; Betten and Mohl, "Discrimination," 385–386.

29. Interview with Frank Rodríguez, MHS, OH.

30. Interview with Juanita Morán, MHS, OH.

31. Statement of Rev. J. A. Ward, MHS, MAC, folder: Our Lady of Guadalupe (1); interview with Manuel Contreras, MHS, OH; Board of Directors, Neighborhood House, Minutes, February 10, 1936, MHS, NH, Box 1, folder: Board Minutes 1933–1939.

32. Minnesota Governor, *Mexican in Minnesota*, 40.

33. Interview with Marcelino and Irene Rivera, MHS, OH; IHRC, II Box 30, folder 1052; IHRC, II Box 26, folder 527; IHRC, II Box 28, folder 545.

34. Interview with Esiquia S. Monita, MHS, OH.

35. "Editorial"; interview with Eduardo Hidalgo, December 16, 1936, and Theodoro Lomelí, Pedro Gutiérrez, and Mauro Esquivel, December 15, 1936, IHRC, CFLPS, reel 62; "Explanation"; Neighborhood House, "Survey of Homes and Businesses, Sixth Ward, 1936," MHS, NH, box 13, folder: Studies.

36. Interview with Guadalupe Cruz, MHS, OH.

37. Sickels, *Around*, 16; Cook, "Poverty"; Comité de reconstrucción, Minutes, Julio 29, 1940, MHS, MAC, Box 1, folder: Research.

38. International Institute, "Mexican Nationality," 6, 12; Neighborhood House, Board of Directors Minutes, June 9, 1932, MHS, NH, Box 1, folder: History.

39. Informe de protección, Chicago, SRE, IV/241 (04) (73-10) "33"/1; Hughes, *Illinois Persons*, xvi, xix; International Institute, "Mexican Nationality," 6, 20.

40. Interview with Carlos and Marcelina Urvina, MHS, OH; IHRC, II, Box 26, folder 527; IHRC, II Box 28, folder 1244.

41. Interviews with Esther M. Avaloz and Louis Medina, MHS, OH; Cook, "Poverty."

42. IHRC, II, Box 30, folder 744; IHRC, II Box 25, folder 714; Flannery, "Immigrants Need"; Deutsch, *No Separate Refuge*, 182–183; International Institute, "Mexican Nationality," 18–19.

43. Cook, "Poverty"; Hoyt, *One Hundred*, 315; Delinquincy Neighborhood House District, 1940, MHS, NH, Box 13, folder: studies; Guild Talk,

January 4, 1937, MHS, GCW, Box 3, folder: Our Lady of Guadalupe; Mary Bishop, Notes on Mexican Settlement in West St. Paul, 1933, MHS, GCW, Box 3, folder: Mission House; *Neighborhood House, St. Paul, Minnesota* (1938), SWHA, NFS, folder: 381.

44. Cook, "Poverty"; Sickels, *Around,* 16, 18; International Institute, "Mexican Nationality," 21.

45. Sickels, *Around,* 20; International Institute, "Mexican Nationality," 17; Neighborhood House, Notes in Preparation for Survey of West Side, and Survey of Homes and Businesses, Sixth Ward, 1936, MHS, NH, Box 13, folder: Studies; Minnesota Governor, *Mexican in Minnesota,* 26.

46. Abbott, *Tenements,* 297; Humphrey, "Mexican Immigrant," 333; Lane, "Extranjeros," 25; IHRC, II, Box 26, folder 712; IHRC, II Box 24, folder 706; Neighborhood House, Notes in Preparation for Survey of West Side, MHS, NH, Box 13, folder: Studies.

47. Abbott, *Tenements,* 298; Betten and Mohl, "Discrimination," 377; Humphrey, "Mexican Immigrant," 332.

48. Cook, "Poverty"; Miss Currie's Report, 1932, MHS, NH, Box 1, folder: History and Purpose; Mary A. Bishop, Notes on Mexican Settlement in West St. Paul, 1933, MHS, GCW, Box 3, folder: Our Lady of Guadalupe; Betten and Mohl, "Discrimination," 373; "A Scene"; "Our Dead"; Cipriano Hernández to Pascual Ortiz Rubio, April 23, 1931, SRE, IV/524.5 (73-10)/19.

49. Laird, "Argentine," 201; International Institute, "A Study," 9; Cook, "Poverty"; Betten and Mohl, "Discrimination," 373; Dr. V. Volk, Saginaw County Health Report, MSA, KS, Box 14, folder 13.

50. International Institute, "Mexican Nationality," 7, 15.

51. International Institute, "Mexican Nationality," 7, 13–14; Rosales and Simon, "Mexican Immigrant," 349; Neighborhood House, "Survey of Homes and Businesses, Sixth Ward, 1936," MHS, NH, Box 13, folder: Studies.

52. "Neighborhood House, St. Paul, Minnesota," MHS, NH, Box 1, folder: Board Minutes 1928–1933; Neighborhood House, Board of Directors Minutes, April 14, 1932, MHS, NH, Box 1, folder: Board Minutes 1928–1933; U.S. Census Bureau, *1930 Census of Population;* International Institute, "Mexican Nationality," 2–4; Neighborhood House, "Survey of Homes and Businesses, Sixth Ward, 1936," MHS, NH, Box 13, folder: Studies.

53. Annual Report, Department of Missions, April, 1935, MHS, MAC, Box 1, folder: Our Lady of Guadalupe (1); IHRC, II, Box 32, folder 896; Comité de reconstrucción, Minutes, February 9, 1940, MHS, MAC, Box 1, folder: Research; International Institute, "Mexican Nationality," 4.

54. Minnesota Governor, *Mexican in Minnesota,* 23.

55. Neighborhood House, Board of Directors, Minutes, May 13, 1937, MHS, NH, folder: Board Minutes 1933–1939.

56. Neighborhood House, Board of Directors, Minutes, March 16, 1939, MHS, NH, folder: Board Minutes 1939–1948.

57. Año Nuevo, "Mexican Chicago," 298–328.

58. Sánchez, "Go After," 250–263; Deutsch, *No Separate Refuge,* 63–86; Barrett, "Americanization," 996–1020; García, *Rise,* 134–136, 175–178, 303; Rodriguez, *Hunger.*

59. International Institute, "Mexican Nationality," 16; interview with Leonard López, MHS, OH; "Guild of Catholic Women Finds New Field Work in Mexican District," MHS, GCW, Box 3, folder: Our Lady of Guadalupe; International Institute, "Mexican Nationality," 16.

60. International Institute, "Mexican Nationality," 16.

61. Oppenheimer, "Acculturation," 440–442; Silverman, "Doing," 40.

62. Interview with Miss Shea, IHRC, CFLPS, Reel 62; IHRC, II Box 28, folder 743; IHRC, II Box 30, folder 744.

63. IHRC, II Box 31, folder 426; IHRC, II, Box 30, folder 524; IHRC, II, Box 24, folder 706.

64. IHRC, II Box 24, folder 707.

65. "A Doctor"; "Mexicans Stage"; "Mexicans Resent"; interview with Juanita Morán, MHS, OH.

66. Schrieke, *Alien,* 51; Oppenheimer, "Acculturation," 440; Duncan and Alanzo, *Guadalupe Center,* 12; Silverman, "Doing," 40; Vobejda, "Heartland"; "Mexican Family Insulted"; interviews with Juanita Morán and Federico Saucedo, MHS, OH; International Institute, "Mexican Nationality," 21.

67. Neighborhood House, Notes from Secretary's Minutes, February 10, 1936, MHS, NH, Box 1, folder: History; Neighborhood House, Board of Director's Minutes, January 29, 1941, MHS, NH, Box 1, folder: Minutes 1939–1948; Cárdenas Coates, *Nuestra Señora,* 11; interview with Teresa Muñoz, MHS, OH; Neighborhood House, 1939 Annual Report, and Notes from Secretary's Minutes, February 16, 1933, MHS, NH, Box 1, folder: History; Neighborhood House, Board of Directors Minutes, January 28, 1931, MHS, NH, Box 1, folder: Minutes 1928–1933; International Institute, "Mexican Nationality," 21; Neighborhood House, Board of Directors Minutes, November 12, 1936, MHS, NH, Box 1, folder: Minutes 1933–1939.

68. Neighborhood House, 1939 Annual Report, MHS, NH, Box 1, folder: History; Fenton, "The Mexicans," 27–28; "Neighborhood House, St. Paul, Minnesota, 1938," SWHA, NFS, folder: 381.

69. Interview with Rev. Thomas M. Lineweaver, December 4, 1936, IHRC, CFLPS, Reel 63; "Celebration of the National"; "May 5th 1862."

70. Diebold, "Mexicans," 95; Sickels, *Around,* 19; Sickels, "International Institute"; International Institute, "Mexican Nationality," 16, 22.

71. International Institute, "Mexican Nationality," 21; IHRC, II, Box 24, folder 757.

72. Mary A. Bishop, "The Mexican Mission of St. Paul," MHS, GCW, Box 3, folder: Our Lady of Guadalupe.

73. Mary A. Bishop, Notes on Mexican Settlement in West St. Paul, Guild of Catholic Women 1933 Report and Notes on Mexican Settlement in

West St. Paul, and Guild Talk, January 4, 1934, MHS, GCW, Box 3, folder: Our Lady of Guadalupe; Macklin and Teniente, "La Virgen," 122; Bishop, "Worker Tells."

74.  Interview with Juanita Morán, MHS, OH; Cárdenas Coates, *Nuestra Señora,* 8–9; Services to Mark Opening Feb. 15 of Mexican Mission, and Mary A. Bishop, Report of the Department of Social Action, May 2, 1938, MHS, GCW, Box 3, folder: Our Lady of Guadalupe; obituary of Rev. Henry Dicks, MHS, MAC, Box 1, folder: Our Lady of Guadalupe; International Institute, "Mexican Nationality," 18; Finnegan, "Mexican Colony."

75.  Notes from Secretary's Minutes, January 14, 1938, MHS, MH, Box 1, folder: History; Mary A. Bishop, Report of the Department of Social Action, May 2, 1938, MHS, GCW, Box 3, folder: Our Lady of Guadalupe; IHRC, II Box 24, folder 1286.

76.  Cárdenas Coates, *Nuestra Señora,* 10; interviews with Guadalupe Cruz, Felicitas Herrera, Federico Saucedo, MHS, OH.

77.  Interviews with Juanita Morán, Federico Saucedo, MHS, OH.

78.  Consul de México, Los Angeles to Dr. J. M. Puig, May 9, 1934, AGN, AR, 244.1/41; "Mexico to Repatriate"; Manuel Ajuria to Luis I. Rodríguez, February 28, 1935, and Comité Pro-México, AGN, LC, 545.3/103; Informe de protección, Chicago, February 1935, SRE, IV/241 (04) (73-10) "35"/1; Eugenio Pesqueira to Luis Rodríguez, March 6, 1935, AGN, LC, 545.3/103; "Labor Leaders."

79.  Edwards, "Kansas City Missouri Diocese 1940," in Duncan and Alanzo, *Guadalupe Center,* 71–75; Roosevelt, "'My Day'"; Bolton, "Socio-Cultural," 10–11.

80.  Oppenheimer, "Acculturation," 444; "Our Educational"; Escobar, "The Forging," 17; Rosales and Simon, "Mexican Immigrant," 353; Humphrey, "Integration," 156.

81.  "Spanish American"; "Mexican Radio"; "Mexican Film."

82.  Interviews with Eduardo Peralta and Alberto Cuellar, December 11, 1936, IHRC, CFLPS, Reel 62.

83.  Rosales and Simon, "Mexican Immigrant," 349; Paz, "Survey," 4.

84.  Diebold, "Mexicans," 94.

85.  Neighborhood House, "Survey of Homes and Businesses, Sixth Ward, 1936," MHS, NH, Box 13, folder: Studies.

86.  "Handling of Funds"; "Celebration of the National"; "Minutes of the Permanent."


## 4. Good Solid Workers

1.  This discussion of the era of monopoly capital is informed in part by Baran and Sweezy, *Monopoly Capital;* Gómez-Quiñones, *Mexican American Labor,* 11, 153–176; and Esser and Hirsch, "The Crisis," 420–421.

2.  Estimates based on Jasso and Tejeda, "Chicano in Kansas," 6; Wolfe,

"Mexican-American"; U.S. Bureau of the Census, *Spanish Origin Population 1970.* Tapia, "Socio-Economic Profile," 7, calculates Mexican-descent population of six midwestern states at 567,000.

3. McWilliams, "Mexican Problem," 14; Año Nuevo, "Mexican Chicago."

4. Minnesota Governor, *Mexican in Minnesota,* 9; International Institute, "A Study," 9; interview with Santos Vásquez and Communist Party, Texas State Convention, Resolution on Mexican Work, July 7, 1940, BL, SJFN, folder 6; Neighborhood House, Board of Directors, *Minutes,* March 16, 1939, MHS, NH, Box 1; Minnesota Governor, *Mexican in Minnesota,* 10–11; Humphrey, "Employment Patterns," 322; Año Nuevo, "Chicano Settlements," 25–26.

5. Rosales and Simon, "Mexican Immigrant," 353; Florence Cassidy, Semiannual Report on Social and Educational Work with Mexicans in Southeastern Michigan, January 1 to June 30, 1945, SCSU, EG, Box 17, folder 10; Neighborhood House Board of Directors, *Minutes,* January 11, 1945, MHS, NH, folder: Minutes 1939–1948; Pierce, "St. Paul's," 74; Vogrin, "Hero Street"; Brower, "A Proud Street," 76.

6. "Mexican Center"; "Mexican Boys"; Neighborhood House, Board of Directors, *Minutes,* January 11, 1945, MHS, NH, Box 1; IHRC, II, Box 27, folder 1260; IHRC, II, Box 30, folders 744 and 1271; IHRC Box 31, folder 1268.

7. Report on Hinsdale camp, SCSU, EG, Box 17, folder 9; Emilio Aldama to J. T. Williamson, February 6, 1945, SCSU, EG, Box 18, folder 8; Ricardo B. Pérez to P. F. Murphy, SCSU, EG, Box 18, folder 9.

8. Ricardo B. Pérez to R. L. Hertzer, August 20, 1945, SCSU, EG, Box 19, folder 1.

9. Emilio Almada to Ralph E. Gates, September 15, 1945, and Ward H. Harris to Emilio Almada, September 5, 1945, SCSU, EG, Box 19, folder 1.

10. IHRC, II, Box 32, folder 1296, and Box 34, folders 1836 and 1135.

11. Matthews, "Migrants Battled"; IHRC, II, Box 27, folder 1240, and Box 30, folder 1006; Santillán, "Rosita," 115–117; ibid., "Midwestern Mexican," 94–98; "Women in Steel," 74–81.

12. Ruiz, *Cannery Women,* 14–19; IHRC, II, Box 28, folder 1244; Humphrey, "Mexican Peasant," 210.

13. Interview with Frank C. Guzmán, MHS, OH.

14. Interview with Teresa Muñoz, MHS, OH.

15. International Institute, "A Study," 2–3; Minnesota Governor, *Mexican in Minnesota,* 28; Sickels, *Around the World,* 19.

16. "Objectives of Renewal Project Outlined," undated clipping, MHS, NH, Box 18, Neighborhood House Scrapbook.

17. International Institute, "A Study," 7–8; Minnesota Governor, *Mexican in Minnesota,* 28–29; interview with Teresa Muñoz, MHS, OH; Diebold, "Mexicans," 98.

18. Finnegan, "Mexican Colony."

19. Martínez, "Historical Development," 3–4; Duncan and Alanzo, *Guadalupe Center*, 13, 39; Shutt, "Silver City," 130, 133; Simmons, "Centennial History," 45; Bogdon, "Bleak Area"; Bolton, "Socio-Cultural," 11.

20. Matthiasson, "Acculturation," 10; U.S. Congress, Senate, *Migratory Labor:* I, 616; Swenson, "Some Characteristics," 5; Shannon and McKim, "Attitudes," 343.

21. Vogrin, "Hero Street."

22. Paz, "Survey," 5; Año Nuevo, "Chicano Settlements," 22–32; Año Nuevo, "Chicano Experience," chapter 1.

23. Paz, "Survey," 5–6; Walton et al., "Political Organization," 20; Chicago, *Chicago's Spanish-Speaking*, 2–4, 7.

24. Año Nuevo, "Chicano Experience," 185; Sue H. Perry, "Report of Study of 50 Mexican Families in the Stockyards District of Chicago," May, 1942, UIC, UCSP, Box 25, folder: "Study"; Halpern, *Killing Floor*, 103; Paz, "Survey," 6–9.

25. Paz, "Survey," 9; Felter, "Social Adaptation," 23.

26. Ropka et al., "Spanish-Speaking," 3; Chicago, *Chicago's Spanish-Speaking*, 2.

27. Paz, "Survey," 5–6; Año Nuevo, "Mexican Chicago," 309; Welfare Council of Metropolitan Chicago, "Background Paper on Services to Children of Migrants," September 14, 1964, CHS, WCMC, Box 624, folder 6; untitled clipping, *Chicago Tribune*, September 24, 1972; Minutes of South Cook County Council for Migrants, October 1, 1959, CHS, WCMC, Box 401, folder 6; DeMuth, "Migrants"; García, "Mexican American People," 41–45, 47; Chicago Research Group, "Study of Mexican-American Community, 1957," WCMC, Box 147, folder 5.

28. U.S. Congress, Senate, *Migratory Labor:* I: 216–217; Leininger, "South Bend," 48, 49, 82, 85; Butler, "South Bend," 25; Fotia and Calvin, "South Bend–Mishawaka," 1–8; Faught, "Chicanos," 316, 318; Council of Community Services, Community Services to Migrant Workers, December 18, 1958, DDE, PCML, Box 5, folder: Indiana; Samora and Lamanna, "Mexican-Americans," 225; Guthrie, Briere, and Moore, *Indianapolis*, 5–11.

29. Ford, "Toledo's Spanish"; John R. Weeks, "The Impact of Neo-Pentecostalism on Spanish-Speaking Catholic Families: The Case of Fremont, Ohio," 1973, SSCC, folder: Toledo, Ohio; interviews with Henry Miranda, Juan Luna, and Secundino Reyes; Macklin, "Americans," 3, 16; Macklin and Teniente, "La Virgen," 121; García, "Mexican American People," 77.

30. Mexican Project, Ecorse, Michigan, and interviews with Mexican Tenants at John R. Fisher Homes, 1943–1944, WPR, DPC, Box 1; Report of 1943 meeting, MHC, MMC; Florence Cassidy, Semiannual Report, January–June 1945, SCSU, EG, Box 17, folder 10.

31. Cárdenas, "Mexican in Adrian."

32. Mexican Project, Pontiac, Michigan, WPR, DPC, Box 1; Haney,

"Migration," 32–33, 40, 180, 210, 280; Choldin and Trout, "Mexican Americans," 6 ff.; interview with Juan J. Castillo.

33. Keller, "Educational Aspirations," 29–30; Rev. James A. Hickey to Most Rev. William Murphy, n.d., MSA, KS, Box 14, folder 13; McCormick, "Migrant"; interviews with María Castellanos and Sister Lucía Medina.

34. Interview with Efraín Marínez; Dorson, "Mexican Michigan," 348–349; M. Pacheco Moreno, "Bandera de Mexico a Lansing, Michigan," September, 1963, JG.

35. Spielberg Benítez, "A Review," 22–23; Berry, "Survey," 1; Choldin and Trout, "Mexican Americans," 363, 365; interview with Rosa Arenas; interview with Jane Gonzales, MHC.

36. International Institute, "A Study," 4; Goldner, "Profile," 107; Choldin and Trout, "Mexican Americans," 42.

37. Minnesota Governor, *Mexican in Minnesota*, 23; International Institute, "A Study," 8–9; IHRC, II, Box 33, folder 1521.

38. Matthews, "Migrants Battled"; Humphrey, "Changing Structure," 625–626; International Institute, "A Study," 5; Rosales and Simon, "Mexican Immigrant," 355; Minnesota Governor, *Mexican in Minnesota*, 23.

39. IHRC, II, Box 30, folders 1763 and 1052; International Institute, "A Study," 8–9; Minnesota Governor, *Mexican in Minnesota*, 23.

40. Interview with Francisco (Kiko) Rangel, MHS, OH; IHRC, II, Box 24, folder 1173.

41. Goldner, "Profile," 107; Caine, "Social Life," 84, 86; Swenson, "Some Characteristics," 10.

42. Interviews with Jesús A. Patlán and Marcelino and Irene Rivera, MHS, OH; Samora and Lamanna, "Mexican-Americans," 226.

43. Goldner, "Profile," 107; interview with Felicitas Herrera, MHS, OH.

44. IHRC, II, Box 30, folder 744.

45. Goldner, "Profile," 107–108; interview with Felicitas Herrera, MHS, OH.

46. Caine, "Social Life," 79, 82.

47. Swenson, "Some Characteristics," 10, SHSW, ARHW; Samora and Lamanna, "Mexican-Americans," 228; Cárdenas and Parra, "La Raza (1973)," 12, 17; Choldin and Trout, "*Mexican Americans*," 182.

48. Minnesota Governor, *Mexican in Minnesota*, 23; Finnegan, "Mexican Colony"; interview with Arturo Coronado Jr. and Elvira Coronado, MHS, OH; Samora and Lamanna, "Mexican-Americans," 230; interview with Carmen Cortina; Paz, "Survey," 23–24.

49. Interview with Francisco (Kiko) Rangel, MHS, OH; Humphrey, "Mexican Peasant," 205; Gordon, *Assimilation*, 109; Chicago, *Chicago's Spanish-Speaking*, 20–21; Mier, Giloth, and Less, "Industrial Employment," 8.

50. Keller, "Educational Aspirations," 119; Choldin and Trout, "Mexican

Americans," 385; International Institute, "A Study," 9; R. Alexander to Mrs. Rich, June 24, 1943, UIC, IPL, folder 74; Johnson, "Minorities"; Paz, "Status," 7–9.

51. Interview with Juan Luna; Cárdenas, "Mexican in Adrian," 348, 349; interview with Federico Saucedo, MHS, OH.

52. Myrdal, *An American Dilemma;* International Institute, "A Study," 12; Hill, "Texas-Mexican," 17.

53. Sickels, "International Institute"; Sickels, *Festival of Nations, St. Paul, Minnesota,* March 10, 1942, MHS; IHRC, II Box 31, folder 870, and Box 32, folders 826 and 1274.

54. Macklin, "Americans," 20; International Institute, "A Study," 7; Choldin and Trout, "Mexican Americans," 366; IHRC, Box 30, folder 1271.

55. Humphrey, "Integration," 162; Humphrey, "Detroit Mexican," 332.

56. Rogers, "Role," 188–189; Macklin and Teniente, "La Virgen," 123–125; "Father Gorman."

57. Salas and Salas, "Mexican Community," 166; "Our Lady of Guadalupe Lays"; Boxleitner, "Years."

58. Humphrey, "Mexican Immigrant," 335 n. 27.

59. IHRC, II, Box 30, folder 744; IHRC, II, Box 31, folders 847, 870; IHRC, II, Box 34, folder 926.

60. Paz, "Survey," 14; "Baile and Tostadas"; Mexican Civic Committee Report, December 13, 1946, CHS, WCMC, Box 147, folder 4.

61. "The First 6 Months of Operation of the Mexican-American Council," CHS, CAP, Box 88, folder 11; Año Nuevo, "Mexican Chicago," 322; Paz, "Status," 10.

62. IHRC, II, Box 30, folders 1006 and 1271.

63. Romo, *East Los Angeles,* 132–135, 140–142; Sánchez, *Becoming,* 93–107; González, *Labor and Community,* 103–107; San Miguel, *Let All,* 33–38; García, *Rise,* 134–136, 286, 303.

64. International Institute, "A Study," 7; U.S. Congress, Senate, *Farm Labor Supply,* 521; Humphrey, "Education," 535; Paz, "Survey," 18.

65. Año Nuevo, "Mexican Chicago," 325; International Institute, "A Study," 6; Matthiasson, "Coping," 264; Chicago, *Chicago's Spanish-Speaking,* 27.

66. Interview with Efraín Marínez; interviews with Dionisia C. Coates, Frank C. Guzmán, MHS, OH.

67. Interviews with Juanita Morán and Dionisia C. Coates, MHS, OH; Neighborhood House, Board of Directors, *Minutes,* April 9, 1962, MHS, NH, Box 1, folder: Minutes 1960–1962; Rosales and Simon, "Mexican Immigrant," 357.

68. IHRC, II, Box 30, folder 744; Paz, "Survey," 18; Choldin and Trout, "Mexican Americans," 50; Walton, Salces, and Belechia, "Political Organization," 24.

69. Humphrey, "Education," 535; International Institute, "A Study," 6.

70. Humphrey, "Mexican Peasant," 95; Manuel Beserra narrative, in Leininger, "South Bend," 70; St. Paul Public Schools, "Seremos hermanos de nombre hasta que aprendamos nuestros idiomas y nuestras culturas," MHS, MAC, Box 1; Goldner, "Two Generations," 105.

71. International Institute, "A Study," 7; Minnesota Governor, *Mexican in Minnesota*, 43; González, *Labor and Community*, 103–107.

72. Interview with Marcelino and Irene Rivera, MHS, OH.

73. Criticisms are cogently made by Kozol, *Savage*, 176, 209, 216, 228; and González, *Labor and Community*, 103–107.

74. Interview with Msgr. Clement Kern; International Institute, "A Study," 11; interview with Federico Saucedo, MHS, OH; IHRC, Box 3, folder 1006; Neighborhood House, Board of Directors, *Minutes*, September 23, 1963, MHS, NH, Box 1, folder: 1963–1964.

75. "Nebraska Village"; Humphrey, "Mexican Peasant," 106; Choldin and Trout, "Mexican Americans," 349; Martínez, "Historical Development," 7–8; Coalición Hispana, "Documentation of FHA, Mortgage, and Insurance Abuses," n.d., UND, GC; Illinois, *Report to the 78th General Assembly*, 23.

76. Samora and Lamanna, "Mexican-Americans," 235; Valdés, *Al Norte*, 108–109; Minnesota Governor, *Mexican in Minnesota*, 61; interview with Juan Luna; Rojo, "Between," 49–50; García, "Mexican American People," 47; Macklin, *Structural Stability*, 94; interview with Juanita Rangel, MHS, OH; García and Rummler, "For Hispanics."

77. Diebold, "Mexicans," 98; Humphrey, "Detroit Mexican," 335.

78. IHRC, II, Box 33, folder 1395; "U.S. Deports"; "Mexican Aliens"; "'Invasion' Spreads"; interview with Jane Gonzales, MHC; "Lobbyists Win"; Max Rabb, "The Wetback and Bracero Programs," DDE, CFCS, Box 4, folder: Cabinet Meeting, January 26, 1955; García, "Operation Wetback."

79. Puente, "Mexican-Americans."

80. "CIO Aids"; Hilario Alemán to Adolfo Ruiz Cortines, September 27, 1954, AGN, ARC, 546.6/55.

81. International Institute, "A Study," 8.

82. Boxleitner, "Years"; García, "Education for Democracy," 34; Humphrey, "Mexican Peasant," 105, 106.

83. Macklin, *Structural Stability*, 80; Samora and Lamanna, "Mexican-Americans," 238; Neighborhood House, Board of Directors, *Minutes*, February 26, 1962, MHS, NH, Box 1, folder: 1960–1962. On the Mexican American generation, see especially Hernández Alvarez, "Demographic Profile," 471–496; and García, *Mexican Americans*.

84. Comité de Reconstrucción, *Minutes*, November 4, December 16, 1940, February 23, March 9, 1941, MHS, MAC, Box 1, folder: Research.

85. "2-Day Fiesta Begins Here Today," and "What's a Little Rain to Mexican Fiesta?" unidentified clippings, MAC, Box 1, folder: Mexican In-

dependence—clippings; "5,000 Take Part"; interview with Crescencia Rangel, MHS, OH.

86. "Loor Eterno a Los Heroes de la Independencia 1810 a 1944," MHS, MAC, Box 1, folder: Mexican Independence—2; "Mexican Fiesta Pays."

87. Interviews with María Morán and Juanita Morán, MHS, OH; "The Guadalupe Fiesta Dancers," MHS, MAC, Box 1, folder: Mexican Independence—2; "Love of Country."

88. "May First Labor"; Rosales and Simon, "Chicano Steelworkers," 267–275.

89. Interview with John V. Riffe, December 14, 1936, IHRC, CFLPS, Reel 62; Rosales and Simon, "Mexican Immigrant," 351; Cohen, *New Deal*, 339; Cassidy, Semiannual Report, 1945, SCSU, Box 17, folder 10.

90. Paz, "Status," 9; Paz, "Survey," 18; Año Nuevo, "Chicano Experience," 26.

91. Bauer, "Delinquency," 1; Paz, "Survey," 8; Rosales and Simon, "Mexican Immigrant," 351–353; Cohen, *New Deal*, 324.

92. Hernández-Fujigaki, "Mexican Steelworkers," 89–92; "The First 6 Months of Operation of the Mexican-American Council," CHS, CAP, Box 88, folder 11; Paz, "Survey," 11–12, 18–20.

93. "Noticias Interamericanas," June 15, 1945, MHS, JT, Box 227, folder 3; Lynd, *Rank and File*, 167; Hernández-Fujigaki, "Mexican Steelworkers," 121–122, 130, 135–136, 139.

94. Paz, "Survey," 11–12, 18–19.

95. Paz, "Status," 8–10; Paz, "Survey," 19–20.

96. Minnesota Governor, *Mexican in Minnesota*, 25; IHRC, II, Box 30, folder 1763.

97. Narrative of Manuel García, in Leininger, *Chicanos in South Bend*, 82–85; Salas and Salas, "Mexican Community," 168; interviews with Gustavo Gaynette and Israel Leyton; García, "Education for Democracy," 37.

98. For laudatory accounts see Allsup, *American G.I. Forum;* Márquez, *LULAC.* For a highly critical assessment, see Parra, Ríos, and Gutiérrez, "Chicano Organizations," 235–253.

99. "Latin League"; Neighborhood House, *Board Minutes,* March 16, 1959, MHS, NH, Box 1, folder: 1957–1959; "3rd Blanco."

100. Interviews with Louis Medina and George Galvin, MHS, OH; Narratives of Manuel García and Concepción Niño, in Leininger, "South Bend," 80–81, 86; "Mexican Dance."

101. Paz, "Survey," 16; Campa, "Immigrant Latinos," 355–356; Rosales and Simon, "Mexican Immigrant," 355; Joe A. Contreras to Alvin Bentley, March 15, 1959, MHC, AB, Box 26, folder: Chicano Farm Labor; interview with Joseph E. Anaya, MHS, OH; García, "Americans All," 201–202; Parra, Ríos, and Gutiérrez, "Chicano Organizations," 239.

102. Chambers, "Mutual Cooperation," 33; interviews with Carlota Arellano and Joseph Anaya, MHS, OH.

103. Interview with Teresa Muñoz, MHS, OH.

104. Interview with Federico Saucedo, MHS, OH.

105. IHRC, II, Box 28, folder 1244; "Rising Flood"; Neighborhood House, Board of Directors, *Minutes,* June 5, 1952, MHS, NH, folder: 1948–1952; James A. Ward, Assets of Our Lady of Guadalupe Parish, September 10, 1956, MHS, MAC, Box 1, folder: Our Lady of Guadalupe—1.

106. Boxmeyer, "Neighborhood House"; Jacobs-White, "West Side," 71; Caine, "Social Life," 73.

107. "3 Mile"; Boxmeyer, "Neighborhood House."

108. Veness, "But It's Not," 153, 225; Russell, "Relocation"; Heinzman, "Good-by."

109. Neighborhood House, Board of Directors, *Minutes,* September 18, 1961, and February 26, 1962, MHS, NH, folder: 1960–1962; Boardman, "Regrouped"; Cárdenas Coates, *Nuestra Señora,* 25; interview with Esther M. Avaloz, MHS, OH.

110. Neighborhood House, Board of Directors, *Minutes,* September 18, 1961, MHS, NH, folder: 1960–1962; "Riverview 'DP's' Seek Moving Aid," *St. Paul Pioneer Press,*" n.d., SWHA, NFS, Box 78, folder 1; "Our Lady of Guadalupe Lays."

111. IHRC, II, Box 30, folder 744.

112. Gordon, *Assimilation,* 108–109, 201.

113. Said, *Culture and Imperialism,* 246.


**5. *El Movimiento***

1. "U to Host"; "Mexican-American Community in St. Paul"; Kyle and Kantowicz, "Kids First," 57; "Latino Progress."

2. Jenkins and Perrow, "Insurgency;" 249–267; Kurtz, "Chicano Student," 2, SHSW, AMHW; Baca, "For Hispanic Kids."

3. "West Siders"; Neighborhood House, Board *Minutes,* February 26, 1962, MHS, NH, Box 1, folder: 1960–1962.

4. Boardman, "Regrouped."

5. Langland, "Old Community"; Boardman, "Regrouped."

6. Frank Hijikata, "Neighborhood House Association Annual Report, 1962," MHS, NH, Box 1, folder: 1963–1964; "Dunedin Terrace."

7. Boxmeyer, "$8.2 Million."

8. "Torre San Miguel" and Neighborhood House, "Torre de San Miguel Homes, May, 1974," MHS, NH, Box 13, folder: Concord Terrace: Histories; "People Do Care"; "Torre to Break"; "HRA's Vista Village"; "Torre De San Miguel," 3–4.

9. "Torre Goes"; Chanco, "West Side's Story"; Moylan, "Housing"; Vaughan, "A Mexican."

10. Veness, "But It's Not," 225–226, 238; Caine, "Social Life," 73–74, 79.

11. Jacobs-White, "West Side," 72; St. Paul Public Schools, "Seremos

hermanos de nombre," MHS, MAC, Box 1, folder: Mexican-American Cultural & Educational Center.

12. Interview with David J. Ramírez, MHS, OH; Ramírez Luna, "Gunpoint Arrest"; Bonner, "Civil"; Rybin, "Agreements"; Diebold, "Mexicans," 98.

13. Wilke, "Pilsen Neighborhood"; Ropka, Ramírez, and de Vise, "Spanish-Speaking," 8, 11–13, UND, MCM; Año Nuevo, "Chicano Settlements," 29.

14. Weeks and Spielberg, "Ethnodemography," 9–10; Valdés, *El Pueblo,* 68–70; Bogdon, "Bleak"; Bolton, "Socio-Cultural," 12–13.

15. Martínez, "Historical Development"; Ladd, "Dodge City"; Vobejda, "Heartland"; interview with Juan J. Castillo.

16. Cain, "Social Life," 113–114; Boardman, "Regrouped"; "El Barrio."

17. Parra, Ríos, and Gutiérrez, "Chicano Organizations," 247–251.

18. Matthews, "Chicanos 'Hungry'"; Kelly, "La Clínica"; Garza, "Carmen Velasquez's Dedication"; Welsh, "Barrio Gets," 26–29.

19. Banas, "On Visit"; Garza, "Barriers"; Reardon and Goering, "Hispanic Groups"; Allsup, "Concerned," 251–262; Strahler, "Alinsky."

20. García, "Agencies"; Gurda, "Cohesiveness," 19, SHSW, ARHW; "Latin American Union," 10.

21. Lupe DeLeón Jr. to Estimados Carnales, December 31, 1973, and Minutes, La Raza Unida Party de Indiana, August 25, 1973, UND, GC.

22. Sánchez, *Expedition;* interview with Rudolph Saucedo, MHS, OH.

23. Interview with Rudolph Saucedo, MHS, OH; Baker, "Brown Power."

24. H.S., letter to the editor, *St. Paul Dispatch,* May 12, 1969; interview with Rudolph Saucedo, MHS, OH; "Mexican Dance," MAC, Box 2, folder: Brown Berets; Baker, "Brown Power."

25. Cárdenas, "East Chicago Youth," UND, GC; interview with Rudolph Saucedo.

26. Baker, "Brown Power"; Parra, Ríos, and Gutiérrez, "Chicano Organizations," 244.

27. Interview with Peter Moreno, MHS, OH; Cook, "Migrants"; Valdés, "Labor," 171–177.

28. Interview with Peter Moreno, MHS, OH; Ediberto González, "Justice for the Spanish-Speaking People," UND, GC.

29. Choldin and Trout, "Mexican Americans," 392; García, "Mexican American People," 55.

30. Florencia Machado, "Service Employment Redevelopment," SHSW, AMHW; Welsh, "Barrio Gets," 26–27.

31. Howard Coan, "History of the Spanish Center," 1–2, 5–7, 14, SHSW, AMHW; Salas, "Reflections," 67.

32. Samora and Lamanna, "Mexican-Americans," 220, 224; Caine, "Social Life," 88–90; Demarest, "Bridging," 21; Garza, "Bringing Drama,"; U.S.

Civil Rights Commission, *Bilingual/Bicultural Education*, 80.

33. St. Paul Public Schools, "Seremos hermanos de nombre," MHS, MAC, Box 1.

34. Grey, "Immigrant," 416–419; Garza, "Bilingual Bill"; Hornblower, "Putting Tongues," 40.

35. Cavaretta and Haynes, "Hispanics Claim"; "Mexican Cultural"; St. Paul Public Schools, "Proposed Mexican-American Cultural Resource Center," St. Paul, 1974, MHS, MAC, Box 1, folder: Mexican-American Cultural and Educational Center; "New School"; interview with María Morán, MHS, OH; Crawford, "Suit."

36. Lewis, "Battling"; "GAP: Guadalupe Area Project," and "Objectives of the Guadalupe Area Project, 1973," MHS, MAC, Box 1, folder: Guadalupe Area Project.

37. Gerald Vizenor, "Guadalupe Area Boutique Offers Items by Poor," *Minneapolis Tribune*, n.d., MHS, MAC, Box 1, folder: Guadalupe Area Project; Hessburg, "Tchoom!"; Guadalupe Area Project Proposal, 1975, MHS, MAC, Box 1, folder: Guadalupe Area Project, 1; Demarest, "Bridging," 21–22.

38. "Mexicans Seek"; "Only Mexican"; Father Adalbert Wolski to Parishioners, June 13, 1971, ASPM, folder: St. Paul–Our Lady of Guadalupe, 1; Cárdenas Coates, *Nuestra Señora*, 31; Mi Cultura Day Center, MHS, Box 1, folder: Mi Cultura Day Center; interview with Sra. Juanita Morán, MHS, OH.

39. "Holy Trinity"; Nash, "Milwaukee Federation," 117; Tan, "St. Agnes."

40. Narrative of María Hernández, in Leininger, "South Bend," 65; Martínez, "Latina Benedictine."

41. Interview with Manuel Contreras, MHS, OH; "The Migrant Tutorial"; Duncan, "LAFC Board."

42. "What Is MIA—Past and Present," MHS, IGB, Box 2, folder: Migrants in Action; Baker, "Bleak Life"; *Migrants in Action: Annual Report 1973*, MHS, MAC, Box 1, folder: Migrants in Action.

43. Tomson, "Field and Dream"; interviews with Frank C. Guzmán, José Valdez, and Peter Moreno, MHS, OH.

44. "Latin American Union," 10; García, "Chicanos in Chicago Heights," 302–303; untitled article, *Adelante*, May 1970, UND, GC; García, "Mexican American People," 51, 56.

45. De La Rosa, "Ombudsman"; Council for Spanish-Speaking People, *1981–83 Biennial Report*, MHS, IGB, Box 2, folder: Spanish-Speaking Affairs Council; "Mission Statement," Spanish-Speaking Affairs Council, SSAC, folder: Spanish-Speaking Affairs Council meeting information package, December 20, 1990; Padilla and Gentile, "Survey Finds," 2.

46. Novak, "Few Minorities"; Cook, "Migrants"; De La Rosa, "Ombudsman"; Chicano Youth Commission Report, Topeka, February 11, 1970, UND, GC.

47. The most complete study on Chicano studies in the Southwest is Muñoz, *Youth.* "Blow Out in Topeka"; Centro Cultural Chicano-Boricua, SHSW, AMHW.

48. Cárdenas, "La Raza," 13–14, UND, GC; La Raza Unida of Wisconsin, "Statistical Analysis" (1973), UND, GC; Latin Community Advisory Board, "Circle Campus vs. the Latin Community of Chicago" (1973), UND, GC.

49. "Mexican Course"; Holman, "More Chicano"; Chicano Studies Department, Proposal for a Major in Chicano Studies, March 8, 1976, MHS, MAC, Box 2, unprocessed; "Report of the University of Minnesota Task Force on Chicano Concerns," December 1, 1976, MHS, IGB, Box 2, folder: University of Minnesota.

50. "U.S.-Mexican students"; Holman, "More Chicano"; "Mexican Course"; Diebold, "Mexicans," 102; Chicano Studies Department, "Proposal for a Major in Chicano Studies," MHS, MAC, Box 2, unprocessed; Wappel, "Chicano Studies Bogs"; "The Report of the University of Minnesota Task Force on Chicano Concerns," MHS, IGB, Box 2, folder: University of Minnesota 1977–1978; notes on presentation by President Nils Hasselmo, Chicano-Latino Advisory Committee, University of Minnesota, May 7, 1994, in possession of author.

51. "U. Latin Americans"; "Chicano Liberation"; González, "Beginnings."

52. Interview with Alfredo González; "U to Host"; Duarte, "Chronology," JD; Holman, "More Chicano."

53. Eduardo Natera and Mike Garza to Hermanos y Hermanas, January 20, 1971, MHS, NH, Box 17, folder: Hispanics; Lemke, "Chicanos Issue"; Brandt, "Officials Stall"; Curriculum Committee, "A Proposal for a Department of Chicano Studies: Departamento de Estudios Chicanos, May 5, 1971," JD; "Chicano Studies"; McDonnell, "Regents Act"; "Chicano Studies Department, March, 1975," MHS, MAC, Box 2, unprocessed; Perry, "Chicano Studies Combine"; interview with Alfredo González.

54. "Chicano Studies Department, March, 1975," MHS, MAC, Box 2, unprocessed; Alfredo M. González, "Chicano Studies Institute: Chicano Studies in Mid-West Higher Education," 1971, JD; interview with Alfredo González; "Mexican Course"; Chicano Studies Department, A Proposal for a Major in Chicano Studies, MHS, MAC, Box 2, unprocessed.

55. Curriculum Committee, "A Proposal for a Department of Chicano Studies," JD; Camarillo, "Mexican-American History Revisited," 43; *Estampas del Valle,* winner of the Premio Casa de Las Americas, is Hinojosa's best-known work in the genre.

56. López y Rivas, "Conquest and Resistance"; López y Rivas, *The Chicanos;* Lucero-Trujillo, "The Dilemma," 324–332; interview with Alfredo González.

57. Saunders, "U Chicanos"; Duarte, "Chronology."

58. Salas and Salas, "Mexican Community," 176–177; Curriculum Committee, "A Proposal for a Chicano Studies Department." JD; Salas, "Impact," 131–147; "Chicano-Boricua Studies Works"; interview with Isabel Salas.

59. Garza, "Hispanic Concerns"; García, "Clemente Students"; Purnell, "Racial Incidents."

60. Kurtz, "Chicano Student"; García, "Chicano Studies"; interviews with Carlos de Onís, John Valadez, and Mario Compean.

61. "Hispanic Students Blast"; "Garza, "UIC's Hispanic."

62. "DePaul Establishes"; "Michigan State Creates Hispanic Institute," UPI Regional News, February 16, 1989.

63. Saunders, "U Chicanos"; interview with Harold Iron Shield.

64. Purnell, "Racial Incidents"; Garza, "Latinos Get"; Garza, "YWCA"; Garza, "Hispanic Concerns."

65. Garza, "Cops"; Flaherty, "Hispanic Leaders"; "U. of I. Defends."

66. "U. of I. Defends"; Flaherty, "Hispanic Leaders"; Garza, "Latinos Get."

67. Carter, "Chicano Students"; Pérez, "M.E.Ch. A."

68. Interview with Federico Saucedo, MHS, OH.

69. Carnoy, Daley, and Hinojosa Ojeda, "Changing Economic Position," 33 ff.

70. David Montgomery and Bert Corona make similar arguments about the 1960s in García, Memories, xiv–xv; Klauda, "Hispanic Community."

71. Bakken, "Chicanos, Professors."

## 6. Completing a Circle

1. The best-known popularization of this model in dominant policy circles is conservative ideologue Chávez, Out of the Barrio. Recent assimilationist accounts include Larson, "Leaving"; McAuliffe, "Migrants Settle"; Hayner, "Area's Ethnic"; "Just Trying"; Campa, "Immigrant Latinos," 352. On the push from Texas, see Meryhew, "One-way."

2. "Urban Trends"; Puente, "Immigration"; Barnes, "Does 'Diversity' Help."

3. Portes and Rumbaut, Immigrant America, 11, 69, 225–226; Rowland, "Jobs Lure Hispanics."

4. Sassen-Koob, Mobility, 1; Sassen-Koob, "Immigrant and Minority," 22; Mayer, "U.S. Firms"; Potts, World Labor Market, 1–5; Braverman, Labor and Monopoly Capital; Torres and Bonilla, "Decline," 86. Useful applications regarding identity and migration, as discussed in this chapter, include Wallerstein, "Construction of Peoplehood," 71–85; Strikwerda and Guerin Gonzales, eds., Politics; Harris, New Untouchables, 1–5.

5. Aponte and Siles, "Latinos," vii–viii, 44–45; James-Johnson, "Population Rise."

6. Barringer, "Minorities"; Hopfensperger, "Children"; González, "Waste Firm."

7. Arias, *Nueva rusticidad,* 104–106.

8. "Justice Finds"; "Extortion of Aliens." *Sure-Tan, Inc., v. National Labor Relations Board* (1984). The decision was weakened by subsequent legislation, administrative decisions, and court rulings.

9. Vobejda, "Heartland."

10. On Latinos, see, e.g., Padilla, *Latino Ethnic Consciousness;* Escobar, "Forging," 5; Fornek, "Latinos Here." On self-identifiers, see, e.g., Davalos, "Ethnic Identity," 99; Cattan, "Diversity," 4. On Mexican increase, see Triana, "Hispanics in Chicago"; Montana and Reardon, "Mexicans Are Expected"; Reardon, "Search"; R. Thomas Gillaspy to Eduardo Wolle, December 17, 1991, SSAC, folder: Undocumented Hispanics in Minnesota; Page, "Hispanics Share."

11. Barringer, "Minorities"; Burke, "Viva Velasquez"; U.S. Census Bureau, *General Population Characteristics 1990.*

12. Garza, "A Region's"; "City Smarting"; Reardon and Montana, "Hispanic Presence"; Montana and Reardon, "Mexicans Are Expected."

13. Reardon, "Communities Defy"; Beijbom, *Swedes in Chicago,* 102–103, 105; Wilke, "Pilsen Neighborhood"; Quintinilla, "Program Builds."

14. Sorrell and Rogovin, *Barrio Murals;* Santana, "Melting Influence"; Kouri, "Near and Far"; Flores, "Portraits"; Pridmore, "Pilsen Mirrors"; Poe, "Hispanic Artists"; Traficante Mills, "In the Eyes."

15. Reardon, "Communities Defy"; Ortiz, "Big Times"; McMurry, "Little Village," 33; Garza and Montana, "Hispanic Areas."

16. Reardon, "Communities Defy"; Kiernan, "Gangs"; Belsie, "Southeast Chicago."

17. Reardon, "Communities Defy."

18. Reardon, "Search"; Reardon and Montana, "Hispanic Presence."

19. Herbers, "Hispanic Gains"; Thomas, "Hispanic Enrollment."

20. Flores, "Diverse Population"; Sulski, "Mature Neighbors"; Knight, "U.S. Charges."

21. Campos Carr, "Mexican Workers," 31–52; Dardick, "Cultural Identity"; Herbers, "Hispanic Gains."

22. Dardick, "Cultural Identity"; Uhler, "Hispanic Joliet"; Garza and Montana, "Hispanic Areas"; Garza, "Hispanics in Elgin"; Garza, "Latinos Carve"; Banas, "School Earns"; Domke, "Suburb Hispanics"; "Who Lives Where."

23. Aponte and Siles, "Latinos," 45; Campbell, "East Chicago Schools"; Krull, "They're Here"; O'Neill, "Local Hotels"; Horne, "Hispanic Center"; Swiatek, "Bringing Home."

24. Slesinger, Parra, and Kanaskie, "Hispanics in Wisconsin, 1980," 1–4; Tracy, "Deportation Cycle"; Perry, "State's Hispanic"; Gilbert, "Hispanics, Asians"; Kirchen, "Textile Union"; Velasco, "Racine's Silent"; "Stereotypes

Decried"; Boultinghouse, "Area Restaurants"; "7 Illegal Aliens"; "Illegal Aliens Cluster."

25. Knorr, "Albert Serrano"; Wingard, "Mexicantown," 14; Valdés, "Historical Foundations," 30–37.

26. U.S. Bureau of the Census, *Social and Economic Characteristics 1970, General Population Characteristics 1980, Social and Economic Characteristics 1990.*

27. "The Midwest: A State-by-State Look"; Santos, "Hispanic Workers," n.p.; Santiago, "Industrial Heartland," 1; "Signs of Life"; Sassen-Koob, *Global City.*

28. U.S. Bureau of the Census, *Social and Economic Characteristics 1990.*

29. Hornung, "Immigrants Drive"; Santos, "Hispanic Workers," n.p.

30. Tai, "Minnesota's Hispanic"; Father Joroszeski to Archbishop Roach, June 17, 1992, ASPM, folder: Hispanic Ministry Office; R. Thomas Gillaspie to Eduardo Wolle, December 17, 1991, SSAC, folder: Undocumented Hispanics; Ojeda-Zapata, "Minnesota Law"; Brandt, "Taking Back."

31. Villalva, "Hispanics Poorer"; Ojeda-Zapata, "Hispanic Community"; "Urban Trends."

32. The complicated process involving extending migrant sending areas into Southern Mexico is discussed in Wright, *The Death of Ramón González.* McAuliffe, "The Mayor"; Doyle, "Residents Face."

33. Henry, "Minnesota Bank"; Kennedy, "Jennie-O"; Green, "Del Valle"; Meryhew, "Hispanics Find"; Spanish Speaking Affairs Council, Executive Director's Report, September 10, 1991, SSAC files; Karlson and Eidman, "Structural Changes," 13–14; Worthington, "Hispanics Drawn"; Herlinger, "Area Hispanic"; Sánchez, "La calle veinte"; Ojanpa, "Madelia's"; McAuliffe, "Housing"; Minnesota Spanish-Speaking Affairs Council, "1992 Biennium Report," SSAC files; Ojeda-Zapata, "Oslo."

34. Goodsell, "Undocumented Workers"; McCord, "Reaching Out"; Freed, "Hispanic Population"; Flannery, "Immigrants Need"; Taylor, "Union Sets"; McMorris, "Former Migrant."

35. Vobejda, "Heartland"; Lamphere, Stepick, and Grenier, eds., *Newcomers,* 25; Sontag, "New Immigrants"; Goodsell, "Undocumented Workers"; Benson, "Good Neighbors," 364–367.

36. Rynearson, "Hiding," 4–10; Librach and Brown, "Success Story"; Dine, "Invisible."

37. Goodsell, "Jobs Take"; McReynolds, "Area Poultry-Plant."

38. Andreas, "Montfort's," 34–39; Karlson and Eidman, "Structural Changes," 5–7; Broadway, "Meatpacking," 321–322.

39. Toner, "Meatpackers"; Andreas, "Montfort's," 34–39; Hedges et al., "New Jungle," 43; Karlson and Eidman, "Structural Changes," 5–10; Anderson, "New Permits"; Gold, "IBP."

40. Broadway, "Meatpacking," 324–325; Benson, "Households," 13; "Meat

Company"; Stych, "A Meaty Job"; "Hormel Prospers." ConAgra reportedly operated 245 plants in June 1996; see "ConAgra to Restructure."

41. Andreas, "Montfort's," 34, 36, 39; Broadway, "Meatpacking," 324; Harris, *New Untouchables,* 39; "Hormel Prospers."

42. Broadway, "Meatpacking," 323; Karlson and Eidman, "Structural Changes," 10–12; Hedges et al., "New Jungle," 39; Cooper, "Heartland's Raw," 12; Andreas, "Montfort's," 35; McEnroe and Schmickle, "For Consumers."

43. Karlson and Eidman, "Structural Changes," 11, 17; Dort, "Employers, Beware"; Aird, "Dynamite Documentaries"; Swiatek, "Bringing Home."

44. In the extensive literature on the Hormel strike, see especially Rachleff, *Hard Pressed;* Green, *On Strike.*

45. McAuliffe, "Asians, Hispanics."

46. Goodsell, "Jobs Take"; Taylor, "Union Sets"; Hedges et al., "New Jungle"; Hawkins, "Most Dangerous," 40.

47. Taylor, "Union Sets"; Arias, *Nueva rusticidad,* 99–110.

48. "Illegal Workers Follow"; Page, "Federal Agents"; Musser, "Foreign Aid," 36; Goldsmith, "Immigration Officials"; Pabst, "Illegal Aliens."

49. Suzukamo, "Project Alleged"; "Illegal Workers Follow"; Musser, "Foreign Aid," 16; Page, "Federal Agents"; Pabst, "Illegal Aliens"; "More Hispanics."

50. "Food, Music"; "New York Mexican"; Smith, "Mexicans in New York," 57–103; Richardson, "This Road."

51. Waldrop; "Newest Southerners," 38; Flippo, "Reborn"; Nifong, "Hispanics and Asians"; Eisele, "N.C. Farms"; Payne, "Southside"; Brumley, "Beyond Border."

52. Cattan, "Diversity," 12; Long, "Dems, Edgar"; Novak, "Minority Hiring"; "192 Minority Police"; Garza, "Hispanics Still"; Stanton, "Town Whites"; Spielman, "Fire, Police"; Glastris, "Seeking Answers."

53. Washington, "Minorities Say."

54. Merrion, "Illinois' Hispanic"; Tai, "Immigrant Entrepreneurs"; Silverman, "Doing," 40; Walkup, "Hispanics"; Wingard, "Mexicantown," 14.

55. Aggergaard, "Chicago's Secret"; Burke, "Viva Velasquez"; Lazaruz, "Old El Paso"; Furore, "A Success."

56. Hartman, "Tortilla Maker"; Butcher, "Food Processing"; Garza and Montana, "Hispanic Areas"; Biddle, "City's Hispanic"; Merrion, "Illinois' Hispanic Firms"; Banker, "Hispanic Firms."

57. Hayner, "Blacks, Latinos"; Garza and Montana, "Hispanic Areas"; Tai, "More Give"; Crewdson, "Illegal Aliens."

58. Crown, "Improving Odds"; Satchell, "Tide"; Garza and McRoberts, "Migrants Find"; Brandon, "Many Migrants"; Garza, "Hispanics Work."

59. Cattan, "Diversity," 7, 12; Aponte and Siles, "Latinos," 20–21.

60. Jacobson, "Bull Sessions," 24; Dauner, "Plaintiffs"; Kilborn, "Coming."

61. Gehrke, "Migrant"; Doyle, "New Hispanic"; Worthington, "Hispanics Drawn"; Tomson, "Field and Dream." On academic achievement, see Banas, "Low Scores"; Hawes, "Hispanic Dropout"; Garza, "Census Puts"; Mendoza, "Schools Doom"; Martínez, "Historical Development," 16; Egler, "Hispanic Dropout"; Pinney, "Study"; Kyle and Kantowicz, "Kids First"; Griffin and Banas, "Dropout Ills."

62. Banas, "College Graduation"; Pearson, "Colleges Getting"; Camper and Becher, "Colleges Trying"; Pinney, "Study"; Vander Weele, "Hispanics' College"; Estrada, "Keep Out."

63. Interview with Mario Compean, April 10, 1990; author's notes from March 3, 1994, CLAC meeting, University of Minnesota.

64. On the bell curve debate, see especially Fraser, *Bell Curve Wars*; and Jacoby and Glauberman, *Bell Curve Debate*. On Moorhead, see "Number of Hispanic."

65. Frievogel, "Black, White"; Celis, "40 Years"; Orfield, "Growth of Segregation," 7; Nicely, "KCK Parents."

66. "Study Says Great Lakes"; Sweet, "Illinois Schools"; "School Group."

67. Orfield, "Growth of Segregation," 1; Griffin and Blake, "Race, Income"; "Hispanics Melt."

68. Oclander, "Mexicans Here"; Garza, "White Teachers"; Egler, "Hispanic Dropout"; Helbig, "State Teaching Colleges"; Smith, "Report Suggests"; Garza, "Hispanic Health"; Grey, "Immigrant Students," 415, 420.

69. Banas, "Illinois Schools' Minority"; Banas, "Minority Teachers"; Helbig, "State Teaching Colleges," Egler, "Hispanic Dropout."

70. Goleman, "An Emerging Theory"; Ogbu, *Minority Status.*

71. Campbell and Kirby, "U.S.: School Bias."

72. Nadler and Donelson, "Affirmative Reaction"; "Americans Rethink"; Wilkerson, "Des Moines Acts"; Frievogel, "Black, White."

73. Puente, "Immigration"; "A Nasty," 28; "Immigration," *National Journal,* 648.

74. Humphrey, "Naturalization," 322.

75. "As Bias Crime"; Montt, "US More Tolerant"; Leon Daniel, untitled report, UPI Domestic News, May 6, 1982; "Skinhead Activism"; Lane, "Bias-Motivated Crime," 15.

76. Wharton, "Mich. Station"; Olvera, "What Is Reverse."

77. Puente, "Immigration"; "Sentiment Sours"; "A Nasty," 28; Kirschten, "The Hispanic Vote." On reports of hostile public opinion in Minnesota, see, e.g., Suzukamo, "Welfare Pressure"; Fishlock, "Clouds Gather"; Kelly, "Hispanics: Outstate"; Meryhew, "State Human"; McAuliffe, "Hispanics Find"; Freed, "Melting Pot."

78. *Regents of the University of California v. Bakke* (1978); Kirschenman and Neckerman, "We'd Love to," 117–119; Farmer and Terrell, "Discrimination," 204; Carnoy et al., "Changing Economic Position," 40.

79. Johnson, "Latino Newcomers"; Aponte and Siles, "Latinos," 75; Garza, "Asian-Americans."

80. On white worker racism, see, e.g., Roediger, *Wages of Whiteness;* Almaguer, *Racial Fault Lines.* On non-working-class employment discrimination, see e.g., Dawson, "Job Discrimination"; Ahern, "Hispanic Group."

81. De La Rosa, "Ombudsman"; Frievogel, "Black, White"; Kilborn, "Backlog."

82. Meryhew, "One-way"; McAuliffe, "Racism Toward"; Garza and McRoberts, "Migrants Find"; Wilmes, "Why Do We"; editorial by Mary Wilson, "Migrants Returning."

83. Wilson, "Migrants Returning"; Wilmes, "Why Do We"; Pierce, "Immigrants No Longer"; Herlinger, "Blooming Prairie"; Jacobson, "Committee Considering."

84. Enstad, "Southeast Wisconsin."

85. Salopek, "Illegal Immigrants"; Coffey, "Legal Immigrants"; Minnesota Department of Human Services, "Use of Public Assistance by Migrant Farm Workers in the Red River Valley," 1990, SSAC files, folder: Politics; Ojeda-Zapata, "Minnesota Law"; Tai, "'Illegals' Soon"; Bill McDonald to Raul DeAnda, April 19, 1990, Spanish-Speaking Affairs Council Board Minutes, July 28, 1990; Wilson, "Migrants Returning."

86. "Housing Suit"; Franchine, "Elsewhere"; "U.S. Says."

87. "Suits: Suburbs Weeding"; Fountain, "Hispanics Charge"; Goering, "Franklin Park's Goal."

88. Cotliar, "Culture Clash."

89. "Senate Committee"; Manning, "Group Says"; Meryhew, "A Pattern."

90. McRoberts, "Town Rejects"; Ring, "Migrant Workers."

91. Garza and McRoberts, "Migrants Find"; McRoberts, "Town Rejects."

92. Ojanpa, "Madelia's"; Meryhew, "Hispanics Find"; Minnesota Human Rights Commission, "Report on Discrimination," 21; Meryhew, "Moorhead Hispanics."

93. "Olivia: Rights Agency"; Polta, "Housing Shortage"; Meryhew, "Hispanics Find"; Minnesota Spanish-Speaking Affairs Council, "1992 Biennium Report"; Minnesota Human Rights Commission, "Report on Discrimination," 21; Doyle, "Residents Face"; interview with Roberto Reyna.

94. Tai, "Immigration Troubles"; Hopfensperger, "Week's Arrests"; Meryhew, "55 Illegal"; "Michigan Hispanics"; González, "Waste Firm"; Jane, "Iowa Ranked"; "'Cowboy' Raids"; Hagerty, "140 Illegal Aliens"; Starr et al., "Target: Illegal Aliens," 45.

95. Kelliher, "Mexican Catholics," 27–28; Sandin, "Immigration Questioning"; Gonzáles, "INS Deports Teenagers."

96. Meryhew, "St. Paul's"; Meryhew, "Moorhead Hispanics"; Wilmes,

"Why Do We"; Suzukamo, "Rights Head"; Wilson, "Migrants Returning"; Bill McDonald to Raul DeAnda, April 19, 1990, in SSAC meeting minutes, July 28, 1990; Bailey, "Judge Reassigned."

97. Oclander, "Latinos Face"; Hlotke, "Elgin Latinos" and "El Protector."

98. Hlotke, "Elgin Hispanics" and "El Protector"; Meryhew, "Moorhead Hispanics"; McAuliffe, "Hispanics Find"; Meryhew, "A Pattern."

99. Rodríguez and Gonzales, "Man's Crime"; Sunderman, "Hispanics Say"; Boellstorff, "Coalition Says"; Hammel, "Refiling."

100. "Salazar Lawyers"; Shnay, "Accused Cop Killer"; Davis, "Missing Evidence"; Shnay, "Extradition Issue"; Shnay, "Salazar: 'I Thought'"; Shnay, "Salazar Witness"; Cotliar, "Jury's Verdict."

101. Papajohn, "Nicarico Case"; Barnum, "Hernández Objects"; Gregory, "Cruz Case"; Rodríguez, "For Cruz"; Possley, "Nicarico Nightmare"; Grady and Bils, "Nicarico Suit."

102. Meddis, "Suit Says"; "Illegal Searches"; Hoffman, "Is Patrol Making."

103. Stockwell, "Workers Walk"; Olen, "Joliet Group"; Tannenbaum, "Sensitivity Training"; Dell' Angela, "Store Raid"; Oclander and Jackson, "Latinos Protest"; "Immigration Rights"; Grove, "Illegal Immigrants."

104. Sánchez, "Anti-immigrant Rhetoric"; Davis, "Hispanics Ask"; Sosa and Schwartz, "Hispanics Call"; Sheppard, "Hispanic Vote"; Griffin and Galván, "City's Hispanics"; Heise and McCaughan, "Mayor's Legacy"; Casuso, "Hispanic Bloc."

105. Edsall and Peterson, "Daley Victory"; Coffey, "Edgar, Daley"; Galván, "City Deals"; Dorning, "Yates Chided"; Dold, "Hispanics Ready."

106. Marx, "Mexicans Have."

107. Tai, "5 Per Cent."

108. Montana, "Staying in Tune"; Borden, "Hispanic Media"; Mullins, "Where Radio's Rally"; Cannariato, "Area Stations."

109. Braxton and Breslauer, "Casting."

110. Borden, "Hispanic Media"; Montana, "For Hispanic Newspapers."

111. Kelliher, "Mexican Catholics," 3; Father Jaroszelski to Archbishop Roach, June 17, 1992, ASPM, folder: Hispanic Ministry; Steller, "Hispanic Worship"; interview with Marcelino and Irene Rivera, MHS, OH; Velasco, "Racine's Silent"; Tai, "Good Neighbor."

112. Father Jaroszeski to Archbishop Roach, June 17, 1992, ASPM, folder: Hispanic Ministry; Steller, "Hispanic Worship"; Dine, "An Invisible Population."

113. Macklin and Teniente de Costilla, "La Virgen," 132–134; Dardick, "Cultural Identity"; Wright, "Her Vision"; Kelly, "Fresh Murals"; Kirby and Garza, "Walls Become."

114. Simbro, "Hispanic Leader"; Thomas, "It's Still"; Davalos, "La Quin-

ceañera"; Macklin and Teniente de Costilla, "La Virgen"; Lorch, "Hispanic Families."

115. Hoekstra, "A Taste."

116. Pérez, "The Teatros"; Broyles-González, *El Teatro Campesino;* La Raza Action Centers, *First Annual Dinner Dance,* May 4, 1973, UND, MCM; Obejas, "Theater Troupes."

117. Interview with Marcelino and Irene Rivera, MHS, OH.

118. Dailey, "Festiva"; Silverman, "Mexican Fest"; Taylor, "Hispanic Celebration"; Gross, "Fiesta Gives"; Wingard, "Mexicantown," 14; Nancrede, "A Hot Time"; "Fiesta del Sol"; Garza, "Liquor Sales."

119. "Food, Music"; Arroyo and Ríos-Bustamante, *Cinco de Mayo.*

120. Rev. Adalbert Wolski to Most Rev. Leo C. Byrne, May 6, 1971, ASPM, folder: Our Lady of Guadalupe (1); Baker, "Migrants in Action"; Magida, "A Lineup."

121. "Food, Music"; Kelly, "Festival"; Villalva, "West Side"; Adams, "Cinco de Mayo."

122. Mexican Independence Celebration Committee, *Bulletin #4* (May 22, 1972), and Mexican American Cultural and Educational Center, *Bulletin #1* (November 15, 1972), MHS, MAC, Box 1, folder: Mexican Independence (2); "162nd Mexican Independence"; Flandrau, "Fiesta," 69–76; "Fiesta Mexicana"; Duchschere, "Mexican-Americans"; "*El Grito* Parade"; Campa, "Immigrant Latinos," 355–356.

123. On the spread of commercialization in Chicago festivals, see Davalos, "La Quinceañera," 215–238; Silverman, "Mexican Fest."

124. Grey, "Immigrant Students," 414; Harris, *New Untouchables,* 1.

## Retrospective

1. Fanon, *Black Skin,* 220.
2. Barrett, "Americanization," 997.

# Bibliography

Archives

AGN  Archivo General de la Nación, Mexico City
    AR—Fondo Abelardo Rodríguez
    LC—Fondo Lázaro Cárdenas
    POR—Fondo Pascual Ortiz Rubio
ASPM  Archives of the Archdiocese of St. Paul and Minneapolis
BL  Bancroft Library, University of California, Berkeley
    PT—Paul Taylor Papers, Mexican Labor in the United States
    PTSJ—Paul Taylor papers, Stuart Jamieson collection
    MG—Manuel Gamio papers
CHS  Chicago Historical Society
    CAP—Chicago Area Project papers
    MED—Mary Elisa McDowell papers
    WCMC—Welfare Council of Metropolitan Chicago papers
CPL  Chicago Public Library
    MRC—Municipal Reference Collection
DDE  Dwight David Eisenhower Library, Abilene, Kansas
    PCML—President's Commission on Migratory Labor
ECHS  East Chicago Historical Society
    RF—American Legion Repatriation files
HFA  Henry Ford Archives, Dearborn, Michigan
    FTS—Ford Trade School, Foreign Student Records
HHL  Herbert Hoover Presidential Library, West Branch, Iowa
    RG 73—PECE/POUR files
IHRC  Immigration History Research Center, University of Minnesota, St. Paul
    II—International Institute of Minnesota, St. Paul, papers
    CFLPS—Chicago Foreign Language Press Survey (microfilm reels 62 and 63)
JD  James Duarte personal files
JG  Jesse Gonzales personal files
MHC  Michigan Historical Collections, Ann Arbor
    AB—Alvin Bentley papers
    MMC—Michigan Migrant Committee reports

MHS  Minnesota Historical Society, Archives and Manuscripts Division, St. Paul
  AC—American Crystal Sugar Company papers
  GCW—Guild of Catholic Women, St. Paul papers
  GNPSF—Great Northern Railway Co., St. Paul, President's subject file
  IGB—Irene Gómez Bethke papers
  II—International Institute of Minnesota, St. Paul papers
  MAC—Mexican American Community of St. Paul papers
  NH—Neighborhood House, St. Paul, papers
  OH—Mexican American History Project, Oral History Interview transcripts
  SMBRA—Sociedad Mutual Beneficia Recreativa Anahuac, St. Paul, papers
MSA  Michigan State Archives, Lansing
  KS—Kim Sigler papers
NA  National Archives, Washington, D.C.
  RG 85—Bureau of Immigration
PHS  Presbyterian Historical Society, Philadelphia
  HMC—Home Missions Council papers
SCSU  Special Collections, Stanford University
  EG—Ernesto Galarza papers, ms. 224
SHSW  State Historical Society of Wisconsin, Madison
  ARHW—Archival Resources on Hispanics in Wisconsin
SRE  Archivo Histórico de la Secretaría de Relaciones Exteriores, Mexico City
SSCC  Spanish-Speaking Catholic Commission files, Notre Dame, Indiana
SSAC  Spanish-Speaking Affairs Council, St. Paul, papers
SWHA  Social Welfare History Archives, University of Minnesota, Minneapolis
  NFS—Neighborhood Federation of Settlements
UIC  University of Illinois at Chicago Archive
  IPL—Immigrants' Protective League papers
  UCSP—University of Chicago Settlement papers
UND  University of Notre Dame
  MCLR—Midwest Council on La Raza records
  MCM—Midwest Chicano materials, compiled and microfilmed by Gilbert Cárdenas
WPR  Walter P. Reuther Library of Labor and Urban Affairs, Detroit
  DPC—Displaced Persons Collection

## Interviews

Sra. Rose Aguilar, July 22, 1980
Sr. José Alfaro, July 30 and August 8, 1980

Srita. Rosa Arenas, June 18, 1984
Prof. Ulf Beijbom, May 14, 1996
Sra. María Castellanos, June 8, 1984
Sr. Juan J. Castillo, June 12, 1984
Sr. Mario Compean, April 10, 1990, and March 7, 1992
Sra. Carmen Cortina, December 1, 1980
Sr. Roberto Cortina, December 1, 1980
Sr. Jaime Duarte, November 12, 1994
Sr. Gustavo Gaynette, August 13, 1980
Sr. Juan Gómez, March 18, 1995
Sra. Irene Gómez-Bethke, March 18, 1995
Sr. Alfredo González, May 16, 1995
Sr. Ramiro González, June 7, 1984
Mr. Harold Iron Shield, November 11, 1994
Msgr. Clement Kern, August 30 and July 7, 1980
Sr. Israel Leyton, August 13, 1980
Sr. Juan Luna, August 31, 1982, and December 25, 1983
Sr. Efraín Marínez, June 6, 1984
Sister Lucía Medina, June 8, 1984
Sr. Henry Miranda, August 27, 1982
Prof. Carlos de Onís, September 23, 1998
Sr. Secundino Reyes, December 25, 1983, and August 27, 1997
Sr. Roberto Reyna, October 25, 1995
Srita. Isabel Salas, August 13, 1980
Prof. John Valadez, September 23, 1998


## Other Sources

"3 Mile, $4 Million Levee Outlined for Riverview." *St. Paul Booster,* March 20, 1959.
"3rd Blanco y Negro Ball's Highlight to Be Coronation." *St. Paul Dispatch,* February 27, 1964.
"7 Illegal Aliens Found at Area Companies." *Milwaukee Journal,* January 22, 1978.
"162nd Mexican Independence Anniversary Celebration." *Neighborhood House News,* September 1972.
"192 Minority Police Officers File Suit in Chicago Alleging Bias in Sergeants Examination." *Jet,* October 10, 1994.
"497 Mexicans Here to Be Repatriated." *Detroit Free Press,* March 20, 1922.
"1,500 Mexicans on Relief in City Will Be Deported." *St. Paul Daily News,* June 15, 1937.
"5,000 Take Part in Mexican Fiesta." *St. Paul Pioneer Press,* September 17, 1943.

Abbott, Edith. *The Tenements of Chicago, 1908–1935.* Chicago: University of Chicago Press, 1936.

"Act of Barbarism." *La Lucha,* April 28, 1934.

Acuña, Rodolfo. *Occupied America: A History of Chicanos.* 3d ed. New York: Harper & Row, 1988.

———. *Anything but Mexican: Chicanos in Contemporary Los Angeles.* New York and London: Verso, 1996.

Adams, Jim. "Cinco de Mayo Brings Fiesta to West St. Paul Streets." *Minneapolis Star Tribune,* May 3, 1987.

Aggergaard, Steve. "Chicago's Secret Is Out: Latin American Taste Abounds in Stores, Restaurants." *Chicago Tribune,* September 16, 1992.

Ahern, Don. "Hispanic Group Assails Ramsey County Hiring Trends, Language Policy." *St. Paul Pioneer Press Dispatch,* January 27, 1987.

Aird, Elizabeth. "Dynamite Documentaries: After Seeing These, You Might Wonder Why They Call It the Land of the Free." *Vancouver Sun,* August 14, 1992.

Albig, William. "Opinions Concerning Unskilled Mexican Immigrants." *Sociology and Social Research* 15 (September–October 1930): 62–72.

Allsup, Carl. *The American G.I. Forum: Origins and Evolution.* Center for Mexican American Studies, Monograph Series No. 6. Austin: University of Texas Press, 1982.

———. "Concerned Latins Organization." In James B. Lane and Edward J. Escobar, eds., *Forging a Community: The Latino Experience in Northwest Indiana, 1919–1975,* pp. 251–262. Chicago: Cattails Press, 1987.

Almaguer, Tomás. *Racial Fault Lines: The Historical Origins of White Supremacy in California.* Berkeley: University of California Press, 1995.

Alonso, Armando C. *Tejano Legacy: Rancheros and Settlers in South Texas, 1734–1900.* Albuquerque: University of New Mexico Press, 1998.

Alvarado, Ernestine M. "Mexican Immigration to the United States." *Proceedings of the National Conference of Social Work* 47 (1920): 479–480.

"Americans Rethink Desegregation." *Chicago Tribune,* November 10, 1995.

Anderson, Benedict. *Imagined Communities: Reflections on the Origin and Spread of Nationalism.* Rev. ed. London and New York: Verso, 1991.

Anderson, Julie. "New Permits Would Alter Treatment of Water." *Omaha World-Herald,* July 11, 1996.

Andreas, Carol. "Montfort's Disposable Meatpackers." *Covert Action* 50 (Fall 1994): 34–39, 62.

Andrews, Gregg. *Shoulder to Shoulder? The American Federation of Labor, the United States, and the Mexican Revolution, 1910–1924.* Berkeley: University of California Press, 1991.

Año Nuevo Kerr, Louise. "The Chicano Experience in Chicago: 1920–1970." Ph.D. dissertation, University of Illinois at Chicago Circle, 1976.

———. "Chicano Settlements in Chicago: A Brief History." *Journal of Ethnic Studies* 2 (Winter 1975): 22–32.

―――. "Mexican Chicago: Chicano Assimilation Aborted, 1939–1954." In Melvin G. Holli and Peter d'A. Jones, eds., *The Ethnic Frontier: Essays in the History of Group Survival in Chicago and the Midwest*, pp. 293–328. Grand Rapids, Mich.: William B. Eerdmans Publishing Co., 1977.

Aponte, Robert, and Marcelo Siles. "Latinos in the Heartland: The Browning of the Midwest." Research Report #5. East Lansing: Julián Samora Research Institute, Michigan State University, 1994.

Arias, Patricia. *Nueva rusticidad Mexicana.* Mexico City: Consejo Nacional para la Cultura y las Artes, 1992.

Aronovici, Carol. "Assimilation." *Annals of the American Academy of Political and Social Science* 93 (January 1921): 134–138.

Arroyo, Luis, and Antonio Ríos-Bustamante. *Cinco de Mayo: Symbol of National Self-Determination.* Encino, Calif.: Floricanto Press, 1991.

"Arte Mexicano Music House." *Mexico,* December 8, 1928.

"As Bias Crime Seems to Rise, Scientists Study Roots of Racism." *New York Times,* May 27, 1990.

"Assaulted Mexican." *La Lucha,* April 28, 1934.

Baca, Eli M. "For Hispanic Kids, Education That Aids Their Assimilation." *Chicago Tribune,* May 2, 1990.

Baca Zinn, Maxine. "Social Science Theorizing for Latino Families in the Age of Diversity." In Ruth E. Zambrana, ed., *Understanding Latino Families: Scholarship, Policy, and Practice*, pp. 177–189. Newbury Park, Calif.: Sage Publications, 1995.

―――. "Sociological Theory in Emergent Chicano Perspectives." *Pacific Sociological Review* 24 (April 1981): 255–272.

"Back to the Homeland." *Survey* 69 (January 1933): 39.

Badillo, David A. "The Catholic Church and the Making of Mexican American Parish Communities in the Midwest." In Jay P. Dolan and Gilberto M. Hinojosa, eds., *Mexican Americans and the Catholic Church 1900–1965,* pp. 239–288. Vol. 1 of the Notre Dame History of Hispanic Catholics in the U.S. Notre Dame, Ind.: University of Notre Dame Press, 1995.

"Baile and Tostadas Make Grande Fiesta at Mexican Civic Center." *Chicago Tribune,* August 12, 1945.

Bailey, David. "Judge Reassigned after Ethnic Remark." *Chicago Daily Law Bulletin,* July 13, 1995.

Baker, Ann. "Bleak Life of Migrant Workers: They Want a Better Break." *St. Paul Pioneer Press,* November 30, 1969.

―――. "Brown Power." *St. Paul Pioneer Press,* July 6, 1969.

―――. "Migrants in Action Wants to Change Its Work Focus." *St. Paul Dispatch,* May 7, 1976.

Bakken, Pearl. "Chicanos, Professors Search for Common Ground." *Minnesota Daily,* October 27, 1972.

Banas, Casey. "College Graduation Rates Low." *Chicago Tribune,* September 28, 1990.

————. "Illinois Schools' Minority Teacher Ratio Threatened, Study Says." *Chicago Tribune,* February 27, 1987.

————. "Low Scores No Surprise in Illinois." *Chicago Tribune,* June 7, 1991.

————. "Minority Teachers Clustered in 2 Cities." *Chicago Tribune,* February 22, 1989.

————. "On Visit, Governor Gets Lesson on Crowded Hispanic Schools." *Chicago Tribune,* November 26, 1985.

————. "School Earns Respect: West Chicago Gets High Marks from U.S. Government." *Chicago Tribune,* June 2, 1993.

Banker, John. "Hispanic Firms Detail Cash Woes." *Business Journal—Milwaukee,* January 17, 1995.

Bannon, John Francis. *The Spanish Borderlands Frontier, 1513–1821.* New York: Holt, Rinehart and Winston, 1970.

Baran, Paul A., and Paul Marlor Sweezy. *Monopoly Capital: An Essay on the American Economic and Social Order.* New York: Modern Reader, 1968.

Barnes, John A. "Does 'Diversity' Help Business?" *Investor's Business Daily,* May 17, 1995.

Barnum, Art. "Hernández Objects to County Jail." *Chicago Tribune,* July 11, 1995.

Barrera, Mario. *Race and Class in the Southwest: A Theory of Racial Inequality.* Notre Dame, Ind.: University of Notre Dame Press, 1979.

Barrera, Mario, Carlos Muñoz, and Charles Ornelas. "The Barrio as an Internal Colony." *Urban Affairs Annual Reviews* 6 (1972): 465–498.

Barrett, James R. "Americanization from the Bottom Up: Immigration and the Remaking of the Working Class in the United States, 1880–1930." *Journal of American History* 79 (December 1992): 996–1020.

Barringer, Felicity. "Minorities on the Move, Often Unpredictably." *New York Times,* June 6, 1993.

"*El Barrio.*" *La Voz,* December 1971.

Barta, Russell. "The Representation of Poles, Italians, Latins and Blacks in the Executive Suites of Chicago's Largest Corporations." Chicago: Institute of Urban Life, 1973.

Bauer, Edward Jackson, "Delinquency among Mexican Boys in South Chicago." M.A. thesis, University of Chicago, 1938.

Beijbom, Ulf. *Swedes in Chicago: A Demographic and Social Study of the 1846–1880 Immigration.* Translated by Donald Brown. Växjö, Sweden: Historika Institutionen at the University of Uppsala and Chicago Historical Society, 1971.

Bell, Bruce B. "Americanization in the Evening Schools." *East Chicago Times,* November 9, 1926.

Belsie, Laurie. "Southeast Chicago." *Christian Science Monitor,* October 20, 1993.

Benson, Janet E. "Good Neighbors: Ethnic Relations in Garden City Trailer Courts." *Urban Anthropology* 19 (Winter 1990): 361–386.

————. "Households, Migration, and Community Context." *Urban Anthropology* 19 (Spring–Summer 1990): 9–29.

Berry, Carol W. "A Survey of the Holland Spanish-Speaking Community." East Lansing: Department of Sociology, Michigan State University, 1970.

Betten, Neil, and Raymond A. Mohl. "From Discrimination to Repatriation: Mexican Life in Gary, Indiana, during the Great Depression." *Pacific Historical Review* 42 (August 1973): 370–388.

Bevans, Charles I., comp. *Treaties and Other International Agreements of the United States of America, 1776–1949,* IX: 791–806. Washington, D.C.: GPO, 1972.

Bichler, Dorothy. "Jewish, Italians, Mexican Americans in St. Paul." St Paul: St. Paul Public Schools, 1974.

Biddle, Fred Marc. "City's Hispanic Businesses Need Help, Study Shows." *Chicago Tribune,* October 6, 1986.

Bishop, Mary A. "Worker Tells of Study Club Organization among Mexicans." *St. Paul Dispatch,* January 23, 1935.

Blackwelder, Julia Kirk. *Women of the Depression: Caste and Culture in San Antonio, 1929–1939.* College Station: Texas A&M University Press, 1984.

Blauner, Robert. *Racial Oppression in America.* New York: Harper & Row, 1972.

"Blow Out in Topeka, Kansas." *Adelante,* May 1970.

Boardman, Kathryn. "Regrouped Mexican Colony Still Calls West Side Home." *St. Paul Dispatch,* January 10, 1963.

Boellstorff, Leslie. "Coalition Says Renteria Case Needs Probing." *Omaha World-Herald,* June 22, 1995.

————. "Conflicting Emotions: Hispanic Festival Doesn't Erase Sorrow in Lincoln." *Omaha World-Herald,* September 16, 1996.

Bogardus, Emory. "The Mexican Immigrant and Segregation." *American Journal of Sociology* 36 (July 1930): 74–80.

Bogdon, Thomas J. "Bleak Area: HUD Men Tell City West Side Has Had It." *Kansas City Times,* April 11, 1972.

Bolton, Herbert Eugene. *The Spanish Borderlands: A Chronicle of Old Florida and the Southwest.* New Haven: Yale University Press, 1921.

Bolton, Santiago. "Socio-Cultural Adjustment of a Mexican-American Community in an Urban Environment." Paper presented at Annual Meeting, Southern Anthropological Society, 1972.

Bonner, Brian. "Civil Rights Ruling Clears Officer." *St. Paul Pioneer Press,* January 15, 1986.

Borden, Jeff. "Hispanic Media Picture: Prosperity, but Ad Base Still Narrow." *Crain's Chicago Business,* September 14, 1992.

Boultinghouse, Chris. "Area Restaurants Haven for Aliens?" *Racine Journal,* April 22, 1978.

Boxleitner, Rev. J. Jerome. "Years Will Not Erase Influence of Good Priest." *Catholic Bulletin,* January 31, 1969.

Boxmeyer, Don. "$8.2 Million West Side Renewal Project Given City Council OK." *St. Paul Dispatch*, March 15, 1968.

———. "Neighborhood House Faces Moving Crisis." *St. Paul Dispatch*, April 5, 1960.

Brading, D. A., and Celia Wu. "Population Growth and Crisis: León, 1720–1860." *Journal of Latin American Studies* 5 (May 1973): 1–36.

Brandon, Karen. "Many Migrants Harvest Jobs Manicuring Suburban Lawns." *Chicago Tribune*, July 3, 1992.

Brandt, Steve. "Officials Stall Chicano Strike Threat." *Minnesota Daily*, November 4, 1971.

———. "Taking Back Corner Is a Real Treat." *Minneapolis Star-Tribune*, September 9, 1996.

Braverman, Harry. *Labor and Monopoly Capital: The Degradation of Work in the Twentieth Century*. New York: Monthly Review Press, 1974.

Braxton, Greg, and Jan Breslauer. "Casting the Spotlight on TV's Brownout." *Los Angeles Times*, March 5, 1995.

Britton, Gertrudis Howe, and Kate Constable. "Our Mexican Patients at Central Free Dispensary." *Nation's Health* 7 (January 1925): 453–458.

Broadway, Michael. "Meatpacking and Its Social and Economic Consequences for Garden City, Kansas, in the 1980s." *Urban Anthropology* 19 (Winter 1990): 321–344.

Bromley, Oxnam G. "The Mexican in Los Angeles from the Standpoint of Religious Forces of the City." *Annals of the American Academy of Political and Social Science* 93 (January 1941): 130–133.

Brower, Monty. "A Proud Street Mourns Its Fallen Sons." *Time* (May 28, 1984): 76.

Broyles-González, Yolanda. *El Teatro Campesino: Theater in the Chicano Movement*. Austin: University of Texas Press, 1994.

Brumley, Al. "Beyond Border States: Booming Economy in Carolinas Luring Hispanic Immigrants." *Dallas Morning News*, November 11, 1996.

Burke, Greg. "Viva Velasquez: Making the American Dream Come True and Sharing It." *Chicago Tribune*, February 28, 1988.

Butcher, Lola. "Food Processing Occupies Vital Role in KC-Area Economy." *Kansas City Business Journal*, October 24, 1988.

"A Butcher Shop in Their Church." *Back of the Yards Journal*, September 23, 1981.

Butler, Edward E. "Change in the Mexican-American Family: A Study in the South Bend Community." Senior essay, University of Notre Dame, 1962.

Caine, Terry Allen. "Social Life in a Mexican-American Community: Social Class or Ethnic Concept." M.A. thesis, University of Minnesota, 1971.

Camarillo, Albert. "Mexican American History Revisited and Corrected." *Center Magazine* 13 (July/August 1980): 40–43.

Camblon, Ruth S. "Mexicans in Chicago." *The Family* 7 (November, 1926): 207–211.

Campa, Arthur. "Immigrant Latinos and Resident Mexican Americans in Garden City, Kansas: Ethnicity and Ethnic Relations." *Urban Anthropology* 19 (Winter 1990): 345–360.

Campbell, Linda P., and Joseph A. Kirby. "U.S.: School Bias Is Rife in Rockford." *Chicago Tribune,* November 4, 1993.

Campbell, Michelle. "East Chicago Schools Face Boycott amid Racism Claims." *Chicago Sun-Times,* February 9, 1996.

Camper, John, and Thomas Becher. "Colleges Trying to Lure Hispanics." *Chicago Tribune,* May 8, 1990.

Campos Carr, Irene, "Mexican Workers in Aurora: The Oral History of Three Immigration Waves, 1924–1990." *Perspectives in Mexican American Studies* 3 (1992): 31–51.

Cannariato, Joe. "Area Stations Bring News and Entertainment to Spanish-Speaking Residents." *Business Journal—Milwaukee,* June 30, 1986.

Cárdenas, Gilbert. "Los Desarraigados: Chicanos in the Midwestern Region of the United States." *Aztlán* 7 (Summer 1976): 153–186.

———. "A Report on East Chicago Youth: Mexican American Youth in East Chicago." 1970. UND, GC.

———. "A Report on La Raza in the Midwest." Notre Dame, Ind.: Centro de Estudios Chicanos e Investigaciones Sociales, University of Notre Dame, 1974. UND, GC.

Cárdenas, Gilbert, and Ricardo Parra. "La Raza in the Midwest and Great Lakes Region." Notre Dame, Ind.: Mid-West Council of La Raza, Institute for Urban Studies, University of Notre Dame, 1973. UND, GC.

Cárdenas, Reymundo. "The Mexican in Adrian." *Michigan History* 42 (Fall 1958): 343–352.

Cárdenas Coates, Dionisia. "Nuestra Señora—Our Very Own, Our Lady of Guadalupe Parish, 1931–1981." N.p.: St. Paul, 1981.

Cardoso, Lawrence A. "Labor Emigration to the Southwest, 1916 to 1920: Mexican Attitudes and Policy." *Southwestern Historical Quarterly* 79 (April 1976): 400–416.

Carlson, Alvar W. "The Settling Process of Mexican Americans in Northwestern Ohio." *Journal of Mexican-American History* 5 (1975): 24–42.

Carnoy, Martin, Hugh M. Daley, and Raul Hinojosa Ojeda. "The Changing Economic Position of Latinos in the U.S. Labor Market since 1939." In Frank Bonilla, comp., *Growing Inequality,* pp. 28–54. Newbury Park, Calif.: Sage, 1993.

Carter, Jerry L. "Chicano Students Start Hunger Strike at SCSU." *St. Cloud Times,* May 8, 1995.

Casuso, Jorge. "Hispanic Bloc Gives Credit to Washington." *Chicago Tribune,* November 30, 1987.

Cattan, Peter. "The Diversity of Hispanics in the U.S. Work Force." *Monthly Labor Review* 116 (August 1993): 3–15.

Cavaretta, June, and V. Dion Haynes. "Hispanics Claim Discrimination in Closing of Bilingual School." *Chicago Tribune,* June 16, 1992.

"Celebration of the National September Festival." *El Nacional,* August 20, 1932.

Celis, William III, "40 Years after Brown Segregation Persists." *New York Times,* May 18, 1994.

Chambers, Sarah. "Mutual Cooperation and Local Leadership among Mexican Immigrants in Minnesota." Senior History thesis, Carleton College, 1985.

Chanco, Ruben. "West Side's Story Can Happen Here." *St. Paul Pioneer Press,* December 27, 1970.

Chávez, Linda. *Out of the Barrio: Toward a New Politics of Hispanic Assimilation.* New York: Basic Books, 1991.

Chicago. Department of Development and Planning. *Chicago's Spanish-Speaking Population: Selected Statistics.* Chicago: Department of Development and Planning, 1973.

"Chicano Liberation Front." *In Amatl in Xicanome,* December 1976.

"Chicano Studies." *La Voz,* December 1971.

"Chicano-Boricua Studies Works to Enroll, Retain Latino Students at Wayne State." *Detroit News,* November 16, 1995.

Choldin, Harvey M., and Grafton D. Trout. "Mexican Americans in Transition: Migration and Employment in Michigan Cities." East Lansing: Rural Manpower Center and Department of Sociology, Michigan State University, 1969.

"CIO Aids Farm Labor." *Economic Outlook* 13 (April 1952): 26.

"City Smarting from Decline While Collar Areas Boom." *Crain's Chicago Business,* July 1, 1991.

Coatsworth, John H. *Growth against Development: The Economic Impact of Railroads in Porfirian Mexico.* DeKalb: Northern Illinois University Press, 1981.

Coffey, Raymond R. "Edgar, Daley Let Immigrant-Bashing Bandwagon Pass." *Chicago Sun-Times,* September 10, 1996.

———. "Legal Immigrants Pay More Than Their Fair Share." *Chicago Sun-Times,* September 12, 1996.

Cohen, Lizbeth. *Making a New Deal: Industrial Workers in Chicago, 1919–1939.* Cambridge: Cambridge University Press, 1990.

"Compatriot Assaulted in South Chicago." *El Nacional,* May 27, 1931.

"ConAgra to Restructure Ops." *Nation's Restaurant News,* June 3, 1996.

Cook, Chris L. "Migrants: The Future Cries Out for Change." *Minneapolis Star,* November 12, 1977.

Cook, Eugene. "Poverty-Tuberculosis-Death." *St. Paul Pioneer Press,* December 1, 1940.

Cooper, Marc, "The Heartland's Raw Deal." *Nation* 264 (February 3, 1997): 11–17.

Córdova, Teresa, Norma Cantú, Gilberto Cárdenas, Juan García, and Christine M. Sierra, eds. *Chicana Voices: Intersections of Race, Class and Gender.* Austin: MAS Publications, University of Texas, 1986.

Cotliar, Sharon. "Culture Clash in Highwood." *Chicago Sun-Times,* September 13, 1993.

———. "Jury's Verdict Frees Salazar in '84 Cop Killing." *Chicago Sun-Times,* November 10, 1996.

"'Cowboy' Raids Assailed by Earl." *Milwaukee Sentinel,* September 17, 1983.

Crawford, William B., Jr. "Suit Attacks Language Barrier." *Chicago Tribune,* April 17, 1988.

Crewdson, John M. "Illegal Aliens Are Bypassing Farms for Higher Pay of Jobs in the Cities." *New York Times,* November 10, 1980.

Crocker, Ruth Hutchinson. "Gary Mexicans and 'Christian Americanization': A Study in Cultural Conflict." In James B. Lane and Edward J. Escobar, eds., *Forging a Community: The Latino Experience in Northwest Indiana, 1919–1975,* pp. 115–134. Chicago: Cattails Press, 1987.

Crown, Judith. "Improving Odds for a Hispanic Workforce." *Crain's Chicago Business,* August 12, 1991.

Dailey, Pat. "'Festiva': Cinco de Mayo Holiday Celebrates a Mexican Victory." *Chicago Tribune,* May 5, 1994.

"Dance." *La Defensa.* November 14, 1936.

Dardick, Hal. "Cultural Identity Emerges in the Suburbs." *Chicago Tribune,* September 16, 1992.

———. "Hispanic Police Select Role Model for Award." *Chicago Tribune,* September 17, 1990.

Dauner, John T. "Plaintiffs Seek Class Action." *Kansas City Star,* December 16, 1995.

Davalos, Karen Mary. "Ethnic Identity among Mexican and Mexican American Women in Chicago, 1920–1991." Ph.D. dissertation, Yale University, 1993.

———. "'La Quinceañera': Making Gender and Ethnic Identitites." *Frontiers* 16, no. 213 (1996): 101–127.

Davis, Robert. "Hispanics Ask Apology for Marzullo Comment." *Chicago Tribune,* January 13, 1983.

———. "Missing Evidence at Issue in Cop Killing." *Chicago Sun-Times,* January 30, 1996.

Dawson, Gary. "Job Discrimination Remains a Problem." *St. Paul Pioneer Press,* November 28, 1988.

De La Rosa, Elena. "Ombudsman for Chicanos Says Few Aware of 'Largest Minority.'" *Minneapolis Tribune,* November 7, 1977.

Dean, R. J. "Detroit's Melting Pot Boils Over." *Survey* 64 (May 15, 1930): 187–188.

De León, Arnoldo. *Ethnicity in the Sunbelt: A History of Mexican Americans in Houston.* Houston: Mexican American Studies Program, University of Houston, 1989.

———. *In Re Rodríguez.* San Antonio: Caravel Press, 1979.

———. *They Called Them Greasers: Anglo Attitudes toward Mexicans in Texas, 1821–1900.* Austin: University of Texas Press, 1984.

Dell' Angela, Tracy. "Store Raid Prompts Immigration Fears." *Chicago Tribune,* July 1, 1996.

Demarest, Donald. "Bridging the GAP." *The Sign* (April 1975): 21.

DeMuth, Jerry. "Migrants Tackle Housing, Their Top Problem." *Chicago Sun-Times,* October 24, 1967.

"DePaul Establishes Hispanic Archives." *Chicago Tribune,* November 18, 1986.

"Detroit Opens Tent City to Care for Evicted Families." *Chicago Tribune,* August 7, 1932.

Deutsch, Sarah. *No Separate Refuge: Culture, Class and Gender on an Anglo-Hispanic Frontier in the American Southwest, 1880–1940.* New York: Oxford University Press, 1987.

Diebold, Susan M. "The Mexicans." In June Drenning Holmquist, ed., *They Chose Minnesota: A Survey of the State's Ethnic Groups,* pp. 92–107. St. Paul: Minnesota Historical Society, 1981.

Dine, Philip. "An Invisible Population." *St. Louis Post-Dispatch,* May 21, 1995.

"A Doctor Makes Insolent Declarations." *Mexico,* October 20, 1928.

Dold, R. Bruce. "Hispanics Ready to Push for School Construction." *Chicago Tribune,* May 23, 1989.

"Dolores Awaits Yule Fiesta: Christmas Eve Party in St. Paul's Mexican Quarter." *St. Paul Pioneer Press,* December 19, 1926.

Dorning, Mike. "Yates Chided for Being a Small Spender." *Chicago Tribune,* August 11, 1996.

Dorson, Richard M. "Mexican Michigan Folklore." *Michigan History* 31 (1947): 443.

Dort, Terrie. "Employers, Beware: Organized Labor Has Right Idea." *Nation's Restaurant News,* May 6, 1996.

Doyle, Pat. "New Hispanic Residents Changing Face of Small Towns." *Minneapolis Star Tribune,* September 6, 1988.

———. "Residents Face Eviction They Say They Can't Afford." *Minneapolis Star Tribune,* February 5, 1995.

Driscoll, Barbara A. "Newspaper Documentary History of the Chicano Community of South Bend." Notre Dame: Centro de estudios chicanos e investigaciones sociales, 1978.

Duarte, James. "Chronology of the Chicano Studies Department 1968–1985." Unpublished study, 1985, JD.

Duchschere, Kevin. "Mexican-Americans Will Celebrate Their Independence Day." *Minneapolis Star Tribune,* September 14, 1991.

Duncan, John T., and Severiano Alanzo. "Guadalupe Center—50 Years of Service." Kansas City, Mo., 1972.

Duncan, Lara. "LAFC Board Votes to Close 2 Offices." *Chicago Daily Law Bulletin,* December 10, 1992.

"Dunedin Terrace Housing Project to Be Dedicated." *St. Paul Dispatch,* May 16, 1966.

Dysart, Jane. "Mexican Women in San Antonio, 1830–1860: The Assimilation Process." *Western Historical Quarterly* 7 (October 1976): 365–375.

"Editorial." *La Defensa,* February 29, 1936.

Edsall, Thomas B., and Bill Peterson. "Daley Victory Spells Trouble for Jackson Coalition." *Washington Post,* March 2, 1989.

Edson, George T. "Mexicans at Albert Lea, Minn." Paul Taylor Collection, Bancroft Library, University of California, Berkeley, 1927. (Cited in notes as Edson, "Albert Lea.")

———. "Mexicans at Davenport, Ia., Moline, Ill., including Bettenforf Ia., Rock Island, East Moline and Silvis." Paul Taylor papers, Bancroft Library, University of California, Berkeley, 1927. (Cited in notes as Edson, "Davenport.")

———. "Mexicans at Fort Madison, Iowa." Paul Taylor Papers, Bancroft Library, University of California, Berkeley, 1927. (Cited in notes as Edson, "Fort Madison.")

———. "Mexicans at Lorain, Ohio." Paul Taylor Papers, Bancroft Library, University of California, Berkeley, 1926. (Cited in notes as Edson, "Lorain.")

———. "Mexicans at Manly, Iowa." Paul Taylor Papers, Bancroft Library, University of California, Berkeley, 1927. (Cited in notes as Edson, "Manly.")

———. "Mexicans in Aurora, Illinois." Paul Taylor Papers, Bancroft Library, University of California, Berkeley, 1926. (Cited in notes as Edson, "Aurora.")

———. "Mexicans in Chicago, Illinois." Paul Taylor Papers, Bancroft Library, University of California, Berkeley, 1926. (Cited in notes as Edson, "Chicago.")

———. "Mexicans in Des Moines, Iowa." Paul Taylor Papers, Bancroft Library, University of California, Berkeley, 1927. (Cited in notes as Edson, "Des Moines.")

———. "Mexicans in Detroit, Michigan." Paul Taylor Papers, Bancroft Library, University of California, Berkeley, 1926. (Cited in notes as Edson, "Detroit.")

———. "Mexicans in East Chicago." Paul Taylor Papers, Bancroft Library, University of California, Berkeley, 1926. (Cited in notes as Edson, "East Chicago.")

———. "Mexicans in Flint, Mich." Paul Taylor Papers, Bancroft Library, University of California, Berkeley, 1926. (Cited in notes as Edson, "Flint.")

————. "Mexicans in Gary, Indiana." Paul Taylor Papers, Bancroft Library, University of California, Berkeley, 1926. (Cited in notes as Edson, "Gary.")

————. "Mexicans in Indiana Harbor (East Chicago), Ind." Paul Taylor Papers, Bancroft Library, University of California, Berkeley, 1926. (Cited in notes as Edson, "Indiana Harbor.")

————. "Mexicans in Joliet, Ill." Paul Taylor Papers, Bancroft Library, University of California, Berkeley, 1926. (Cited in notes as Edson, "Joliet.")

————. "Mexicans in Mason City, Iowa." Paul Taylor Papers, Bancroft Library, University of California, Berkeley, 1927. (Cited in notes as Edson, "Mason City.")

————. "Mexicans in Milwaukee, Wisc." Paul Taylor Papers, Bancroft Library, University of California, Berkeley, 1926. (Cited in notes as Edson, "Milwaukee.")

————. "Mexicans in Minneapolis and St. Paul." Paul Taylor Papers, Bancroft Library, University of California, Berkeley, 1927. (Cited in notes as Edson, "Minneapolis and St. Paul.")

————. "Mexicans in New York City." Paul Taylor Papers, Bancroft Library, University of California, Berkeley, 1926. (Cited in notes as Edson, "New York City.")

————. "Mexicans in Omaha, Nebraska." Paul Taylor Papers, Bancroft Library, University of California, Berkeley, 1927. (Cited in notes as Edson, "Omaha.")

————. "Mexicans in Our North Central States." Paul Taylor Papers, Bancroft Library, University of California, Berkeley, 1927. (Cited in notes as Edson, "North Central.")

————. "Mexicans in Our North Central States—Summary." Paul Taylor Papers, Bancroft Library, University of California, Berkeley, 1927. (Cited in notes as Edson, "Summary.")

————. "Mexicans in Philadelphia, Pa." Paul Taylor Papers, Bancroft Library, University of California, Berkeley, 1926. (Cited in notes as Edson, "Philadelphia.")

————. "Mexicans in Pontiac, Mich." Paul Taylor Papers, Bancroft Library, University of California, Berkeley, 1926. (Cited in notes as Edson, "Pontiac.")

————. "Mexicans in Saginaw." Paul Taylor Papers, Bancroft Library, University of California, Berkeley, 1926. (Cited in notes as Edson, "Saginaw.")

————. "Mexicans in Sioux City, Iowa." Paul Taylor Papers, Bancroft Library, University of California, Berkeley, 1927. (Cited in notes as Edson, "Sioux City.")

————. "Mexicans in Sugar Beet Work in the Central West." Paul Taylor Papers, Bancroft Library, University of California, Berkeley, 1927. (Cited in notes as Edson, "Central West.")

————. "Mexicans in the Pittsburgh, Pa., District." Paul Taylor Papers, Bancroft Library, University of California, Berkeley, 1926. (Cited in notes as Edson, "Pittsburgh.")

———. "Mexicans in Toledo, Ohio." Paul Taylor Papers, Bancroft Library, University of California, Berkeley, 1926. (Cited in notes as Edson, "Toledo.")

———. "Mexicans in Waukegan, Illinois." Paul Taylor Papers, Bancroft Library, University of California, Berkeley, 1926. (Cited in notes as Edson, "Waukegan.")

———. "Northern Sugar Beet Mexicans." Paul Taylor Papers, Bancroft Library, University of California, Berkeley, 1927. (Cited in notes as Edson, "Northern Sugar.")

Edwards, Frank S. *A Campaign in New Mexico with Colonel Doniphan.* Philadelphia: Carey and Hart, 1847.

Egler, Daniel. "Hispanic Dropout Rate Critical: Task Force." *Chicago Tribune,* March 24, 1985.

Eisele, Stella M. "N.C. Farms Bountiful to Mexicans." *Des Moines Register,* July 23, 1995.

Enstad, Robert. "Southeast Wisconsin Paying for State's Welfare Generosity." *Chicago Tribune,* May 25, 1986.

Escobar, Edward. "Forging of a Community." In James B. Lane and Edward J. Escobar, eds., *Forging a Community: The Latino Experience in Northwest Indiana, 1919–1975,* pp. 3–24. Chicago: Cattails Press, 1987.

Esquivel, Servando I. "The Immigrant from Mexico." *Outlook* 125 (May 19, 1920): 131.

Esser, Josef, and Joachim Hirsch. "The Crisis of Fordism and the Dimensions of a 'Postfordist' Regional and Urban Structure." *International Journal of Urban and Regional Research* 13 (September 1989): 417–437.

Estrada, Richard. "Keep Out: Immigrants with Low Job Skills." *Chicago Tribune,* August 7, 1995.

"Explanation." *La Lucha,* June 2, 1934.

"Extortion of Aliens Investigated." *St. Paul Pioneer Press,* September 22, 1992.

Fanon, Frantz. *Black Skin, White Masks.* New York: Grove Press, 1967.

———. *The Wretched of the Earth.* New York: Grove Press, 1963.

Farmer, Amy, and Dek Terrell. "Discrimination, Bayesian Updating of Employer Beliefs, and Human Capital Accumulation." *Economic Inquiry* 34 (April 1996): 204–219.

"Father Gorman Going to Findlay." *Toledo Blade,* April 13, 1951.

Faught, Jim D. "Chicanos in a Medium-Sized City: Demographic and Socioeconomic Characteristics." *Aztlán* 7 (Summer 1976): 307–326.

Felter, Eunice. "The Social Adaptations of the Mexican Churches in the Chicago Area." M.A. thesis, University of Chicago, 1941.

Fenton, Agnes M. "The Mexicans of the City of Milwaukee—Wisconsin." Milwaukee: YMCA and International Institute, 1930.

"Festival." *Mexico,* November 28, 1928.

"Fiesta del Sol Starts Today in Pilsen." *Chicago Sun-Times,* July 28, 1994.

"Fiesta Mexicana." *St. Paul Downtowner,* September 11, 1975.

Finnegan, John R. "Mexican Colony Flourishes Despite Housing Shortage." *St. Paul Pioneer Press,* November 25, 1951.

Fishlock, Trevor. "Clouds Gather over the Prairie." *Worthington Sunday Telegraph,* October 4, 1992.

Flaherty, Roger, "Hispanic Leaders Back U. of Illinois Protesters." *Chicago Sun-Times,* May 22, 1992.

Flandrau, Grace. "Fiesta in St. Paul." *Yale Review* 33 (September 1943): 69–76.

Flannery, James Allen. "Immigrants Need a Place to Start." *Omaha World-Herald,* May 29, 1995.

Flippo, Leslie Denton. "Reborn in the USA: Newcomers from Mexico Contribute to Dalton's Economy and Culture." *Chattanooga Times,* June 28, 1995.

Flores, Veronica. "Diverse Population Is Learning to Coexist." *Chicago Sun-Times,* March 28, 1993.

———. "Portraits of Pilsen: Murals Reflect Sense of Pride among Latinos." *Chicago Sun-Times,* August 15, 1993.

"Food, Music and Dance: Celebrating Mexico, Olé—A Growing Mexican Community Brings Cinco de Mayo to New York." *Newsday,* April 29, 1994.

Ford, Harvey S. "Toledo's Spanish Mission: Help for Newcomers." *Toledo Blade,* January 13, 1957.

Fornek, Scott. "Latinos Here are Epitome of Diversity." *Chicago Sun-Times,* September 16, 1992.

Fotia, Elizabeth R., and Richmond Calvin. "The Mexican-Americans of the South Bend–Mishawaka Area." South Bend: Indiana University–South Bend, Ethnic Studies Heritage Program, 1975.

Fountain, Monica. "Hispanics Charge Housing Law Bias." *Chicago Tribune,* August 2, 1994.

Franchine, Philip. "Elsewhere in the Suburbs." *Chicago Sun-Times,* September 11, 1994.

Fraser, Steve. *The Bell Curve Wars: Race, Intelligence and the Future of America.* New York: Basic Books, 1995.

Freed, Kenneth. "Hispanic Population on Rise." *Omaha World-Herald,* February 18, 1996.

———. "Melting Pot of Perceptions." *Omaha World-Herald,* February 18, 1996.

Frievogel, William H. "Black, White and Brown: Desegregation Ruling Established a Legal Landmark, Unkept Promises." *St. Louis Post-Dispatch,* May 15, 1994.

Furore, Kathleen. "A Success Story Worth Repeating: Velasquezes Back Where They Started: At Helm of Azteca." *Chicago Tribune,* November 28, 1993.

Galván, Manuel. "City Deals Immigration Officials a Blow." *Chicago Tribune,* March 8, 1985.

Gamio, Manuel. *The Mexican Immigrant: His Life Story.* Chicago: University of Chicago Press, 1931.

———. *Mexican Immigration to the United States: A Study of Human Migration and Adjustment.* Chicago: University of Chicago Press, 1930.

García, Carolina. "Agencies Rip Aid-Cut Plan." *Milwaukee Journal,* September 9, 1982.

———. "Chicano Studies Department for UW Urged." *Milwaukee Journal,* February 21, 1982.

García, Carolina, and Gary C. Rummler. "For Hispanics, Life Can Be a Long Migration." *Milwaukee Journal,* July 17, 1983.

García, Edwin. "Clemente Students Stage Walkout: Ouster of Librarian Sought amid Charges of Racism." *Chicago Tribune,* September 27, 1988.

García, Gus C. "Education for Democracy." In *Report of the Conference on the Mexican American in Chicago,* pp. 32–50. Chicago: Community Relations Service, 1949.

García, Juan R. "History of Chicanos in Chicago Heights." *Aztlán* 7 (Summer 1976): 291–306.

———. *Mexicans in the Midwest, 1900–1932.* Tucson: University of Arizona Press, 1996.

———. "Midwest Mexicanos in the 1920s: Issues, Questions, and Directions." *Social Science Journal* 19 (April 1982): 89–99.

García, Juan R., and Angel Cal. "El círculo de obreros católicos 'San José,' 1925 to 1930." In James B. and Edward J. Escobar, eds., *Forging a Community: The Latino Experience in Northwest Indiana, 1919–1975,* pp. 95–114. Chicago: Cattails Press, 1987.

García, Juan Ramón. "A History of the Mexican American People in the Chicago Heights, Illinois Area." Chicago Heights: Prairie State Community College, 1975.

———. "Operation Wetback: Midwest Phase." Paper presented at NACS Midwest FOCO Conference, November 1981.

García, Mario. "Americans All: The Mexican American Generation and the Politics of Wartime Los Angeles." In Rodolfo O. de la Garza et al., eds., *The Mexican American Experience,* pp. 201–212. Austin: University of Texas Press, 1985.

García, Mario T. *Memories of Chicano History: The Life and Narrative of Bert Corona.* Berkeley: University of California Press, 1994.

———. *Mexican Americans: Leadership, Ideology, and Identity, 1930–1960.* New Haven: Yale University Press, 1989.

García, Richard A. *Rise of the Mexican American Middle Class: San Antonio, 1929–1941.* College Station: Texas A&M University Press, 1991.

Garis, Roy L. "A Brief Review of Immigration Legislation." In Madison Grant and Charles Stewart Davis, eds., *The Alien in Our Midst,* pp. 114–121. New York: Galton Publishing Co., 1930.

Garza, Melita Marie. "Asian-Americans Far Outpace Other Minorities in Income." *Chicago Tribune,* July 14, 1994.

———. "Barriers Defined to U.S. Citizenship." *Chicago Tribune,* April 25, 1994.

———. "Bilingual Bill Called Unconstitutional." *Chicago Tribune,* February 7, 1995.

———. "Bringing Drama to the School Reform Story." *Chicago Tribune,* January 18, 1993.

———. "Carmen Velasquez's Dedication Is the Key to the Medical Center Pilsen Calls Its Own." *Chicago Tribune,* July 17, 1994.

———. "Census Puts Latinos in a Bittersweet Light." *Chicago Tribune,* October 20, 1994.

———. "Cops Remove Latino Protesters at U. of I." *Chicago Tribune,* May 6, 1992.

———. "Hispanic Concerns Surface at U. of I." *Chicago Tribune,* May 6, 1992.

———. "Hispanic Health Care Spotty, Professor Says." *Chicago Tribune,* March 12, 1993.

———. "Hispanics in Elgin Seek Power." *Chicago Tribune,* March 22, 1991.

———. "Hispanics Still Underrepresented on Nation's Police Force." *Chicago Tribune,* June 28, 1992.

———. "Hispanics Work, but They Are Still in Poverty, Study Reports." *Chicago Tribune,* March 8, 1993.

———. "Latinos Carve Their Own Spot in the Suburbs." *Chicago Tribune,* August 30, 1994.

———. "Latinos Get Promises from U. of I." *Chicago Tribune,* April 9, 1992.

———. "Liquor Sales Banned at Festival in Pilsen." *Chicago Tribune,* May 27, 1993.

———. "A Region's New Look: Latinos Flock to Midwest, Make Their Presence Felt." *Chicago Tribune,* March 7, 1995.

———. "So American, So Hispanic." *Milwaukee Journal,* June 26, 1987.

———. "UIC's Hispanic Program Would Speak to 90s Needs." *Chicago Tribune,* May 13, 1992.

———. "White Teachers Remain the Rule in Suburb Schools." *Chicago Tribune,* October 28, 1992.

———. "YWCA at Forefront of U. of I. Fight." April 14, 1992.

Garza, Melita Marie, and Flynn McRoberts. "Migrants Find Hatred in Harvard." *Chicago Tribune,* July 21, 1991.

Garza, Melita Marie, and Constanza Montana. "Hispanic Areas on the Grow: Dreams of Owning Homes, Businesses Helping These Communities to Flourish." *Chicago Tribune*, September 11, 1993.

Gehrke, J. T. "Migrant No More; Family Settles in St. James." *Mankato Free Press*, November 24, 1990.

Gilbert, Craig. "Hispanics, Asians Boost South Side's Population and Diversity." *Milwaukee Journal*, March 22, 1991.

Gilbert, James Carl. "A Field Study of Mexico and the Mexican Repatriation Movement." M.A. thesis, University of Southern California, 1934.

Glastris, Paul. "Seeking Answers to Racial Disparity in Tests." *Rocky Mountain News*, August 19, 1994.

Glenn, Evelyn Nakano. "From Servitude to Service Work: Historical Continuities in the Racial Division of Paid Reproductive Labor." *Signs* 18 (Autumn 1992): 1–43.

"Go to School in a Box Car." *Toledo Blade*, April 30, 1920.

Goering, Laurie. "Franklin Park's Goal Is to Age Gracefully." *Chicago Tribune*, September 5, 1994.

Gold, Scott. "IBP Inc./Hog-Processing Plant in Duplin County: Environmental Rules Challenged." *Wilmington Star-News*, February 2, 1995.

Goldner, Norman. "The Mexican in a Northern Urban Area: A Profile of an Ethnic Community." *Proceedings of the Minnesota Academy of Sciences* 29 (1961): 102–111.

———. "The Mexican in the Northern Urban Area: A Comparison of Two Generations." M.A. thesis, University of Minnesota, 1959.

Goldsmith, Julie. "Immigration Officials Arrest 65 Workers." *Indianapolis Star*, July 10, 1996.

Goleman, Daniel. "An Emerging Theory on Blacks' IQ Scores." *New York Times*, April 10, 1988.

Gómez-Quiñones, Juan. *Mexican American Labor, 1790–1990*. Albuquerque: University of New Mexico Press, 1994.

Gonzales, Cindy. "INS Deports Teenagers, Doesn't Tell Their Parents." *Atlanta Journal and Constitution*, November 26, 1992.

———. "Waste Firm Raid a First in Region." *Omaha World-Herald*, December 11, 1996.

González, Alfredo M. "The Beginnings of Chicano Studies in Minnesota." *Roots* 21 (Fall 1992): 15–18.

González, Gilbert G. *Labor and Community: Mexican Citrus Worker Villages in a Southern California County, 1900–1950*. Urbana and Chicago: University of Illinois Press, 1994.

González, Narciso. "The Problem of La Cruz Azul and Mexicans of Chicago." *Mexico*, April 5, 1930.

González Navarro, Moisés. "Efectos sociales de la crisis de 1929." *Historia Mexicana* 19 (abril–julio 1970): 536–558.

Goodsell, Paul. "Jobs Take Them Well North of Border." *Chicago Tribune,* October 16, 1992.

———. "Undocumented Workers Flock to Meatpacking Jobs." *Dallas Morning News,* October 27, 1992.

Gordon, David M., Richard Edwards, and Michael Reich. *Segmented Work, Divided Workers: The Historical Transformation of Labor in the United States.* Cambridge: Cambridge University Press, 1982.

Gordon, Milton. *Assimilation in American Life: The Role of Race, Religion, and National Origin.* New York: Oxford University Press, 1964.

Gosse, Van. *Where the Boys Are: Cuba, Cold War America and the Making of a New Left.* London and New York: Verso, 1993.

Grady, William, and Jeffrey Bils. "Nicarico Suit Looms in DuPage." *Chicago Tribune,* June 29, 1996.

Gramsci, Antonio. "Americanism and Fordism." In *An Antonio Gramsci Reader: Selected Writing, 1916–1935,* pp. 275–299. Edited by David Forgacs. New York: Shocken Books, 1988.

———. "The Intellectuals." in *Selections from the Prison Notebooks,* pp. 5–23. New York: International Publishers, 1971.

Grant, Bruce. "Little Mexico in Chicago: Gayety, Color and Strumming Guitars." *Chicago Sun-Times,* May 26, 1935.

Grant, Laurens. "Spanish Center Speaks with Voice of Caring." *Chicago Tribune,* November 15, 1992.

Green, Hardy. *On Strike at Hormel: The Struggle for a Democratic Labor Movement.* Philadelphia: Temple University Press, 1990.

Green, Susan. "Del Valle a Willmar: Settling Out of the Migrant Stream in a Rural Minnesota Community." Working Paper #19. East Lansing: Julián Samora Research Institute, Michigan State University, 1994.

Gregory, Ted. "Cruz Case Does Little to Debate on Death." *Chicago Tribune,* November 2, 1996.

Grey, Mark A. "Immigrant Students in the Heartland: Ethnic Relations in Garden City, Kansas, High School." *Urban Anthropology* 19 (Winter 1990): 409–427.

Griffin, Jean Latz, and Casey Banas. "Dropout Ills More Severe in Recount." *Chicago Tribune,* February 7, 1985.

Griffin, Jean Latz, and John Blake. "Race, Income Called Key to School Failure." *Chicago Tribune,* June 22, 1987.

Griffin, Jean Latz, and Manuel Galván. "City's Hispanics Strengthen Coalition with Blacks." *Chicago Tribune,* April 10, 1987.

"*El Grito* Parade." *Minneapolis Star Tribune,* August 28, 1993.

Gross, Andale. "Fiesta Gives KC a Chance to Learn Hispanic Culture." *Kansas City Star,* September 17, 1995.

Grove, Ben. "Illegal Immigrants Face INS Crackdown: Rights Groups Protest as Roundups Boost Pace across Region." *Chicago Tribune,* May 12, 1995.

Guerin-Gonzales, Camille. *Mexican Workers and American Dreams: Immigration, Repatriation, and California Farm Labor, 1900–1939.* New Brunswick: Rutgers University Press, 1994.

Gurda, John. "The Cohesiveness of the Latin Community on Milwaukee's Near South Side." Milwaukee, 1976. SHSW, ARHW.

Guthrie, Charles, Dan Briere, and Mary Moore, *The Indianapolis Hispanic Community.* Indianapolis: University of Indianapolis Press, 1995.

Hagerty, Thomas J. "140 Illegal Aliens Arrested in State." *Milwaukee Journal,* September 21, 1987.

Halpern, Rick. *Down on the Killing Floor: Black and White Workers in Chicago's Packinghouses, 1904–54.* Urbana and Chicago: University of Illinois Press, 1997.

Hammel, Paul. "Refiling of Charges Considered in Renteria Case." *Omaha World-Herald,* October 18, 1995.

Handlin, Oscar, ed. *Immigration as a Factor in American History.* Englewood Cliffs, N.J.: Prentice-Hall, 1959.

"Handling of Funds from Festivals Questioned." *Mexico,* November 23, 1929.

Haney, Jane B. "Migration, Settlement Pattern, and Social Organization: A Midwestern Case Study." Ph.D. dissertation, Michigan State University, 1978.

Harris, Nigel. *The New Untouchables: Immigration and the New World Worker.* London: I. B. Tauris, 1995.

Hartman, Holli. "Tortilla Maker Banks on Corn." *Des Moines Register,* December 6, 1993.

Hawes, Christine. "Hispanic Dropout Rate Still Edges Up, U.S. Report Says." *Chicago Tribune,* September 17, 1992.

Hawkins, Dana. "The Most Dangerous Jobs." *U.S. News and World Report* 121 (September 23, 1996): 40–41.

Hayner, Don. "Area's Ethnic Separation Fades: Intermarriage, Mexican Influx Blur the Boundaries." *Chicago Sun-Times,* June 7, 1992.

———. "Blacks, Latinos on an Economic Treadmill in '80's." *Chicago Sun-Times,* June 26, 1992.

Hedges, Stephen J., Dana Hawkins, and Penny Loeb. "The New Jungle." *U.S. News and World Report* 121 (September 23, 1996): 34–45.

Heinzman, Don. "Good-by Neighborhood House." *St. Paul Dispatch,* October 2, 1962.

Heise, Kenan, and Dan McCaughan. "Mayor's Legacy a New Direction for Chicago Politics." *Chicago Tribune,* November 26, 1987.

Helbig, Bob. "State Teaching Colleges Show Dearth of Minorities." UPI Regional News, April 22, 1990.

Henry, Shennon. "Minnesota Bank Gets 'Outstanding' Rating after Employees Lend a Hand." *American Banker,* October 21, 1993.

Herbers, John. "Hispanic Gains in Suburbs Found." *New York Times,* June 28, 1991.

Herlinger, Chris. "Area Hispanic Population Grows Rapidly." *Rochester Post-Bulletin,* April 12, 1991.

———. "Blooming Prairie Hispanic Center May Ease Prejudice." *Rochester Post-Bulletin,* February 16, 1988.

Hernández Alvarez, José. "A Demographic Profile of the Mexican Immigration to the United States, 1910–1950." *Journal of Inter-American Studies* 8 (July 1966): 471–496.

Hernández-Fujigaki, Jorge. "Mexican Steelworkers and the United Steelworkers of America in the Midwest: The Inland Steel Experience (1936–1976)." Ph.D. dissertation, University of Chicago, 1991.

Hessburg, L. J. "Tchoom! Nun Sparks Controversy, Admiration." *Minnesota Daily,* September 29, 1977.

Hill, George W. "Texas-Mexican Migratory Agricultural Workers in Wisconsin." Bull. No. 6. Madison: Wisconsin Agricultural Experiment Station, 1948.

Hill, Howard C. "The Americanization Movement." *American Journal of Sociology* 24 (May 1919): 609–642.

Hinojosa, Rolando. *Estampas del Valle y otras obras: Sketches of the Valley and Other Works.* Berkeley: Quinto Sol, 1973.

"Hispanic Students Blast UIC Policies." *Chicago Tribune,* April 30, 1992.

"Hispanics Melt, but Don't Rise to Top of the Pot." *Milwaukee Journal,* May 23, 1984.

Hlotke, Suzanne G. "El Protector Delivers His Message." *Chicago Tribune,* August 7, 1994.

———. "Elgin Latinos Say Their Civil Rights Are Victims of City's War on Gangs." *Chicago Tribune,* November 5, 1993.

Hoekstra, Dave. "A Taste of Lowrider Culture in Chicago." *Chicago Sun-Times,* May 28, 1993.

Hoerder, Dirk, ed. *Labor Migration in Atlantic Economies: The North European and North American Working Classes during the Period of Industrialization.* Westport, Conn.: Greenwood, 1985.

Hoffman, Dennis. "Is Patrol Making Race-Based Stops?" *Omaha World-Herald,* October 13, 1994.

Holman, Jeff. "More Chicano Students Sought." *Minnesota Daily,* November 17, 1970.

"Holy Trinity—Our Lady of Guadalupe—Milwaukee, Wisconsin." White Plains, N.Y.: Monarch Publishing, 1975.

Hopfensperger, Jean. "Children in Need: In Inner Cities and Outstate, Economic Hardships Come Early and Achingly for Many in Minnesota." *Minneapolis Star Tribune,* October 25, 1992.

———. "Week's Arrests by INS Highest in a Decade." *Minneapolis Star Tribune,* August 21, 1993.

"Hormel Prospers by Getting Into Processed Food Lines." *Los Angeles Times,* December 7, 1992.

Hornblower, Mark. "Putting Tongues in Cheek: Should Bilingual Schooling Be Silenced?" *Time,* October 9, 1995, 40.

Horne, Terry. "Hispanic Center Handles Changes." *Indianapolis News,* September 15, 1994.

Hornung, Mark. "Immigrants Drive Areas That Work." *Chicago Sun-Times,* December 29, 1993.

Horowitz, Ruth. *Honor and the American Dream: Culture and Identity in a Chicano Community.* New Brunswick: Rutgers University Press, 1983.

"Housing Suit Filed." *Newsday,* March 26, 1993.

Hoyt, Homer. *One Hundred Years of Land Values in Chicago.* Chicago: University of Chicago Press, 1933.

"HRA's Vista Village Completed in 1973." *St. Paul Metro Sun,* February 13, 1974.

Hughes, Elizabeth Ann. *Illinois Persons on Relief in 1935.* Chicago: WPA, 1937.

———. "Living Conditions of Small Wage-earners in Chicago." Chicago: Chicago Department of Welfare, 1925.

Humphrey, Norman Daymond. "The Changing Structure of the Detroit Mexican Family: An Index of Acculturation." *American Sociological Review* 9 (December 1944): 622–626.

———. "The Detroit Mexican Immigrant and Naturalization." *Social Forces* 22 (March 1944): 332–335.

———. "The Education and Language of Detroit Mexicans." *Journal of Educational Sociology* 17 (May 1944): 534–542.

———. "Employment Patterns of Mexicans in Detroit." *Monthly Labor Review* 68 (November 1945): 913–924.

———. "Ethnic Images and Stereotypes of Mexicans and Americans." *American Journal of Economics and Sociology* 14 (April 1955): 305–313.

———. "The Housing and Household Practices of Detroit Mexicans." *Social Forces* 24 (May 1946): 433–437.

———. "The Integration of the Detroit Mexican Colony." *American Journal of Economics and Sociology* 3 (January 1944): 155–166.

———. "The Mexican Peasant in Detroit." Ph.D. dissertation, University of Michigan, 1943.

———. "Mexican Repatriation from Michigan: Public Assistance in Historical Perspective." *Social Service Review* 15 (September 1941): 497–513.

———. "The Migration and Settlement of Detroit Mexicans." *Economic Geography* 19 (July 1943): 357–361.

———. "Some Marriage Problems of Detroit Mexicans." *Applied Anthropology* 3 (December 1943): 13–15.

———. "The Stereotype and Social Types of Mexican-American Youths." *Journal of Social Psychology* 22 (1945): 69–78.

"Illegal Aliens Cluster around Milwaukee." *Madison Capital Times,* January 23, 1979.

"Illegal Searches Used in Illinois." *New York Times,* September 9, 1994.

"Illegal Workers Follow Building-Boom Trail." *Engineering News-Record,*
    August 29, 1985.

Illinois. Legislative Council. Spanish Speaking Peoples Study Commission.
    *Report to the 78th General Assembly.* Springfield, 1972.

"Immigration Rights Protest." *Chicago Sun-Times,* June 3, 1995.

"Immigration." *National Journal* 24 (March 14, 1992): 648.

"Impudence of Policemen." *El Nacional,* January 7, 1931.

*In Re Camille.* 6F. 256, 257 (C.C.D. Or 1880).

International Institute. "The Mexican Nationality Community in St. Paul: A
    Study Made in February to May 1936." IHRC, II, Box 13, folder 200.
    (Cited as International Institute, "Mexican Nationality").

————, and Neighborhood House. "A Study of the Mexican Community in
    St. Paul." Released 1946. IHRC, II, Box 13, folder 201. (Cited as Interna-
    tional Institute, "A Study").

"'Invasion' Spreads, 'Wetbacks' Move into Industrial Midwest." *Washington
    Post,* July 16, 1951.

Jacobs-White, Kris. "West Side St. Paul: Mexican-Americans on the Flats."
    *Common Ground Magazine* 4 (June 1975): 70–74.

Jacobson, Anne. "Committee Considering Legal Action." *Albert Lea Tribune,*
    April 27, 1990.

Jacobson, Don. "Bull Sessions?" *Business Dateline* 23 (January 1992): 24.

Jacoby, Russel, and Naomi Glauberman. *The Bell Curve Debate: History,
    Documents, Opinions.* New York: Times Books, 1995.

James-Johnson, Alva. "Population Rise Sped Up." *Omaha World-Herald,*
    March 9, 1996.

Jane, Norman. "Iowa Ranked 4th in INS Crackdown." *Des Moines Register,*
    September 6, 1996.

Jasso, Paula, and Tejeda, Eddie. "The Chicano in the State of Kansas." Paper
    presented at the Midwest Conference of La Raza, April 1970, UND,
    MCM.

Jenkins, J. Craig, and Charles Perrow. "Insurgency of the Powerless: Farm
    Worker Movements (1946–1972)." *American Sociological Review* 42 (April
    1977): 249–267.

Johnson, Carrie. "Minorities: War Made Racism Harder to Swallow." *Omaha
    World-Herald,* September 6, 1995.

Johnson, Eric. "Latino Newcomers Are Changing Face of Iowa Towns." *Los
    Angeles Times,* May 27, 1993.

Johnson, Fred R. "Detroit Out of Work." *Survey* 46 (April 23, 1921): 106–107.

Jones, Anita. "Conditions Surrounding Mexicans in Chicago." M.A. thesis,
    University of Chicago, 1928. Reprint ed., San Francisco: R&E Research
    Associates, 1971.

————. "Mexican Colonies in Chicago." *Social Service Review* 2 (Decem-
    ber 1928): 579–597.

Jones, Robert C., and Wilson, Louis R. "The Mexican in Chicago, 1928–
    1931." *The New Home.* CFLPS, Reel 62.

"Just Trying to Fit In: They Feel Work Ethic Makes American Dream Reality." *Chicago Tribune,* July 31, 1996.

"Justice Finds Illegal Aliens Entitled to Protection of Federal Labor Law." *New York Times,* June 26, 1984.

Kallen, Horace M. "Democracy versus the Melting-Pot: A Study of American Nationality." *Nation* 100 (February 18 and 25, 1915): 190–194, 220.

Kanellos, Nicolás. "Fifty Years of Theater in the Latino Communities of Northwest Indiana." *Aztlán* 7 (Summer 1976): 255–265.

———. "Mexican Community Theater in a Midwestern City." *Latin American Theater Review* 7 (Fall 1973): 43–48.

"Kansas City Urged to Aid Mexican Colony." *Kansas City Journal-Post,* March 28, 1926.

Karlson, Nick, and Vernon Eidman. "Structural Changes in Meat Packing and Processing: The Pork Sector." Staff Paper P91-31. St. Paul: University of Minnesota, Department of Agricultural and Applied Economics, 1991.

Keller, Robert Andrew. "The Educational Aspirations and Achievements of Mexican-Americans in a Northern Community—A Historical-Descriptive Study." Ph.D. dissertation, Wayne State University, 1971.

Kelliher, Thomas G., Jr. "Mexican Catholics and Chicago's Parishes, 1955–1976." Cushwa Center for the Study of American Catholicism Working Papers Series 25, No. 2. Notre Dame, Ind.: Cushwa Center for the Study of American Catholicism, University of Notre Dame, 1993.

Kelly, Sean T. "La Clinica Serves Hispanic Community's Health Needs." *St. Paul Pioneer Press,* April 17, 1985.

———. "Festival to Link Hispanic Heritage, West Side Businesses." *St. Paul Pioneer Press,* April 10, 1985.

———. "Fresh Murals to Capture West Side's Heritage, Hope." *St. Paul Pioneer Press,* May 29, 1985.

Kelly, Suzanne P. "Hispanics: Outstate Families Suffer a Backlash." *Minneapolis Star Tribune,* July 24, 1992.

Kennedy, Tony. "Jennie-O to Invest in Turkey Plant." *Minneapolis Star Tribune,* May 26, 1994.

Kiernan, Louise. "Gangs Getting Younger, but No Less Deadly." *Chicago Tribune,* May 27, 1993.

Kilborn, Peter T. "Backlog of Cases Is Overwhelming Job-Bias Agency." *New York Times,* November 26, 1994.

———. "Coming to America: Hispanic Workers Run Highest Risk of Job Injury." *Houston Chronicle,* February 18, 1992.

Kirby, Joseph, with Melita Marie Garza. "Walls Become Canvas for Masterpieces." *Chicago Tribune,* September 16, 1992.

Kirchen, Rich. "Textile Union Seeks Representation at Three Local Kleen Test Plants." *Business Journal—Milwaukee,* April 2, 1990.

Kirschenman, Joleen, and Kathryn M. Neckerman, "'We'd Love to Hire Them, but . . .': The Meaning of Race for Employers." In Fred L. Pincus and Howard J. Ehrlich, eds., *Race and Ethnic Conflict: Contending Views on Prejudice, Discrimination, and Ethnoviolence*, pp. 115–123. Boulder: Westview Press, 1994.

Kirschten, Dick. "The Hispanic Vote—Parties Can't Gamble That the Sleeping Giant Won't Awaken." *National Journal*, November 19, 1983.

Kiser, George C., and David Silverman. "Mexican Repatriation during the Great Depression." *Journal of Mexican-American History* 3 (1973): 139–164.

Klauda, Paul. "Hispanic Community Adapts to Change." *Minneapolis Star Tribune*, March 28, 1987.

Knight, Robert M. "U.S. Charges Berwyn Realty Law Shuns Hispanics." *Chicago Sun-Times*, June 12, 1993.

Knorr, David. "Albert Serrano: At the Crossroads of Two Cultures." *Grand Rapids Business Journal*, October 10, 1988.

Kouri, Charles. "Near and Far: Close-in Pilsen Is a Journey to Another Land." *Chicago Tribune*, September 3, 1993.

Kozol, Jonathan. *Savage Inequalities: Children in America's Schools*. New York: Harper, 1991.

Krull, John. "They're Here to Stay." *Indianapolis Star*, July 12, 1996.

Kurtz, Donald V. "Chicano Student Activists: One Segment of Emerging Brown Power." Center for Latin America, University of Wisconsin–Milwaukee, 1973. SHSW, AMHW.

Kyle, Charles, and Kantowicz, Edward. "Kids First—Primero Los Niños: Chicago School Reform in the 1980's." Springfield: Illinois Issues, Sangamon State University, 1992.

La Raza Unida of Wisconsin. "Statistical Analysis on the Status of the Chicano on the University of Wisconsin System." Madison: La Raza Unida of Wisconsin, 1973.

"Labor Leaders Give An Interesting Conference." *La Defensa*, May 30, 1936.

Ladd, Scott. "Dodge City: Violence Thing of the Past." *Newsday*, August 2, 1990.

Laird, Judith Ann Fincher. "Argentine, Kansas: The Evolution of a Mexican American Community, 1905–1940." Ph.D. dissertation, University of Kansas, 1975.

Lamar, Rinaldi I. "The Identity of Mexican Americans in Argentine, Kansas City, Kansas." M.A. thesis, University of Kansas, 1985.

Lambert, Louisa. "Tank Town: Mexicans in Minnesota." *Hamline Piper* 15 (May 1935): 24–31.

Lamphere, Louise, Alex Stepick, and Guillermo Grenier, eds. *Newcomers in the Workplace: Immigrants and the Restructuring of the U.S. Economy*. Philadelphia: Temple University Press, 1994.

Lane, James B. "Extranjeros en la Patria: Mexican Immigrants." In James B. Lane and Edward J. Escobar, eds., *Forging a Community: The Latino Experience in Northwest Indiana, 1919–1975*, pp. 25–30. Chicago: Cattails Press, 1987.

Lane, Virginia. "Bias-Motivated Crime: A Summary of Minnesota's Response." St. Paul: Minnesota Board of Peace Officer Standards and Training, 1990.

Langland, Carl G. "Old Community Ties Lure Nearly Half of Displaced Families Back to West Side." *St. Paul Pioneer Press,* January 27, 1963.

Larson, Tom. "Leaving Migrant Life: Many Settle, Seek Jobs in Central Minnesota." *St. Cloud Times,* July 3, 1989.

"Latin American Union for Civil Rights." *IFCO News* 3 (November–December 1972): 10.

"Latin League Plans Dinner." *St. Paul Dispatch,* May 30, 1960.

"Latino Progress Slow in Chicago." *Chicago Tribune,* May 25, 1979.

Lazaruz, George. "Old El Paso Takes Pillsbury Back to the Border." *Chicago Tribune,* October 17, 1996.

Leininger, Julie. "Chicanos in South Bend: Some Historical Narratives." Notre Dame, Ind.: Centro de Estudios Chicanos e Investigaciones Sociales, Inc., 1976.

Leitman, Spencer. "Exile and Union in Indiana Harbor: Los Obreros Católicos 'San José' and *El Amigo del Hogar,* 1925–1930." *Revista Chicano Riqueña* 2 (invierno 1974): 50–57.

Lemke, Bill. "Chicanos Issue 72-hour Ultimatum." *Minnesota Daily,* October 27, 1971.

Lewis, Dorothy. "Battling Nun Wins Poverty Fund Fight but Still Needs Equipment." *St. Paul Dispatch,* May 13, 1966.

Librach, Phyllis Brash, and Susan K. Brown. "Success Story: County Hispanics among Wealthiest." *St. Louis Post-Dispatch,* March 21, 1993.

"Lobbyists Win 'Wetback' Fight." *International Teamster,* March 1952.

Long, Ray. "Dems, Edgar Clash on Hiring Practices: Watchdog Unit Formed; Bias Charges Fly." *Chicago Sun-Times,* July 31, 1993.

López y Rivas, Gilberto. *The Chicanos: Life and Struggles of the Mexican Minority in the United States.* New York: Monthly Review Press, 1973.

———. "Conquest and Resistance: The Origins of the Chicano National Minority." Palo Alto: R&E Research Associates, 1979.

Lorch, Donatella. "Hispanic Families Go All Out to Celebrate Girls' 15th Birthday." *Minneapolis Star-Tribune,* February 11, 1996.

"Love of Country Inspires Mexican Folk Dancers." *St. Paul Dispatch,* September 11, 1975.

Lucero-Trujillo, Marcela Christine. "The Dilemma of the Modern Chicana Artist and Critic." In Dexter Fisher, ed., *The Third Woman: Minority Women Writers of the United States,* pp. 324–332. Boston: Houghton Mifflin, 1980.

Lynd, Alice. *Rank and File: Personal Histories by Working-Class Organizers.* Boston: Beacon Press, 1974.

Macklin, Barbara June. "Americans of Mexican Descent: A Toledo Study." Toledo: Board of Community Relations, 1958.

————. *Structural Stability and Culture Change in a Mexican-American Community.* New York: Arno Press, 1976.

Macklin, June, and Alvina Teniente de Costilla. "La Virgen de Guadalupe and the American Dream: The Melting Pot Bubbles on in Toledo, Ohio." In Stanley A. West and June Macklin, eds., *The Chicano Experience,* pp. 111–143. Boulder: Westview Press, 1979.

Magida, Phyllis. "A Lineup of Cinco de Mayo Celebrations." *Chicago Tribune,* May 2, 1986.

Manning, Rick. "Group Says Bias Exists on Homeowners' Insurance." *Milwaukee Courier-Journal,* May 12, 1994.

Márquez, Benjamin. *LULAC: The Evolution of a Mexican American Political Organization.* Austin: University of Texas Press, 1993.

Martínez, Arthur D. "The Historical Development of the Mexican-American Community of Dodge City, Kansas." Presented at the Western Social Science Association Conference, Denver, Colorado, April 1982.

Martínez, Demetria. "Latina Benedictine Nun Made a Personal Option for the Poor." *National Catholic Reporter,* December 17, 1993.

Martínez, Elizabeth, and Ed McCaughan. "Chicanas and Mexicanas within a Transnational Working Class" in *Between Borders: Essays on Mexicana/Chicana History,* pp. 31–60, edited by Adelaida del Castillo. Encino, Calif.: Floricanto Press, 1990.

Martínez, Thomas M. "Chicanismo." Paper prepared for the Chicano Studies Institutes, Summer, 1970.

Marx, Gary. "Mexicans Have Pent-up Political Clout." *Chicago Tribune,* March 27, 1989.

Matthews, Tom. "Chicanos 'Hungry' for Recognition." *St. Paul Dispatch,* October 12, 1970.

————. "Migrants Battled Stereotypes." *St. Paul Dispatch,* October 14, 1970.

Matthiasson, Carolyn Weesner. "Acculturation of Mexican Americans in a Midwestern City." Ph.D. dissertation, Cornell University, 1968.

————. "Coping in A New Environment: Mexican Americans in Milwaukee, Wisconsin." *Urban Anthropology* 3 (Fall 1974): 262–277.

"May 5th 1862." *La Alianza,* May 1936.

"May First Labor Activities." *El Nacional,* April 29, 1933.

Mayer, Nancy. "U.S. Firms Losing Love for Mexico." *San Francisco Chronicle,* July 10, 1993.

McAuliffe, Bill. "Asians, Hispanics Moving to Rural Areas: Firms Attracting Them with Jobs, Social Programs." *Minneapolis Star Tribune,* December 12, 1990.

————. "Housing for Migrants Tough to Find in Blooming Prairie." *Minneapolis Star Tribune,* September 6, 1988.

————. "The Mayor of Migrants." *Minneapolis Star Tribune,* September 5, 1993.

———. "Migrants Settle In: Ex-Field Workers Buy Homes, Find Year-round Jobs." *St. Paul Pioneer Press,* November 26, 1989.

———. "Racism toward Hispanics Alleged in Albert Lea." *Minneapolis Star Tribune,* May 2, 1990.

McCall, Colonel George Archibald. *New Mexico in 1850: A Military View.* Edited by Robert W. Frazer. Norman: University of Oklahoma Press, 1968.

McConnell, Clarence E. "Poor Man's Paradise below Rio Grande Beckons Prodigals from Field and Factory." *Detroit Free Press,* November 13, 1932.

McCord, Julia. "Reaching Out to Hispanics: Language, Culture Differences Challenge Midlands Churches." *Omaha World-Herald,* September 10, 1994.

McCormick, Kenneth. "Migrant Workers Crowd Miserable Hovels in Beet Fields of Saginaw Area." *Detroit Free Press,* May 30, 1948.

McCulley, John. "The Spanish-speaking: North from the Rio Grande." *Reporter* 3 (December 26, 1950): 25–28.

McDonnell, Lynda. "Regents Act on Chicano Studies Department and Remaining New Budget." *Minnesota Daily,* February 14, 1972.

McDowell, John. "A Study of Social and Economic Factors Relating to Mexicans in the United States." New York: Home Missions Council, n.d. PHS.

McEnroe, Paul, and Sharon Schmickle, "For Consumers, It's Luck of the Draw." *Minneapolis Star Tribune,* August 8, 1993.

McKay, R. Reynolds. "The Federal Deportation Campaign in Texas: Mexican Deportation from the Lower Rio Grande during the Great Depression." *Borderlands Journal* 5 (Fall 1981): 95–120.

———. "Texas Mexican Repatriation during the Great Depression." Ph.D. dissertation, University of Oklahoma at Norman, 1982.

McLean, Robert N. "Hard Times Oust the Mexican." *Mexican Life* 7 (September 1931): 19–21.

———. "The Mexican Return." *Nation* 135 (August 24, 1932): 165–166.

———. *The Northern Mexican.* New York: Home Missions Council, 1930. Reprint ed. San Francisco: R&E Research Associates, 1971.

———. "Tightening the Mexican Border." *Survey* 64 (April 1, 1930): 28–29, 54–56.

McMorris, Robert. "Former Migrant Worker Sows Hope for Hispanics." *Omaha World-Herald,* September 10, 1994.

McMurry, Scott. "Little Village Hits Big." *Chicago Magazine* 44 (October 1994): 33.

McReynolds, Steve, "Area Poultry-Plant Jobs Attract 'Little Mexico.'" *Joplin Globe,* December 21, 1991.

McRoberts, Flynn. "Town Rejects Hate, Offers Hope." *Chicago Tribune,* October 24, 1992.

McWilliams, Carey. "The Mexican Problem." *Common Ground* 8 (Spring 1948): 3–17.

———. *North from Mexico: The Spanish-speaking People of the United States.* New York: Greenwood Press, 1968. Orig. Philadelphia: J. B. Lippincott, 1949.

"Meat Company Taking on Modern Image." *Marketing News,* January 4, 1993.

Meddis, Sam Vincent. "Suit Says Suspect 'Profiles' Are Racist." *USA Today,* September 1, 1994.

Memmi, Albert. *The Colonizer and the Colonized.* New York: Orion Press, 1965.

Mendoza, Manuel. "Schools Doom Young Hispanics, Study Says." *Milwaukee Journal,* December 20, 1990.

Mendoza, Valerie M. "They Came to Kansas Searching for a Better Life." *Kansas Quarterly* 25:2 (1994): 97–106.

Merrion, Paul. "Illinois' Hispanic Firms Register Robust Growth." *Crain's Chicago Business,* May 27, 1991.

Meryhew, Richard. "55 Illegal Immigrants Are Arrested in Minnesota." *Minneapolis Star Tribune,* April 16, 1993.

———. "Hispanics Find Bias, Hostility Outstate: State Task Force Offers Solution." *Minneapolis Star Tribune,* June 3, 1994.

———. "Moorhead Hispanics Face Specter of Racism." *Minneapolis Star Tribune,* April 4, 1993.

———. "One-way Ticket to Despair: Migrants Face Grinding Hardship in Madelia." *Minneapolis Star-Tribune,* October 1, 1992.

———. "A Pattern of Discrimination in Willmar?" *Minneapolis Star Tribune,* August 9, 1992.

———. "St. Paul's West Side Will Try to Tell Its Story." *St. Paul Pioneer Press,* May 4, 1985.

———. "State Human Rights Chief Says Moorhead Schools Are Hostile to Minorities." *Minneapolis Star Tribune,* September 3, 1993.

"Message from the Mexican Consul." *El Nacional,* May 14, 1932.

"Mexican Aliens Seized in Chicago to Be Returned." *Rocky Mountain News,* June 13, 1948.

"Mexican Boys Inducted." *St. Paul Dispatch,* January 1, 1943.

"Mexican Center Smooths Way in a Strange Land." *Chicago Tribune,* August 12, 1945.

"Mexican Course to Be First of Kind at University." *Minnesota Daily,* November 23, 1970.

"Mexican Cultural Center Planned." *St. Paul Pioneer Press,* November 4, 1971.

"Mexican Dance Will Help Some Student Go to U." *St. Paul Dispatch,* April 20, 1959.

"Mexican Family Insulted by Immigration Agents." *El Nacional,* August 13, 1932.
"Mexican Fiesta Pays Tribute to Homeland." *St. Paul Pioneer Press,* September 16, 1959.
"Mexican Film." *Mexico,* December 29, 1928.
"Mexican Journeys to Bethlehem." *Literary Digest* 77 (June 2, 1923): 103–104.
"Mexican Labor Colony at Bethlehem, Pa." *Monthly Labor Review* 33 (October 1931): 74–78.
"Mexican Laborers for Bethlehem Steel Company." *Literary Digest* 80 (June 2, 1923): 103.
"Mexican Migrants." *Survey* 73 (March 1937): 82–83.
"Mexican Population Here Reduced by 300." *Saginaw Daily News,* September 9, 1931.
"Mexican Radio Program." *El Nacional,* April 4, 1931.
"Mexican Workers Victimized in Deportation Swindle." *Michigan Worker,* November 20, 1932.
"The Mexican-American Community in St. Paul." *Minneapolis Tribune,* August 5, 1973.
"Mexicans Resent Yankee Slur." *Mexico,* March 11, 1930.
"Mexicans Seek School Funds." *Minneapolis Tribune,* December 12, 1948.
"Mexicans Stage Own Opera." *Chicago Daily News,* March 7, 1930.
"Mexico to Repatriate Thousands." *Los Angeles Times,* May 7, 1934.
"Michigan Hispanics Win Legal Challenge." *Chicago Tribune,* March 3, 1989.
"The Midwest: A State-by-State Look at Changes." *USA Today,* May 2, 1991.
Mier, Robert, Robert Giloth, and David Less. "Industrial Employment Opportunities and the Hispanic Community: The Case of Pilsen." Chicago: School of Social Sciences, University of Illinois at Chicago, 1979.
"The Migrant Tutorial Program." *La Voz,* June 1973.
Minnesota. Governor. Governor's Interracial Commission. *The Mexican in Minnesota.* St. Paul, 1948.
———. Human Rights Commission. Chicano/Latino Task Force. *Report on Discrimination.* St. Paul, 1994.
"Minutes of the Permanent Committee." *El Mexicano,* April 20, 1934.
Mirandé, Alfredo. *The Chicano Experience.* Notre Dame, Ind.: University of Notre Dame Press, 1985.
Montana, Constanza. "For Hispanic Newspapers, Battle for Credibility." *Chicago Tribune,* October 2, 1989.
———. "Staying in Tune with Hispanics." *Chicago Tribune,* July 17, 1989.
Montana, Constanza, and Patrick Reardon. "Mexicans Are Expected to Gain." *Chicago Tribune,* June 9, 1991.
Montt, Lucia. "US More Tolerant of Racism, Civil Rights Leaders Say." *Christian Science Monitor,* September 26, 1989.
"More Hispanics Call N.C. Home." *Asheville Citizen-Times,* April 24, 1995.

"More Mexicans Attacked." *El Nacional,* May 20, 1931.

Moylan, Martin J. "Housing Project Revival." *New York Times,* April 23, 1989.

Mullins, Robert. "Where Radio's Rally in Touch with Local Listeners." *Business Journal—Milwaukee,* April 9, 1994.

Muñoz, Carlos, Jr. *Youth, Identity, Power: The Chicano Movement.* New York: Verso, 1989.

Musser, R. S. "Foreign Aid: Despite Some Business People's Concerns, Kansas City's Latest Wave of Immigrants Gives More Than It Takes from Local Economy." *Ingram's* 19 (February 1993): 36.

Myrdal, Gunnar. *An American Dilemma.* New York: Pantheon, 1962. (Orig. 1944).

Nadler, Richard, and Tom Donelson. "Affirmative Reaction: Problems with School Desegregation in Kansas." *National Review,* September 15, 1989.

Nancrede, Sally Falk. "A Hot Time Promised at Mexican Fest." *Indianapolis Star,* March 3, 1995.

Nash, J. Madeline. "The Milwaukee Federation of Independent Community Schools." In Don Davies, ed., *Schools Where Parents Make a Difference,* p. 117. Boston: Institute for Responsive Education, 1976.

"A Nasty Turn on Immigrants." *Newsweek,* August 23, 1993, 28.

"Nebraska Village Bars Mexicans from Residential Areas." *Chicago Tribune,* November 26, 1941.

Nelson, Raymond E. "The Mexican in South Chicago." BL, PT, carton 1, folder: Mexican in South Chicago.

"New School to Annex Mexican-American Cultural Center." *St. Paul Dispatch,* May 30, 1974.

"New York Mexican Community Registers Big Growth." *Notimex,* September 7, 1992.

Nicely, Steve. "KCK Parents Embrace Plan to End Busing." *Kansas City Star,* December 15, 1995.

Nifong, Christina. "Hispanics and Asians Change the Face of American South." *Christian Science Monitor,* August 6, 1996.

Nissen, Todd. "Creating One of the Nation's Largest Contract Packagers." *Corporate Report Minnesota* 25 (January 1994): 23–24.

Nordahl, Pers. *Weaving the Ethnic Fabric: Social Networks among Swedish-American Radicals in Chicago, 1890–1940.* Stockholm: Almquist & Wiksell, 1994.

Nostrand, Richard L. *The Hispano Homeland.* Norman: University of Oklahoma Press, 1992.

Novak, Tim. "Few Minorities Get Piece of State Jobs Pie in Illinois." *St. Louis Post-Dispatch,* April 5, 1994.

———. "Minority Hiring Lags in Illinois: Jobs at State Agencies Don't Reflect the Law." *St. Louis Post-Dispatch,* April 19, 1993.

"Number of Hispanic Students Increasing." *Fargo-Moorhead Forum,* May 21, 1989.

Obejas, Achy. "Theater Troupes Taking Their Place on Center Stage." *Chicago Tribune,* September 16, 1992.

Oclander, Jorge."Latinos Face Up to High DUI Rate." *Chicago Sun-Times,* August 8, 1994.

———. "Mexicans Here Seek Bigger Role in Schools." *Chicago Sun-Times,* October 11, 1994.

Oclander, Jorge, and Brian Jackson. "Latinos Protest Immigration Raids: Rising Fear of Deportations Sparks Father's Day March." *Chicago Sun-Times,* June 19, 1995.

Ogbu, John U. *Minority Status and Schooling: A Comparative Study of Immigrant and Involuntary Minorities.* New York: Garland, 1991.

Ojanpa, Brian. "Madelia's 'Fairy Tale' Has a Nightmarish Tinge." *Mankato Free Press,* November 24, 1990.

Ojeda-Zapata, Julio. "Hispanic Community Gains Greater Diversity with Recent Arrivals." *St. Paul Pioneer Press,* March 3, 1991.

———. "Minnesota Law Ends Undocumented Workers' Aid." *St. Paul Pioneer Press,* October 1, 1993.

———. "Oslo: Former Migrant Workers Merge into Lifestyle of Small, Rural Town." *St. Paul Pioneer Press,* April 7, 1991.

Olen, Helaine. "Joliet Group Plans Probe of Brutality." *Chicago Tribune,* January 6, 1992.

"Olivia: Rights Agency Studying Complaints That Motel Discriminates against Hispanics." *Minneapolis Star Tribune,* August 11, 1988.

Olsson, Lars. "Labor Migration as a Prelude to World War I." *International Migration Review* 30 (Winter 1996): 875–900.

Olvera, Joe. "What Is Reverse Discrimination?" *El Paso Times,* August 6, 1992.

O'Neill, John R. "Local Hotels Recruit Entry-level Employees." *Indianapolis Star,* January 14, 1996.

"Only Mexican School Opens with 70 Pupils." *St. Paul Dispatch,* September 12, 1961.

"Open Grants to Mexicans Who Return to Homeland." *Mexico,* March 29, 1930.

Oppenheimer, Reuben. "The Deportation Terror." *New Republic* 69 (January 13, 1932): 231–234.

Oppenheimer, Robert. "Acculturation or Assimilation: Mexican Immigrants in Kansas, 1900 to World War II." *Western Historical Quarterly* 16 (October 1985): 429–448.

Orfield, Gary, with the assistance of Sara Schley, Diane Glass, and Sean Reardon. "The Growth of Segregation in American Schools: Changing

Patterns of Separation and Poverty since 1968." Alexandria, Va.: National School Boards Association, 1993.

Ortiz, Lou. "Big Times for Little Village: Mexican Americans Take Pride in Robust Economy." *Chicago Sun-Times,* May 2, 1994.

"Our Dead." *La Defensa,* June 27, 1936.

"Our Educational Work." *La Alianza,* April, 1936.

"Our Lady of Guadalupe Lays Corner Stone." *Minneapolis Star,* October 4, 1960.

Pabst, Georgia. "Illegal Aliens Answer Call of Good Life." *Milwaukee Journal,* January 22, 1978.

Padilla, Félix. *Latino Ethnic Consciousness: The Case of Mexican Americans and Puerto Ricans in Chicago.* Notre Dame, Ind.: University of Notre Dame Press, 1985.

Padilla, Steve, and Angela Gentile. "Survey Finds 20 Hispanic State Commissions." *La Voz del Llano,* April 1985, 2.

Page, Clarence. "Hispanics Share 'American' Values." *Chicago Tribune,* September 1, 1991.

Page, Robert. "Federal Agents to Disregard Aliens during Harvest." UPI Regional News, June 22, 1983.

Palmer, Susan L. "Building Ethnic Communities in a Small City: Romanians and Mexicans in Aurora, Illinois." Ph.D. dissertation, Northern Illinois University, 1986.

Papajohn, George. "Nicarico Case Leaves Aurora Hispanics in Turmoil." *Chicago Tribune,* December 31, 1985.

Parra, Ricardo, Víctor Ríos, and Armando Gutíerrez. "Chicano Organizations in the Midwest: Past, Present and Possibilities." *Aztlán* 7 (Summer 1976): 235–253.

Payne, Doug. "Southside International." *Atlanta Journal and Constitution,* August 24, 1995.

Paz, Frank X. "Mexican-Americans in Chicago: A General Survey." Chicago: Council of Social Agencies, 1948.

———. "Status of the Mexican American in Chicago." In Report of the Conference on the Mexican American in Chicago, pp. 6–12. Chicago: Community Relations Service, 1949.

Pearson, Rick. "Colleges Getting Few Minorities." *Chicago Tribune,* November 29, 1990.

"People Do Care in Co-op Community." *St. Paul Pioneer Press,* December 26, 1971.

Pérez, Daniel. "The Teatros: More Polish, Less Politics." *Los Angeles Times,* February 2, 1986.

Pérez, Hilary, "M.E.Ch. A. Ends Nine Day Hunger Strike with Signed Agreement." *La Prensa de Minnesota,* May 18, 1995.

Perry, Gail. "State's Hispanic Children Suffering." *Madison Capital Times,* September 3, 1992.

Perry, Suzanne. "Chicano Studies Combine Education, Service." *Minnesota Daily,* September 27, 1972.

———. "St. Paul's Lower West Side." M.A. thesis, University of Minnesota, 1971.

Pierce, Neal R. "Immigrants No Longer Welcome." *Cleveland Plain Dealer,* May 23, 1993.

Pinney, Gregory W. "Study: College Is Slim Chance for Minority 9th-graders." *Minneapolis Star Tribune,* April 26, 1994.

Poe, Juanita. "Hispanic Artists Flourish in Pilsen Galleries." *Chicago Tribune,* December 16, 1992.

Polta, Anne. "Housing Shortage Probed." *West Central Tribune,* August 17, 1991.

Portes, Alejandro, and Rubén Rumbaut. *Immigrant America: A Portrait.* Berkeley, Los Angeles, and Oxford: University of California Press, 1990.

Portes, Alejandro, and Sassen-Koob, Saskia. "Making It Underground: Comparative Material on the Informal Sector in Western Market Economies." *American Journal of Sociology* 93 (July 1987): 30–61.

Possley, Maurice. "The Nicarico Nightmare: Admitted Lie Sinks Cruz Case." *Chicago Tribune,* November 5, 1995.

Potts, Lydia. *The World Labor Market: A History of Migration.* Translated by Terry Bond. London: Zed Publishers, 1990.

Pridmore, Jay. "Pilsen Mirrors the Art in 'The Other Mexico' Exhibit." *Chicago Tribune,* August 13, 1993.

Puente, María. "Immigration 'Issue of the 90s.'" *USA Today,* September 30, 1993.

Puente, Teresa. "Mexican-Americans Stake Claim on Past: Families Trace Midwest Roots to before Turn of Century." *Chicago Tribune,* September 22, 1995.

Purnell, Florestine. "Racial Incidents 'Happen All the Time.'" *USA Today,* December 4, 1990.

Quintinilla, Ray. "Program Builds Pilsen: Home Dream Is Fulfilled." *Chicago Tribune,* June 13, 1994.

Rachleff, Peter. *Hard Pressed in the Heartland: The Hormel Strike and the Future of the the Labor Movement.* Boston: South End Press, 1993.

Ramírez, Socorro M. "A Survey of the Mexicans in Emporia, Kansas." M.A. thesis, Wichita State University, 1950.

Ramírez Luna, David. "Gunpoint Arrest." *La Voz,* June 1972.

Reardon, Patrick T. "Communities Defy Racial Patterns of City." *Chicago Tribune,* September 16, 1992.

———. "Search for Better Life Brought Different Waves of Immigrants." *Chicago Tribune,* September 11, 1991.

Reardon, Patrick T., and Laurie Goering. "Hispanic Groups Charging Census Efforts Have Fizzled." *Chicago Tribune*, September 14, 1990.

Reardon, Patrick T., and Constanza Montana. "Hispanic Presence Booms in Suburbs." *Chicago Tribune*, March 18, 1991.

*Regents of the University of California v. Bakke*, 438 U.S. 265 (1978).

Reisler, Mark. "The Mexican Immigrant in the Chicago Area during the 1920's." *Journal of the Illinois State Historical Society* 66 (Summer 1973): 144–158.

———. *By the Sweat of Their Brow: Mexican Immigrant Labor in the United States, 1900–1940*. Westport, Conn.: Greenwood Press, 1976.

"Relief Efforts on Behalf of Needy Mexicans." *El Nacional*, December 17, 1930.

"A Repatriation Program." *La Defensa*, January 18, 1936.

"Return of Mexicans to Homeland." *El Nacional*, May 28, 1932.

Richardson, Lynda. "This Road to New Rochelle Begins in the Hills of Mexico." *New York Times*, July 7, 1992.

Ring, Wilson. "Migrant Workers in McHenry Fighting the Odds to Be Paid." *Chicago Tribune*, July 25, 1992.

"Rising Flood Waters Halt Auto, Rail Traffic." *St. Paul Dispatch*, April 14, 1952.

Rodríguez, Alex. "For Cruz, 'Nightmare' Is Over." *Chicago Sun-Times*, November 5, 1995.

———. "Suburb Hispanics Skip Politics." *Chicago Sun-Times*, June 19, 1994.

Rodríguez, Navor. "Sintesis historica de la colonia Mexicana de Joliet, Ill., U.S.A." *Perspectives in Mexican American Studies* 2 (1989): 149–179.

Rodriguez, Richard. *Hunger of Memory: The Education of Richard Rodriguez*. Toronto: Bantam Books, 1982.

Rodríguez, Roberto, and Patrisia Gonzales. "Man's Crime of Appearing Hispanic Fatal." *Fresno Bee*, November 9, 1994.

Roediger, David E. *The Wages of Whiteness: Race and the Making of the American Working Class*. London: Verso, 1991.

Rogers, Sister Mary Helen. "The Role of Our Lady of Guadalupe Parish in the Adjustment of the Mexican Community to Life in the Indiana Harbor Area." M.A. thesis, Loyola University of Chicago, 1952.

———. "The Role of Our Lady of Guadalupe Parish in the Adjustment of the Mexican Community to Life in the Indiana Harbor Area, 1940–1951." In James B. Lane and Edward J. Escobar, eds., *Forging a Community: The Latino Experience in Northwest Indiana, 1919–1975*, pp. 187–200. Chicago: Cattails Press, 1987.

Rojo, Emilia Angela. "Between Two Conflicting Cultures: A Phenomenological-Participatory Investigation of the Enduring Struggle of a Mexican-American Community." Ph.D. dissertation, University of Michigan, 1980.

Romo, Ricardo. *East Los Angeles: History of a Barrio.* Austin: University of Texas Press, 1983.

Roosevelt, Eleanor. "'My Day' in Kansas City." *Kansas City Star,* November 6, 1939.

Ropka, Gerald, Ruth Ramírez, and Pierre de Vise. "The Spanish-Speaking Peoples of Chicago." Working paper study vol. 9, Chicago Regional Hospital, 1973. CPL, MRC.

Rosales, Francisco Arturo. "Mexican Immigration to the Urban Midwest during the 1920s." Ph.D. dissertation, Indiana University, 1978.

———. "Mexicanos in Indiana Harbor during the 1920's: Prosperity and Depression." *Revista Chicano-Riqueña* 4 (otoño 1976): 88–98.

———. "Mexicans, Interethnic Violence, and Crime in the Chicago Area during the 1920s and 1930s: The Struggle to Achieve Ethnic Consciousness." *Perspectives in Mexican American Studies* 2 (1989): 59–97.

———. "The Regional Origins of Mexicano Immigrants to Chicago during the 1920s." *Aztlán* 7 (Summer 1976): 187–201.

Rosales, Francisco Arturo, and Daniel T. Simon. "Chicano Steelworkers and Unionism in the Midwest, 1919–1941." *Aztlán* 6 (Summer 1975): 267–275.

———. "Mexican Immigrant Experience in the Urban Midwest: East Chicago, Indiana, 1919–1945." *Indiana Magazine of History* 72 (December 1981): 333–357.

Rowland, Debra. "Jobs Lure Hispanics to DuPage." *Chicago Tribune,* June 30, 1991.

Ruiz, Vicky. *Cannery Women, Cannery Lives: Mexican Women, Unionization and the California Food Processing Industry, 1930–1950.* Albuquerque: University of New Mexico Press, 1987.

Russell, Falsum. "Relocation Aid for Riverview Homes Pushed." *St. Paul Pioneer Press,* November 16, 1961.

Rutter, Larry G. "Mexican Americans in Kansas: A Survey and Social Mobility Study, 1900–1970." M.A. thesis, Kansas State University, 1972.

Ryan, Oswald, "Who Shall Inherit the United States?" *Michigan Educational Journal* 5 (October 1928): 291.

Rybin, Virginia. "Agreements Could End Trejo Case." *St. Paul Pioneer Press,* March 26, 1986.

Rynearson, Ann. "Hiding within the Melting Pot: Mexican Americans in St. Louis." Ph.D. dissertation, Washington University, 1980.

"S. M. Carmen and Her Court of Honor." *Mexico,* September 15, 1928.

Said, Edward W. *Culture and Imperialism.* New York: Alfred A. Knopf, 1993. Vintage Books Edition, 1994.

St. John de Crèvecoeur, J. Hector. *Letters from an American Farmer and Sketches of 18th-Century America.* Edited with an introduction by Albert E. Stone. New York: Penguin Books, 1981.

Salas, Gumecindo, and Salas, Isabel. "The Mexican Community of Detroit." In *La Causa Chicana*, pp. 161–178. New York: Family Service Association of America, 1972.

Salas, Isabel. "The Impact of Chicano-Boricua Studies on Cultural Identity." In National Association for Chicano Studies, ed., *The Chicano Struggle: Analysis of Past and Present Efforts*, pp. 131–147. Binghamton, N.Y.: Bilingual Press, 1984.

Salas, Jesús. "Reflections on Urban Life." In Richard Wisniewski, ed., *Teaching about Life in the City*, pp. 61–73. Washington, D.C.: National Council for the Social Studies, 1972.

Salazar, Rubén. "What Is a Chicano?" *Los Angeles Times*, February 1, 1969.

"Salazar Lawyers File Extradition Appeal." *Chicago Tribune*, March 9, 1996.

Salopek, Paul. "Illegal Immigrants at Hope." *Chicago Tribune*, May 19, 1996.

Samora, Julián, and Richard A. Lamanna. "Mexican-Americans in a Midwest Metropolis: A Study of East Chicago." In James B. Lane and Edward J. Escobar, eds., *Forging a Community: The Latino Experience in Northwest Indiana, 1919–1975*, pp. 215–250. Chicago: Cattails Press, 1987. (Orig. Los Angeles: Graduate School of Business, University of California, 1967.)

San Miguel, Guadalupe, Jr. *"Let All of Them Take Heed": Mexican Americans and the Campaign for Educational Equality in Texas, 1910–1981*. Austin: University of Texas Press, 1987.

Sánchez, David. *Expedition through Aztlán*. La Puente, California: Perspectiva Publications, 1978.

Sánchez, George. *Becoming Mexican American: Ethnicity, Culture and Identity in Chicano Los Angeles, 1900–1945*. New York and Oxford: Oxford University Press, 1993.

———. "'Go After the Women': Americanization and the Mexican Immigrant Woman, 1915–1929." In Ellen Carol DuBois and Vicki L. Ruiz, eds., *Unequal Sisters: A Multicultural Reader in Women's History*, pp. 250–263. New York: Routledge, 1990.

Sánchez, Marcela. "'La calle veinte' Is Hispanic EGF Area." *Grand Forks Herald*, June 8, 1992.

Sánchez, Mary. "Anti-immigrant Rhetoric Stirs Many to Become Citizens, Vote." *Kansas City Star*, March 17, 1996.

Sánchez, Rosaura. "The History of Chicanas: Proposal for a Materialist Perspective." In Adelaida R. del Castillo, ed., *Between Borders: Essays on Mexicana/Chicana History*, pp. 1–29. Encino, Calif.: Floricanto Press, 1990.

———. *Telling Identities: The Californio Testimonios*. Minneapolis: University of Minnesota Press, 1995.

Sandin, Jo. "Immigration Questioning Argued." *Milwaukee Journal*, January 28, 1971.

Santana, Rosa María. "A Melting Influence: Sales Areas Shrinking for Paleteros as City Hits Ice Cream Vendors." *Chicago Tribune*, July 19, 1994.

Santiago, Anne M. "Life in the Industrial Heartland: A Profile of Latinos in the Midwest." Research Report #2. East Lansing: Julián Samora Research Institute, Michigan State University, 1990.

Santillán, Richard. "Midwestern Mexican American Women and the Struggle for Gender Equality: A Historical Overview, 1920's–1960's." *Perspectives in Mexican American Studies* 5 (1995): 79–119.

———. "Rosita the Riveter: Midwest Mexican American Women during World War II, 1941–1945." *Perspectives in Mexican American Studies* 2 (1989): 115–147.

Santos, Richard. "Hispanic Workers in the Midwest: A Decade of Economic Contrast 1970–1980." Working Paper #2. East Lansing: Julián Samora Research Institute, Michigan State University, 1989.

Sassen-Koob, Saskia. *The Global City: New York, London, Tokyo*. Princeton, N.J.: Princeton University Press, 1991.

———. "Immigrant and Minority Workers in the Organization of the Labor Process." *Journal of Ethnic Studies* 8 (Spring 1980): 1–34.

———. *The Mobility of Labor and Capital: A Study in International Investment and Labor Flow*. Cambridge: Cambridge University Press, 1988.

Satchell, Michael. "Tide of Aliens Flows on Unseen." *Milwaukee Journal*, December 15, 1974.

Saunders, Mary Jane. "U Chicanos Plan Demonstration." *St. Paul Dispatch*, July 8, 1976.

"A Scene of Tragedy." *El Nacional*, May 14, 1932.

Schrieke, Bertram. *Alien Americans: A Study of Race Relations*. New York: Viking Press, 1936.

"Senate Committee Hears Allegations of Redlining." *Federal & State Insurance Week*, May 16, 1994.

"Sentiment Sours as Rate of Arrival Rises." *USA Today*, July 14, 1993.

Sepúlveda, Ciro. "La Colonia del Harbor: A History of Mexicanos in East Chicago, Indiana, 1919–1932." Ph.D. dissertation, University of Notre Dame, 1976.

Sepúlveda, Ciro Haroldo. "The Origins of the Urban Colonias in the Midwest 1910–1930." *Revista Chicano-Riqueña* 4 (otoño 1976): 99–109.

———. "Research Note: Una Colonia de Obreros: East Chicago, Indiana." *Aztlán* 7 (Summer 1976): 327–336.

Servín, Manuel, ed. *The Awakened Minority: The Mexican Americans*. Beverly Hills: Glencoe Press, 1974.

Shannon, Lyle, and Judith L. McKim. "Attitudes toward Education and the Absorption of Immigrant Mexican-Americans and Negroes in Racine." *Education and Urban Society* 6 (May 1974): 333–354.

Sheppard, Nathaniel, Jr. "Hispanic Vote Seen as a Key in Chicago Mayoral Race." *New York Times,* April 11, 1983.

Shnay, Jerry. "Accused Cop Killer Set for Retrial after Civil Suit's Dismissed." *Chicago Tribune,* February 10, 1996.

———. "Extradition Issue Fails for Salazar." *Chicago Tribune,* September 25, 1996.

———. "Salazar: 'I Thought He Was Going to Shoot Me.'" *Chicago Tribune,* October 26, 1996.

———. "Salazar Witness Called Off: Judge Won't Allow Expert's Testimony." *Chicago Tribune,* October 30, 1996.

Shutt, Edwin Dale II. "'Silver City,' a History of the Argentine Community of Kansas City, Kansas." M.A. thesis, Emporia State College, 1976.

Sickels, Alice L. *Around the World in St. Paul.* Minneapolis: University of Minnesota Press, 1945.

———. "The International Institute in the Field of Folk Arts." Paper presented at the National Conference of International Institutes, Grand Rapids, Michigan, May 25, 1940.

"Signs of Life in the Neighborhoods." *Chicago Tribune,* June 19, 1994.

Silverman, David. "Mexican Fest Getting Feisty." *Chicago Tribune,* July 27, 1993.

Silverman, Robin. "Doing the Right Thing: Entrepreneur and Civil Rights Activist Ana Rioja Speaks Out against Injustice." *Ingram's* 18 (November 1992), 40.

Simbro, William. "Hispanic Leader Kept Battling On." *Des Moines Register,* February 27, 1997.

Simmons, Donald H., ed. "Centennial History of Argentine: Kansas City, Kansas, 1880–1980." Kansas City, Kans.: Simmons Funeral Home, 1980.

Simon, Daniel T. "Mexican Repatriation in East Chicago, Indiana." *Journal of Ethnic Studies* 2 (Summer 1974): 11–23.

Skendzel, Eduard Adam. *Detroit's Pioneer Mexicans: A Historical Study of the Mexican Colony in Detroit.* Grand Rapids: Littleshield Press, 1980.

"Skinhead Activism on Rise, Report Says." UPI Regional News, July 13, 1993.

Slavín Ruiz, Leon, and Alberto Moreau. *Los latino-americanos en los Estados Unidos: La situación de los trabajadores en Norte America.* New York: Vida Obrera, 1929.

Slesinger, Doris P., Pilar A. Parra, and Nancy J. Kanaskie. "Hispanics in Wisconsin, 1980." *Population Notes* 18 (September 1986): 29–57.

———. "20,000 Mexicans Find Michigan Home." *Detroit News,* August 1, 1926.

Smith, Maureen M. "Report Suggests How Schools Can Close Learning Gap." *Minneapolis Star Tribune,* May 10, 1994.

Smith, Michael M. "Beyond the Borderlands: Mexican Labor in the Central Plains, 1900–1930." *Great Plains Quarterly* 1 (Fall 1981): 239–251.

———. "Mexicans in Kansas City: The First Generation, 1900–1920." *Perspectives in Mexican American Studies* 2 (1989): 29–57.

———. *The Mexicans in Oklahoma.* Norman: University of Oklahoma Press, 1980.

Smith, Robert C. "Mexicans in New York: Membership and Incorporation in a New Immigrant Community." In Gabriel Haslip-Viera and Sherrie L. Baver, eds., *Latinos in New York: Communities in Transition,* pp. 57–103. Notre Dame, Ind.: University of Notre Dame Press, 1996.

Sontag, Deborah. "New Immigrants Test Nation's Heartland." *New York Times,* October 10, 1993.

Sorrell, Victor A., and Rogovin, Mark. *The Barrio Murals: Murales del Barrio.* Chicago: Mexican Fine Arts Center, 1987.

Sosa, Norma, and Donald M. Schwartz, "Hispanics Call Alien Raids Racist." *Chicago Sun-Times,* April 28, 1982.

"Spanish American Radio Hour." *Mexico,* May 10, 1930.

Spielberg Benítez, Joseph. "A Brief Review of the Background and History of Hispanic Peoples in Grand Rapids." Presented to Hispanic Forum, Grand Rapids Junior College, March 1, 1978.

Spielman, Fran. "Fire, Police Exams Leave Racial Divide." *Chicago Sun-Times,* January 27, 1996.

Spoor, May J. "Work with the Mexican Groups." *Proceedings of the National Conference of Catholic Charities* 11 (1925): 213–221.

"St. Paul Is City of Charity Welfare Officials Declare." *St. Paul Pioneer Press,* December 19, 1926.

Stanton, Sam. "Town Whites Blind to Racism." *Sacramento Bee,* July 26, 1993.

Stapp, James A. "Down Where the Melting Pot Boils: Omaha Shelters a Large Colony of Mexicans Who Came Here Seeking Opportunity." *Omaha Bee-News,* March 18, 1928.

Starr, Mark, et al. "Target: Illegal Aliens." *Newsweek,* May 10, 1982, 45.

Steller, Tim. "Hispanic Worship: Cities Spanish Speakers Seek Protestant Churches." *Minneapolis Star Tribune,* June 6, 1993.

"Stereotypes Decried on Illegal Immigrants." *Milwaukee Sentinel,* December 2, 1978.

Stockwell, Jean. "Workers Walk Out at Heartland." *Marshall Independent,* May 8, 1993.

Stoddard, Lothrop. *Re-Forging America: The Story of Our Nationhood.* New York and London: Charles Scribner's Sons, 1927.

Strahler, Steven R. "Alinsky Activists Look Homeward." *Crain's Chicago Business,* February 20, 1995.

Street, Paul. "The Logic and Limits of 'Plant Loyalty': Black Workers, White Labor, and Corporate Racial Paternalism in Chicago's Stockyards." *Journal of Social History* 29 (March 1996): 659–681.

Strikwerda, Carl, and Camille Guerín-Gonzales, eds. *The Politics of Immigrant Workers: Labor Activism and Migration in the World Economy since 1830.* New York: Holmes and Meier, 1993.

"Study Says Great Lakes Schools Are Segregated." *AsianWeek,* October 23, 1992.

Stych, Ed. "A Meaty Job: Hormel Is Still Spam—and a Lot More." *Providence Journal-Bulletin,* December 8, 1992.

"Suits: Suburbs Weeding Out Minorities." *Dubuque Telegraph Herald,* August 29, 1996.

Sullenger, T. Earl. "Ethnic Assimilation in Omaha." *Sociology and Social Research* 19 (July–August 1935): 545–554.

———. "The Mexican Population of Omaha." *Journal of Applied Sociology* 8 (May–June 1924): 289–293.

Sulski, Jim. "Mature Neighbors Now Becoming Fountains of Youth: New Influx of Families Boosts Berwyn, Cicero." *Chicago Tribune,* March 30, 1994.

Sunderman, Gloria. "Hispanics Say System Didn't Work." *Omaha World-Herald,* June 21, 1995.

*Sure Tan v. National Labor Relations Board.* 467 U.S. 883 (1984).

Suzukamo, Lee. "Project Alleged to Exploit Migrants." *St. Paul Pioneer Press,* June 22, 1988.

———. "Rights Head Says Hispanic's Rights Violated." *St. Paul Pioneer Press,* December 9, 1988.

———. "Welfare Pressure Charged on Migrants." *St. Paul Pioneer Press,* December 30, 1987.

Sweet, Lynn. "Illinois Schools among Most Segregated in U.S." *Chicago Sun-Times,* December 14, 1993.

Swenson, Russell. "Some Characteristics of the Spanish-Speaking Community of Waukesha, Wisconsin." Milwaukee, 1974. SHSA, ARHW.

Swiatek, Jeff. "Bringing Home the Bacon." *Indianapolis Star,* June 25, 1995.

Tai, Wendy S. "5 Per Cent in State Speak Other Languages at Home." *Minneapolis Star Tribune,* August 30, 1992.

———. "Good Neighbor: Program Gives Emergency Aid to Hispanic Immigrants." *Minneapolis Star Tribune,* September 9, 1993.

———. "'Illegals' Soon Will Lose Aid." *Minneapolis Star Tribune,* August 15, 1993.

———. "Immigrant Entrepreneurs Prove a Strong Force in Urban Renewal." *Minneapolis Star Tribune,* September 19, 1994.

———. "Immigration Troubles Rising: Arrests in Minnesota Double Over Year." *Minneapolis Star Tribune,* September 21, 1993.

———. "Minnesota's Hispanic Rainbow: Spanish-Speaking Population Grows in Numbers, Diversity." *Minneapolis Star Tribune,* November 6, 1992.

————. "More Give Than Take: Study Finds Immigrants Get Little Return on Their Taxes." *Minneapolis Star Tribune,* June 9, 1992.

Takaki, Ronald. *Strangers from a Different Shore: A History of Asian Americans.* New York: Penguin, 1989.

Tan, Cheryl L. "St. Agnes Offers West Side Kids Lessons for Life." *Chicago Tribune,* July 16, 1995.

Tannenbaum, Fred. "Sensitivity Training for Officers to Help Fight Racism in Waukegan." *Chicago Tribune,* December 22, 1993.

Tapia, María. "Socio-Economic Profile of the Spanish Speaking in Lake County, Indiana." APRISA, 1973. UND, GC.

Taylor, John. "Union Sets Sights on IBP: Fremont Local 22 Targets Lexington." *Omaha World Herald,* May 30, 1996.

Taylor, Kimberly Hayes. "Hispanic Celebration Teaches, Promotes, Preserves Culture." *Minneapolis Star Tribune,* September 16, 1994.

Taylor, Paul Schuster. *Mexican Labor in the United States: Bethlehem, Pennsylvania.* University of California Publications in Economics, 7:1. Berkeley: University of California Press, 1931.

————. *Mexican Labor in the United States: Chicago and the Calumet Region.* University of California Publications in Economics 7:2. Berkeley: University of California Press, 1932.

————. *Mexican Labor in the United States: Migration Statistics, IV.* University of California Publications in Economics 12:3. Berkeley: University of California Press, 1934.

————. "Note on Streams of Mexican Migration." *American Journal of Sociology* 36 (September 1930): 287–288.

————. *A Spanish-Mexican Peasant Community: Arandas in Jalisco.* Berkeley: University of California Press, 1933.

Tennayuca, Emma, and Homer Brooks. "The Mexican Question in the Southwest." *The Communist* 18 (March 1939): 257–268.

Thomas, Doug. "It's Still the Season for Soccer." *Omaha World-Herald,* November 18, 1996.

Thomas, Jerry. "Hispanic Enrollment Soars in the Suburbs." *Chicago Tribune,* October 11, 1993.

Thomson, Charles A. "The Man from Next Door: The Mexican Who Is Filling the Cheap Labor Vacuum." *Century Magazine* III (January 1926): 275–282.

Tomson, Ellen. "Field and Dream." *St. Paul Pioneer Press,* July 31, 1994.

Toner, Ann. "Meatpackers Need Study, Officials Say." *Omaha World-Herald,* November 21, 1996.

"Torre de San Miguel Cooperative Mixes People Cultural, Economically." *Business Voice* (August 1971): 3–4.

"Torre Goes Co-op." *Neighborhood House News,* January–February, 1971.

"Torre to Break Ground." *Neighborhood House News,* December 1970.

Torres, Andres, and Bonilla, Frank. "Decline within the Decline: The New York Perspective." In Rebeca Morales and Frank Bonilla, eds., *Latinos in a Changing U.S. Economy,* 86–102. Newbury Park: Sage, 1993.

Tracy, John. "Deportation Cycle Seems Endless." *Milwaukee Sentinel,* July 6, 1979.

Traficante Mills, Maryann. "In the Eyes of the Beholder: Pilsen's 'Casa' Also a Home to Photographer." *Chicago Tribune,* November 10, 1993.

"Train Carries 430 Mexicans." *Saginaw Daily News,* November 23, 1932.

Triana, Armando R. "Hispanics in Chicago: Demographic Changes and Behavioral Characteristics at the Workplace." Presented at the Chicago chapter, American Statistical Association Conference, March 25, 1980. CPL, MRC.

Turner, Frederick Jackson. *The Frontier in American History.* Reprint ed. New York: Holt, Rinehart and Winston, 1947.

"U. Latin Americans Helped." *Minnesota Daily,* February 12, 1970.

"U. of I. Defends Action in Sit-ins: Minority Students Say Police Used Unnecessary Force." *Chicago Tribune,* October 15, 1992.

"U.S. Deports 26 Mexicans by Airplane." *South Bend Tribune,* May 21, 1946.

"U.S. Says Illinois Town Denied Hispanics Housing." *Orlando Sentinel,* March 26, 1993.

"U.S.-Mexican Students Sought for University." *Minnesota Daily,* May 24, 1968.

"U to Host Chicano Conference." *Minnesota Daily,* December 2, 1970.

Uhler, David. "Hispanic Joliet Area Gets Boost." *Chicago Tribune,* November 4, 1992.

United States Bureau of the Census. *1920 Census of Population.*

———. *1930 Census of Population.*

———. *1940 Census of Population.*

———. *1960 Census of Population.*

———. *General Population Characteristics 1980.*

———. *General Population Characteristics 1990.*

———. *Persons of Hispanic Origin 1990.*

———. *Persons of Spanish Origin 1970.*

———. *Social and Economic Characteristics 1970.*

———. *Social and Economic Characteristics 1990.*

United States Chamber of Commerce. "Mexican Immigration." (1930). BL.

United States Civil Rights Commission. Illinois State Advisory Committee. *Bilingual/Bicultural Education: A Privilege or a Right?* Springfield, Ill.: U.S. Commission on Civil Rights, 1974.

United States Congress. House. Committee on Immigration and Naturalization. *Immigration from Countries of the Western Hemisphere.* 70th Cong., 1st Sess. Washington, GPO, 1928.

————. "Our Present Immigration Policy Should Be Upheld." *Congressional Record.* 69th Cong. 2nd Sess. January 18, 1927, p. 1904.

————. *Seasonal Agricultural Laborers from Mexico.* 69th Cong., 1st Sess. Washington: GPO, 1926.

————. Select Committee to Investigate the Interstate Migration of Destitute Citizens. *Interstate Migration of Destitute Citizens,* 10 vols. 76th Cong. 3d Sess. Washington: GPO, 1940–1941.

————. *Western Hemisphere Immigration.* 71st Cong. 2d Sess. Washington: GPO, 1930.

United States Congress. Senate. Committee on Agriculture and Forestry. *Agricultural Labor Supply.* 71st Cong. 2d Sess. Washington: GPO, 1930.

————. *Farm Labor Supply Program.* 80th Cong., 1st Sess. Washington: GPO, 1947.

————. Committee on Labor and Public Welfare. Subcommittee on Labor and Labor-Management Relations. *Migratory Labor.* 82nd Cong. 2nd Sess. Washington: GPO, 1952.

United States Industrial Commission. *Report on Agriculture and Agricultural Labor,* X. Washington, D.C.: GPO, 1901.

"Urban Trends: Twin Cities Warning Gleaned from Census." *Minneapolis Star Tribune,* October 4, 1993.

Valdés, Dennis Nodín. *Al Norte: Agricultural Workers in the Great Lakes Region, 1917–1970.* Austin: University of Texas Press, 1991.

————. *El pueblo mexicano en Detroit y Michigan: A Social History.* Detroit: College of Education, Wayne State University, 1982.

————. "Historical Foundations of Latino Immigration and Community Formation in 20th Century Michigan and the Midwest." In Refugio I. Rochín, ed., *Immigration and Ethnic Communities: A Focus on Latinos,* pp. 30–37. East Lansing: Julián Samora Research Institute, 1996.

————. "Labor." In *The Hispanic Almanac: From Columbus to Corporate America,* pp. 155–185. Detroit: Visible Ink Press, 1994.

————. "Mexican Revolutionary Nationalism and Repatriation during the Great Depression." *Mexican Studies/Estudios Mexicanos* 4 (Winter 1988), 1–23.

————. "Perspiring Capitalists: Latinos and the Henry Ford Service School, 1918–1928." *Aztlán* 12 (Autumn 1981): 227–239.

Vander Weele, Maribeth. "Hispanics' College Enrollment Soars 95 Percent in 11 Years." *Chicago Sun-Times,* July 4, 1992.

Vargas, Zaragoza. *Proletarians of the North: A History of Mexican Industrial Workers in Detroit and the Midwest, 1917–1933.* Berkeley: University of California Press, 1993.

Vaughan, Peter. "A Mexican Community Preserves Its Heritage." *Minneapolis Star,* March 20, 1972.

Velasco, Catherine Ann. "Racine's Silent Community." *Racine Journal Times,* April 29, 1990.

Veness, April Renee. "'But It's Not Supposed to Feel Like Home': Ethnicity and Place on the West Side of St. Paul." Ph.D. dissertation, University of Minnesota, 1984.

Villalva, Lydia. "Hispanics Poorer, Study Shows." *St. Paul Pioneer Press,* February 12, 1986.

———. "West Side Merchants Expect Festival Bonuses." *St. Paul Pioneer Press & Dispatch,* April 30, 1986.

Villar, María de Lourdes. "From Sojourners to Settlers: The Experience of Mexican Undocumented Migrants in Chicago." Ph.D. dissertation, Indiana University, 1989.

———. "Rethinking Settlement Processes: The Experience Of Mexican Undocumented Migrants in Chicago." *Urban Anthropology* 19 (Spring–Summer 1990): 63–79.

Vobejda, Barbara. "The Heartland Pulses with New Blood." *Washington Post,* August 11, 1991.

Vogrin, Bill. "Hero Street: Mexican-Americans Cut a Path to Patriotism." *Chicago Tribune,* March 14, 1988.

Waldrop, Judith. "The Newest Southerners." *American Demographics* 15 (October 1993): 38–43.

Walkup, Carolyn. "Hispanics: Learning the Language of Success." *Nation's Restaurant News,* September 20, 1993.

Wallerstein, Emmanuel. *Capitalist Agriculture and the Origins of the European World-Economy in the Sixteenth Century.* New York: Academic Press, 1974.

———. "The Construction of Peoplehood: Racism, Nationalism, Ethnicity." In Etienne Balibar and Immanuel Wallerstein, eds., *Race, Nation, Class: Ambiguous Identities,* pp. 71–85. New York: Verso, 1991.

———. "Culture as the Ideological Battleground of the Modern World-System." In Etienne Balibar and Immanuel Wallerstein, eds., *Race, Nation, Class: Ambiguous Identities,* pp. 31–55. New York: Verso, 1991.

———. *Historical Capitalism.* London: Verso, 1983.

Walton, John, Luis Salces, and Joanne Belechia. "The Political Organization of Chicago's Latino Communities." Evanston: Center for Urban Affairs, Northwestern University, 1977. CPL, MRC.

Wappel, Pat. "Chicano Studies Bogs with Paperwork, but Strides toward Goals." *Minnesota Daily,* January 28, 1974.

Warnshius, Paul Livingston. "Crime and Criminal Justice among the Mexicans of Illinois." National Commission on Law Observance and Enforcement, *Report on Crime and the Foreign Born,* no. 10, pp. 265–329. Washington, D.C., 1931.

Washington, Wayne. "Minorities Say Diversity Push Benefits White Women." *Minneapolis Star Tribune*, June 21, 1994.

Weber, David J. *The Spanish Frontier in North America*. New Haven and London: Yale University Press, 1992.

———, ed. *Foreigners in Their Native Land: Historical Roots of the Mexican Americans*. Albuquerque: University of New Mexico Press, 1973.

Weber, David Stafford. "Anglo Views of Mexican Immigrants: Popular Perceptions and Neighborhood Realities in Chicago, 1900–1940." Ph.D. dissertation, Ohio State University, 1982.

Weeks, John R., and Joseph Spielberg. "The Ethnodemography of Midwestern Chicano Communities." Presented at Annual Meeting of the Population Association of America, 1973.

Welsh, Teresa. "The Barrio Gets Ready." *The Detroiter*, February 1975, 26–29.

West, Stanley A. "Cinco *Chacuacos:* Coke Ovens and a Mexican Village in Pennsylvania." In Stanley A. West and June Macklin, eds., *The Chicano Experience*, pp. 63–82. Boulder: Westview Press, 1979.

———. *The Mexican Aztec Society: A Mexican-American Voluntary Association in Perspective*. New York: Arno Press, 1976.

"West Siders Protest Public Housing Plan." *St. Paul Dispatch*, May 27, 1960.

"Wetbacks Head for Midwest." *AFL News*, October 25, 1951.

Wharton, Dennis. "Mich. Station Draws Ire of Hispanic Org." *Daily Variety*, January 5, 1995.

"Who Lives Where in the Suburbs." *Chicago Sun-Times*, June 7, 1992.

Wilke, David E. "Pilsen Neighborhood Thrives on Change through the Years." *Chicago Tribune*, June 8, 1986.

Wilkerson, Isabel. "Des Moines Acts to Halt White Flight after State Allows Choice of Schools." *New York Times*, December 16, 1992.

Wilmes, Michael. "Why Do We Subsidize the Wealthy?" *Agri-News*, May 26, 1994.

Wilson, Mary. "Migrants Returning to Moorhead Create All Kinds of Social Problems." Undated editorial, *Fargo-Moorhead Forum*, in appendix, Spanish-Speaking Affairs Council board meeting, May 24, 1990, SSAC files.

Winant, Howard. *Racial Conditions: Political Theory, Comparisons*. Minneapolis and London: University of Minnesota Press, 1994.

Wingard, Gail. "Mexicantown Dream." *Detroiter*, May 1992, 14.

Wolf, Eric. "Perilous Ideas: Race, Culture, People." *Current Anthropology* 35 (February 1994): 1–12.

Wolfe, Warren. "The Mexican-American Community of St. Paul." *Minneapolis Tribune*, August 15, 1971.

"Women in Steel: They are Handling Tough Jobs in Heavy Industry." *Life* 15 (August 9, 1943): 75–81.

Worthington, Rogers. "Hispanics Drawn to Minnesota: More Farm Workers from Texas Coming and Staying." *Chicago Tribune,* December 24, 1990.

Wright, Angus. *The Death of Ramón González: An Agricultural Dilemma.* Austin: University of Texas Press, 1990.

Wright, Kristi. "Her Vision Filled a Need: El Museo Latino Is First for Midlands." *Omaha World-Herald,* September 17, 1995.

Zamora, Emilio. *A History of the Mexican Worker in Texas.* College Station: Texas A&M University Press, 1993.

# Index